Railroads for Rent

RAILROADS FOR RENT

The Local Rail Service
Assistance Program

William R. Black

INDIANA UNIVERSITY PRESS

Bloomington

Manufactured in the United States of America

Library of Congress Cataloging in Publication Data

Black, William R. (William Richard), 1942–
    Railroads for rent.

    Bibliography: p.
    Includes index.
    1. Railroads—United States—Finance.   2. Federal
aid to transportation—United States.   3. Railroads—
United States—Branch lines.   4. Railroads—United States
—Freight.   5. Railroads and state—United States.
I. Title.
HE1061.B57   1985   385'.1   84-48546
ISBN 0-253-34774-2

1   2   3   4   5   90   89   88   87   86

This book is dedicated to

THOMAS D. BLACK
(1914–1981)
Monongahela Railway

CHARLES A. BLACK
(1890–1934)
Monongahela Railway

THOMAS W. BLACK
(1870–1956)
Baltimore and Ohio Railroad

father, grandfather, and great-grandfather,
for more than a century of service to the railroads.

Contents

Preface

A great deal has been written regarding the bankruptcy of the Penn Central and the formation of Conrail. Interest in these events goes beyond rail buff nostalgia for the events were respectively the largest bankruptcy in American business history and the largest corporate reorganization ever attempted. Yet all these phrases describe are a larger bankruptcy and a larger attempt to reorganize. In effect, the events, though the largest at the time, were simply more of the same. Some of those involved in the formation of Conrail viewed it simply as a large rail merger with the need to eliminate duplication.

Hidden away in the legislation creating Conrail was a section entitled "rail service continuation subsidies." It was this program and its implementation that were truly unique and new to the rail sector, and these form the subject matter of this study.

To some degree this is a very personal study. I became involved in evaluating the impact of the Regional Rail Reorganization Act on Indiana less than a month after enactment of that legislation. There followed nearly two years of analysis and planning for the State of Indiana. The last several months of this time were spent in the role of Director of Rail Planning for the Public Service Commission of the state. I left Indiana in November of 1975 to join the activation task force of the Consolidated Rail Corporation. Following the start-up of Conrail in 1976 I returned to Indiana University. I have served as a rail planning consultant to railroads, states, and the federal government since my return.

These points are notable not so much as autobiography, but more as an explanation for the sources utilized here. Much of what is contained here is not accessible to the general researcher; these include minutes from meetings, memorandums, letters, and the like. These materials were accessible to me simply because I took part in many of the events and organizations noted here.

This monograph recounts the history of the local rail service assistance program from its incorporation in federal legislation to its "termination" a decade later. But there is more than history here. The major goals of this study were to identify what we have learned from this program, how the program developed from a perceived need (as opposed to a real need), how it grew, and what can be considered its successes and failures. In effect, this is as much an evaluation of the legislation and the program it created as it is a history.

I believe the governmental and railroad positions I have held bring insight and a large degree of objectivity that are often missing in studies of this nature. It is believed that this is reflected in the pages that follow.

This research has benefitted from the assistance of numerous individuals and agencies, and it is only proper to acknowledge their roles here. Foremost among the individuals are Otis R. Bowen, Governor of Indiana from 1973 to 1981, and Edward G. Jordan, Chairman of the Consolidated Rail Corporation from 1975 to 1979. I sincerely appreciate the trust these individuals had in me and the opportunity that each made possible for me to be involved with the program.

Among the agencies that were very helpful are: the Railroad Divisions of the Public Service Commission of Indiana and the Indiana Department of Transportation; the Public Affairs Departments of the Penn Central Transportation Corporation and the Consolidated Rail Corporation; the Superintendent of Stations for Conrail; and, the staff of the Office of State Assistance Programs of the Federal Railroad Administration.

The research was facilitated by a sabbatical leave from Indiana University during the fall of 1982. That leave was spent as a guest scholar at the Brookings Institution in Washington, D.C. which gave me access to their library as well as the library of the U.S. Department of Transportation, and the financial dockets of the Interstate Commerce Commission.

One must also note the wise counsel received over the years from William J. Watt, Chairman of the Transportation Coordinating Board, State of Indiana, James McClellan of the Norfolk-Southern Corporation, Robert V. Wadden of Conrail, George M. Smerk of Indiana University, John Dring, formerly of the Public Service Commission of Indiana, and three fellow geographers who have worked with me during the past decade in much of what is recounted here: James R. Blaze of Conrail, Bruce W. Pigozzi of Michigan State University, and James F. Runke, formerly Secretary of the Kentucky Department of Transportation.

To all of the individuals and agencies I am sincerely grateful. I am sure that this study has benefitted from their respective contributions: direct and indirect. Any faults that remain are solely attributable to the author.

Chapter 1

INTRODUCTION

The passage of the Regional Rail Reorganization Act of 1973 resulted in the creation of a program of local rail freight service continuation subsidies that represented a significant departure from the traditional role of government in this area. Although it is true that all levels of government had a role in the initiation and development of the rail system of the United States, during the present century agencies of the federal and state governments have been the protestors of the railroads' abandonment and rate increase petitions, regulators of rail safety, and guardians of the public welfare ensuring that monopolistic railroads did not exploit the public. This governmental role of adversary changed with the passage of the reorganization act.

With regard to light-density branch lines the railroads have had the responsibility for continuing their local rail service, absorbing the losses from such operations, or presenting arguments for why the "public convenience and necessity" would permit the abandonment of such operations. With the passage of the reorganization act the uneconomical branch lines would continue to receive rail service provided by private sector rail operators, however, the losses from such operations became the responsibility of the local, state, and federal governments.

Of course the reorganization act did far more than create a local rail service subsidy program. At the time it was the enabling legislation for the largest corporate reorganization in American business history. This reorganization has already resulted in tens of thousands of pages by others and it will be treated here only in so far as it relates to the subsidy program under examination.

There is no question raised here as to whether the railroads should be subsidized in this country; this is taken as given. All transport modes in the United States have been subsidized during this century and, if anything, the railroads have not received an equitable share of these funds. It has been impossible for most of the railroads to compete with other transport modes and maintain their equipment and right-of-way. If such competition is to exist, then the railroads must be able to compete on a comparable basis. This mandates the elimination of subsidies to waterborne and highway carriers, or the provision of such subsidies to railroads. But the local rail freight subsidy program is not a railroad subsidy program; it is a shipper subsidy program.

For several decades railroads have been forced to operate uneconomical branch lines and to internally cross-subsidize the costs of these operations. Some might argue that it was possible to abandon such lines through formal procedures before the Interstate Commerce Commission (ICC), however, the record is clear that only extremely poor lines could be abandoned in this manner. With the passage of the reorganization act the nation entered a period of external cross-subsidization where at the request of a state the federal government would cover the cost of deficit operations with federal funds. The problem did not change. The funding mechanism did not change. Only the source of funds changed.

The numerous transport subsidy programs that are currently funded by the federal government should have at least one characteristic in common: they should be subsidizing operations that are more efficient based on some criterion, or they should be assisting operations that represent the most efficient means of providing a social service that might not otherwise be provided. It is a benchmark of the age of affluence when government begins to subsidize transport modes so that a choice is available. Over the past decade there were numerous cases where cities subsidized a dial-a-ride system when a local taxi company would have performed the same service at a lower cost. In the present context it may very well be more economical to subsidize the shipper's truck costs in excess of rail costs, rather than providing the option of a choice of modes.

It is the perspective of this study that a short-term subsidy program is perfectly in order. Such a program would give shippers time to adjust to an alternate mode or allow planners a period to reanalyze the viability of a rail line. However, a long-term program of operating subsidies is not justifiable and does not represent an economically efficient solution to the problem of light-density lines.

This study summarizes and documents how the program of local rail service continuation subsidies developed. In addition to this historical dimension the study also evaluates the program and what has been learned from it. The chapters which follow survey the legislation that was proposed, the planning studies that were undertaken and the methodologies utilized to assess viability. The activities of the different federal agencies, the railroads and bankrupt estates, and the states are summarized as they relate to the program and the role of each of these is identified. A review of the negotiations that took place between the states and railroads regarding operating agreements is also presented along with a detailed case study on management fees for such operations. The early trends of the program's branch line traffic are reviewed along with more recent data in order to evaluate the successes of the program. Problems identified and the steps taken to correct these are summarized. Several major evaluations of the program are summarized and critiqued. The problems that continued to plague the program are also examined. Following a summary of the financial aspects of the program there is an examination of some research questions that can now be answered based on experience of the program. The study concludes with some policy recommendations regarding the structure of future rail assistance programs.

Chapter 2 of this study examines the legislative proposals that emerged as a solution to the problem of bankrupt carriers in the Midwest and Northeast. The five House bills and the two Senate bills presented are discussed from the perspective of the local rail service subsidy program. The Regional Rail Reorganization Act that resulted from these proposals is presented along with the minor amendments to the act during 1974 and 1975. Major amendments to the act incorporated in the Rail Revitalization and Regulatory Reform Act of 1976 are also reviewed. The chapter illustrates the changes in the legislation which resulted in a temporary program of assistance becoming a long-term subsidy program.

Chapter 3 presents the various plans related to light-density line (LDL) or branch line abandonment. These began with the identification of "potentially excess track" in the Secretary of Transportation's Report and culminated in the *Final System Plan* of the United States Railway Association (USRA). These plans ranged from radical to moderate in terms of the proposed number of miles of track to be abandoned.

Determination of whether a line of track was profitable or not necessitated a measurement system capable of assessing such viability or profitability. The Federal Railroad Administration (FRA) started with an abstract statistical approach to the problem. Several states proposed methods which were in many ways superior to the FRA approach. However, the United States Railway Association developed a methodology far superior to others in existence at that time. The Rail Services Planning Office (RSPO) of the ICC improved on this by adding refinements not included in the original USRA approach. Chapter 4 discusses these methods noting the strong points of each as well as the weaknesses. Alternative approaches to the viability measurement problem are also discussed.

Each of the federal agencies in the rail area played a role in the reorganization. Although the major branch line function of the USRA was accomplished with the publication of their *Final System Plan* they continued to have a strong voice in this area. RSPO, the ICC, and FRA had major roles in the interim between acceptance of the *Plan* and initiation of subsidized rail service. Chapter 5 identifies the activities of USRA and the federal agencies in the branch line area. Each of these had their strengths, as well as weaknesses, and these are also noted in this chapter.

If the local rail service assistance program was going to work it needed the cooperation and assistance of the bankrupt estates and the operating railroads. With the exception of the Consolidated Rail Corporation (Conrail), the new railroad created by the reorganization, this cooperation did not exist. The development of Conrail and the basis for its policy in this area are summarized in chapter 6. Some of the railroads sought to avoid the subsidy program while the bankrupt estates generally avoided the negotiation of rail property leases with the states. As will be noted the operating railroads were skeptical of the program for several reasons, and the estates were anxious to get involved but not if it jeopardized legal proceedings underway at the time.

The reorganization act called for a major role to be played by the states in the rail planning area. In an attempt to present a stronger voice the states formed the Conference of States on Regional Rail Reorganization in the spring of 1974. The accomplishments of this group and its failures are noted in chapter 7. With one or two exceptions the states knew little or nothing of a technical nature about railroads and this chapter also summarizes the manner in which the states reacted to their new role. The policy positions of the different states and the rationale for these positions, where they are identifiable, are also reviewed.

Numerous issues emerged during the negotiations between Conrail and the states in which it was to operate under subsidy. Among these issues were: Who would bear the liability risk for the operations? What crew size would "subsidized trains" have? If profits were generated who would retain these? Who would be responsible for maintenance, rehabilitation, safety waivers? How much control could the states have over rail operations? Should the railroad receive a management fee? What standards of performance would have to be met by the railroad? These questions and how they were resolved form the content of chapter 8. A detailed analysis of one of the issues, management fees, forms the subject matter of chapter 9. Although the states were also involved in negotiations with other railroads these were minor in comparison to the Conrail negotiations.

In chapter 10 the monthly traffic trends for branch lines in the local rail service program are examined. This analysis examines traffic trends after about two years of operation and after the program ended. It is clear that the program was unable to build traffic or for that matter even maintain the initial low levels. Instead, traffic significantly decreased from year to year on most lines.

By 1978 the Congress was aware that it had some problems with the program and a new series of legislative changes began. The 1978 Local Rail Service Assistance Act significantly broadened the program. Appearance of the Reagan Administration brought the first signs that the program was headed toward termination. These events are reviewed in chapter 11.

Chapter 12 summarizes the three major evaluations that were completed regarding the local rail service assistance program. It is noted that these failed to identify some of the major problems with the program and the remainder of this chapter examines these. Some of these problems concern conflicts with the initial legislation, but there are also discussions of problems resulting from implementation of the program by the Federal Railroad Administration. Logical problems with a pre-abandonment rehabilitation program and the use of benefit cost analysis are examined in some detail.

The final price tag for implementation of the program was well in excess of a billion dollars with about two thirds of this being federal funds. Only a portion of this was from the Federal Railroad Administration since several federal agencies took an active role in different aspects of the program. Chapter 13 summarizes the appropriation and allocation history of the program from fiscal year 1976 through fiscal year 1983. This chapter also examines several research and planning questions that existed during the reorganization planning and attempts to indicate the answers to these questions based on the huge volume of research completed during the last decade. In a few cases the research has not been undertaken but the data are available to analyze the questions and the results of such analyses are presented in this chapter as well.

In the final chapter (14) there is a discussion of whether a program is necessary for those shippers that are about to lose rail service due to abandonment. Assuming that such a program has merit the remainder of the chapter identifies the major attributes of such a program and suggests certain tests for determining the nature of the assistance and the length of such assistance. It is noted that in several cases it might be far more reasonable to provide subsidy funds for the differential between prior rail costs and the cost of providing the service by motor carriers.

Chapter 2

LEGISLATIVE DEVELOPMENT
OF THE RAIL SERVICE
CONTINUATION PROGRAM

The Penn Central Transportation Company was formed by the merger of the Pennsylvania Railroad Company and the New York Central Railroad Company on February 1, 1968. In less than three years the new railroad filed for reorganization under Section 77 of the Bankruptcy Act. An additional three years of analysis resulted in the conclusion that the railroad could not be reorganized into a for-profit corporation without substantial financial assistance from the federal government.[1]

In early 1973 Congress began to propose and deliberate different legislative solutions to this problem. This chapter reviews, contrasts, and summarizes several of the legislative proposals that emerged in 1973 and resulted in the Congress passing the Regional Rail Reorganization Act in December of that year. Of primary concern in this chapter are the proposals for the program of local rail service continuation and related sections of these bills, and the adopted legislation. Amendments to the program are also reviewed.

The House Proposals

Five bills were proposed and reviewed in as many months by the Subcommittee on Transportation and Aeronautics of the House Committee on Interstate and Foreign Commerce.[2] Two of these bills (H.R. 6591 and H.R. 8526) were introduced by Representatives Harley O. Staggers (West Virginia), who was chairman of the committee, and Samuel L. Devine (Ohio). The other three bills (H.R. 7373, H.R. 9069, and H.R. 9142) were introduced by Representatives Bertram Podell (New York), Brock Adams (Washington), and Dick Shoup (Montana), respectively.

The Staggers-Devine ICC Bill

H.R. 6591 was introduced at the request of the Interstate Commerce Commission on April 4, 1973. This bill would have given the ICC the primary responsibility for solving the Northeast rail crisis. The basic mechanism to accomplish this was a three year lease of the bankrupt properties to the federal government. The ICC was to identify the core railroad system which would be retained in a new rail system.

Title IV of that bill was concerned exclusively with "local rail services." It included major revisions of the Interstate Commerce Act provisions covering abandonment and joint use of track. For example, under the bill railroads filing for an abandonment could have this approved within ninety days by the ICC if there were no protests to the abandonment. If there was a protest or complaint the ICC was instructed to postpone the abandonment for a period not to exceed eight months. If at the end of that period a state decided it wished to subsidize the operation of the line, the abandonment could again be postponed for six months to allow subsidy negotiations to be completed between the state and railroad. In effect, the states could legally resist any proposed abandonment for at least seventeen months using provisions of the bill.

If a state decided to subsidize a line it could request federal funds which were to be provided on a 70 percent federal and 30 percent state or local matching grant basis. The bill authorized the appropriation of $50 million in federal funds for this purpose.

The bill also required railroads to prepare a list of "low density rail lines" and other lines that they might wish to abandon. If a line was on this list for a period of eighteen months and there was no opposition to abandonment then the line could automatically be abandoned on request of the railroad. Since "any person" could object, this would have been a useless task. In addition, the railroads could simply list everything they might be interested in abandoning and as a result the list would not have provided any insight to state planners or others.

The ICC could refuse to allow operation of a line under subsidy if it determined that such an operation was not required in the interest of public convenience and necessity, or that such operation would impair the ability of a carrier to perform its other services. Under this bill the subsidy program was limited to not more than three years for any particular line of railroad. This suggests a transitional program was envisioned by the ICC.

The Podell Bill

Representative Podell's bill called for liquidation of the bankrupt estates, and acquisition and operation by a new federal authority (to be called Federail). This authority would hold the bankrupt railroads in place as individual operating units for two years while it determined the most economical method of operation.

The bill did not contain any provisions for local rail service continuation, however, it did postpone all abandonments for one year. During this period the new authority would identify lines to be retained and lines to be abandoned and submit a report on these to the Congress. Sixty days later the authority could seek abandonment using existing procedures of the ICC.

The Staggers-Devine DOT Bill

The U.S. Department of Transportation (DOT) had a major role in the drafting of H.R. 8526, which was introduced in June of 1973. The bill reflected the Nixon administration's desire to see a private sector solution to the Northeast rail problem with a minimum of federal funds involved. Operations of the bankrupt carriers would be taken over by the Northeast Railroad Corporation, a for-profit corporation.

Under this legislation DOT would identify the core rail system for the Northeast United States, and the corporation would have the responsibility for restructuring and modernizing the system. It is apparent that the idea was to create a profitable system that would attract private capital since only minimal federal funds were authorized.

There were no major provisions for local rail service continuation in this bill. Any lines not identified in the core system report prepared by DOT could be abandoned after providing sixty days notice. The corporation formed was to retain this sixty day notice capability throughout its first two years of operation, however, the railroad had to hold the line for 120 days to make sure that no party wished to acquire or subsidize its future operation. The bill did not include any provision for federal subsidy monies, or any penalties for a railroad which refused to operate under subsidy.

The Adams Bill

The national rail problem as well as the Northeast rail crisis were attacked in H.R. 9069. Under this legislation DOT would supply its recommended regional plan to the Northeast Transportation Commission (NETC) within 30 days of enactment. NETC would then take one year to prepare a final rail system plan. A preliminary plan would be submitted within ten months and the Congress would have veto power over the final plan that would be submitted at a later date.

Rail operations would be provided by the Northeast Rail Corporation (NERC), and financing would be provided by the Federal National Railway Association (FNRA), both of which were to be created by the legislation.

DOT was authorized to provide 70 percent federal matching funds for operating subsidies on lines that otherwise would be abandoned by the restructuring. However, the legislation required the DOT to evaluate each state's requests for reimbursement and consider the need for such service, the impacts of abandonment, and the benefits that would come from subsidizing the line(s).

This bill also provided $50 million for operating subsidies, but limited subsidy contracts to a term not to exceed two years. If, after two years, the initial contract had expired and a new contract was not negotiated the line could be abandoned in 90 days. This bill prohibited DOT from reimbursing a state that had not adopted enabling legislation for its involvement in this program.

The bill called for guidelines to facilitate abandonment after a 90 day notice to the ICC. Hearings were to be held if merited and a six month postponement could be granted if analysis and investigation were necessary. An additional six months could be granted to allow states to develop mechanisms for eliminating deficits on lines approved for abandonment. The possible abandonment list of H.R. 6591 became a diagram of lines in this bill. This was to be supplied by the railroads.

The Shoup Bill

On June 29, 1973, Representative Dick Shoup of Montana introduced H.R. 9142, which had been drafted by the Union Pacific Railroad Company.[3] This bill was similar to the Adams' bill although not as broad. It called for the creation of a Federal National Railway Association (FNRA) for financial backing and a new for-profit operating railroad to be called the Northeast Rail Corporation.

FNRA would formulate a plan for a profitable railroad which would then be submitted to the Congress. Lines not included in the plan could have service discontinued thirty days after the plan was approved. A line could be abandoned six months following discontinuance unless a subsidy was offered by some party. This bill also provided 70 percent matching funds for the subsidies. The DOT could distribute their funds after they considered the impact of possible abandonment, the need for service, practicality, costs, benefits and alternatives. The legislation also provided an authorization of $50 million for the subsidy program.

The Senate Proposals

The Hartke Bill

On February 27, 1973, Senator Vance Hartke of Indiana, who was Chairman of the Surface Transportation Subcommittee of the Committee on Commerce, introduced S. 1031. The bill was co-sponsored by several senators from the Northeast including Kennedy of Massachusetts, Weicker of Connecticut, and Williams of New Jersey. As the initial Senate proposal to the rail crisis in the Northeast it was considerably different

from the House proposals that followed it. It is apparent that Hartke and
the other sponsors of the bill saw the major problem as the inability of the
railroads to maintain and rehabilitate track.[4]

The bill proposed the creation of a Northeast Rail Line Corporation.
This would be a not-for-profit corporation which would acquire the
bankrupt rail line in the Northeast and be responsible for its rehabilitation, maintenance, and modernization. It would not operate trains but it
would provide the track on which others would operate. The corporation
would receive funds through user charges and these in turn would
provide the capital for any necessary restructuring. This portion of the
legislation was similar to "consolidated facilities" proposals that were
discussed two years later.

The legislative proposal also required the preparation of a complete list
of low traffic volume lines (less than one million gross ton-miles of traffic
annually) by the corporation within 120 days after enactment. If the
corporation wanted to abandon any line it would have to send out a notice
of this proposed action 120 days prior to the effective date of such
abandonment. A protest period and an investigation period were provided. If conditions merited, an abandonment decision could be postponed for up to nine months. After nine months the ICC would issue its
decision. If the line was not necessary and the ICC approved its abandonment, the line could be abandoned on 60 days notice. If a state or anyone
decided they wanted the line retained and operated under subsidy, they
would have to inform the corporation of this during the 60 day period.
They would also have to offer to cover 50 percent of the corporation's
losses from such operations.

Senator Hartke, as Chairman of the Surface Transportation Subcommittee, presided over hearings on this bill in February, March, May
and June. Representatives of DOT, the ICC, railroads and shippers
appeared as witnesses. Numerous revisions were suggested.

The Hartke-Ribicoff Bill

S.2188 was the legislation that resulted from the Senate hearings. It
was introduced in July by Senator Hartke and Senator Ribicoff of Connecticut. If anything this Senate bill was an attempt to put off solving the
problem, which may explain its lack of additional co-sponsors. The bill
called for the creation of a new office in the Interstate Commerce
Commission to be called the Rail Emergency Planning Office (the Office).
This office was charged with the identification and planning of a new rail
system in the Northeast. The Office was to receive recommendations
from an "advisory council for the rail emergency region," which was also
created and defined in the bill.

DOT was charged with preparing an initial report on essential rail
services in the region within 60 days after enactment. This would be
followed eight months after enactment by a preliminary identification

plan prepared by the Office. The Office would be responsible for holding hearings on its preliminary plan. By ten months after enactment the Office would have to complete the proposed final plan and submit it to the ICC. They would have to approve or amend the plan within eleven months after passage of the act.

There was no local rail service program in this bill although it addressed, in passing, the abandonment issue. Basically, the bill proposed that abandonments could not take place if anyone opposed them for up to one year after the date of enactment. A subsidy program, if one was to be created, would possibly be created under Section 13(a). This section called upon the Congress to prepare necessary implementation legislation within 60 days after receiving the Office's report; this would be fourteen months after enactment.

The legislative proposals summarized above are indicative of the congressional anxiety to resolve the rail crisis in the Northeast; there were other proposals. Nevertheless, included in the proposals discussed above are the rudiments of what was to become the Regional Rail Reorganization Act. Let us briefly examine how this occurred.

Moving Toward a Solution

Of the bills considered by the House, the DOT and Adams' proposals were the two which held the greatest support of the nine members of the House's Subcommittee on Transportation and Aeronautics. When the vote came there was a tie with Shoup of Montana holding the deciding vote. According to Joseph Albright, "Adams decided on the spot that the Union Pacific bill was a pretty good vehicle for mark-up after all, and he promptly steered his four votes behind it."[5] What had been the Shoup bill became the Shoup-Adams bill.

As is evident from the previous discussion the Hartke-Ribicoff Senate bill (S. 2188) would have postponed the problem for a year; it was not a solution. The Shoup-Adams House bill on the other hand was an action oriented piece of legislation that proposed a method of solving the problem and it cleared the House with a vote of 306 to 82.

When the Subcommittee on Surface Transportation of the Senate began hearings in November of 1973 it had two bills before it: the Hartke-Ribicoff bill (S. 2188) and the Shoup-Adams bill (H.R. 9142). Also discussed was a document entitled "the rail services act of 1973" and referred to as Working Paper No. 1. This latter document was prepared by the professional staff of the Subcommittee and represented a Senate version of the Shoup-Adams House bill. It later became S. 2767.

The hearings lasted three days and the witnesses were, by and large, supportive of the mechanism provided in H.R. 9142 and the working paper. Representative Brock Adams entered a statement into the record for his fellow congressman, Dick Shoup, which characterizes these hearings very well: "It is fair to say that H.R. 9142 has very broad support in Congress, among the railroads, with labor, and with those who must depend on rail service."[6] He also noted that there had only been one dissenting voice from the beginning; this was the Department of Transportation, which expressed concern about the cost of the proposed solution to the taxpayers.

Of course it would have been unusual if the witnesses failed to support the legislation. Governor Shapp of Pennsylvania was the only governor at the hearings and he raised numerous questions regarding the abandonment issue and local rail service subsidies. On the other hand there were five railroad presidents in attendance and four other roads were represented by their trustees or vice presidents. The major rail unions and brotherhoods, all of which supported the legislation, were also present. Neither railroads nor labor were treated poorly by the legislation and their support should have been expected.

The Senate hearings concluded on November 19, 1973. At that time the problem was turned over to the House and Senate conferees so that they could pound out a mutually acceptable piece of legislation. The House took up the conference report on December 20 and approved it by a vote of 284 to 59 with 89 members not voting. The following day the Senate approved the conference report by a vote of 45 to 16 with 39 senators not voting. The bill was then sent to the White House.

For several months President Nixon had been concerned about some of the proposals being discussed as possible solutions to the Northeast rail crisis. He had always been in favor of a "private sector" solution and the DOT bill (H.R. 8526) that had been introduced by Staggers and Devine reflected such a solution. But that bill had proven to be unacceptable to the Congress.

During his message to the Congress on national legislation goals in September, President Nixon had indicated his position when he stated:

> . . . While we are always open to suggestions for improvement in our proposal, I feel that some of the alternatives which have been aired in the Congress—especially those which would merely postpone action or would saddle the Federal Government with a heavy financial burden, or could lead to quasi-nationalization—are beyond the pale of acceptability.[7]

On November 3, 1973, Nixon signed the Amtrak Improvement Act of 1973, and he took the opportunity to let the Congress know that his position had not changed. He noted:

> . . . Federal action to shore up the financial condition of major Northeast and Midwest railroad freight lines must take the form of a *private* solution that would impose only a minimal and finite financial burden on the taxpayers . . . I simply could not sign any legislation which purported to solve this problem through massive, open ended subsidies or through quasi-nationalization.[8]

As the House considered the conference report on December 20 the Administration's attitude toward the proposed legislation was raised. Representative Shoup, one of the co-sponsors of H.R. 9142, stated:

> Mr. Speaker, as the gentleman will recall, during the previous discussion . . . the spector of a possible presidential veto raised its ugly head several times.
>
> I have received assurance from the Department of Transportation that with the provisions of the bill that is now before the House, they have no objections and will recommend signature by the President.[9]

Representative Brock Adams, the other sponsor of the bill, confirmed that the White House found the bill acceptable.[10]

Although the bill did not echo the private sector solution advocated by Nixon, the Watergate plagued President signed the Regional Rail Reorganization Act of 1973" (the 3R Act) into law on January 2, 1974. At the time he stated:

> . . . the act authorizes the issuance of up to $1.5 billion in federally guaranteed obligations and authorizes more than $500 million in direct Federal payments that can be used for interim cash assistance to the bankrupt railroads, for protection of displaced rail employees, and for interim local rail service subsidies to ease the impact of the restructuring process. While some of these expenditures are higher than I believe they should be, I feel the overall act strikes a responsible balance between the burden on the taxpayer and the gains to the Nation that will flow from a healthier private sector rail freight system.[11]

At an earlier time Nixon would have probably been able to influence the content of legislation more than is evident from the above, but his popularity was decreasing. Watergate had grown to become a major national issue and it was probably occupying more and more of the President's time. Some evidence of this is provided by the fact that two days after signing the act, Nixon sent a letter to Senator Sam Ervin, Chairman of the Select Committee on Presidential Campaign Activities, which was investigating the Watergate problem. In the letter the President refused to supply materials that Ervin's committee had requested by subpoena.[12]

The 3R Act

The 3R Act was conceptually similar to the Shoup-Adams bill. Although the law had fewer sections and the names of the various agencies were changed, its origin was recognizable.

Title I contained general provisions including the Congress's policy position, its findings, and the purpose of the act. The findings noted that service was being provided by railroads that were bankrupt; that the service could be terminated at any time; that the public convenience and necessity required adequate and efficient rail service; that continuation of rail service was in the national interest; that rail service and rail transportation offered advantages over alternate modes; and that these needs could not be met without federal action.

In response to these findings the act stated that its purposes were: (1) the identification of a rail system in the region which was adequate to meet the needs of the public; (2) the reorganization of the railroads in the region into an economically viable system; (3) the establishment of the United States Railway Association (USRA) instead of the Federal National Railway Association; (4) the establishment of the Consolidated Rail Corporation; (5) to assist states and others in preserving rail lines that would be terminated; and (6) to accomplish these with minimum cost to the general taxpayer.

Title II created USRA, the government corporation which was to carry out the major planning required by the act. Among its specific responsibilities it was directed to:

(1) prepare a survey of existing rail services in the region, including patterns of traffic movement; traffic density over identified lines; pertinent costs and revenues of lines; and plant, equipment, and facilities (including yards and terminals);

(2) prepare an economic and operational study and analysis of present and future rail service needs in the region; the nature and volume of the traffic in the region now being moved by rail or likely to be moved by rail in the future; the extent to which available alternate modes of transportation could move such traffic as is now carried by railroads in reorganization; the relative economic, social, and environmental costs that would be involved in the use of such available alternate modes, including energy resource costs; and the competitive or other effects on profitable railroads;

(3) prepare a study of rail passenger services in the region, in terms of scope and quality;

(4) consider the views of the Office and of all government officials and persons who submit views, reports, or testimony under Section 205 (d)(1) of this title or in the course of the proceedings conducted by the Office;

(5) consider methods of achieving economies in the cost of rail system operations in the region including consolidation, pooling, and joint use and operation of lines, facilities, and operating equipment; relocation; rehabilitation and modernization of equipment, track, and other facilities; and abandonment of lines consistent with the anticipated economic, social, and environmental costs and benefits of each such method;

(6) consider the effect on railroad employees of any restructuring of rail services in the region;

(7) make available to the Secretary, the Director of the Office and

appropriate committees of the Congress all studies, data, and other information acquired or developed by the Association.

Section 203 directed railroads in the region to supply planning data and information as requested by USRA. The Secretary of the Department of Transportation was directed to prepare a report "containing his conclusions and recommendations with respect to the geographic zones within the region in and between which rail service should be provided and the criteria upon which such conclusions are based" in Section 204.

Section 205 created the Rail Services Planning Office (RSPO), a new office in the ICC. Although analogous to the Rail Emergency Planning Office proposed in S. 2188 by Senator Hartke, the RSPO was not the primary planning agency as the senator had proposed. Instead, the RSPO was to be an evaluator of the work of USRA. It was to hold hearings on all federal and USRA plans; determine and publish standards for determining "the revenue attributable to the rail properties," the "avoidable costs of providing rail service," and a "reasonable return on the value," as those terms were used in the act; and, assist states and others in determining what lines to subsidize and to establish criteria to be considered in such a decision.

RSPO was also authorized to employ and utilize the services of attorneys to protect the interests of communities and rail users that might not otherwise be adequately represented. The result of this provision was the creation of the Office of Public Counsel of the RSPO.

Section 206 identified the goals which were to guide the preparation of a Final System Plan by USRA. USRA was to create a financially self-sustaining rail system in the region, which would meet the needs and service requirements of the region. In preparing the plan USRA was to try to preserve the existing patterns of rail service, as well as tracks in fossil fuel areas. The plan was also intended to retain and promote rail competition in the region. Although the USRA plans were excused from the provisions of the National Environmental Policy Act of 1969, it was to consider the environmental impact of alternative plans and actions. The plan developed was to be efficient and, in addition, attempt to minimize job losses and unemployment.

Congress required that this Final System Plan should designate which rail properties of the bankrupt estates would be transferred to Conrail; would be offered for sale to another railroad; would be acquired in some manner by Amtrak; would be acquired in some manner by a state or local or regional transportation authority; or, would be offered for use as some other public purpose. The plan was also to designate which rail properties of the solvent railroads might be transferred to Conrail. The legislation also specified the principles that were to govern such transfers.

Under Section 207 USRA was given 300 days to prepare and release a Preliminary System Plan. This was to be followed by hearings conducted by RSPO. The latter agency was to prepare a critique and evaluation of this preliminary plan. USRA was given an additional 150 days to submit the Final System Plan to the Congress. The remainder of Title II defined the financial role of USRA and authorized appropriations for the activities to be undertaken.

Title III of the act established the Consolidated Rail Corporation, a for-profit railroad corporation, and identified the railroad's powers and duties. The procedures that would govern valuation of the rail properties and conveyance were covered in Section 303.

Section 304 laid out the principles governing the termination of rail service. Specifically, service could be discontinued if the Final System Plan did not designate rail service to be operated on the properties, and if the appropriate trustees issued (not sooner than 30 days after the effective date of the plan) a notice to affected parties that it intended to discontinue service in not less than 60 days. Once the service was discontinued the line could be abandoned not sooner than 120 days after the discontinuance of service on the line after giving 30 days notice. If the Final System Plan determined that properties could be used for other public purposes, the trustees would have to hold these properties for 180 days from the date on which a notice of a proposed abandonment was issued. The trustees could have bypassed this latter requirement by offering to sell the property for public purposes on reasonable terms.

There were limitations placed on the abandonment flexibility noted above. Specifically, two years after the effective date of the Final System Plan or more than two years after the final rail service continuation subsidy was received the railroad would have to seek regular ICC abandonment approval.

After the plan was approved service could not be discontinued and properties could not be abandoned if a shipper, state, the United States, a local or regional transportation authority, or any responsible person offered to subsidize continued operation. The subsidy would cover the difference between the revenue attributable to the line and the avoidable cost of providing service. This would be paid to the operator plus a reasonable return on the value of such properties would be paid to the owner of the property. If the line was being subsidized for rail passenger service at the time the act was passed, or if an offer was made to purchase the rail properties, they were not to be discontinued or abandoned.

If a subsidy was offered, the government or person offering the subsidy was required to enter into an operating agreement with Conrail or any responsible person capable of providing the service. Offers to purchase rail lines were to be accompanied by offers of subsidy in order to protect the owner in the event that the property was not acquired.

Section 304(e) gave the ICC authorization to allow Conrail to abandon any rail properties which were found to be unnecessary after two years of operation. At the same time the ICC could request Conrail to operate additional rail service in the region or authorize abandonment of properties not being operated.

In order to prevent financial erosion of the estates, Section 304(f) permitted interim abandonment of lines, i.e., abandonment of lines during the planning process, provided this was approved by USRA and not reasonably opposed by any state, or local or regional transportation authority.

Title IV addressed the local rail service continuation or subsidy program. The congressional rationale for this program was based on (1) energy shortages that were facing the nation, (2) the energy efficiency of railroads and their relatively low pollution level, (3) the fact that abandonment would conflict with long term energy and environmental goals, and (4) the belief that "under certain circumstances the cost to the taxpayers of rail service continuation subsidies would be less than the cost of abandonment of rail service in terms of lost jobs, energy shortages and degradation of the environment." These justifications for the program were weak. In particular, the only definitive statements are (2) and (4). However, point (2) is not necessarily correct on lines with very light traffic. In addition the economic methodology for assessing point (4) has never been developed to the satisfaction of most researchers working in this area.

The rail service continuation subsidy program was to be administered by the Secretary of Transportation, who in turn designated the Federal Railroad Administration to perform in this capacity. Subsidies were to be made up of 70 percent federal funds and 30 percent state or local funds. Those funds appropriated for the program were to be split equally between two types of assistance: entitlement and discretionary. Each state was entitled to receive from the entitlement funds an amount equal to the ratio of its total rail mileage to the total rail mileage in the region. However, no state was to receive less than three percent or more than ten percent of these funds. The discretionary funds, as the term implies, were to be distributed to the states or authorities for subsidies or acquisitions at the discretion of the secretary (FRA). During the November Senate hearings previously noted, several parties had expressed concern that under the proposed legislation all subsidy monies were to be distributed at the discretion of the secretary. This was probably the reason for splitting the funds and placing half of these in the entitlement class.

In order to be eligible to receive the subsidy monies a state had to establish a state rail plan, and designate an agency to administer and coordinate the plan and provide for the equitable distribution of subsidies. The state agency was to have the authority and administrative jurisdiction to oversee the program, employ personnel, carry out research, and hold hearings. The state also had to provide assurances that it could manage the necessary fiscal accounting and that it would comply with regulations issued by the secretary for the subsidy program. These regulations were to be issued within 90 days after enactment of the legislation.

Although the legislation called for the states to be paid an amount equal to its entitlement, this apparently ran contrary to certain U.S. Treasury regulations and the FRA refused to make such payments. The legislation also limited the term of negotiated contracts to two years and required all recipients of subsidy monies to keep thorough records, which could be examined or audited by the General Accounting Office. If a state was found to be not eligible for the program the FRA could withhold that state's payments until it complied with the regulations.

Title IV also authorized the appropriation of $90 million for the subsidy program for each of the two years following the effective date of the Final System Plan. As noted, these funds were to be split between entitlement and discretionary categories. The subsidies to be paid were to be calculated in accordance with the RSPO methodology to be developed under section 205(d)(3) of the act.

Section 403 covered acquisition and modernization loans for the use of state or transportation authorities. These loans were to be provided by USRA at the direction of the secretary and could cover 70 percent of the purchase price or project cost. However, any recipient of such a loan would no longer be eligible for operating subsidies.

The bulk of the remainder of the act, which is primarily Title V, is directed toward employee protection. This is one of the longer titles of the act and it is easy to see why the act had the support of labor unions. Since this section is only of peripheral interest to the program of local rail service continuation, it is not summarized here.

Amendments to the 3R Act in 1974 and 1975

It became evident to many that the time limits imposed by the legislation for planning the new system would be difficult to meet under the best of circumstances. However, the failure of the Nixon administration to appoint the USRA board left the rail planners without major policy direction. As a result the Congress extended the timing of the USRA planning phase by joint resolution on October 26, 1974.[13] The Preliminary System Plan was to be released 300 days after the act was signed; this became 420 days. Initially, the Final System Plan was to go to the ICC within 420 days after enactment of the 3R Act; this became 540 days. Since the planning phase was increased by 120 days, USRA's appropriation was also increased from $26 million to $40 million by the amendments.

Several states were disturbed that lines which had been supported by them in the past would not be eligible for assistance under the 3R Act. The act was amended to make eligible any line not designated for continuation in the Final System Plan; any line which had been supported during the previous five years by a state, authority, or local government; or any lines abandoned after the date of enactment.

One other technical correction was included in the October amendments. Under the original legislation if property was acquired with a Section 403(a) loan, the recipient was no longer eligible to receive subsidy monies. This was worded in such a way that a state acquiring one line with a loan would be unable to subsidize any other lines. The intent was to prevent a given line from being acquired and subsidized with Title IV monies, and the legislation was so amended.

In January and February of 1975 another series of amendments was passed.[14] The significant amendments of this set: authorized additional payments to the trustees of the bankrupt carriers in order to keep these carriers operating; provided for continuation of the RSPO; and increased the flexibility of loan guarantees under Sections 213 and 215.

Amendments of the Rail Revitalization and Regulatory Reform Act

Although there was a general sigh of relief by most parties when the Congress did not reject the *Final System Plan*, none of the principals involved in the reorganization believed that it could be accomplished without supplemental legislation. During the months of November and December of 1975 hearings were held in the House and Senate on Senate Bill 2718, entitled the "Railroad Revitalization and Regulatory Reform Act of 1976" or as it was later called, the 4R Act. The House and Senate accepted the bill on December 18, 1976, however, it was generally believed that the bill would be pocket vetoed over the Christmas holiday. As a result the bill was held in committee and was not sent to President Ford.

Secretary of Transportation William Coleman was disturbed by several provisions of the bill and as a result the House and Senate reexamined and revised the legislation in an attempt to satisfy him. This occupied most of January, but on the 23rd of the month the bill was sent to the White House. The 4R Act was signed into law by the President on February 5, 1976.[15]

Heralded by many as the most significant rail reform legislation in a quarter of a century, the new act amended parts of the Interstate Commerce Act, the Department of Transportation Act, the Urban Mass Transportation Act of 1964, and the Regional Rail Reorganization Act of 1973. The amendments to the 3R Act were concerned primarily with the financial aspects of the reorganization and the local rail service continuation program. The discussion here will focus primarily on changes in the latter program or changes related to the initiation of that program.

The fact that legislation to implement the *Final System Plan* was not enacted until February resulted in a thirty day postponement of the conveyance of bankrupt properties to Conrail (March 1, 1976 to April 1, 1976). Under the 3R Act lines not to be conveyed could be discontinued no sooner than 90 days after the *Final System Plan* was approved by the Congress. This would have been February 7, 1976. However, the line could not be discontinued if a subsidy was offered. If a subsidy was offered, an operator would have to be found to provide the service. Conrail was not to be an operating railroad until March 1 and the estates were concerned that they would be designated to provide the service. As a result the discontinuance notices had an effective date of February 27, 1976. Postponement of the conveyance created the same problem by postponing the discontinuance to the day of conveyance.

The question of who would operate the subsidized service was addressed in Section 304(d) of the 3R Act as amended by the 4R Act. It stated that the subsidizer could designate as the operator: (1) Conrail if its property was connected to the line, unless the ICC determined that another railroad could provide the service more efficiently or economically; (2) any other railroad connected to the line, if Conrail was not so connected or if these other railroads could provide the service more efficiently or economically; or, (3) any responsible person or government entity willing to operate the service.

There was a general concern by the states that the railroads would refuse to operate under subsidy, and Section 304(d) was an attempt to resolve this problem. Conrail had already indicated a willingness to provide service on such lines, but it had no desire to perform service if it would need trackage rights to get to the line. Ironically, the connection provisions in this section of the law were advocated by Conrail and the Chessie System. The latter road assumed that trackage rights utilized by the Penn Central were being conveyed automatically to Conrail, hence Conrail would "connect" with certain lines. However, not all lines were being transferred and Conrail instructed their conveyance team not to acquire such rights in several areas because of the subsidy program.

The amended Section 304(d) also provided that the operator of subsidized rail service was to be paid a management fee. The amount of the fee was to be determined by the RSPO. The need for such a fee was accepted by most parties. The railroads that would be providing the service would do so on an avoidable cost basis and there would be no profit gained from such operations and, therefore, no incentive to provide good service. States wanted improved service and viewed the fee as an incentive to that end. Railroads also saw costs that were not covered by the program, and it was believed that the fee would help to defer some of these.

This section also provided that the designated railroad could refuse to enter an operating agreement if that "agreement would substantially impair such railroad's ability to serve adequately its own patrons or to meet its outstanding common carrier responsibilities." It is very doubtful that a Class I railroad could utilize such a provision, and it was probably intended as a way of protecting smaller railroads.

The trustees of the bankrupt railroads were not anxious negotiators. As owners of the property over which subsidized service would operate, they were entitled to receive a reasonable return on the value of such properties if they had lease arrangements with the subsidizers. Although a lease sounded rather simple, the problem was that it indirectly addressed the "valuation" question. USRA had valued the properties much lower than the trustees of the bankrupt roads believed was acceptable and they had, in turn, taken the Association to court over the question. States viewed the value on the low side as did USRA, and the trustees saw the value as greater than these parties would admit. Therefore, it did not appear that leases could be negotiated to the satisfaction of all parties to allow operators onto the railroad properties.

The amended act addressed this problem by simply stating that the trustees "shall permit rail service," if an operating agreement was in place. It also gave the ICC authority to act if leases were not in place by the day of conveyance. Although the ICC had such authority under Section 1(16)(b) of the Interstate Commerce Act to direct rail service, this authority was restated in terms of a designated railroad.

In the event that operating subsidy negotiations were a total failure, the 3R Act was amended (Section 402(a)(3)) to permit the secretary of transportation to enter into agreements with the railroads designated to provide the service, or with the trustees for property leases. This particular provision was permissive rather than mandatory and the FRA did perform this function for a short period after the program started.

The amended act continued to have the subsidy monies distributed by the secretary (FRA) to the states, but nearly all other financial aspects of the program changed. The procedures for allocating entitlement funds had been the ratio of total miles of rail line in a state to total miles in the region. This was changed to become the total miles eligible for subsidy in the state compared to total miles eligible in the region. The various bills had placed a minimum of not less than one and one half percent of the total available funds for a given state. However, the smaller New England states had this changed to a minimum of three percent during markup of the bill.

The discretionary assistance program of the 1973 act was scrapped in the amended act. All funds were to be distributed on the basis of the entitlement criterion noted above.

During the hearings several individuals advocated a change in the 70 percent federal and 30 percent state (or local) matching funds formula. Some witnesses believed the program should be 100 percent federally funded, others said it should be 90/10 and so forth. As amended the act provided 100 percent federal money for the first year and 90/10 the second year. DOT was opposed to the 100 percent subsidy as were some states. DOT's concern was that the program would remain at the high level. Some states on the other hand believed that they would lose control of the program if they had no financial role in it.

The criteria for eligible rail was also changed in the amended act. As before those rail lines not designated for continuation in the *Final System Plan* were eligible. Rail services which were owned, leased or operated by the states also became eligible. In addition, intermodal facilities needed to handle freight which had been moved by rail, as well as yards, shops and docks became eligible for assistance. The identification of intermodal facilities was a major breakthrough in terms of the rationality of the program, however, it was countered by the nonsensical proposal that the shops, yards and docks were to be eligible for subsidy. The latter amendment was allegedly proposed by the Ohio congressional delegation as a method of saving jobs that would be lost with massive abandonments of the Erie-Lackawanna in Ohio. The reactions of Conrail and state planners to this provision were identical: How do you subsidize a yard or shop or dock if it no longer has rail traffic? At least this provision was limited to one year so that some sanity prevailed.

There were numerous other amendments that were related to the events that occurred in the first two years of the reorganization act. One of these established on a permanent basis (or so it seemed at the time) the Office of Public Counsel and empowered it to represent the interests of communities and users of rail service in hearings before the Commission and other federal agencies involved in rail transportation. Several other amendments focussed on rail commuter operations and provided subsidies for these.

Although not an amendment to the 3R Act, the 4R Act set in place the legislation for a nationwide rail freight service continuation program. This was a congressional "something for everyone" move. There were only a few areas outside the Northeast/Midwest region where an abandonment problem existed, and it is strange that the Congress did not even wait until the results of the 3R Act subsidy program were in before making the program national. Perhaps it is not so strange since regional legislation, such as the 3R Act, is often followed by national legislation of the same nature. An example of this from the 1960's was the Appalachian Regional Development Act which was followed by the Public Works and Economic Development Act.

The national rail continuation program was scheduled to begin July 1, 1976, and the federal share of the subsidy was set at 100 percent for the first year, 90 percent for the second year, 80 percent for the third year, and 70 percent for the fourth and fifth year. The program in the Midwest and Northeast was scheduled to end after two years (April 1, 1978) and the states in that program were to then join the national program.

Among the interesting aspects of the nationwide program was the requirement that railroads had to file a map and list with the ICC showing lines which were potentially subject to abandonment. No line could be abandoned unless it had been on the list for four months, even though shippers might not object to the abandonment. If the ICC approved the abandonment and a subsidy was offered, the ICC could postpone the abandonment for six months to give the potential subsidizer time to reach an operating agreement with the railroad. These latter provisions are analogous to some of the provisions of proposed legislation during 1973, when the reorganization act was being drafted.

The state eligibility and planning requirements of the 3R Act were also made applicable to the nationwide program. The federal funding authorized for the two subsidy programs was $180 million for the two year regional program and $360 million for the five year national program. It was believed that unless the rail problems of the country became acute, this level of funding would be sufficient to handle the problem.

A final provision of the 4R Act that was related to the rail continuation program was the establishment (by August 8, 1976) of a rail bank program in agricultural and fossil fuel areas. The idea of "mothballing" part of the national rail system made considerably more sense than continuing rail operations under subsidy in several cases, and it was certainly more economical. The Congress authorized $6 million for acquiring or leasing lines under this program, but the program was never implemented by the FRA.

Some Concluding Thoughts on the Process

This is the legislative background of the local rail service continuation program that began on April 1, 1976. After the program began there was additional legislation and this will be discussed later. The legislation enacted and summarized above serves as an excellent illustration of how congressional attempts to solve a relatively minor regional problem of an interim nature, i.e., to enable rail users in the Midwest and Northeast to make arrangements to use alternate modes, developed into a five year national program of operating assistance and a capital program that continues at the time of this writing.

It is not a contradiction to say that there is very little legislatively wrong with the program. It is true that a limitation should have been placed on how long a line could be operated under subsidy; a two year limit had appeared in the earlier legislative proposals. However, in the absence of such a limit this could have been handled by state decision makers or the U.S. DOT. In addition, shippers and receivers were the true beneficiaries of the program, yet they were not required to contribute to the local share of the subsidy. Once again the states could have required this, but only a few did.

The Congress reacted to what they sensed was a very political issue. It was a political issue primarily because local areas perceived the loss of rail service as an economic problem. Whether the economic problem was more apparent than real may never be known.

It is ironic that the political issue developed into a major political problem by action of the Congress. First, the 3R Act inferred that the light density branch line problem was a significant component in the bankruptcy of the eastern railroads, when it was not. Second, the act also required several planning and evaluation reports in the branch line abandonment area. Third, it stipulated that hearings would be held on lines recommended for abandonment by the FRA or USRA plans, and in the event of public apathy regarding these plans it created the Office of Public Counsel to stir up interest. To some extent the Congress was successful in creating the proverbial mountain from a mole hill.

NOTES TO CHAPTER 2

1. See the "Foreword" of the United States Railway Association's *Preliminary System Plan, Vol. I*, Washington, D.C.: U.S. Government Printing Office, 1975.

Several other railroads in the Midwest and Northeast were also bankrupt. These carriers were the Ann Arbor, Erie Lackawanna, Boston and Maine, Central of New Jersey, Lehigh Valley, Reading and Lehigh and Hudson River.

2. U.S. Congress. House. Committee on Interstate and Foreign Commerce. *Northeast Rail Problems, Legislative Proposals*. Washington, D.C.: U.S. Government Printing Office, 1973.

3. Joseph Albright. "A Hell of a Way to Run a Government." *New York Times*, November 3, 1974.

4. U.S. Congress. Senate. Surface Transportation Subcommittee of the Committee on Commerce. *Northeastern Railroad Transportation Crisis*, Serial 93-8, Washington, D.C.: U.S. Government Printing Office, 1973.

5. Joseph Albright. *op. cit.*

6. U.S. Congress. Senate. Surface Transportation Subcommittee of the Committee on Commerce. *Northeastern and Midwestern Railroad Transportation Crisis*. Serial 93-8, Part 3, Washington, D.C.: U.S. Government Printing Office, 1974, p. 870.

7. Richard M. Nixon. "Special Message to the Congress on National Legislative Goals." September 10, 1973. *Public Papers of the Presidents of the United States, 1973*. Washington, D.C.: U.S. Government Printing Office, 1975, pp. 762–763.

8. Richard M. Nixon. "Statement on the Signing of the Amtrak Improvement Act of 1973." November 3, 1973. *Ibid.* pp. 914–915.

9. *Congressional Record*, 119, Part 33, p. 42947.

10. *Ibid.*

11. Richard M. Nixon. "Statement on Signing of the Regional Rail Reorganization Act of 1973," January 2, 1974. *Public Papers of the President of the United States,, 1974. op. cit.*, pp. 1–2.

12. *Ibid.*, pp. 5–6.

13. Public Law 93–488, enacted October 26, 1974.

14. Public Law 94–5, enacted February 28, 1975.

15. Public Law 94–210, enacted February 5, 1976.

Chapter 3

NATIONAL RAIL PLANS AND
THE PUBLIC'S RESPONSE

The planning process presented in the Regional Rail Reorganization Act for reorganizing the bankrupt rail carriers in the Midwest and Northeast involved seven steps. These steps are presented below in chronological order.

1. The secretary of transportation was directed to submit a report containing his conclusions and recommendations for rail service within and between the several geographic areas in the region, and describing the methodology utilized to reach these conclusions and recommendations. This report was to be submitted thirty days after enactment of the legislation.

2. The Rail Services Planning Office of the ICC was charged with holding hearings on the report and preparing an evaluation of the secretary's recommendations.

3. Based on the secretary's report, the RSPO evaluation, as well as other work performed by the United States Railway Association, the latter agency was to prepare a Preliminary System Plan.

4. Once again RSPO would hold hearings, and based on these and its own analysis it would prepare an evaluation of the Preliminary System Plan.

5. USRA was to then prepare a Final System Plan incorporating the RSPO recommendations.

6. The Interstate Commerce Commission would then review the Final System Plan and prepare an evaluation of the plan for the Congress.

7. The Congress would then review the USRA Final System Plan and the ICC evaluation. If they did not act to reject the plan by a given date the plan would stand as approved by the Congress.

This chapter summarizes the studies prepared, and the hearings conducted as part of the planning process outlined above. As the primary concerns here are the light density lines and the rail service continuation program these are the foci of the discussion.

The Secretary's Report

The first planning study to be completed under the 3R Act was the *Secretary's Report on Rail Service in the Midwest and Northeast Region* as required by Section 204.[1] This report was to be submitted to the Congress 30 days after enactment of the act. It should come as no surprise to the reader to know that the study was nearly ready for the printer when the act was signed. One only has to recall that such a report requirement was included in legislation that had been proposed in the spring of 1973. Apparently, such a report seemed like a good idea to the U.S. DOT because the study was begun far in advance of the 3R Act.

The report consisted of two volumes. Volume I was concerned with general recommendations and methodology, and Volume II included local rail service zone reports for the seventeen states and the District of Columbia affected by the act. This second volume was so large that is was divided into two parts of nearly 400 pages each. The methodology and recommendations volume on the other hand comprised a little more than ten percent of the entire study.

The methodology utilized in the *Secretary's Report* (which is discussed in more detail in chapter 4) identified a significant amount of rail in the region as potentially excess as displayed in Table 3.1. Nearly 16,000 miles of rail line in the region was identified as falling into this excess category; this represented more than 25 percent of the rail line in the region. Track that seemed duplicative, or tracks which did not have sufficient local traffic were identified with orange ink in the study and it was soon dubbed the "orange-line report" or the "orange-line exercise."

It is hard to understand exactly what the FRA had in mind when it prepared the report. From a planning perspective FRA assumed that it was analyzing a single system in the region and not a subsystem. The result of this assumption was that lines of solvent carriers serving the region were examined along with lines of the railroads in reorganization and in several cases the former were identified as "potentially excess track." As reasonable as the assumption was in an abstract planning theory context, it ran contrary to economic reality and perhaps beyond the intent of the Congress since the act did not provide for abandoning the track of solvent carriers. Why then was this approach taken? Why identify such a large amount of track as potentially excess and why should some of this involve track of profitable carriers in the region?

In retrospect it seems apparent that the report was not directly keyed into the reorganization process. More than likely it was based on legislation drafted nearly a year before the reorganization act was signed into law. Why the report recommended such a high level of abandonment is also something about which one can only conjecture, but the following seems quite plausible. FRA knew that abandonment was not a popular action with the public. They also realized from the earliest draft legisla-

TABLE 3.1

Summary of Secretary's Recommendations

State	Total Track (miles)	Potentially Excess (Miles)	Percent of Total
Connecticut	664	175	26
Delaware	291	75	26
District of Columbia	30	---	--
Illinois	10,822	2,650	24
Indiana	6,405	2,350	37
Maine	1,666	75	5
Maryland	1,110	225	20
Massachusetts	1,430	475	33
Michigan	6,159	2,275	37
New Hampshire	817	400	49
New Jersey	1,742	300	17
New York	5,595	1,875	34
Ohio	7,804	2,500	32
Pennsylvania	8,273	1,450	18
Rhode Island	146	25	17
Vermont	766	250	33
Virginia	3,895	275	7
West Virgnia	3,569	200	6
Total for Region	61,184	15,575	25

Source: Secretary of Transportation, Rail Service in the Midwest and Northeast Region, Vol. I, op. cit., p. 3.

tion that they would not be the planners of the reorganized rail system in the region. At least they would not have a direct role. It is reasonable to assume that FRA, in attempting to make the job easier for the Federal National Railway Association or the United States Railway Association (as it was finally called) would play the role of the heavy; advocating a high level of abandonment. If subsequent studies by the new planning agency called for less abandonment, that new agency would be viewed as "good guys" relative to what the FRA had proposed. If this was the rationale it was not quite fair to the public. Regardless of its good intentions the plan almost backfired.

Secretary Brinegar of the U.S. Department of Transportation acknowledged in his introductory letter to the report the work and contributions of James Hagen, William Loftus, James McClellan and Gerald Davies of the FRA. When it became known that several of these individuals might join the USRA staff, the public became generally concerned. These individuals were viewed as the radical pro-abandonment people from

FRA, and it was hoped that USRA would be more reasonable and moderate in its recommendations than the FRA had been. Although some senators considered action to prevent FRA to USRA moves, no action was taken.

Whether FRA's approach to their report was proper is something open to debate. It is clear that they achieved the desired end. At the same time the "overkill" approach turned the RSPO hearings into the most popular rail event of 1974.

The Hearings

For most state governments rail abandonment prior to the 3R Act was a creator of paperwork. Only on rare occasions did the states attend hearings on proposed abandonments, and even then they rarely testified. A line could be proposed for abandonment, a hearing scheduled and completed, and an ICC order issued without any substantial state government involvement. Under existing law the state was informed of these events; they just did not become involved.

The FRA hearings changed this apathetic attitude. These hearings, held throughout the seventeen state region, drew 12 governors, 20 members of the U.S Senate, and 77 members of the House of Representatives. In some states the number of representatives from the state government nearly equalled the shippers. As RSPO summarized: "Over 3,800 persons testified at the 32 hearings which the office held between March 4 and July 11. The record of public participation amounts to nearly 50,000 pages, including hearings transcripts, exhibits, and statements sent directly to Washington independently of any hearings."[2] The attitude expressed by the state representatives as well as others in attendance was overwhelmingly negative.

This type of reaction could not have been anticipated by the developers of the "overkill" strategy at FRA. When governors and senators testify the news media follows. Their words become the evening news or tomorrow's front page. Abandonment became an issue and nearly everyone opposed it. States that were uncommitted had to take a stand and advocate a position with regard to the FRA report. Several states took an anti-abandonment position and once this action was taken the states continued to support that policy. Therefore, it does not seem that the FRA report was of any assistance to USRA and it probably made the latter's job more difficult.

The testimony presented at the hearings has been summarized by the RSPO and this will not be repeated here.[3] In view of the fact that the FRA report did not become part of the USRA plans, it is reasonable to ask if the report served any useful purpose. The report did focus public attention on the rail problems and it resulted in states beginning to think about the problems of the bankrupt railroads and, in some cases, proposing or supporting difficult solutions to the problems. However, since the 3R Act specified a very clear rail planning role for the states it is likely that this interest would have developed without the FRA report.

If the reader is an advocate of rail preservation then the FRA report was crucial to that position. Its proposals were so extreme that groups were formed to preserve rail service that would not have been formed otherwise, and many divergent groups found they were united in their opposition to the report. It is very doubtful that such forces would have ever united in response to the more moderate USRA plans.

Preliminary System Plan

USRA was formed and began work on their Preliminary System Plan (PSP) during the spring of 1974. They continued work on the plan through the summer and into the fall. It became evident that they would not have the PSP completed in the 300 days given for its preparation in the statute. The primary reason for the delay was most often attributed to President Nixon's failure to appoint all the members of the USRA Board of Directors. This was reported to the Congress which, as previously noted, reluctantly gave USRA an additional 120 days to complete the plan.

The *PSP* was finally released on February 26, 1975.[4] USRA had analyzed 9,600 miles of so called light-density line and the *PSP* recommended that 3,400 miles of this should be included in Conrail. It further stated that a little more than 6,000 miles not included in Conrail would be analyzed further to determine if they would be included in Conrail, operated under subsidy, or acquired by solvent railroads in the region. The results of the *PSP* planning effort in terms of its impact on the states are displayed in Table 3.2.

Comparatively, the *PSP* was much more acceptable to the public than the FRA report had been. After all the region had saved 10,000 miles of track in the *PSP* in comparison with the earlier report. USRA had also looked at the impact of proposed abandonments on communities, the environment, and energy needs. With regard to community impact they noted:

> From an overall regional standpoint, the Association found that abandonment of certain light-density lines would not have a serious impact on the local community but that harm could be done in specific instances.[5]

They further noted that "the increased cost of adjusting from rail to truck would be small relative to overall cost."[6] Similarly, in the energy-environment area they found that trucks could be more efficient on branch lines from 7 to 50 miles long with traffic of more than five but less than 18 cars per day. In essence, what the *PSP* said was that the critical

TABLE 3.2

Summary of Preliminary System Plan Findings

State	Total Bankrupt Track* (miles)	To Be Included in Conrail	Available for Subsidy or Further Study
Connecticut	596	446.4	142.5
Delaware	257	194.0	57.2
District of Columbia	13	13.0	-----
Illinois	1,322	659.3	353.5
Indiana	2,845	1,927.1	714.8
Maine	-----	-------	-----
Maryland	450	206.9	195.0
Massachusetts	768	534.7	208.9
Michigan	2,163	780.9	1,332.7
New Hampshire	-----	-------	-------
New Jersey	1,324	956.8	211.6
New York	2,980	1,973.9	824.4
Ohio	3,572	2,230.5	940.3
Pennsylvania	5,467	3,947.8	891.7
Rhode Island	109	51.7	57.3
Vermont	-----	-------	-------
Virginia	81	16.8	59.8
West Virginia	370	172.2	51.1
Total for Region	22,317	15,155.0	6,040.2

Source: USRA News Release, February 26, 1975.

*Mileage owned or operated under lease by railroads in reorganization. Erie Lackawanna mileage is not included. Mileage does include approximately 1,000 miles of out of service rail line.

factor in their decision-making was whether there was sufficient traffic for a line to be viable. Their consultants had informed them that the other factors were not relevant.

A major shortcoming of the *PSP* concerned the Erie-Lackawanna Railroad. Although originally considered as a railroad in reorganization under the act, the trustees of this railroad decided that it would attempt to reorganize independently of the 3R Act mechanism under Section 77 of the Bankruptcy Act of 1933.[7] By January of 1975 these trustees concluded that an income based reorganization was not possible under the latter and they requested inclusion under the 3 R Act rubric. Although this was easy enough to accomplish USRA had already completed most of the work on the *PSP*. As a result only cosmetic changes were made in the *PSP* to incorporate the fact that the Erie-Lackawanna Railroad was to be included under the USRA plan. Unfortunately, the general mainline structure of what would become Conrail was already established by that time and it is unlikely that this railroad was ever truly considered as a mainline candidate by USRA.

Hearings and the RSPO Evaluation

With the reduction in track under consideration for abandonment (from the *Secretary's Report* to the *PSP*), there was a corresponding decrease in the public's interest as reflected in the hearings conducted by the RSPO. The number of witnesses appearing was only one-half (about 1900) of what it had been for the FRA report and the testimony presented was also considerably shorter.[8] These reductions occurred even though the days of hearings increased from the initial 32 days for the FRA report to 87 days for the *PSP*. It is clear that the USRA preliminary plan was far less disturbing to shippers, railroads and state policy makers.

As could be expected the light-density lines were the focus of the hearings and 1400 of the 1900 witnesses testifed on this subject. Witnesses were also concerned about other aspects of the plan, such as industry structure, coordination projects with solvent railroads, passenger service, financial structure and the environment, however, the branch lines dominated the sessions.

Those testifying in the light-density line area expressed their concern over the methodology of the plan and the data utilized by USRA. They also expressed the opinion in several cases that the social, energy, and environmental concerns were being ignored in comparison with the economic viability goals of the act.

Much of the criticism at the hearings on the light-density lines was due to a lack of understanding on the part of the witnesses. This was particularly the case in the data and cost areas. Witnesses on several occasions presented information that showed their annual rail freight bill was in excess of the revenues being attributed to lines by USRA. What shippers failed to realize was that in most cases several railroads divide a shippers freight bill and in the light-density line case, the number presented in the *PSP* represented revenue that would be retained by Conrail. Witnesses also took issue with the costing; this was particularly so in the area of maintenance-of-way. They noted quite properly that the USRA figures were in excess of what the railroads had spent on the lines in recent years. However, USRA was not planning to create a system plagued with deferred maintenance. Their maintenance costs were normalized and represented what the railroad should spend annually, not what the bankrupt railroads were spending. Not all of the criticism had its foundation in a poor understanding of the plan or railroad practices.

Several witnesses took issue with USRA's use of system average costing. They disliked such an approach to off-branch and on-branch costing. The off-branch cost methodology issue was subsequently taken into the courts. The on-branch costs would have undoubtedly been more acceptable if they were actual costs rather than estimated costs, and although some witnesses wanted to oppose the plan until such costs were collected, this was not practical.

As noted in chapter 2 the initial subsidy ratio of 70 percent federal and 30 percent state/local funding was changed in 1976. Much of the impetus for such a change came from these hearings. It was noted by some that the ratio should be 90 percent federal and by others that it should be 100 percent federal. Witnesses also objected to the two year limit on the program; they thought a permanent program should be established.

It was noted that the agricultural sector would probably be hurt the worst by the abandonments. This was undoubtedly true. Given the national energy situation at the time several witnesses urged that light-density lines should be retained in fossil fuel areas.

In their summary of the testimony RSPO noted that:

"potential loss of service on light-density lines remains the central concern of most communities and users of rail service. Witnesses expressed their exasperation that this issue continues to dominate the planning process. Few were satisfied with the Association's position. The testimony reveals that the public believes the line analysis methodology is arbitrary and unreasonable and the data so thoroughly inadequate as to render a majority of the light-density line calculations incorrect. Witnesses once again reaffirmed the belief that massive branch line abandonment, in any form, is not the answer to ensuring Conrail's financial viability.[9]

The RSPO evaluation of the testimony does not differ to any great extent from the testimony presented. They recommended:
1. USRA should scruntinize their estimation methods.
2. USRA should evaluate lines as part of a system, and each line or mile of track should be evaluated in terms of its contribution to the system.
3. The data should be reviewed for accuracy.
4. USRA should consider growth potential on the lines.
5. Out-of-service lines should be placed back in service before abandonment decisions are made.

They further suggested changes in the *Preliminary System Plan* to resolve several of the other protests from the hearings. A major part of the RSPO effort went into the analysis of light-density lines. Although they noted additional information by line where it was available they did not make specific recommendations on each line.

The Final System Plan

On July 28 of 1975 USRA issued the first reports of its *Final System Plan (FSP).*[10] The final plan had analyzed approximately 11,883 miles of light-density lines and recommended the inclusion of 4,968 miles of this track in Conrail.[11] USRA noted that 88 percent of the traffic on the lines under analysis would be retained on the lines being included in the restructured system. A summary of the *FSP* recommendations by state appears as Table 3.3.

The lines being abandoned would have resulted in an operating loss of

TABLE 3.3

Summary of Final System Plan Recommendations

State	CRC[*]	AVS	OSNA	OS	Total
Connecticut	111.6	69.6	.2	6.6	188.0
Delaware	2.1	3.5	15.4	4.3	25.3
District of Columbia	-----	-----	-----	-----	-----
Illinois	476.3	177.0	54.9	102.0	810.2
Indiana	501.2	507.6	124.1	107.6	1240.5
Maine	-----	-----	-----	-----	------
Maryland	4.2	66.1	38.5	7.3	116.1
Massachusetts	162.0	115.9	2.1	1.4	281.4
Michigan	486.4	762.9	294.2	21.7	1566.1
New Hampshire	-----	-----	-----	-----	------
New Jersey	220.3	183.3	10.5	32.5	446.6
New York	454.4	792.5	78.1	99.0	1425.0
Ohio	638.6	856.9	55.8	124.0	1675.3
Pennsylvania	958.1	716.1	82.2	444.9	2201.3
Rhode Island	17.0	9.3	13.1	1.7	41.1
Vermont	-----	-----	-----	-----	------
Virginia	-----	-----	32.7	-----	32.7
West Virgnia	135.0	23.7	0.0	2.0	160.7
Conn. - Mass.	29.5	47.8	0.0	0.0	77.3
Conn. - R.I.	49.1	0.0	0.0	0.0	49.1
Del. - Md.	30.3	15.9	69.2	0.0	115.4
Del. - Pa.	21.5	0.0	27.3		48.8
Ill. - Ind.	224.8	26.9	0.0	3.8	255.5
Ind. - Ky.	70.7	0.0	0.0	0.0	70.7
Ind. - Mich.	4.3	15.1	25.7	0.0	45.1
Ind. - Ohio	23.2	158.0	0.0	0.0	181.2
Md. - Pa.	32.3	32.2	0.0	117.2	181.7
Md. - Va.	0.0	0.0	63.5	0.0	63.5
Md. Va. - WVa.	41.1	0.0	0.0	0.0	41.1
Mich. - Ohio	44.3	34.3	3.8	0.0	82.4
Mich. - Wisc.	0.0	23.5	0.0	0.0	23.5
N.J. - N.Y.	144.3	0.0	0.0	0.0	144.3

Source: USRA News Release, July 28, 1975.

[*]CRC - To be transferred to Conrail or another railroad
  AVS - Available for subsidy
 OSNA - To be transferred to another Railroad or subsidized
   OS - Out of service
Total - Total mileage under analysis

$33 million if they were transferred to Conrail. This figure, however, does not include an estimated $51 million that would have been necessary to rehabilitate the lines to a level that permitted safe operations.[12]

USRA also attempted to respond to the criticisms in the RSPO evaluation of their preliminary plan. Among the subjects addressed were maintenance costs, net salvage value, traffic volumes and revenues, crew size, trip frequency and service time. The maintenance costs in USRA's plans were set at greater than the $1,000 a mile, which was noted by the RSPO standards as a minimum maintenance level. Their rationale was that the $1,000 was too low and would not permit the lines to be maintained. There can be little question that they were correct in their rejection of this standard. Net salvage value represented the cost of ownership of the rail lines. In other words if the lines were abandoned and the track, ties, and so on were scrapped and the monies from the sale of these were invested (at an assumed rate of 8.3 percent), the railroad would get a return of approximately $2,000 a mile annually. It was this figure that formed the basis for USRA's net salvage value.

In numerous cases revenues in the *FSP* were revised based on better information received from the RSPO. Traffic growth potential was incorporated in some cases and errors in traffic volumes were corrected. One type of problem that USRA could not solve is illustrated by the situation where traffic originated on a Reading Company line, moved to a Penn Central Transportation Company line, and terminated on an Ann Arbor Railroad Company line. In other words traffic moving over multiple bankrupt carriers frequently did not result in a correct total (Conrail) revenue, but included only the originating, or as the case might have it, terminating carrier revenue. This was a far more significant problem in the eastern states which had several of the smaller bankrupt railroads. It was not resolved to any great extent by the *FSP*.

RSPO and witnesses at the hearings had noted that crew size on some lines was too large in a number of cases. USRA responded by setting all crew sizes at four individuals. This probably weakened the analysis since it excluded the use of firemen (in the most common case) on the light-density lines. Operationally, it would not be possible to exclude firemen from such lines.

To those who noted that trip frequency could be reduced and thereby generate savings in operating costs USRA noted that this could result in a loss of traffic. Nevertheless, they reviewed the traffic and adjusted trip frequency where this seemed reasonable. The savings generated by this adjustment were not sufficient to "save" any line. There were also some errors in how long it would take to provide service to certain branch lines. Where these were unreasonable or unrealistic they were changed.

RSPO had generally attacked the entire analytical methodology of the *PSP* and USRA's basic response was that they believed that it was the best approach available, which was just another way of saying they were going to use it anyway.

ICC Evaluation

Although the RSPO was created as a division of the Interstate Commerce Commission, RSPO had a relatively free hand in its duties under the reorganization act.[13] The ICC also made this observation in the introduction to their evaluation of the *Final System Plan*, stating further that they did not necessarily agree with the RSPO on all issues.[14] The ICC had more or less total control in the branch line abandonment area for more than half a century. Now USRA was on the scene and in little more than a year had identified nearly 7,000 miles of light-density lines as candidates for abandonment. During the planning process the ICC had received approval of its 34 carload per mile rule, however, USRA was rejecting lines with 90 carloads per mile. Finally, there was some question of whether the ICC through its failure to approve abandonment requests of bankrupt carriers had actually contributed to their bankruptcy. One could hardly have expected the complete endorsement of any USRA plan by the ICC.

The ICC in their evaluation critiqued the USRA methodology including their procedure for segmenting lines, their misunderstanding of transit shipments,[15] and their treatment of costs. USRA had analyzed the transit shipment situations and by and large had found these to be unprofitable. However, the ICC correctly noted USRA's failure to treat such revenues in an equitable manner. With regard to costs, the ICC did not care for the use of estimates and system averages, the inclusion of overhead costs as an avoidable cost, the treatment of return on value as a branch line cost, and the failure to consider cost savings resulting from increased efficiency and reduced levels of service. Data quality was also of some concern to the ICC. On nearly all of these points the Commission's assessment was correct in this writer's opinion. Nevertheless, the ICC evaluation concluded:

> From the information now available, it is the Commission's view that any flaws that remain in the light-density line analysis are not so serious as to require rejection of the Final System Plan, and we recommend unequivocally that the Plan not be rejected by the Congress on this ground.[16]

The Commission believed that if certain lines were restudied and found to be profitable then they should be included in or transferred to Conrail. They also included several legislative proposals in their evaluation report; these were designed to clarify the light-density line area.

More USRA Reports and the Congress

Some of the operations and facilities planning was not completed in time for inclusion in the *Final System Plan*. This was issued as a supplemental report in September of 1975.[17] Also included in this report were discussions of the community and environmental impacts of the discontinuances which were called for in the *Final System Plan*.

The *FSP* had called for an industry structure composed of Conrail and the Chessie. The latter railroad would take over the eastern portion of the Erie-Lackawanna Railroad, nearly all of the Reading Company lines, and the Penn Central coal lines in West Virginia. If something happened to prevent this transfer, then USRA's backup plan was "Unified Conrail" or "Big Conrail," which would place parts of all the bankrupt railroads under Conrail. The *Supplemental Report* included a description of the pro forma financial performance, operating plan and rehabilitation plan for the Unified Conrail alternative.

As written the 3R Act did not require congressional action for approval. Rather, an explicit act of Congress would be necessary to reject the plan. Such action was to occur by November 9 of 1975 or the plan would stand as accepted by the Congress. At the time of its submission to the Congress in July the *FSP* had about an even chance of being approved by that body. However, as time passed it became apparent that the Chessie System and the Southern Railway were concerned about deficiency judgement protection in the event that the bankrupt estates were able to get a favorable ruling on the valuation of their properties. That is, USRA had valued the properties at one level and this was the selling price to Conrail and the other solvent railroads. The estates on the other hand had taken the valuation question to court saying that the properties were worth much more than USRA had stated. If the court ruled in the estates favor, or at any value greater than what USRA was selling the property for, then the buyer would have to pay the difference (or deficiency). Chessie and the Southern wanted protection against such additional payments. This protection would require additional legislation.

As November 9 approached the chances of congressional rejection of the plan increased. In fact if the Chessie and Southern were not going to participate some states and others wanted the plan rejected because the alternative would be the "Unified Conrail" structure. Nevertheless, the plan was not rejected despite attempts to do this. It is apparent that the Congress realized that it could pass the necessary legislation to protect acquiring railroads, or for any other technicality related to conveyance of the properties. It is also known that many congressional leaders were unwilling to give additional funds to the bankrupt estates in the absence of a plan.

In December of 1975 USRA issued an official errata supplement to the *Final System Plan*, and this was of more significance to the branch lines than their previous supplement.[18] In particular, certain lines that had been designated for transfer to other railroads had questionable futures in the event those acquisitions did not take place. The options were generally "transfer to Conrail" or "available for subsidy" and the errata clarified certain situations where ambiguity existed.

Summary

In less than two years after passage of the 3R Act the nation saw a report on rail services in the Midwest and Northeast, and a preliminary and final plan for alleviating the problems with that service. A multitude of hearings were held. Witnesses critiqued, protested, brought forth new evidence and otherwise attempted to clarify parts of the plans and reports that affected them. Although there were questions during the *PSP* hearings that certain information from the FRA hearings was being ignored by USRA, this apparently was resolved by the time the *FSP* appeared.

Congress approved the *Final System Plan* and USRA clarified certain aspects of that plan. Conveyance of the properties to Conrail and the beginning of the branch line subsidy program were visible on the horizon.

NOTES TO CHAPTER 3

1. Secretary of Transportation, *Rail Service in the Midwest and Northeast Region, Vol. I, II, III,* (Washington, D.C.: The U.S. Department of Transportation), February 1974.

2. Rail Services Planning Office, Interstate Commerce Commission. *The Public Response to the Secretary of Transportation's Rail Services Report, Vol. III, Midwestern States,* (Washington, D.C.: U.S. Government Printing Office), February 1975, p. 1; other RSPO volumes issued were *New England, Vol. I,* August 1974; and *Mid-Atlantic States, Vol. II,* October 1974; and *Evaluation of the Secretary of Transportation's Rail Services Report,* May 1974.

3. *Ibid.*

4. U.S. Railway Association, *Preliminary System Plan, Summary, Vol. I, Vol. II,* (Washington, D.C.: U.S. Government Printing Office), February 1975; a *Supplement* was issued in May of 1975.

5. *USRA News Release,* p. 6, February 26, 1975.

6. *Ibid.*

7. Title II, U.S.C., Section 77.

8. Rail Services Planning Office, Interstate Commerce Commission, *Evaluation of the U.S. Railway Association's "Preliminary System Plan".* (Washington, D.C.: U.S. Government Printing Office), April 28, 1975; *Supplemental Report,* June 1975.

9. *Ibid.*

10. U.S. Railway Association, *Final System Plan, Vol. I, Vol. II,* (Washington, D.C.: U.S. Government Printing Office), July 26, 1975.

11. Of the 11,883 miles, 10,692 miles were in service and 1,191 miles were out of service. The plan recommended inclusion of 4,935 miles from the former group and 33 miles from the latter group. See: USRA, *Final System Plan, op. cit.,* Vol. II. p. 25.

12. *Ibid.*

13. The Commission was charged with reviewing coordination projects proposed under the USRA planning process. See: *Ex Parte No. 293 (Sub. No. 4)*, "Acquisition of Rail Properties by Profitable Railroads in the Region as Proposed by the United States Railway Association," decided May 16, June 17, and July 16, 1975.

14. Interstate Commerce Commission, *Evaluation of the U.S. Railway Association's Final System Plan*, (Washington, D.C.: U.S. Government Printing Office), August 25, 1975.

15. Transit shipments or privileges involve charging a through rate for a move that may stop and be processed and subsequently transhipped to its final destination. The ICC charged that the through rate division should be considered as part of the line revenue.

16. Interstate Commerce Commission, *Evaluation of the U.S. Railway Association's Final System Plan, op. cit.*, p. 47.

17. U.S. Railway Association, *Final System Plan, Supplemental Report*, Washington, D.C.: U.S. Government Printing Office), September 1975.

18. U.S. Railway Association, *Final System Plan, Official Errata Supplement to Vol. I and Vol II*, (Washington, D.C.: U.S. Government Printing Office), December 1, 1975.

Chapter 4

THE ASSESSMENT OF RAIL LINE VIABILITY

As noted in the previous chapter much of the criticism of the *Secretary's Report* and the USRA plans was directed toward the methodologies those plans had utilized to assess whether a branch line was profitable. At the outset of the planning process it is doubtful if anyone had a firm understanding of the costs involved in providing rail service and only a few agencies had access to carload revenue information. A decade later these rail costs are still a subject of some controversy. Methods of determining revenues on the other hand are relatively acceptable, but there remain some questions as to how much of that revenue should be attributed to the line that originated the traffic and how much should be attributed to the line that terminated the traffic.

This chapter summarizes and surveys the salient aspects of the methodologies developed during the planning process by some of the different state and federal agencies involved in the reorganization. An in-depth treatment of each of these may be found in the sources noted in the chapter.

The FRA Approach

The secretary of transportation's report on *Rail Service in the Midwest and Northeast Region* did not represent a new approach to the measurement of branch line viability. Instead, it represented an application on a rather large scale of a methodology that had been developed for the FRA several months earlier by the consulting firm of R.L. Banks and Associates.[1] The method was not developed for planning purposes, but as a check on the validity of the ICC "34 carload" rule.

The 34 carloads per mile rule was a standard issued by the ICC in January of 1972.[2] Specifically, the ICC regulation issued permitted abandonment of a rail line if traffic on that line was less than 34 carloads per mile per year and if there were no public objections to abandonment and the requirements of the public convenience and necessity were minimal. The Commonwealth of Pennsylvania and the Congress of Railway Unions sought and received an injunction against the use of the new 34 carload standard before it could be applied.[3]

Nevertheless, the FRA contracted with R.L. Banks and Associates to determine if such a standard or abstraction could be used to predict whether branch line operations were profitable or not. Due to the absence of detailed data for branch lines, the Banks group utilized a hypothetical sample of branch lines. Such a sample had variable line lengths, carloads per mile, train speeds, average hauls and trips per year. The lines had these attributes assigned to them based on characteristics of railroads serving different regions of the country. Using standard costs applied to the aforementioned attributes, revenues and costs were assigned to the hypothetical lines. The study then proceeded to examine the differences in total line revenues and costs in order to determine line profits and losses. An attempt was then made to estimate this profit or loss, or the viability criterion, based on attributes of branch lines that are generally available such as cars per mile per year, gross ton-miles per mile of line, length of line, loaded car miles, and cars originated or terminated.

One of the models derived by this analysis was:

$$P = - 6400 - 6457\ X_3 + 125.7\ X_5$$

where P was the measure of profit or loss, X_3 was the length of the rail line, and X_5 was the number of cars originated or terminated. Several models of this type were developed for the different regions of the United States (Eastern, Western, and Southern), and the reader is referred to the Banks report for further detail. Assessing the Banks methodology in and of itself, it should be noted that it represented an operational approach to an unsolvable problem given the data available. It used historical information and as a result it would have been difficult to utilize in a predictive situation. In addition, a railroad would not know if the parameters of the model varied with time, but in an inflationary period it is unlikely that these would be stable. If one were willing to accept this approach, the hypothetical data base and the assumptions involved, then it would be possible to crudely estimate for a given point in time the viability of a light-density or branch line.

FRA was willing to accept the approach and make these assumptions and the result was the utilization of this methodology in the *Secretary's Report*. The actual methods were reduced to the graphic device of Figure 4.1. In the figure the DOT Upper Criteria line represents the carloads necessary for a given branch line length in order to assure profitability. It is basically rail lines that fall in the area below this line that are more than likely non-viable, or of questionable viability, and therefore worthy of further analysis. The Banks report and the methods derived did support the ICC 34 carload criterion as a base level for probable viability. FRA worked from the upper criteria line which represented something more on the order of 70 carloads per mile in the preparation of the *Secretary's Report*.

RELATIONSHIP OF RAIL LINE LENGTH
AND TRAFFIC VOLUMES
FOR FINANCIALLY VIABLE LOCAL SERVICE OPERATION

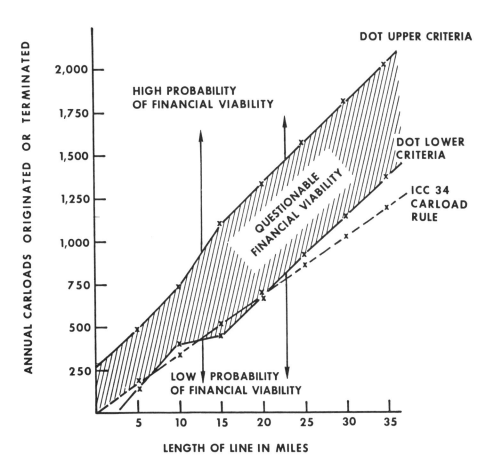

SOURCE: FEDERAL RAILROAD ADMINISTRATION RESEARCH
REPORT OE-73-3 - DEVELOPMENT AND EVALUATION
OF AN ECONOMIC ABSTRACTION OF LIGHT DENSITY
RAIL LINE OPERATIONS

Figure 4.1

New York State Approach

Louis Rossi of the New York Department of Transportation was responsible for the development of that state's approach to light-density line viability measurement.[4] The system developed had several advantages over the R.L. Banks approach.

Rossi's approach may be viewed as consisting of three components: revenues, on-branch costs, and off-branch costs. Revenues attributable to the branch line were the product of total revenues for the branch line and a proportion representing traffic that would be lost (.742) to the rail carrier if the line were abandoned. In other words the assumption was that 25.8 per cent of the traffic would be retained by the railroad even if the line were abandoned.

On-branch costs were viewed as consisting of the following cost items: (1) maintenance of way, (2) maintenance of equipment, (3) transportation, (4) traffic, (5) general, (6) payroll taxes, (7) property taxes, (8) per diem and (9) capital costs. New York created cost standards for each of these cost elements.

Off-branch costs were treated differently. These would be the costs of handling the car after it had left the branch line. Rossi noted that "because the branch line operations are so minor in nature, the only off-branch, main-line costs considered to be valid are car ownership costs."[5] These averaged from $38 a car for the Lehigh Valley Railroad Company to $74 a car for the Erie-Lackawanna Railroad. Rossi acknowledged that there could be other off-branch costs identifiable and where these were identifiable they should be included.

Indiana Approach

Indiana was aware of the work performed by R.L. Banks and Associates and the work of Rossi in New York. The basic problem with these methods was that they seemed to rely on branch line data which were not available or not reliable for Indiana. In particular the Banks formula implied a type of precision estimate that was unrealistic and probably impossible to obtain in the early days of the reorganization planning process.

Attempts were made to develop standards using the railroad annual reports filed with state governments. After a few simple experiments it was obvious that these values were too large to represent the costs on branch lines. The procedure finally utilized was based on attributes of the Banks and New York methods.

The Indiana approach began with the determination of maintenance costs. All available and active abandonment petitions for Indiana were reviewed and the maintenance cost for each branch line in 1971 was recorded. Although more recent years were available it seemed unlikely that these would reflect a viable maintenance program. More than 292 miles of branch line were represented in the petitions available. Using these data the average maintenance cost per mile of branch line was calculated at $1,186 and allowing for a six per cent annual inflation rate this yielded a 1974 maintenance cost of $1,413 per branch line. The New York study had suggested a figure of no greater than $1,700 per mile for lightly used branch lines where a distinct maintenance-of-way crew was not necessary. Since the latter was rarely the case in Indiana and since the staff did not want to under estimate maintenance, the $1,700 New York figure was adopted.

Table 4.1 gives the percentage of total costs attributable to each of a number of different cost categories for branch lines as presented in the Banks report. Indiana utilized the maintenance figure of 54.3% since it was based on 250 branch line studies and was the largest and probably the most stable figure in the table. Since the Banks percentage also included taxes these were added to the $1,700 maintenance figure. In the Indiana case these were an average of $340 per mile which yielded a total cost of $2,040.

This $2,040 was then assumed to equal 54.3% of the total branch line

TABLE 4.1

Percentage by Major Cost Element
of Total Branch Line Expense

Expense Items	All Districts	Eastern District	Southern District	Western District
Maintenance of Way Expenses and Return on Investment Expense on Right of Way	54.3%	55.5%	62.6%	44.9%
Train-mile Expense	15.6	15.4	12.8	18.6
Train & Engine Crew Expense	9.9	9.7	8.4	11.4
Locomotive Unit Hour Expense	8.7	9.5	6.8	9.8
Per Diem Expense (Time)	7.3	6.6	6.1	9.2
Cars Originated & Terminated Expense	2.7	1.9	2.0	4.1
Locomotive Fuel Expense	1.0	1.0	0.8	1.1
Car-mile Expense	0.6	0.5	0.5	0.9

Source: R. L. Banks and Associates, Development and Evaluation of an Economic Abstraction of Light Density Rail Line Operations, (Federal Railroad Administration, U.S. D.O.T.; Washington, D.C.), Report FRA-OE-73-3, June 1973, p. 89.

costs. A multiplier of 1.84162 was used to yield total on-branch costs of
$3,757 per mile. The per mile cost standards used in the Indiana study
were therefore:

Maintenance	$1,700
Taxes	340
Operating Costs	1,717
	$3,757

Indiana did not consider any off-branch costs. They argued that the traffic
was so little that these costs could effectively be viewed as zero. They
further assumed that abandonment would result in no traffic being
retained by the rail carrier and, therefore, attributed all originating and
terminating revenue to the branch.

The Indiana methodology was in many ways too simple, and it significantly underestimated the costs which were revealed by later studies.
The method did identify, under the most liberal of conditions, those lines
which the state could abandon rather than subsidize. In addition the
method did incorporate the best data available for planning purposes at
the outset of the reorganization process. In the spring of 1975 Indiana
changed its methodological approach to one based on the USRA method
described later in this chapter. The basic difference between that new
Indiana method and the USRA method was that the former included
locally derived cost factors as well as several impact areas in their line
analyses.

RSPO Methodology

The Rail Services Planning Office (RSPO) had the statutory responsibility under the 3R Act of developing a method for determining the
payments for lines that would be operated under subsidy. Section
304(c)(2) of the act stated that the payment would be equal to "the
difference between revenue attributable to such rail properties and the
avoidable costs of providing service, plus a reasonable return on the value
of such properties." RSPO was to determine the "revenue attributable to
the rail properties," the "avoidable costs of providing service," and "a
reasonable return on value" as those phrases were used in the act.
Therefore, their mission was not to develop a method of assessing branch
line viability, but indirectly that was the product developed.

Revenues were defined as the actual revenue for all traffic originating
and terminating on the branch.[8] Bridge or overhead traffic was to be
assigned on a mileage prorate basis to the branch. All other possible
revenue sources were also considered and assignable to the branch on an
actual, passenger-mile or car-mile basis.

The "avoidable costs of providing service" were simply those costs that would be avoided if the branch line were abandoned. As an illustration, the cost of fuel utilized in serving a branch line would be avoided if that line were abandoned. On the other hand, the salary of the railroad's president would not be affected by abandonment of a branch line and, therefore, his or her salary would not be an avoidable cost (unless the railroad only had the one branch line as its total system). Although in this illustration it is rather easy to distinguish these cost elements, the problem is usually not this simple in practice. RSPO was to determine the avoidable components of off-branch costs, on-branch costs, and the return-on-value.

It is important to note that in practice there were two different RSPO methods. The first was an estimation process to be utilized in forecasting the avoidable costs of service or the amount of the subsidy necessary for a given line. The second was an accounting procedure wherein costs were translated into ICC accounts for annual report and final billing purposes.[9]

Off-branch costs were to be estimated using a ratio of off-branch costs on the entire railroad to revenues for that railroad. Although not a precise estimate, it was assumed that this ratio would give a realistic estimate of the off-branch costs for a given segment of track.

On-branch costs included (1) routine maintenance-of-way and structures, (2) rehabilitation, (3) maintenance of equipment, (4) transportation, (5) taxes and (6) miscellaneous costs. If the subsidizer and railroad were unable to agree on a level of maintenance, then $1,000 per mile was to be used. Rehabilitation costs included those costs necessary to get the line to meet FRA Class I safety standards. Subsidizers could have requested a higher level of rehabilitation within 10 days after filing their notice of intent to subsidize a given line.

Maintenance-of-equipment was estimated using ICC accounts for only a few of the costs in that general area, i.e., those concerned with the costs of repairing rolling stock. The superintendence, shops, machinery, and repair of that machinery were not included. Once again it was believed that the railroad would have to cover these costs even if the line were abandoned.

Transportation costs for the branch were treated by the RSPO if they were assignable to branch operations. The transportation accounts not included were superintendence (account 371), yard enginemen (380) and yard supplies and expenses (389). Taxes on property were also included in the on-branch costs as were revenue taxes.

Miscellaneous expenses were included to cover direct outlays necessary during the subsidy year. An administrative cost for the railroad providing the service was included here; it was set equal to one-half per cent of the revenue on the branch.

Many other ICC accounts were considered as representing costs that were not avoidable, e.g., all superintendence accounts, small tools and supplies (271), all stationery and printing costs, all traffic expenses (350–360), and all general operating expense accounts (450–462).

Considerable credit has to be given to the RSPO for the standards developed, however, these standards do have their problems. As one high level official at RSPO noted: "If we had it to do all over again we would just include all of the accounts." Obviously, not all of the accounts are avoidable, or are they? The answer must be in the affirmative if a short line railroad is created for the sole purpose of providing service under subsidy. This situation was probably not considered at the outset of the process to establish the RSPO standards or it is likely such an approach would have been taken.

The USRA Method for Assessing Viability

In order to evaluate and assess the viability of light-density lines USRA also had to develop a method of measuring the costs and revenues of serving those lines. It is important to understand that USRA was not particularly interested in evaluating the profitability of lines operated by the bankrupts, or with estimating the subsidy necessary for continued service. The question was more one of if the lines were operated as part of the new Conrail system would they be viable.

The basic steps in their procedure were:
1. Establish total branch line generated revenue.
2. Subtract the following cost items in the order given:
   a. on-branch operating costs
   b. on-branch maintenance costs
   c. on-branch return on net salvage value
   d. on-branch overhead costs
   e. off-branch operating costs, and
   f. up-grading costs.[10]

USRA defined revenue in a manner not unlike RSPO's method. However, one shortcoming of the USRA method was its inability to incorporate revenue from moves involving multiple bankrupt carriers (as noted earlier). RSPO did incorporate this capability in its subsidy estimates for 1976.

On-branch operating costs included locomotive costs, commodity specific car costs, caboose costs, and crew costs. Most of these and other costs were developed through the application of statistically derived cost factors to line specific data. The cost factors or standard costs utilized by USRA were derived from different sources, however, the ICC's Rail Form A and individual carriers R-1 annual report forms were the principal sources. This was also the case with the RSPO methods. A list of some of the cost factors utilized by USRA appears in Table 4.2.

In the area of on-branch maintenance, relevant cost factors were applied to the branch line, siding, and yard track mileage. These costs

TABLE 4.2

RAILROAD COST FACTOR DATA

Factor	Dollars
Locomotive cost per hour	16.3900
Two-man crew cost per hour	17.9900
Three-man crew cost per hour	25.5100
Four-man crew cost per hour	33.0400
Five-man crew cost per hour	40.9900
Station employee annual cost	15,140.0000
Caboose cost per mile	.0420
Caboose cost per day	8.7000
Regular indirect maintenance cost factor	.3834
Variable maintenance: tunnels and subways	.0011
Variable maintenance: bridge, tressel, culvert	.0426
Steel, gross scrap value per mile	29,912.5000
Good ties, gross scrap value each	5.0000
Dismantling and removal cost per mile	9,000.0000
Rate of return on net scrap value	.0830
Maintenance of way supervision	150.0000
Upgrading: turnouts	1,033.6001
Upgrading: grade crossings	5,367.0508
Upgrading: cost per tie inserted	32.3800
Upgrading: cost per mile of track	33,856.1016
Gross ton-mile unit costs	.0029
Maintenance, siding and yard tracks	2,939.0000
Acres of land per track mile	7.2700
Land value per acre	500.0000

Source: United States Railway Association, 1976

were a function of traffic density, length, and the existence of unusual cost factors such as bridges, tressels, and so forth. Costs included labor, materials, and machinery.

PORTION OF THE COLUMBUS-MADISON
SECONDARY TRACK

USRA Line No. 590

Penn Central

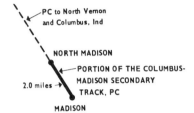

This portion of the Columbus-Madison Secondary Track, formerly part of the Pennsylvania RR, extends from *North Madison* (Milepost 42.9) to *Madison, Ind.* (Milepost 44.9), a distance of *2.0 miles*, in Jefferson County, Ind. Madison is the end of this line. The continuation of this line extends northwestward from North Madison (see Line No. 589).

Traffic and Operating Information

Stations (with their 1973 carloads) served by this line:

Madison [1] _____	178
Total carloads generated by the line_____	178
Average carloads per week_____	3.4
Average carloads per mile_____	89.0
Average carloads per train_____	3.4
1973 operating information:	
Number of round trips per year_____	52
Estimated time per round trip (hours)_____	3
Locomotive horsepower_____	1,200
Train crew size_____	4

[1] Includes only traffic segment.

Public Comments on Preliminary System Plan

See comment on USRA Line No. 589.

The Governor's Rail Task Force analyzed the line from Columbus to Madison, almost twice as long as the N. Vernon to N. Madison segment and much longer than N. Madison to Madison. It says that the Columbus to Madison line is a 45-mile line but is not operated as such. A bridge is out at Scipio necessitating local service on an as-needed basis for that station. The same applies for Elizabethtown. In serving Madison, therefore, the line actually runs over segment 619 to Seymour, then over the Chessie (B&O) tracks to North Vernon and then to Madison. "The circuitous routing," the task force says, "is detrimental to the viability of the North Vernon-Madison Line. Beyond the above, industries currently located in Madison need to have rail service due to the size of products produced. Based on the profitability of this line, the state recommends its inclusion in the Final System Plan and transfer to ConRail."

Figure 4.2A

Information for Line-Transfer Decision

Revenue received by PC_____		$53,222
Average revenue per carload_____	$299	
Variable (avoidable) cost of continued service:		
Cost incurred on the branch line_____	29,876	
Cost of upgrading branch line to FRA class I: (1/10 of total upgrading cost)_____	6,830	
Cost incurred beyond the branch line_____	31,154	
Total variable (avoidable) cost_____		67,860
Net contribution (loss): total_____		(14,638)
Average per carload_____		(82)

This line would require upgrading to meet the requirements of the Federal Railroad Administration's minimum safety standards (Class I track, which has a maximum safe operating speed of 10 m.p.h.). Based on available information, this upgrading would include the replacement of a total of 1,278 crossties (an average of 639 crossties per mile).

The service characteristics for this line differ significantly from the service on Line No. 589. No adjustments could be made in the level of service or time per trip.

Service to this line generated a loss of $14,638 in 1973. Recovery of this loss would require approximately a 66-percent increase in traffic or a 28-percent rate increase.

Disposition

This portion of the Columbus-Madison Secondary Track is *not* designated for transfer to Consolidated Rail Corp. and is available for subsidy pursuant to section 304 of the Act. Public officials have recommended that certain rail rights-of-way be used for other public purposes if rail service is discontinued. For line-specific recommendations, see section C of this appendix.

Figure 4.2B

USRA also included a return on net salvage value cost factor in their methodology. Essentially, this was "an estimate of the opportunity cost to the carrier of continued operation.[11] In other words if the value of the line were invested in a different area, this was the return that could be expected. To determine this value USRA estimated the salvage value of the steel rail and track supplies, and ties and subtracted from this the removal costs. Land value was also included. To this value an 8.3 per cent rate of return was applied.

On-branch overhead costs included several cost elements which were generally considered as unavoidable in the RSPO standards. These were the supervision for maintenance and train crews, and the clerical support costs, cost of employee injuries, and property damage.

Perhaps the most controversial aspect of the USRA costing was their treatment of off-branch costs. Included were carload ton-mile costs, switching costs, loss and damage costs, car-day and car-mile costs, and clerical costs per car. It was argued by several planners outside of USRA that only freight car costs should have been included since all other costs were unavoidable if they occurred on the mainline system. This argument in marginal costing, although refreshing, was viewed by USRA as inapplicable. Although the argument has merit for a single branch line, USRA was analyzing close to 10,000 miles of branch line and they could not view the entire 10,000 miles in a marginal cost framework.

The final component of the USRA costing procedure was upgrading costs. The crucial factor for most of the lines was upgrading to meet FRA Class I safety standards. The method included the necessary number of ties, miles of track, and turnout and grade-crossing repairs that would be necessary to bring the line to the Class I standard. It was assumed that such upgrading would occur over a ten year period and as a result only 1/10 of the upgrading costs were included in the viability analysis. An illustration of the final product of this analysis appears in Figure 4.2.

It is impossible to give adequate recognition to the thoroughness of the USRA viability methodology. It is also impossible to cover the operational aspects of this method in the space available and the reader is directed to USRA's publication on this subject.[12] Nevertheless, it is necessary to evaluate the method in light of USRA's statutory responsibility and in comparison with the RSPO method.

The congressional mandate that was given USRA called for their evaluation to take into consideration the social, economic, energy, and environmental impacts of their plan for the restructured rail system. USRA's response to this was a series of consultant reports on these subjects.[13] However, these were never incorporated into the planning process per se, but served more as indications that the USRA planners had looked at the potential impact areas. There was no attempt to integrate these criteria into their decisions regarding line retention. The attitude at USRA was that if these impacts were significant then the lines affected should be subsidized by the state and federal governments; this, they argued, was the rationale for the subsidy program of Title IV. As acceptable as this argument is on the surface, it loses its validity when one considers the two year subsidy program that was in place during the USRA planning process. After two years the impacts would still occur.

Concluding Observations

As noted elsewhere in this study there was a genuine concern and confusion on the part of the public and state planners as to why two avoidable cost methodologies would yield different results. The differences are understandable and reasonable in several areas (e.g., maintenance and upgrading) given the missions of RSPO and USRA. It is true that RSPO was to evaluate the USRA plan and perhaps interaction between the agencies was viewed as undesirable. However, it seems apparent that the units could have at least coordinated their efforts in the identification of which costs were avoidable and which were unavoidable. The final product and the planning process would have benefited from such interaction.

Of the two procedures RSPO's has more attributes of an avoidable cost methodology than does the USRA approach. In fact, USRA's incorporation of overhead costs, and clerical and superintendence costs are not defensible in an avoidable cost methodology; at least not in an abstract theoretical context.

History is sometimes the only clarifier of such conflicts and it is of interest to note that in practice, the overhead, clerical, and superintendence costs were avoided by Conrail in performing service under subsidy. At the same time there were at least an equal number of instances where such costs were unavoidable to Conrail. Perhaps more than anything else this illustrates the general ambiguity of the avoidable cost concept in theory and practice.

Notes to Chapter 4

1. R.L. Banks and Associates, *Development of an Economic Abstraction of Light Density Rail Line Operations*, Final Report under contract DOT-FR-30020 for the Federal Railroad Administratin, June 1973.

2. Interstate Commerce Commission, *Ex Parte No. 274 (Sub. No.1)*, "Abandonment of Railroad Lines," effective January 18, 1972.

3. The ICC standard was later upheld by the U.S. Supreme Court, but it was never utilized.

4. Louis Rossi, *Report on Profitability of New York State Branch Lines*, (Albany, New York: N.Y. State Dept. of Transportation), February 13, 1974.

5. *Ibid*, p. 4.

6. This is presented in Governor's Rail Task Force, *USRA Segments in Indiana: State Analysis and Recommendations*, (Bloomington, Ind.: Center for Urban and Regional Analysis), August 1974.

7. This is described in more detail in: B.W. Pigozzi, R.N. Martin, and H.J. Schuler, *Indiana Rail Plan: Methodology Review*, (Bloomington, Ind.: Center for Urban and Regional Analysis, Rail Planning and Policy Series, No. 2), October 1976.

8. The reader interested in the precise method used for each category and account, as well as the accounts included, is referred to: Interstate Commerce Commission, Rail Services Planning Office, "Standards for Determining Rail Service Continuation Subsidies," *Federal Register*, Vol. 40, pp. 1624–1636; pp. 14186–14190.

9. The accounts are described in: Interstate Commerce Commission, *Uniform*

System of Accounts for Railroad Companies, Issue of 1968, as revised Nov. 1, 1974 as printed in 49 CFR - 1200–1299.

10. United States Railway Association, *Preliminary System Plan, Vol. II,* (Washington, D.C.: U.S. Government Printing Office), 1975, p. 346.

11. *Ibid.,* p. 349.

12. Gerald K. Davies, *et al., Viability of Light Density Rail Lines: The United States Railway Association's Analytic Policies and Procedures,* (Washington, D.C.: USRA), March 1976.

13. Battelle Columbus Laboratories, *An Environmental Assessment of the Potential Effects of the Railroad System Plan,* (Columbus, Ohio: Battelle); CONSAD Research, *Analysis of Community Impacts Resulting from the Loss of Rail Service,* (Pittsburgh, Pa.: CONSAD), October 1974; PIEC, *Community Impacts of the Abandonment of Railroad Service,* (Washington, D.C.: PIEC), December 1974; Wilbur Smith and Associates, *Economic Study of Alternative Modes for Rail Traffic and Their Costs,* (Washington, D.C.: Wilbur Smith and Associates), 1974.

Chapter 5

ACTIVITIES OF THE USRA AND
FEDERAL AGENCIES

At the national level there were three major agencies involved in the branch line problem. These were the United States Railway Association (USRA), the Federal Railroad Administration of the U.S. Department of Transportation (FRA), and the Rail Services Planning Office (RSPO) of the Interstate Commerce Commission (ICC). In this chapter we will examine the activities of these agencies during the seven year period from passage of the Regional Rail Reorganization Act in 1974 until about 1981. The major emphasis will be on their respective roles during the planning and start-up of the local rail service continuation program. A fourth agency, the ICC, working outside the structure of the RSPO also played a role at this time and this will be examined.

USRA[1]

Most of the proposals for legislation that were summarized in chapter 2 noted that there would be a special agency created to plan the restructured system in the Northeast. After reviewing these proposals one is left with the impression that the Congress lacked confidence in the ICC's ability to expeditiously plan anything. The FRA might have been viewed as capable by some, but if it was to prepare the initial report on rail service in the region there was a belief that others, working independently, should develop the plan. At least that was the idea.

What the Congress had not thought out was where this "new" planning agency was to secure its planners. There were very few sources for large scale regional transport planners and even fewer sources for rail planners of this type. Either they would have to be hired from the rail industry or from the FRA. States at the time did not have sufficient expertise to be viewed as a labor pool. Therefore, when the USRA light-density line area was being staffed most of the key individuals came from the FRA. Two of these, Jim McClellan and Gerald Davies, had critical roles at the FRA in the preparation of the *Secretary's Report on Rail Service in the Midwest and Northeast* and they were acknowledged by the Secretary, Claude S. Brinegar, in the preface to that document.

Another individual that had a key role in the preparation of the

Secretary's Report was James Hagen; he joined USRA as its Vice President for Operations and Facilities Planning. Hagen later became the President of USRA. However, shortly after Hagen's initial move from FRA, President Nixon put forth the name of Arthur D. Lewis as his nominee for the position of chairman of the board and chief executive officer of USRA. Senator Vance Hartke (D - Indiana), Chairman of the Subcommittee on Surface Transportation, refused to confirm Lewis.[2] Hartke's concern was that USRA was to have a board of directors composed of government and non-government members. President Nixon would not forward names of the seven non-government nominees. As a result recommendations by USRA staff would be reviewed only by DOT and the other governmental board members. Since the key USRA planners had come from the FRA area of DOT Hartke believed that the plan that would evolve from such a process would be biased. However, by refusing to confirm Lewis prior to the appointment of the non-governmental board members Hartke was able to prevent this from occurring. One of the negative effects of this action was that it was July before the board was in place and USRA had some policy direction.

During the interim period USRA was busy securing data that could be analyzed to assess the viability of the Northeast rail system. Contracts were also let for inventories of the facilities of the six bankrupt roads that were to form Conrail.

In September, Ed Jordan, the president of USRA, went before the House Appropriations Subcommittee on Transportation and asked the Congress for an increase in the USRA appropriation from $26 million to $40 million, and an additional 120 days to prepare the Preliminary System Plan.[3] With regard to the funds requested there was little rationale offered except to say that more money was necessary. The time extension was based on the four month delay in naming the USRA board of directors since the board had to approve both appointments to certain positions as well as major contracts. Each of these requests was granted by the Congress in the form of a Senate Joint Resolution signed by President Ford on October 26 of 1974.[4]

It was November when USRA issued its first annual report to the Congress.[5] The report summarized the reorganization act, the organizational structure of USRA and its financial commitments, as well as the planning approach to be used. Also included in the report were sections on interim abandonments and litigation involving USRA. With regard to the local rail service area, the interim abandonments and branch line planning process are of interest.

The interim abandonment issue was incorporated in the original 3R Act (Sec. 304 (f)) as a procedure for abandoning or discontinuing lines during the USRA planning process. While logic would suggest that all branch lines should be subjected to the planning process underway, the bankrupt estates also had to be able to protect the value of their property in order to assure that the value of that property did not erode away (a process referred to at the time as interim erosion). The Special Court, a single, three-judge, federal district court which presided over all judicial proceedings with respect to USRA's plans, felt the interim erosion potential was exaggerated and it believed that USRA should not approve any interim abandonments if any affected state, local, or regional transportation authority "reasonably opposed such action."

The result of these provisions and rulings is effectively summarized by noting that the bankrupt estates requested interim abandonments on 152 line segments between the passage of the act and June of 1975. USRA approved ten of these which were unopposed or supported by state or local governments. They did not act on the 142 remaining segments viewing them as "reasonably opposed."[6]

The planning process for branch lines that was proposed by USRA took most of the state planners by surprise. The analytical process to be followed would identify and categorize all light density lines on the basis of economic viability. These categories were:

(1) lines that produce a return on investment and have sufficient current revenues to cover all operating, normalized maintenance, and rehabilitation costs;

(2) lines that were able to cover operating costs and minimal maintenance in the short run but not normalized maintenance or rehabilitation costs;

(3) those lines where projections of definite growth in revenue demonstrates long or short term viability;

(4) lines that fail these prior three steps but are capable of operating at a profit if operated by another carrier;

(5) those lines for which states should consider whether social, energy or environmental impact would justify a subsidy in lieu of abandonment.[7]

The surprise was not in the economic criteria to be used by USRA; this was expected. But its use to the exclusion of everything else was a surprise. In effect, what USRA was saying was that they were going to transfer to Conrail only lines that fell in category 1. This became even more evident in charts released at a later time. Lines that couldn't cover normalized maintenance and rehabilitation could be supported by federal/state subsidies; this was category 2. The possibility of category 3 lines, those with a projection of definite growth in revenue, was itself a contradiction—an estimate of something definite. Few lines would make it into Conrail in this manner. It could be that some lines might be profitably operated by other carriers (category 4), but there would not be sufficient time to work out most of the agreements necessary for this to occur. Finally, the last category was for all those lines that would result in negative social, energy or environmental impacts if abandoned. The problem with the final category was that these impact areas were men-

tioned in the legislation as areas to be avoided. It was USRA that was
making the decision that these negative impact lines could be avoided by
having them subsidized by the states and federal government. The states
believed the legislation called for the inclusion of these lines in Conrail
and numerous arguments erupted between the states and USRA based on
this perspective. The states, for example, believed that preserving the
nation's energy goals (as vague as they were and continue to be) was a
national responsibility and should be funded by the federal government
exclusively. USRA did not really disagree with this, but they did not
believe that Conrail should have to bear that burden.

During the fall of 1974 USRA held technical seminars in Washington,
D.C. to acquaint state planners and policy makers with the methodology
being utilized to evaluate the branch lines as well as other aspects of the
plan being developed.

On February 26, 1975, the *Preliminary System Plan* was released to the
public. As previously noted, hearings were held on the plan by the Rail
Services Planning Office in 27 cities in the Midwest and Northeast. Rail
sources at the time indicated that reactions to the plan were mixed and
that is true if negative and very negative are viewed as mixed reactions.
John Fishwick, president of the Norfolk and Western, described the
proposed solution as a poor one, while Milton Shapp, governor of
Pennsylvania, described it as "the rape of the industrial Northeast unless
Congress stops it."

It is conjectural as to whether USRA paid any attention to the testimony given during these hearings. Much attention was given to USRA
claims that the testimony was being placed on computer so that testimony
related to each line could be compiled. However, there is no clear
evidence that USRA did anything more than a thorough analysis and
caught some errors that had appeared in prior reports. In her study of the
impact of the public on the planning process, Mitchell notes, "Gerald
Davies, a member of USRA in the Office of Strategic Planning, maintained to me that USRA rejected all testimony from the hearings after the
Secretary's report. He characterized it mostly as 'local Chamber of
Commerce' propaganda.'"[8] While this is certainly true, it is also true that
the quality of the testimony submitted by the public increased over time.

There were revisions to the plan and a *Final System Plan* was completed and sent to the Congress on July 26, 1975. Under the legislation
the plan would be approved unless the Congress acted specifically to
reject it.

Realizing that the *Plan* was the only visible solution to the Northeast
rail problem, the Congress began to work at making it more palatable.
Senator Richard Schweicker (R - Pa.) proposed that there should be a
moratorium on abandonments. Senator Clifford P. Chase (R - N.J.)
introduced a bill that called for 100 percent federal subsidies for all lines

not conveyed to Conrail. Senator Hartke, chairman of the Surface Transportation Subcomittee, pointed out that there would be a clear need for legislation prior to implementing the *Plan.*

It was Rep. Fred B. Rooney (D - Pa.), chairman of the House Commerce Subcommittee on Transportation and Commerce, who presided over congressional hearings on the plan in September 1975.[9] The hearings were held in two parts. The first focussed on system configuration, branch lines and abandonments, coordination projects, marketing, manpower and passenger service. The second part centered on the financial needs of Conrail and the rail industry in general. It is not apparent that these hearings had any direct effect on USRA's *Plan,* however, they did have an impact on the implementation of that plan through the Rail Revitalization and Regulatory Reform Act (4R Act).

In September of 1975, USRA issued a *Supplemental Report and Errata* to the *Final System Plan.* It contained USRA's estimates of the community employment and environmental impacts of the plan, as well as financial projections for Unified Conrail. The errata was simply a refinement of data in the plan. In November, USRA's *Final System Plan* went into effect when neither the House or Senate took action to return it to USRA for revisions.

There followed five months of documenting the methods and models used and the preparation of documents for the conveyance of real property to Conrail. In the property transfer area, the light-density lines again played a role albeit indirect. Since such a mass of property was to be conveyed it seemed that it would almost be impossible to inventory and describe all of this prior to conveyance day. As a result the conveyance documents were drawn up in such a way as to convey all of the estate property in a given jurisdiction except for certain lines and parcels that were specifically excluded. Also to be transferred were office space, records, files, data processing equipment, rolling stock and so forth. According to USRA "the conveyance documents included," in total over 2,000 separate documents consisting of some 30,000 pages, plus 6,000 pages of computer printouts and 5,000 maps."[10]

In the fall of 1975 USRA was of considerable aid in setting up the light-density line area at Conrail. They did this primarily through the duplication and transferral of individual line files that had been used by USRA. In addition, the computer programs of USRA were amended by Conrail in order to give them the capability of estimating subsidies on given lines. The agency was also instrumental in working with Conrail's branch line personnel in the legislative area and some of the amendments embodied in the 4R Act used this route to become law.

Of course USRA's role was far from completed when Conrail began operations in the spring of 1976. Through a financial agreement required by the 3R Act (Section 216), USRA became the banker of Conrail. As such, it was to review all requests for funds made by Conrail. It was also required, under law, to monitor Conrail's performance; a role which continues at the time of this writing.

FRA

For reasons which are not clear, the FRA was never seriously considered as the agency to solve the rail crisis in the Midwest and Northeast. A review of the legislation in chapter 2 indicates that the FRA was identified as the chief planning agency in the Staggers-Devine bill (H.R. 8526), but then DOT had drafted that bill. The only other attention given to FRA (or DOT to be more specific) was in the Hartke-Ribicoff bill (S. 2188), where DOT was identified as an agency to develop a preliminary report on rail service. They retained this role in the final legislation and this became the *Secretary's Report on Rail Service in the Midwest and Northeast Region.* Of course any designation of DOT in the rail area was a designation of the FRA and it is this latter agency and its role in the branch line question that is of concern here.

FRA had been responsible for planning the Amtrak system and it could be that the Congress felt they had made enough mistakes at that time.[11] It is known that numerous senators were unhappy with the Amtrak plan. Alternatively, it could have been that the FRA did not have sufficient personnel to undertake the preparation of the plan. Though it is clear that a substantial number of employees were to finally join USRA, these were not identified as government employees and at a time when the growth of government was a political issue this mechanism must have been attractive to the Congress.

When the *Secretary's Report* was released, the overwhelming reaction to that document was negative as has been noted. Extremal in its recommendations, impossible to implement, and based on a rather elementary methodology, the FRA made very few friends with what was soon dubbed "the orange line report."

The role of the FRA following the issuance of the *Secretary's Report* was essentially that of administrator. On behalf of the secretary of transportation, the FRA was charged with setting up procedures and requirements regarding applications for federal funds from states or others in order to keep branch lines in service under the local rail service continuation program of the 3R Act. The agency was also the source of funds for the bankrupt estates as they requested funds to keep operating during the interim between the passage of the act and the start-up of Conrail. In addition, FRA retained its rail safety functions which it had had since its creation as part of the new Department of Transportation in 1966, and this function was also relevant in the branch line area.

Following the release of the *Secretary's Report*, the FRA began losing staff members to USRA which was being staffed at the time. The movements of McClellan, Davies, and Hagen to USRA have been noted. The only other major FRA official involved in the preparation of that report was William Loftus. Loftus remained with the FRA and was of vital importance in resolving numerous conflicts in the rail assistance area during the next several years.

THE RULES AND REGULATIONS

During the Spring of 1974 the FRA published its procedures and requirements regarding the "continuation of local rail services" and called for comments on these by June 4, 1974.[12] It was the agency's role to translate the generality of law into specific operating procedures. In the case of the Regional Rail Reorganization Act the law was rather specific so that there was very little discretion on the part of the FRA as to what was required of the states in the rail subsidy or rail service continuation area. Revised rules and regulations which took into consideration the comments received were published in January of 1975.[13]

A few months later FRA issued its procedures and requirements governing the acquisition and modernization loan assistance of the 3R Act's Section 403.[14] It will be recalled that this section of law provided loans to states for purchasing or rehabilitating rail lines. Since the act also provided matching grant funds under Section 402 for these same purposes the provision of loans was not viewed as very attractive by the states.

Revised requirements governing the service continuation and loan programs were issued the following January.[15] With regard to the subsidy area the regulations covered the following points:
1. Rail freight services for which the program could be used.
2. Which states in the country were eligible for entitlement and discretionary funds.
3. The nature, management, and allocation procedure for entitlement and discretionary funds.
4. Planning requirements under the act for each state, and the required contents of plans submitted.
5. Financial, recording and auditing requirements for funds under the program.

Although the provisions of the act were amended by the 4R Act, the rules and regulations of January 1975, which did not differ substantially from later regulations, were in effect when the states submitted rail plans in December of 1975. Revised regulations which incorporated amendments from the 4R Act did not appear until March of 1976.[16]

Of course the FRA was busy on a number of other fronts during the years of 1974 and 1975. It was a period when FRA had to continually grant monies to the estates in order to keep them going: there was $1.2 million to the Central of New Jersey, $30 million to the Penn Central, $7 million to the Erie, the list went on. FRA had also promised the states a rail planning manual to assist them with the preparation of their state rail plans. The first of these appeared in September of 1975, less than three months before the plans were due, and was a little too general to be of use.[17] A much better effort was completed in 1977. It was far more specific than its predecessor and assumed a level of information that was no longer available to planners in 1977.[18] These reports did little to endear the FRA to the states.

SAFETY WAIVERS

As early as November of 1975 the FRA was taking an active role in attempting to smooth the path that subsequent state-railroad negotiations would follow during the first three months of 1976. One of the first issues concerned the question of safety waivers for lines that would be operated under subsidy. The issue brought the FRA into disagreement with members of Conrail's activitation task force. Conrail realized that most of the subsidized lines did not measure up to FRA Class I safety standards, and that most of the lines had been operated under safety waivers. Such waivers permitted a railroad to operate lines at less than Class I speed, which was ten miles per hour, provided that they would take certain precautions. In the problem area there were three entities involved: Conrail, the states, and the bankrupt estates. Conrail maintained that they did not own the lines, would not operate the lines if they had a choice in the matter, and did not control the monies that would be necessary to upgrade the lines to safe levels. As a result they did not want to be responsible for requesting safety waivers. They felt that the states, as the units that had control of rehabilitation funds and wanted the lines operated, should be responsible for this. The estates, as owners of the lines, were at best a poor second in terms of who should request the waivers on subsidized lines.

The formal FRA position was expressed in a memo in January of 1976.[19] It stated that Conrail did not have to provide service unless it was satisfied that the line met FRA Class I standards or unless Conrail accepted a safety waiver on the line. Conrail was informed that it could cease operations if it determined that there were discrepencies on a line unless rehabilitation or safety waivers were in effect. The memo continued: "As Conrail is the agency which controls levels and scheduling of maintenance, it has the obligation to ensure that the line meets the required safety class or has a safety waiver." It added, "Conrail must request the waiver and may not refuse to operate if a subsidy is offered on a line operating with a waiver." Of course the levels of maintenance and rehabilitation were to be set by the states and, indirectly, by the FRA, who had to approve state rail plans, but the agency seemed little concerned with this fact.

Further complicating the general problem was the stated position of FRA that they would require that all lines come up to the Class I level by January of 1977. In order to accomplish this the FRA would have to disperse far more money for rehabilitation than they wanted to initially. It also meant that some states would have to expend more funds for this than they had planned.

The problem remained unresolved for more than two months until Conrail agreed to request the waivers. Officials of the FRA informally assured the railroad that they should not be overly concerned regarding the waivers since limited funding either by FRA or the states would be sufficient cause not to have the work performed. These same officials indicated that from their perspective the states that planned on ten percent rehabilitation during the first year of operations, while the lines' potential viability was being reviewed, were practicing sound economic planning from the viewpoint of the agency. It is an established fact that rehabilitation funds for subsidized lines moved very slowly for the first year and a half of subsidized service, and it is unknown if this was FRA policy or ineptitude. In any event, the safety waiver conflict was resolved, but there was something intrinsically disturbing about the agency charged with railroad safety saying, in essence, that they would look the other way.

CROSS-SUBSIDIES

The FRA has also taken positions on a number of other issues that were later negotiated between the states and Conrail. One of these was the liability question which sought to determine the level of risk on subsidized lines. This is discussed in some detail in the chapter on negotiations. Another area where FRA became involved was in the development of management fees and this is also discussed elsewhere. A final point was the question of cross-subsidies and the FRA position on this question is worthy of note.

Cross-subsidies, or the covering of losses with the profits from other areas, is a well established practice for those transportation modes that have operated under government regulation. In the rail context it may be illustrated by certain unprofitable branch lines having those losses covered by profitable lines elsewhere on the same system. If operations are very profitable for the company as a whole such cross-subsidies are no burden to the rail corporation. However, if the operations are marginal or just break even, cross-subsidies can become the proverbial straw. At the time of the negotiations prior to the start-up of Conrail the general philosophy in the rail industry was that cross-subsidies would have to go and government at the federal level agreed.

In early December of 1975, it appeared to FRA that the potential funds needed by the state programs being proposed would run considerably in excess of appropriations. It was for this reason that FRA advocated a cross subsidy type of arrangement wherein the losses on some subsidized branch lines could be covered by the profits on other "subsidized" lines that turned out to be profitable. The idea did not originate with FRA; it had been around for several months.[20]

FRA continued to advocate this passing of what they viewed as "profits" to lines incurring deficits well into January. Conrail opposed this and was joined in its opposition by the ICC's Rail Services Planning Office. It was noted by these two that the entire question of costs had been defined as "avoidable" costs and the fact that these might run below the total revenues on a branch line did not mean that the line was profitable. If the costs had been defined as fully allocated costs and these were less than revenues then the railroad would be making a profit. But this was not the case. The standards issued by the RSPO failed to consider certain long term costs and, therefore, it was meaningless to talk of profit. The FRA finally accepted the Conrail and RSPO argument.

OTHER ACTIVITIES

William S. Coleman, Secretary of the U.S. Department of Transportation, took an active interest in the circumstances related to labor problems on the Delmarva peninsula. This also involved FRA staff members as an attempt was made to resolve the impasse created by the unwillingness of labor unions to agree to terms proposed by the Southern Railway and Chessie System related to their acquisitions. These negotiations failed much to the chagrin and disgust of the Secretary.

Following the start-up of Conrail the FRA began preparations for the national branch line program incorporated in the 4R Act. New rules and regulations were needed. In addition, the FRA issued a report in August of 1976 that sought to classify lines of Class I U.S. railroads into categories and designating individual rail lines into these categories "so that investments in track can be directed where they will do the most good."[21] There was also a series of seminars held around the country with the objective of informing those outside the Midwest and Northeast regions what the new program was all about.[22]

After two years of operations in the 3R Act region, the regional local rail service program was collapsed into the national program. Appropriations for the seven years of the program's life appear in Table 5.1. Approximately 340 million dollars were involved in the little more than four years between April 1, 1976, and September 30, 1980. Although total authorizations for the program were $542 million, this amount has yet to be totally appropriated.

Hearings on the Local Rail Service Assistance Act of 1978 were held after the program was in place and operating. They were not as positive as many would have liked them to be. It was stated during these hearings that:

> Federal funds are being spent under the current law to attempt to salvage the worst lines in the railroad system, at high cost, and with little, if any potential for success.[23]

Strangely enough, rather than cancelling the program, the Congress extended it. Rather than narrowing the potential lines that could be assisted, they broadened the line eligibility criteria of the program and now allowed lines that had not been abandoned to be eligible for rehabilitation or modernization. At the same time they decided to put an end to the waste in the operating subsidy area; this part of the program was scheduled to end on September 30, 1981. In addition to this, all projects except for the operating subsidy projects were to be submitted to a benefit-cost analysis. When an FRA staff member was later asked why the operating subsidy line projects were excluded from the benefit-cost analysis, he responded, "We knew that none of the projects had benefits exceeding their costs."

In the fall of 1978 FRA's Office of State Assistance Programs, then directed by Madeline S. Bloom, initiated a comprehensive evaluation of the effectiveness of the local rail service assistance program.[24] This evaluation is summarized elsewhere, but it is fair to say that the report went out of its way to identify positive points regarding the program. These could not have been easy to find.

The program continued through 1980 and into 1981. Shortly after Ronald Reagan moved into the White House, Robert W. Blanchette became administrator of the Federal Railroad Administration. Putting Blanchette in charge of any federal program that grew out of the Regional Rail Reorganization Act was like turning over a community's taverns to the W.C.T.U. Blanchette's negativism regarding such programs was notable when he served as a trustee of the bankrupt Penn Central. When he appeared before the House committee's budget authorization hearings in March of 1981, he called for termination of the entire program.[25] In September of 1981 the federally subsidized branch line program ended; the other program elements continue at this writing.

RSPO

"There is established, on the date of enactment of this Act, a new Office in the Commission to be known as the Rail Services Planning Office."[26] With this phrase the RSPO had been created by the Regional Rail Reorganization Act. RSPO's mission at the time of enactment was to serve as a review agency for some of the major reports required by the act. As such it was responsible for conducting public hearings on the *Secretary's*

Report on Rail Service in the Midwest and Northeast Region, as well as
USRA's *Preliminary System Plan* and issuing reports on each of these
documents.

In addition to these tasks the RSPO was to:

> . . . publish standards for determining the "revenue attributable to the rail
> properties," the "avoidable costs of providing service" and "a reasonable
> return on value," as those phrases are used in section 304 of this Act . . .[27]

There can be little doubt that the major function of the RSPO during the
pre-conveyance period was to develop these standards, which were
referred to at the time simply as the "RSPO standards."

Surprisingly, many participants in the rail planning process did not
have a firm understanding of what these subsidy standards were to be
used for. Put quite simply, they were to be used as an interim formula for
estimating the first year subsidy payment for a line operated under the
new rail service continuation program. On numerous occasions individuals reacted to the output of this process as though it were carved in
stone, whereas in reality decreasing maintenance levels or increasing
service frequency would change the numbers substantially.

The RSPO standards had another role as well. They identified, using
standard railroad accounting codes, the extent to which each cost item on
a railroad was to be allocated, or in some cases not allocated, to a branch
line. This was an obvious necessity in estimating a subsidy and it also had
the practical value of allowing railroads operating lines to know exactly
what could be billed to the subsidizer and how. It was in other words a
branch line accounting system for the railroad.

On February 25, 1974, the RSPO issued its first "Notice of Proposed
Rulemaking and Order" to establish the subsidy standards.[28] The standards appeared nearly eleven months later.[29] These were not to be the
final standards since the RSPO opened the rulemaking on four different
occasions in the next two years in order to determine whether certain
costs should or shouldn't be permitted as avoidable costs.[30] This
prompted one official of the agency to comment that if they had it to do all
over again, they would just include everything as an avoidable cost and
then listen to arguments as to why certain accounts should be dropped.
"At this rate we will have all accounts included soon," he added. It did not
become quite that bad, but while most items included up to March 26,
1976 were reasonable, the items included after that date lack the logical
basis of the earlier standards. This point will be returned to later.

Passage of the Rail Revitalization and Regulatory Reform Act in 1976
resulted in some significant changes for the RSPO. In the two years
following enactment of this law, RSPO became involved in several
different studies. Two of the better known of these were a rail merger
study[31] and a study of Amtrak route restructuring.[32]

The agency was not completely out of the branch line area. In 1978 it completed a joint project with the National Conference of State Rail Officials concerning liability coverage on subsidized lines, and published an "abandonment brochure" and an "abandonment information manual." It did little more in the branch line area after that time.

One other function of the RSPO as identified in the 1973 act was that it would:

> . . . employ and utilize the services of attorneys and such other personnel
> as may be required in order to properly protect the interests of those
> communities and users of rail service which, for whatever reason, such as
> their size or location, might not otherwise be adequately represented in the
> course of the hearings and evaluations which the Office is required to
> conduct and perform under provisions of this Act.[33]

This function was realized through the creation of the Office of Public Counsel within the RSPO. Although part of the RSPO it was allowed to function almost independently of it as a unit to represent the public. As an experiment it was probably successful and two extensive reviews of the public counsel function have appeared in the literature.[34]

The ICC

Although RSPO was part of the Interstate Commerce Commission (ICC), it almost functioned independently of it. To some extent this separation was real: the act clearly distinguishes the "Commission" from the "Office." The Congress saw the need for an office that could perform certain functions that had not been performed before. It did not simply assign these tasks to the ICC. Perhaps because the monolithic commission was considered a slow agency among a field of slow moving bureaucracies, it was passed over, but not completely. The ICC still had certain functions to perform under the act and other functions which it retained as guardian of the Interstate Commerce Act.

More specifically the legislation enacted in 1973 stated that the Commission was to be in charge of staffing RSPO (Section 205); assessing the transfers to take place under the *Final System Plan* (Section 206); and, reviewing and evaluating that final plan for the Congress (Section 207). Perhaps the Commission's strongest role appeared in Section 601 which specified the Commission's powers to order "emergency service." If the entire process began to fail, the ICC would emerge as the most important agency.

There were cases of active involvement on the part of the ICC during the planning process. It was concerned that the "western roads" had no idea what lines would continue to have service. The Commission believed that shippers who would be receiving rail service under a subsidy arrangement should also be informed of this. Although representatives of the Penn Central and Conrail did not necessarily feel that either group, western roads or subsidized shippers and receivers, were in the dark regarding these events, they agreed to supply the ICC with all necessary information so that these two "problems" could be avoided. This occurred at a meeting at the ICC on January 26, 1976.

There was also a question as to exactly what the responsibilities were of designated operators; these were the railroads that would perform subsidized service. It was feared by Conrail, for one, that getting out of the position of designated operator might be as complicated as abandoning lines under the traditional ICC procedure. To clarify this point the Commission released a notice on March 5, 1976, that gave designated operators "the right to commence and terminate service pursuant to the terms of agreement between the parties . . ."[35] The flexibility of the Commission was commendable, however, the notice did not require carriers to inform the Commission of a service termination. They now had no idea when rail service was no longer being offered on a line by a designated operator and this continued to be the case until the end of the assistance program.

The final major act of the Commission in the reorganization process came in the middle of March, a mere two weeks before the start-up of Conrail. Although negotiations between potential operators and states were proceeding about as well as could be expected, the same could not be said for negotiations between the trustees of the bankrupt carriers and the states regarding the lease agreement that would permit the operator onto the line. As the Commission stated it:

> . . . in the absence of such lease agreements trustees having control over such properties may be reluctant to permit access to and use of their rail properties by designated operators; that their refusal to do so would result in disruptions of service which would have serious economic consequences to both shippers and the communities served by these lines;[36]

The Commission went on to order the trustees to:

> . . . permit entry onto rail properties for which a rail service continuation payment operating agreement has been executed to allow continuation of rail service, free of all interference by the Trustees.

A Concluding Comment

These were the governmental agencies at the federal level that were involved in the reorganization and, in particular, in the branch line area. Each was vital in ensuring that the planning process worked and the plan and legislation were implemented. Although many of the problems attacked by these agencies could reoccur tomorrow with a rail bankruptcy in another part of the country, it does not appear that an USRA-FRA-RSPO type solution will be utilized again. Each agency has shrunk to a small proportion of what it was at the peak of the program. In order to attack any problem of magnitude considerable staffing would be necessary.

NOTES TO CHAPTER 5

1. A comprehensive history of the formation and activities of the USRA is available in: John E. Harr, *The Great Railway Crisis: An Administrative History of the United States Railway Association*, National Academy of Public Administration. March 1978.

2. John E. Harr, *The Great Railway Crisis: An Administrative History of the United States Railway Association, op. cit.* p. 223.

3. United States Railway Association, *Annual Report June 30, 1974, with a Supplemental Report Through October 1974*, Washington, D.C.: U.S.G.P.O., Nov. 1974, p. 39.

4. Regional Reorganization Act, Amendments, P.L. 93–488, 93rd Congress, 2nd Session, Report, October 26, 1974.

5. United States Railway Association, *Annual Report, June 30, 1974 with a Supplemental Report Through October, 1974*, Washington, D.C.: U.S. Government Printing Office, November 13, 1974.

6. United States Railway Association, *Second Annual Report, June 30, 1975*, Washington, D.C.: U.S. Government Printing Office, October 2, 1975, p. 9.

7. United States Railway Association, *Annual Report, June 30, 1974, op. cit.*, p. 55–56.

8. See: Susan Mitchell, "Public Participation: The Regional Rail Reorganization Approach (I Think I Can . . . I Know I Can)," *ICC Practioner's Journal*, Vol. 44, No. 1 (1976), p. 46.

9. U.S. Congress. House. *USRA Final System Plan*, Hearings before the Subcommittee on Transportation and Commerce, Com. Int. & For. Com, 94th Cong. 1st Sess., Serial 94–44, September 9–11, 22–26, 1975.

10. United States Railway Association, *Third Annual Report, June 30, 1976*, Washington, D.C.: U.S. Government Printing Office, September 30, 1976, p. 14.

11. See: George W. Hilton, *Amtrak, The National Railroad Passenger Corporation*, Washington, D.C.: American Enterprise Institute for Public Policy Research, 1980, pp. 19–20.

12. Department of Transportation, Federal Railroad Administration, "Continuation of Local Rail Services: Procedures and Requirements Regarding Filing of Application," *Federal Register*, Vol. 39, No. 67, pp. 12528–12532, April 5, 1974.

13. Department of Transportation, Federal Railroad Administration, "Continuation of Local Rail Service: Procedures and Requirements Regarding Applications and Disbursements," *Federal Register*, Vol. 40, No. 19, pp. 4232–4237, January 28, 1975.

14. Department of Transportation, Federal Railroad Administration, "Acquisi-

tion and Modernization Loan Assistance: Procedures and Requirements for Filing of Applications and Disbursements," *Federal Register*, Vol. 40, No. 169, pp. 39898–39901, August 29, 1975.

15. Department of Transportation, Federal Railroad Administration, "Rail Service Continuation Subsidies and Modernization of Rail Properties: Loan Assistance," *Federal Register*, Vol. 41, No. 11, pp. 2524–2529, January 16, 1976.

16. Department of Transportation, Federal Railroad Administration, "Assistance to States and Persons in the Northeast and Midwest Region for Local Rail Services Under Section 402 of the Regional Rail Reorganization Act of 1973," *Federal Register*, Vol. 41, No. 45, pp. 9692–9699, March 5, 1976.

17. Federal Railroad Administration, *Rail Planning Procedures Report*, prepared by the State of Wisconsin, Department of Transportation, Report RFA - 40025 - 75, September 1975.

18. Federal Railroad Administration, *Rail Planning Manual*, Vol, I, Guide for Decision-Makers, Vol. II, Guide for Planners, Reports FRA-RFA-76-06, FRA-RFA-78-01, prepared by JWK International Corp. and Roger Creighton Assoc., Inc., December 1976 and July 1978.

19. Federal Railroad Administration, "Comments on Conrail Operating Agreements," undated but received by Conrail during week of January 12, 1976.

20. See, for example, W.R. Black and James F. Runke, *The States and Rural Rail Preservation: Alternative Strategies*, Lexington, KY.: The Council of State Governments, October 1975, pp. 72–73.

21. U.S. Secretary of Transportation, *Preliminary Standards, Classification and Desination of Lines of Class I Railroads in the United States*, August 1976; and, *Final Standards, Classification, and Designation of Lines of Class I Railroads in the United States*, Vol. I and II, Washington, D.C., 1977.

22. Council of State Governments, *Proceedings of the Regional Rail Planning Seminars, Fall 1976*. Co-sponsored with the Federal Railroad Administration, Lexington, KY: 1977.

23. U.S. Congress, Senate, "Local Rail Services Act of 1978," Report to accompany S. 2981, 95th Cong., 2nd Sess., Report No. 95–1159, p. 5.

24. Ernst and Whinney, *Evaluation of the State Rail Assistance Program Findings and Guidelines for Program Evaluation and Financial Management*, prepared for the Office of State Assistance Programs, Federal Railroad Administration, January 1980.

25. U.S. Congress, House, *Local Rail Services Assistance Act Authorization*, Hearing before the Subcommittee on Commerce, Transportation and Tourism of the Committee on Energy and Commerce, 97th Congr., 1st sess. Serial 97–23, March 17, 1981, p. 4.

26. See: Public Law 93–236, 93rd Congr., HR 9142, 2 January 1974.

27. *Op. cit.*

28. Interstate Commerce Commission, Rail Services Planning Office, "Rail Service Continuation Subsidies: Standards for Determination," *Federal Register*, Vol. 39, 7182, February 25, 1974.

29. Interstate Commerce Commission, Rail Services Planning Office, "Standards for Determining Rail Service Continuation Subsidies, *Federal Register*, Vol. 40, No. 5, pp. 1624–1636, January 8, 1975.

30. See: 40 FR 14186, March 28, 1975; 41 FR 3402, January 22, 1976; 41 FR 12836, March 26, 1976.

31. Interstate Commerce Commission, Rail Services Planning Office, *Rail Merger Study*, Issue Papers and Final Report, 10 Vol., 1977.

32. Interstate Commerce Commission, Rail Services Planning Office, *Report to the President and Congress on the Effectiveness of the Rail Passenger Service Act of 1970*, March 15, 1978.

33. *Op. cit.*

34. See: Mitchell, *op cit..*, and T.S. Bloch and R.J. Stein. "The Public Counsel Concept in Practice: The Regional Rail Reorganization Act of 1973, *"William and Mary Law Review*, Vol. 16, No. 2, 1974, pp. 215–236.

35. Interstate Commerce Commission, "Trustees Directed to Make Rail Properties Available for Continued Rail Service," *Ex Parte No. 293 (Sub. No. 10)*, Service Date: March 17, 1976.

36. Interstate Commerce Commission, Notice: "Continuation of Rail Service Under Subsidy by Designated Operator," Service Date: March 8, 1976.

Chapter 6

CONRAIL, THE ESTATES, AND
OTHER RAILROADS

The general reaction of the rail industry to the concept of subsidizing branch lines was favorable. If the lines weren't the major problem of the industry, this didn't really matter. They were a problem and as a result they supported the idea of offering subsidies for their continued operation. However, as the concept became more of a program, the railroads were not really sure that they wanted to be involved with it.

In this chapter the goal is to acquaint the reader with the activities of the railroads as they relate to the rail continuation program. The creation and activities of Conrail are given considerable attention since that railroad became the key to whether the program would get off the ground. Equally important were the activities and policies of the bankrupt Penn Central estate; however, in their case, legal problems clouded their actions. The attitudes of other railroads and the roles of the emerging short lines are also reviewed here.

Conrail

The 3R Act called for the creation of Conrail within 300 days after enactment and this was accomplished during the fall of 1974.[1] The Consolidated Rail Corporation was incorporated in the State of Delaware by the USRA Executive Committee. It was June of 1975 before any substantive activity started at Conrail. At that time Edward G. Jordan, who had been president of USRA, was named president of the new rail corporation. In late summer, Richard D. Spence, formerly vice president of operations for the Southern Pacific Railroad, was named president and chief operating officer of Conrail, and Jordan became chief executive officer and chairman of the corporation.

At about the same time David R. McCarthy, who had previously been a special assistant to the under secretary of transportation at the U.S. Department of Transportation and responsible for staffing USRA, joined the corporation in a similar capacity. He was to lead the search for staff of the activation task force.

The activation task force was the group that was to assure that everything worked on conveyance day. Initially, there were thirteen components that formed the task force. Each of these components was headed by a team leader (see Figure 6.1). The number of teams expanded as the process identified new tasks that had to be performed. For example, Title V, the labor protection section of the 3R Act, created sufficient work to be split off as a separate group.

Each team was responsible for planning the activities in their respective areas that had to be accomplished prior to conveyance day. As such, each had their own staff members working individual parts of the conveyance problem. Jordan and Spence chaired weekly staff meetings where progress, problems, strategies, accomplishments and future plans were laid out by each team leader. Generally, major policy was set by Jordan and Spence, but it was not uncommon for individual team leaders to have a considerable amount of control over day-to-day decisions in their respective areas.

Figure 6.1

ACTIVATION TASK FORCE

Team	Team Leader
State Negotiations	William R. Black
Activation Planning	Robert H. Clement
Passenger Negotiations	C. Garry Collins
Labor Relations	Alvin E. Egbers
Management Control	Robert Evanson
Personnel Administration	James R. Frick
Computer Systems/Data Processing	Robert E. Lingquist
Staffing	David McCarthy
Solvent Railroad Negotiations	Calvin H. Nelson
Operations Planning	Hugh L. Randall
Procurement	J.A. Smith
Sales/Marketing	James R. Sullivan
Public Affairs	Mark B. Sullivan
Capital and Rehabilitation Planning	Carl N. Taylor
Conveyance	Michael J. Timbers
Legal	Richard B. Wachenfield
Financial Accounting	Robert V. Wadden
Administration	Tobias V. Welo

STATE NEGOTIATIONS

"State negotiations" was the label given to the team in charge of light density lines and the subsidy program at Conrail. At the beginning of the activation process the team consisted only of the author. In a very short time James R. Blaze was added to the team. Blaze had directed rail studies for the Chicago Area Transportation Study (CATS) prior to joining the Department of Transportation of the State of Illinois. He left Illinois in the summer of 1974 to join the United States Railway Association. His work with USRA had been primarily in the state relations and strategic planning divisions. One of the missions of USRA was to provide for the implementation of the Final System Plan and Blaze was responsible for drafting one of the earliest versions of a state - railroad operating agreement.

Michael Kenney, who was in the trackage rights and agreements area of USRA, joined Blaze in meeting with some of the states as early as October of 1975 when they were both at USRA. Kenney later became the Conrail team leader responsible for negotiations with "solvent" (the non-bankrupt) railroads in the Northeast. On at least one occasion James R. Sullivan of the Penn Central joined the group in such a meeting with state officials. Sullivan also later joined the activation task force of Conrail as the team leader in charge of "sales and marketing." Prior to this, in the early 1970's, he was responsible for developing the "prepaid revenue supplement" program at the Penn Central.[2] This was a type of subsidy arrangement and, therefore, Sullivan was quite familiar with the subsidized rail service concept.

The states in the region had not developed any affection for USRA or the Penn Central during the planning process, and they did not hesitate to point this out to Jordan when the USRA and Penn Central personnel appeared in their states. They had assumed they would be negotiating with Conrail for subsidized service. It is quite likely that this potential conflict area resulted in this author being hired by Conrail. He was known to USRA as the director of rail planning for the State of Indiana. Indiana had been cooperative with USRA and based most of its decisions on objective analyses, i.e., the state was not opposed to the entire process as were some others in the region.

Aside from Blaze and the author, the state negotiations team had two other members: Richard Huffman and Thomas Heiber. Both individuals had worked in the "light-density lines" area of strategic planning at USRA. They were intimately familiar with the USRA methodology, and the line segments that were available for subsidy. In addition they had previously worked for the Chessie System and brought to the team some familiarity with railroad operations.

The duties of each of the individuals varied over time, but some idea of the responsibilities of each individual may be obtained from Figure 6.2.

Figure 6.2

STATE NEGOTIATIONS - FUNCTIONAL RESPONSIBILITIES

William R. Black . . . . Team Management
                                     Negotiations
                                     Trustee or Estate Contacts
                                     State Relations
                                     LDL Insurance
                                     Contract Development
                                     State Taxation
                                     Legislative Amendments
                                     FRA Communications
                                     RSPO Communications

James R. Blaze . . . . Chessie and Solvent Communications
                                     LDL-AVS Inventory and Records
                                     Distribution
                                     Local Government Inquiries
                                     Shipper Inquiries
                                     Trackage Rights
                                     Coordination Projects

Thomas Heiber . . . . Short Line Proposals
                                     Marketing/Economic Analysis
                                     Cost Estimation/Sub-Segment Analysis
                                     State Rail Plans
                                     Safety Waivers
                                     Rehabilitation Programs
                                     Maintenance Programs

Richard Huffman . . . . Branchline Accounting
                                     Labor-Manpower Coordination
                                     RSPO Standards - Submissions
                                     Operations - Coordination
                                     Consultant Liaison
                                     Line Designations

This figure identifies the major functional responsibilities about midway through the activation process (about January 1976).

At the outset of the activation process, there were five major projects identified in the state negotiations area. The first of these was the further development and polishing of the basic negotiating agreement. This would be followed by the second major project: the actual process of negotiating agreements with states and others for subsidized rail service. A third project involved transferring the detailed branch line files and information system from USRA to Conrail. In order to keep records of the costs and revenues on the subsidized lines, a new accounting system would have to be developed and this was the fourth project. There was one other major task or project and this was a communication and coordination project with other divisions of the activation task force. It was recommended by Conrail management that this task be dropped because these were implied functions of the task force or team approach being followed. Although this was certainly true, it was also true that the state negotiations or light-density lines (LDL) area was different from every other area of the activation task force. Robert Wadden, the team leader for finance and later vice president and treasurer of Conrail, understood this better than most. He noted that all of the activation problems, labor relations, rehabilitation, financial, and so forth, were attacked any time a rail merger took place, but subsidized freight service was something new. It was an area where new ground could be broken. He also added, "It is the only area where the corporation is guaranteed not to lose money." However, these differences were not understood very well by others at Conrail.

Every area of the activation task force had problems that they had to solve, and given enough time they could accomplish this. If state negotiations had a problem, it was only on rare occasions that they could solve it alone. Whether a branch line could be operated in a particular manner necessitated communication with "operations" and "labor". For a line to be rehabilitated by the end of the summer of 1976 required coordination with the "rehabilitation" team. As each team was busy working on problems in their respective areas of the new 17,000 mile system, the state negotiations team was planning the complete operations of a separate and new 3,000 mile system composed entirely of subsidized lines.

There was also a problem in that other areas of Conrail's activation did not understand the holdup in LDL information. There was never any assurance, until operating agreements were in place, that a given set of lines was going to be operated under subsidy. Therefore, it was impossible to respond to requests for subsidized lines' rehabilitation needs, or a budget estimate for revenues and costs on the LDL's, or whether a crew would be necessary in a given area for subsidized service. In effect, the states had complete control over this area of Conrail's activation planning until agreements were signed in March of 1976.

Returning to the major tasks to be undertaken by the state negotiations group, one of these concerned the development of an accounting system. There were those who believed that this function overlapped similar functions being executed by the finance area of Conrail. Admittedly, it made sense to transfer this item to the finance area since that area housed practically all of the accounting expertise of the task force. State negotiations continued to play a role in the area and assisted in the development of an accounting manual for branch lines, and the instructing of operations personnel regarding the necessary information to be collected.

THE PREVAILING ATTITUDE

Jordan and Spence had completely different backgrounds and concerns at Conrail. Jordan had to give primary consideration to the legislative and political atmosphere surrounding the corporation and conveyance.

Spence's concerns were in assuring that the operations were ready on conveyance day. The two were polar opposites in many ways, yet the outcome of these differences appeared to be a cooperative balance. Each individual knew a viable rail system could emerge from "the wreck of the Penn Central" and the other eastern bankrupts. They knew this; there was no doubt in their minds. Indeed, each gave the impression that there was no other outcome that they were willing to consider.

So far as is known no one ever had the nerve to ask Spence what he would do if one of his trains disappeared on conveyance day as had occurred when the Pennsylvania Railroad and the New York Central had merged less than a decade before. Spence's concerns were for the operations of the railroad and a smooth start-up. The impression was that he would accept the sun rising in the west before he would entertain something wrong with the operation of the railroad.

Jordan on the other hand was the person who had answers. From his background as president of the USRA, he was very much aware of the financial aspects of the *Final System Plan* and the outlook for future viability of the corporation. On one occasion he was asked to address a meeting of the state rail officials at Saratoga Springs, New York. He was also asked to respond to questions which the state representatives might have regarding the new railroad. Peter Metz, assistant secretary of transportation for the Commonwealth of Massachusetts, began a question with, "Assuming that Conrail does not become profitable . . ." Jordan quickly interrupted, "I am unwilling to accept that initial premise." No one questioned that Jordan was indeed sincere in this response. He was capable of addressing several hundred skeptical shippers who had gone through interrupted service periods when the Penn Central merger took place and convince the vast majority of these that this would not happen with Conrail.

The positive attitudes of Jordan and Spence were sufficient to convince members of the activation task force that Conrail would indeed become a viable railroad. At the same time, no one on the task force would have considered doing anything that could result in a negative financial impact on the corporation. On numerous occasions, the federal agencies involved made comments that Conrail would become another Amtrak. This attitude was unacceptable to Jordan and Spence. When a new cost item was identified as part of the activation process and a staff member made a casual remark that it would need a little more federal money, Jordan responded that the money was an USRA loan and every penny was going to be repaid.

Jordan and Spence were not as directly involved in the light-density line area as some thought. The initial negotiating instrument was reviewed by each and they made their concerns known. Quite simply, Spence would not allow the states to run his railroad, and Jordan would not condone any action that would strain the financial prospects of

Conrail. Each believed that Conrail should be "made whole" for the subsidized service that it would provide in accordance with the provisions of the 3R Act.

Although there were no conflicts between the state negotiations group and Spence, there was one area where the group did not necessarily agree with Jordan. The specific issue was crew size on branch lines that were to be operated under a subsidy arrangement. The author was of the opinion that this was an excellent place to make a stand on this question. The states wanted smaller crews; the crews would be paid with federal and state funds; the Congress would clearly back any attempt to keep the cost of the program down. Unfortunately, Jordan was unwilling to discuss the issue even on a philosophical basis. He saw any attempt to move to smaller crews as the potential basis for a major strike and he believed that such a strike could have wrecked the conveyance and Conrail. In retrospect and knowing what the labor unions did on the Delmarva Peninsula, there is every possibility that Jordan was right to be concerned. However, what the reaction of the unions would have been to small crews on subsidized lines will never be known.

DIFFICULTIES WITH NEGOTIATIONS

The major issues that developed during the negotiations with the states were resolved by the state negotiations group. If the issue appeared significant, it was reviewed by Jordan. This was true, for example, of the excess revenue and insurance solutions discussed in the negotiations chapter. At no time were any of the group's positions reversed by such a review.

The negotiations which had begun in October in some cases were drawn out until March. Two or three states would sequentially go through the negotiations and tentative agreements would be reached with them. Then the first state would talk to the third, and the latter would want a particular clause that the former had received in its agreement. In this manner the negotiations with the individual states moved very slowly. On the other hand, negotiating with all states at the same time proved to be an impossible situation on the two occasions that it was attempted and, as a result, this latter approach was discarded.

By the middle of February it was apparent that something would have to be done to speed up the state negotiations. On February 18, 1976, the following memorandum was delivered to the states at a meeting in Hartford, Connecticut:

> Due to the failure of States and other subsidizers to conclude operating agreements for continued rail service with the Consolidated Rail Corporation, the Corporation must take the following actions:
> (1) All jobs on lines available for subsidy and not incorporated in Conrail will be abolished by April 1, with notification by March 15;

(2) All stations on lines available for subsidy will be deleted from the existing tariffs (in progress);

(3) All equipment to be utilized by the Corporation in providing rail service under subsidy is being removed from these lines (in progress);

(4) Plans currently being prepared and distributed to field supervisors for Day One operation do not include plans for subsidized service.

In addition, the Corporation will not be able to undertake active maintenance or rehabilitation involving replacement of materials, e., ties, bolts, etc., for several months on lines operated under subsidy due to the lag time between placement of orders and deliveries.

It is our sincere hope that we can still provide rail service under Title IV of the Regional Rail Reorganization Act of 1973, as amended. However, at this point in time, CRC has not been designated as the railroad to provide this service by any State or potential subsidizer, and, we have not been offered a subsidy by any party. As a result, CRC will incur unnecessary costs if the actions outlined here are not taken.

The reaction to the memo was strong and hostile, but it was kept under control except for a few comments about "blackmail." Although some thought that the memo was a bluff, everything mentioned in the memo was true. It was ridiculous for the states to think that they could sign agreements at the last minute and have operations start on time. If nothing else the memo pointed out the complexity of starting subsidized operations in all of the states. Within ten days all of the states had designated Conrail as its operator and the negotiations began in earnest after that time.

There was still some difficulty in getting signed contracts from the states. It was rumored and later confirmed that the states had agreed among themselves not to sign agreements with Conrail until each state was satisfied with the operating agreement. This delayed finalizing agreements until Michigan signed its first contract with Conrail on March 18, 1976. All agreements were in place prior to the start-up of operations on April 1.

The Estates and the Subsidy Program

Early in the fall of 1975 the states, Conrail, and the FRA decided that there should be two separate agreements for the subsidy program: the operating agreement between the states and railroads and the lease agreement between the states and the owners of the rail properties. At the time, RSPO did not particularly endorse the two agreement approach, but argued unsuccessfully for a single three-party contract. As events developed, it is fortunate that the two agreements' approach was taken.

In order to understand the situation that developed between the bankrupt estates and their trustees, and the states, it is necessary to go back to the *Final System Plan* of July, 1975. The USRA plan had placed a value of $422 million on the estates to be conveyed to Conrail. This figure was arrived at by determining the current scrap value of the properties in 1975 (this was $3.6 billion) and the assuming it would take 20 years to liquidate this amount of property. USRA then discounted the $3.6 billion back twenty years to current values (as of January 1, 1976).[3]

The Penn Central trustees, among others, argued that this discounted net liquidation valuation theory was not appropriate. The method yielded a valuation which was too low and they believed the property alone was worth something in the neighborhood of $7.4 billion. Creditors and investors of the estates requested that the Special Court, created by the 3R Act to resolve disputes of this sort, determine the true value of the property. That court was presided over by Judge Henry J. Friendly of the United States Court of Appeals for the Second Circuit. The case began on April 1, 1976, and more than a year and one-half later the Special Court admitted that they were having trouble resolving the valuation question.[4]

Three years later during the fall of 1980 the Penn Central estate and the federal government agreed to a $2.113 billion settlement. Actually, the settlement was for $1.46 billion with interest accounting for an additional $650 million. It was the largest settlement in U.S. history. Part of the reason for the settlement being reached so soon was due to a recommendation by the Special Court that the parties agree to these terms. In addition, Stephen Berger, the chairman of USRA, noted that the litigation had been costing USRA and therefore the federal government almost $20 million a year in legal fees.[5]

Returning to the subsidy program, it can be seen that so long as the valuation question was under litigation or contested, it would be difficult to set a value for the property for purposes of the lease agreements with the states. In this regard the trustees were reluctant to move ahead; however, the government also moved very slowly. Each was afraid that any valuation that differed from their posited value in the legal case underway might sacrifice their position in future court actions. Initially, the Penn Central Transportation Company (PCTC) believed that a reasonable lease value would be about $2,700 per route mile. However, the FRA thought the value should be more in the neighborhood of $2,100 dollars per mile.

Representatives of the states, RSPO, and FRA had numerous negotiating sessions with David Kelso McConnell, counsel for the PCTC trustees, in an attempt to resolve the issue. The objective of these sessions was to set a lease value that would not necessarily equate with the property value. One of the alternatives that had the greatest promise was a form of trackage rights agreement, where payment would be a function of traffic moving over the line. This actually seemed acceptable to all parties in the negotiating session. However, when McConnell presented the approach to the trustees they rejected it.

Writing in March of 1976, the Office of Public Counsel of RSPO noted:

Negotiations on the lease agreements have bogged down over the issue of valuation of properties. Neither the trustees, nor the states, nor the federal government are anxious to agree to a value for the subsidized lines which will prejudice their court case before the special court concerning the ultimate value of the transferred rail properties. For the same reason, binding arbitration is also unsatisfactory.[6]

This problem with the lease agreement continued through March necessitating action by the ICC. On the 16th of March, they issued an order directing the trustees of the bankrupt estates to permit entry onto their property for rail operations covered by an operating agreement under the rail service continuation program.[7] The Commission displayed its pessimism by making the order effective until lease agreements were executed. Therefore, the absence of the lease agreements was not a barrier to continued operations under the subsidy program.

On October 19, 1976, President Ford signed into law the Rail Transportation Improvement Act.[8] This law, which in committee was referred to as the "Son of Conrail" bill, included a provision that was essential to the lease agreement situation. Section 205 of that law amended the 3R Act (Section 304(d)) by stating that "no determination of reasonable payment for the use of rail properties of a railroad in reorganization in the region, and no determination of value of rail properties of such a railroad (including supporting or related documents of any kind) which is made in connection with any lease agreement, contract of sale, or other agreement or understanding which is entered into after a date of enactment of the Rail Transportation Improvement Act . . . shall be admitted as evidence, or used for any other purpose, in any civil action, or any other proceeding for damages or compensation arising under this Act." This was intended to eliminate the value barrier to reaching consensus on a lease agreement; however, it did not have that immediate impact on the process.

First it was necessary to have the approval of Judge John P. Fullam of the reorganization court. New York State had been negotiating with the Penn Central Transportation Company trustees and it appeared that a model lease had been drafted that was acceptable to both parties. This lease was submitted along with a petition from the trustees for approval of the New York agreement. Writing on April 25, 1977, Judge Fullam approved the petition, and the model lease. He further wrote:

The Trustees are authorized to enter into substantially similar agreements with New York and other states and Commonwealths with respect to line segments not covered by this agreement and not conveyed to Conrail or profitable railroads . . .[9]

Negotiations began between the other states and the appropriate estates

based on the New York-Penn Central model and by the end of the year
these agreements were in place throughout the region.

It should be noted that although the trustees had been requesting
$2,700 per route mile and the FRA had posited $2,100 per route mile, the
final compromise value was $2,475 per route mile in most of the agree-
ments signed in 1977 and backdated to April 1, 1976. A major problem
with the leases occurred during later negotiations when it was agreed that
the lease values would increase based on inflationary trends. The impact
of this was substantial as reflected in Table 6.1 for seven lines in Indiana.
As can be seen in the table, the lease values increased significantly over
the five year period covered.

Related Trustee Problems and Concerns

The estates had other problems related to the subsidy program. The 3R
Act had incorporated a provision that would enable them to file notices of
discontinuance of service to be effective 90 days after approval of the
Final System Plan by the Congress in November of 1975. This would have
made the notices effective on or about February 7 of 1976. However, at
the time Conrail was not to start operations until February 27, 1976. The
trustees were concerned that they might be ordered to operate under
subsidy during the intervening 20 days. They had no real desire to do

TABLE 6.1

PENN CENTRAL CORPORATION LEASE VALUES

FOR SEVEN INDIANA BRANCH LINES*

USRA No.	Length (route miles)	1976	1977	Subsidy Year 1978	1979	1980
399	16.0	$39,600	$39,600	$36,282	$ 57,541	$ 71,043
401a	19.1	$47,300	$47,300	$36,787	$ 58,343	$ 71,888
417	1.5	$ 3,700	$ 3,700	$11,183	$ 17,735	$ 21,980
523	6.38	$15,800	$15,800	$20,223	$ 32,072	$ 39,681
554	14.31	$35,400	$35,400	$44,383	$ 70,390	$ 87,115
571	26.15	$64,800	$64,800	$72,108	$114,360	$141,394
589	25.90	$63,400	$63,400	$98,059	$155,517	$192,586

*Source: Division of Railroads, Department of Transportation,
State of Indiana

this. As a result, the notices were changed to take effect on February 27. This would have resolved the problem if the Rail Revitalization and Regulatory Reform Act had been signed prior to January 1, however, the failure of that to occur resulted in a postponement of conveyance day and the start-up of Conrail. Fortunately, this delay was anticipated by the drafters of the 4R Act and they made the discontinuances effective the day of conveyance.

In January of 1976 the trustees of the Penn Central attempted to sell certain properties which were not to be conveyed to Conrail. Since some of these properties might be operated under subsidy, the states and others had no desire to see the track and ties carried away. The sale was undoubtedly prompted by the general cash flow situation of the estate at the time and it was halted by the courts.[10]

The "cash flow crisis" (as it was called) was attributable in part to a slump in the automobile industry and a coal strike in the fall of 1974. Traffic volume on the Penn Central was down 15 percent in January of 1975 compared to January of 1974. Of course the railroad had been systematically losing money: $197.9 million in 1972, $189 million in 1973, 1200 million in 1974, and an estimated $340 million in 1975.[11] Those who complained that the railroad was losing a million dollars a day were not far off the mark.

The maintenance programs of all the railroads in reorganization had been affected by shortages in parts and capital. Rumors circulated that the Penn Central was using some of its locomotives for parts, a process referred to as cannibalizing, in order to repair other locomotives during the months before conveyance. Conrail emphasized that it was to be conveyed an operating railroad implying that there would be nothing left that worked by conveyance day.

Simple cash was not abundant at the Penn Central. At the end of 1974 that railroad had a year end cash balance of $17.3 million.[12] This seems like a significant amount until one realizes that it would probably not be enough to meet a weekly payroll for the railroad.

Of course all of the railroads in reorganization had been receiving substantial amounts of money from the federal government in order to enable them to continue operating until Conrail took over control of the operations. These funds were either cash grants from the Federal Railroad Administration or loans from the United States Railway Association.[13]

The Chessie System and the Southern Railway

The primary reason for the involvement of the Chessie System and the Southern Railway in the solution proposed by the United States Railway Association in their *Final System Plan* was the belief that there would not be adequate competition in the region if Conrail was the only major carrier involved; Conrail might have a monopoly in the region. Therefore, USRA's planners sought to get these two railroads involved in the plan. Of the two it would appear that the Chessie was the more vigorous in responding to USRA designations that they take over certain lines.

As early as mid-January of 1975 the Chessie had offered a financial arrangement to USRA that called for $20 million in cash and $95 million in Baltimore and Ohio Railroad bonds for the lines offered them in the *Final System Plan.*[14] By November, Chessie's board of directors had approved the acquisition which had been refined to 2,185 route miles plus trackage rights over an additional 744 miles. The price tag had been revised to $54.5 million.[15] The board also conditioned its approval on agreements with unions, and traffic and financial arrangements, but the later had already been agreed to by USRA. Of course there was another concern of the Chessie board as well as others and this was the need for additional legislation by the Congress which would approve the USRA price for the properties to be conveyed to Conrail and others. This legislation would also have to provide protection for Chessie against any possible future "deficiency judgement" by the courts regarding the adequacy of the USRA established price. In other words if the courts later ruled the USRA price was too low and raised it, Chessie did not want to have to make up the difference. As Hays Watkins, chairman and chief executive officer of the Chessie System stated before the Senate's Sub-committee on Surface Transportation: ". . . Chessie cannot and will not, be a party to open ended purchase contracts."[16]

The needed deficiency judgement protection was provided in the 4R Act which was enacted on February 5 of 1976. However, even prior to that date there were indications that all was not going well in the labor negotiations of Chessie and the Southern with their respective unions.[17] Although the problem was initially identified as some difficulty related to what rules the workers would come under after acquisition, the problem turned out to be more extensive than this. It is true that there was some question as to whether employees would have to follow practices or work rules of the acquiring railroad or the previous (now bankrupt) railroad for which they had worked. The Congress was aware of the labor difficulty and had inserted provisions in the 4R Act that gave the solvent railroads seven days (after enactment) to complete any labor agreements necessary for the lines to be sold to them. On February 12 it was announced that "the Chessie System and the Southern Railway, unable to reach agree-ment with rail unions over work rules, have withdrawn from the northeast restructuring."[18]

Although most of the unions had reached agreements with the rail-roads, the Brotherhood of Railway and Airline Clerks, known as BRAC (and the United Transportation Union)[19] had held out. BRAC declined to sign the labor agreements because of three main points according to reports. These were:

(1) Refusal of the firms to approve a cost of living escalator which the union said would cost workers $400 a year; however, the question of such compensation was the subject of an industry wide dispute and both Southern and Chessie ultimately would be required to follow whatever general settlement was reached.

(2) Refusal of the union to agree to work rule changes asked by the Southern and Chessie such as the right to move workers or to lay them off with pay if they elected not to move. Under the new Conrail, BRAC would have to work under similar requirements.

(3) Refusal of the Southern to provide workers in the Wilmington area with commuter passes on government funded regional commuter lines; passes not provided by the Pennsy and not contemplated by Conrail.[20]

William Jones, the *Washington Post* reporter who was the source of this report appears to be suggesting that the three major issues of contention were major non-issues, and that there was more to the impasse than the casual observer would notice. Attempts by the Congress, Secretary of Transportation William T. Coleman, and Labor Secretary W.J. Usery to get the negotiations to continue were successful and the talks continued until late in March, but sufficient agreements were not reached to permit the Southern and Chessie acquisitions.[21]

The net results of failure to reach the necessary labor agreements were:

1. A larger Conrail system than envisioned by the *Final System Plan* and, as a result, in some people's eyes, less competition;

2. Operation of most of the Delmarva Peninsula lines by Conrail as subsidized light-density branch lines; and

3. An ICC study ordered by the Congress that would state why the acquisitions were not consumated and recommend what actions to take regarding rail service on the Delmarva Peninsula.

With regard to the third item, that study was completed in April of 1977.[22] It identified the major problem with the negotiations to be wages and rates of pay. Southern agreed to preserve the rates of pay for those individuals holding 75 positions coming to it from the Penn Central (where the rate was higher), but it would not agree to apply that PC rate of pay to the positions.

The report continues:

The Southern feared that such concessions would force them to accept higher rates of pay and more restrictive work rules on the rest of Southern's system, and they pointed out that if Southern had operated with the PC's 1974 transportation ratio or compensation ratio on its system, Southern's $88 million net profit that year would have been more than a $37 million loss.[23]

The unions would not agree to reduced rates of pay for these positions and that, in effect, was the reason why the Southern portion of the *Final System Plan* failed to materialize.

Two general observations occur to most individuals who examine this situation in any detail. The first is whether the railroad labor unions should have been allowed to essentially alter the will of Congress by altering a plan that they had implicitly approved. The second observation results from an examination of traffic figures on the Delmarva Peninsula. It is, basically, why would the Southern even consider acquiring these lines and the rather sparse traffic that would come with them. It had all the attributes of an acquisition that was not thought out very well.

The Norfolk and Western Railway (N&W)

USRA's *Preliminary System Plan* recommended a three-carrier system for the region (Conrail, N&W, and Chessie) that would have given the Norfolk and Western the bankrupt Erie-Lackawanna from Buffalo, New York to Newark, New Jersey by way of Binghamton, New York. However, as USRA noted in the *Final System Plan* "under the terms and conditions proposed and within the time constraints of the Act, the Association was unable to reach an agreement with Norfolk and Western for participation of that railroad in major industry structure acquisitions."[24]

Although minor lines were conveyed to the N&W it is not difficult to imagine the major obstacle in failing to reach agreement on a greater involvement for this railroad. That obstacle was probably John P. Fishwick, president of the N&W. Fishwick would have been comic relief if he wasn't so convinced that he was right. He ridiculed USRA's private sector solution as de facto nationalization.[25] He also considered the $2.1 billion that Conrail would start with as a significant underestimate. He believed the figure would have to be more in the neighborhood of $10 billion. Regarding the $2.1 billion, he stated "we figured that amount of money is the total sum of the earnings of the N&W before taxes from 1930 to 1975. In other words it took us 45 years of productive operation to make as much as Conrail got from the government's pocket with one congressional act.[26] Fishwick was also concerned over trucks, barges, and the St. Lawrence Seaway since he believed that these were responsible for the "decline of railroads in the East." To be sure there was some truth in everything Fishwick had to say, and that is probably what irritated the USRA planners and congressional leaders who had designed the solution.

The Short Lines

On February 19, 1976, it was necessary for the state negotiations group at Conrail to issue a memorandum to the states in the region regarding short line railroads. It stated:

> The volume of proposals for the creation of short line railroads has increased substantially in the past few weeks. CRC does not have sufficient staff to perform the divisions analysis on all of these proposals prior to conveyance. As a result, whenever we are approached by short line entrepreneurs, we will request that they be designated by the State as the operator and that their proposal be consistent with the State Rail Plan.

Although this did cut down the number of proposals received, there continued to be a significant volume.

Perhaps Lionel, Marx, and others are to blame for the fact that there are a large number of adults who have always wanted to run their own railroad. That being the case there was never a better opportunity than during the rail reorganization process that led to the start-up of Conrail. There were several reasons for the popularity of this approach.

First, the states realized that if their branch lines were to be operated by Conrail under a subsidy agreement, the crews would most likely consist of the same Penn Central or other bankrupt carrier employees that in many cases had driven the rail traffic away. Second, Conrail as a new railroad would have enough problems so that it would not be able to give individual branch lines the attention that the states thought they deserved. Third, because Conrail would be operating under subsidy, it would do only what it was paid to do under the RSPO standards. Marketing was not an allowable (and therefore "avoidable") cost under the standards and therefore little growth in traffic could be expected. Fourth, there was no doubt that the labor costs of a short line could be substantially less than those of Conrail. Fifth, short lines were continually "talked up" as the way to go and several research and informational reports during 1974 and 1975 had advocated this approach.[27] There were other reasons applicable to specific situations, but these are representative of the attractiveness of the option.

For the most part the states moved too slowly when it came to short lines and most of these were not in place by April 1, 1976, when the new operations of Conrail started and the bankrupts ceased to offer service. Those short lines that were in place and had been granted "designated operator" status by the ICC appear as Table 6.2. These six roads accounted for just under 400 miles of track (398.7) and except for 5.1 miles operated by the Delaware and Hudson, the remainder of the subsidized lines were operated by Conrail.

Of the short lines noted in the table, the Ogdensburg Bridge and Port Authority was later replaced by the National Railway Utilization Corporation, which was subsequently replaced by the North Country Railroad Corporation in 1980, and this in turn gave way to the Ontario Eastern Railroad Corporation in 1982. Although this short line did lose money, it lost less than most of its counterparts. Perhaps the most notorious of these short lines is the Michigan Northern. Its actions provoked the rail industry as well as the state government of Michigan.[28]

TABLE 6.2

THE SHORT LINE DESIGNATED OPERATORS

Railroad	State	USRA Lines	Length (miles)
Ogdensburg Bridge and Port Authority	NY	89a	19.0
Providence and Worcester Co.	CT	674	16.9
		41	1.1
Hillsdale County Railway Co., Inc.	MI	398	6.3
		401	15.1
		402	14.6
		404	14.7
		692a/693a	17.1
Bath and Hammondsport Railroad Co.	NY	1239	22.1
Lackawaxen and Stourbridge Railroad Co.	PA	1238	25.7
Michigan Northern Railway Co.	MI	454	128.0
		454a	73.9
		461	18.5
		470	25.7

Source: Interstate Commerce Commission

It is clear from the record that some of the short lines started since 1976 are far from profitable even given the potential savings of non-union labor practices and wage rates. Why would anyone get into such a business? In order to answer this question it is necessary to examine the RSPO standards of December 21, 1976.[29] There were four items revised by those standards that make the operation of a short line on a former USRA line very attractive.

First, there was the question of superintendence cost. The RSPO concluded that the fairest approach to take with this cost item was to provide that the actual, direct superintendence costs be included in the standards, based on the number of hours actually devoted to the branch line where such supervision was necessary. If we are talking about a short line railroad that is being operated over a single USRA line then all superintendence costs were considered as "avoidable costs" and were thus allowable for reimbursement.

Second, there was an administrative fee provided. The administrative fee had previously been set at 0.5 percent of the total annual revenue attributable to a branch line. Some of the short line railroads, as well as Conrail, complained that this was not enough. On the basis of the comments received by RSPO that agency decided that this should be increased to one percent of the revenue attributable to the line.

A third point was the management fee that had been set in previous standards as 4.5 percent. RSPO insisted that this was not intended to be a ceiling and that it was viewed as the lowest value that Conrail or other designated railroads could receive for "managing" the branch lines. "Moreover, responsible persons,' including short line operators designated by a subsidizer, are in a preferred position, since unlike Conrail or other designated railroads, they are under no legal compulsion to continue service on the subsidized light-density lines. For this reason we would not expect to disapprove a short line operator fee, which exceeded 4.5 percent, even though it was not tied to incentive provisions."

A final point has to do with the cost item of "traffic and general expenses". In short, the RSPO allowed all actual traffic and general expenses "if the size of the railroad's operation is increased by more than 25 percent as a result of operating the subsidized service." In case there was any ambiguity the RSPO went on to state explicity that "a new carrier, formed to operate a subsidized line . . . which did not exist at the start of the subsidy program" would satisfy its definition.[30]

One has to look very carefully to determine exactly what short line costs would not be covered by the RSPO standards. In addition, the presence of an administrative fee and a management fee could be viewed in the short line case merely as profit. Depending on the negotiated level of the management fee it became apparent that a short line venture could be very attractive.

Why was this the case? Why the apparent favoritism toward short lines? Surprisingly, it does not appear that there was any conspiracy or collusion involved. The standards had evolved as a very logical system of whether costs were or were not avoidable. If you follow this logic it is only natural that you will conclude that all the costs of a short line established to serve one of the USRA branch lines are avoidable. The fact that operators could not go broke, except in cases of poor management, and were guaranteed a profit will perhaps explain the attractiveness of short line ventures.

As for the number of short lines that have been spawned by the subsidy program, there were a total of 49 railroads issued certificates as designated operators.[31] Excluding Conrail, the Delaware and Hudson, the Providence and Worcester, and the false starts of the Ogdensburg Bridge and Port Authority type, it would appear that there have been about 35 new short lines formed to serve lines that were not conveyed to Conrail or a solvent railroad. This does not include those short lines that have acquired branch lines prior to April 1, 1976. It is known that there are several roads of this type. Given that federal operating subsidies ended in September of 1981, it is apparent that states are now supporting a number of these roads. The exact number is not known since operators may simply stop service; they do not have to go through an abandonment process or even return their certificate as a designated operator and as a result there are no records in this area.[32]

The Railroads in Retrospect

Looking back over the period from the passage of the 3R Act in 1974 to the present, the behavior of the railroads and the rail industry in response to this program borders on apathy. Conrail in a realistic sense had little choice but to cooperate in the branch line area. The other railroads, Chessie, Southern, Norfolk and Western, as well as the bankrupt railroad estates, did very little to assist in the branch line area, or for that matter, in the entire reorganization. Perhaps the most vigorous of the railroads in responding to the problem were the individual short lines. However, the short lines had nothing to lose from their involvement as the program was structured, and therefore, their actions are understandable. In the final analysis, it is unlikely that more than ten percent of these lines will continue as viable short lines.

Of course there were many other railroads not mentioned here that played a significant role in the reorganization, however, their role in the branch line area was not very important. As for the other bankrupt estates they were willing, by and large, to let the Penn Central resolve problems and then emulate those solutions.

Although it would be nice to say that the railroads and government working together solved the branch line problem, it is apparent that government and public funds managed to cope with the problem in spite of the rail industry.

NOTES TO CHAPTER 6

1. Members of the Committee at the time were: Arthur D. Lewis, Chairman; Claude S. Brinegar, Secretary of Transportation; George M. Stafford, Chairman of the ICC; William W. Scranton, former governor of Pennsylvania; and Gale B. Aydelott, Chairman and President of the Denver and Rio Grande Western.

2. James R. Sullivan, "The Prepaid Revenue Supplement Program," in the Federal Railroad Administration's, *Symposium on Economic and Public Policy Factors Influencing Light Density Rail Line Operations*, Washington, D.C.: U.S.G.P.O., 1973.

3. For a more detailed discussion of the procedure involved the reader is referred to the *Final System Plan, op. cit.*, Vol. 1, pp. 119–155.

4. "Special Court Suggests Flexible Guidelines in Conrail Valuation Case," *Traffic World*, Vol. 172, No. 4, Whole Number 3679, pp. 86–87. 1977.

5. "Penn Central's Estate Agrees to $2.1 Billion Payment for Property," *Traffic World*, Vol. 184, No. 8, Whole Number 3840, 1980, p. 114.

6. Office of Public Counsel, *Report of the Office of Public Counsel*, Washington, D.C.: Rail Services Planning Office, Interstate Commerce Commission (March 1976).

7. *Ex Parte No. 293 (Sub-No. 10)*, Order: Trustees Directed to Make Properties Available for Continued Rail Service, Interstate Commerce Commission, March 16, 1976.

8. Public Law 94–555.

9. *In re Penn Central Transportation Company*, Bky. No. 70–347, Order of Judge John P. Fullman, No. 2927, April 25, 1977.

10. "Sale, Assets Transfer by 7 Railroads Barred," *Philedelphia Inquirer*, December 24, 1975.

11. U.S. Congress, House, *Regional Rail Reorganization Act Amendments of 1975*, Report of the Committee on Interstate and Foreign Commerce, 94th Congress, 1st Session, Report No. 94–7, February 10, 1975, p.7.

12. *Ibid.*, p. 7.

13. Further discussion of these funds may be found in: Congressional Budget Office, *Railroad Reorganization: Congressional Action and Federal Expenditures Related to the Final System Plan of the U.S. Railway Association*, Washington, D.C.: U.S.G.P.O., Background Paper No. 2, January 15, 1976.

14. Association of American Railroads, *Information Letter*, No. 2171, July 23, 1975.

15. *Ibid.*, No. 2180, November 26, 1975.

16. U.S. Congress, Senate, *Railroads–1975*, Hearings before the Subcommittee on Surface Transportation of the Committee on Commerce, 94th Congress, 1st Session, Serial No. 94–31, Part 4, September 9, 10, 11, 18, 19, 1975, p. 1403.

17. "Southern, Chessie Having Problems Getting Labor Pacts for Bankrupts," *Journal of Commerce*, (New York), January 30, 1976.

18. "Labor Impasse Blocks Sale of Track in Northeast to Chessie and Southern," *Traffic World*, Vol. 165, No. 7, Whole Number 3591, February 16, 1976.

19. Helen Ericson, "Talks on Northeast Rail Track Purchases Slated," *Journal of Commerce*, (New York), February 25, 1976.

20. William H. Jones, "Rail Plans Dealt Blow by Failure on Union Pact," *Washington* (D.C.) *Post*, February 13, 1976.

21. William H. Jones, "Public-Be-Damned Attitude," *Washington* (D.C.) *Post*, March 24, 1976.

22. Interstate Commerce Commission, *Rail Transportation Services on the Delmarva Peninsula*, Washington, D.C., April 19, 1977.

23. *Ibid.*, p. 38.

24. *Final System Plan.*, *op. cit.*, p. 17.

25. U.S. Congress, Senate, *Railroads–1975*, *op. cit.*, p. 1373.

26. Bruce Ellison, "Conrail is a Threat, N&W Official Says," *Cleveland Plain Dealer*, March 19, 1976.

27. See, for example, William R. Black and James F. Runke, *The States and Rural Rail Preservation: Alternative Strategies*, Lexington, KY.: The Council of

State Governments, October 1975; or, Wisconsin Department of Transportation. *Short Line Railroads Operation–As An Alternative to Loss of Rail Service–Pros and Cons*. Madison, Wisconsin, November 1975.

28. Rush Loving, Jr., "Michigan's Wacky Ride on the Little Railroad That Couldn't," *Fortune*, October 23, 1978, pp. 42–44.

29. Interstate Commerce Commission, "Standards for Determining Rail Services Continuation Subsidies: Report and Order," *Federal Register*, Vol. 41, No. 246, Dec. 21, 1976, pp. 55686–55694.

30. *Ibid.*, p. 5689.

31. Interstate Commerce Commission, Designated Operator Docket File, Washington, D.C.

32. It would appear that this problem should have been resolved by: Interstate Commerce Commission, "Common Carrier Status of States, State Agencies and Instrumentalities, and Political Subdivisions," *Finance Docket 28990F*, Served August 7, 1980, although this does not appear to be the case.

Chapter 7

ACTIVITIES OF THE STATES

As is apparent from the legislation in chapter 2, there was a clear requirement that the states should be involved in the reorganization process generally and the light-density line program specifically. This requirement was interpreted in about as many different ways as there were states and the purpose of this chapter is to summarize some of the activities of the states from the passage of the reorganization act through the beginning of subsidized rail freight service. In some cases the summary goes beyond that point in time in order to note significant events or to evaluate state programs.

Any discussion of the states and their role would be deficient if it did not include a review of the activities of the Conference of States on Regional Rail Reorganization. An ad hoc group formed at about the same time as the Conference was the USRA Technical Advisory Committee. These two groups and their early views and activities leadoff the discussion of state activities below. This is followed by summaries of the activities of individual states in response to the reorganization.

The Conference of States

When the reorganization act was signed into law in January of 1974 only a few states were familiar with the rail systems within their borders, however, they did realize the need and potential advantages of interstate cooperation. An informal meeting of concerned state officials was held at Columbus, Ohio in the spring of 1974. The states in attendance were Ohio, Illinois, Wisconsin, Michigan, Pennsylvania and New York. A discussion of technical aspects of the reorganization act as it affected the states was the primary topic of the meeting. The decision was made to try and expand the group so that all states affected by the act would be represented.[1]

The group was far more organized by the time of its second meeting in late June of 1974 at Buffalo, New York. Fourteen of the states affected by the reorganization were in attendance, and four were absent.[2] The major issues discussed by the group were:

  (1) the need for a cooperative, comprehensive, coordinated, and
       continuing (4-C) planning process for rail reorganization;

(2) the necessity for a homogeneous USRA-RSPO methodology for assessing branch line viability;

(3) data needs of the states for planning;

(4) the failure of some states to get responses from federal agencies and USRA;

(5) the need for an immediate determination of what lines would go into Conrail;

(6) whether a time extension should be granted to USRA for preparation of their plans;

(7) whether all railroads should be entitled to receive branch line subsidy monies; and

(8) if rehabilitation funds provided in Sections 213 and 215 of the act should be released immediately to the railroads.

Without exception the group consensus was either positive or in favor of corrective action on each of these points.

Following meetings of the Conference an executive committee would either prepare documents including the resolutions passed or their concensus positions and then forward these to the appropriate parties involved with the specific issue or issues. These parties were often USRA, RSPO, ICC, FRA, the Office of Public Counsel of RSPO, Conrail, members of Congress and so forth. Some resolutions involving proposed changes in legislation were sent to all parties.

By the time of its third meeting (held in Boston on August 6–7, 1974), the group of states recognized the need to formally constitute itself and its procedures. It was at this time that the group identified itself as the Conference of States on Regional Rail Reorganization. Members of the Conference were the states affected by the reorganization act.[3] Bylaws were adopted by the new group and these are not unlike the bylaws of other organizations. One possible exception to this statement was in the area of what constituted a consensus position. Up to this point a consensus was the unanimous support of all the states. It would now become a position supported by 12 of the 18 states. Specifically, the bylaws read:

Twelve states must be represented to constitute a quarum. To be considered a consensus position of the organization an issue must be approved by twelve (12) member states. To be considered the unanimous position of the organization, the issue must be approved by all of the voting members present.[4]

This is a significant point to be aware of for the issues that were to come up later and the states involved.

It was not clear at the time whether the policy of one geographic area would be in conflict with the policy of another area. For example, were the long or short range goals of the New England states different from those of the four major Midwest states (Ohio, Indiana, Michigan, and

Illinois)? It seemed to some that there should be a difference in philosophies, but the geographical transport policy research necessary to identify this had not then, and has not yet, been undertaken.

The Conference and Its Concerns

The major issues discussed at the Buffalo meeting are worthy of further clarification since they continued to occupy the interest of the Conference for several months.

CONFLICT OF USRA-RSPO METHODS

The need for a homogeneous methodological approach in analyzing the viability of light-density lines was one such issue. The USRA and RSPO had each developed different methods of assessing viability. The former was concerned with identifying branch lines to go into Conrail, while the RSPO was concerned with estimating the amount of subsidy for a specific line. There was the possibility that the USRA methods would exclude a branch line from Conrail, which the RSPO methods would identify as a profitable line, or at least as a line not in need of subsidy. The opposite could also occur. Practice is frequently the only test of whether a conflict exists and in this case the different methods did not create insurmountable problems. This was due in part to the RSPO standards, which stated that any line excluded from Conrail that their methods showed as profitable could be subsidized for one dollar a year.[5] Although this took care of a practical problem it did not remove the stigma that the line was an abandonment candidate, or the later view that the line, if not conveyed to Conrail, had been abandoned.

DATA ISSUES AND CONFIDENTIALITY

Data needs were also a concern of the Conference. The railroads in the region were not interested in working with each state and their desire was to have USRA in charge of data distribution. USRA on the other hand was having a difficult time getting the data from all railroads. Data which they did receive was not as "clean" as desirable and they spent some time attempting to get this in a usable form. In addition there was a legal question regarding the confidentiality of the data.

Data compiled by railroads on inbound and outbound traffic by commodity type, and the origin and destination of such traffic represent confidential information. Even in the case of bankrupt railroads, their data would reveal information on traffic forwarded to other rail carriers and the latter roads could consider this as proprietary information. If the railroads were agreeable to distributing such data there was still the question of whether the shippers would agree to release it. In the shipper case such data could reveal the magnitude of production at a given location and the distribution costs of the firm; two essential pieces of information for a possible competitor of the firm. The major concern of the railroads and USRA was that someone (probably a shipper) would take them to court for releasing this type of data.

USRA finally made data available to the states for bankrupt railroads in the region. In order to protect itself USRA required each state to sign a confidentiality statement promising not to release the information. Data on the solvent railroads operating in the region were never released by USRA.

There is no question that proprietary information for some firms has been made public over the past several years by the rail planning process at the state and federal levels. However, not one shipper has taken anyone to court over the issue. It would appear that if there is a question of whether a line will be abandoned, subsidized, or in this case included in Conrail, then the firm is not so concerned about data on its operation being released.

THE 120 DAY EXTENSION

The consensus of the Conference was that USRA should be granted a 120 day extension for the preparation of the Preliminary System Plan. This extension was necessitated according to USRA by the failure of President Nixon to appoint the members of the USRA board of directors, which left the USRA staff without major policy direction. Two of the fourteen states present at the Conference meeting (Chicago, September 1974) where the issue was discussed in detail did not support the extension; these were Indiana and New Jersey. They argued that the creation of Conrail and the resolution of uncertainty as to the future of branch lines were important and should not be delayed. The consensus prevailed.

OTHER ISSUES

The total number of individual issues examined by the Conference is legion. To a large extent the group sought to resolve policy issues of genuine concern to all the member states, however, this was not always the case. On one occasion the group had been reviewing several different industry configurations for the railroad corporation that was to emerge as the end product of the *Final System Plan*. These were generally referred to as "Strategic Options" and they are discussed in some detail in the USRA *Preliminary System Plan*.[6] New York State favored the "Penn Central Unmerged" option, which was also called "Multiple Conrails." That state was also a strong advocate of preserving competition in the Eastern Terminal area, which is analogous to the option they favored. It is fair to say that most of the states lacked concern on this issue. Indiana favored "Big Conrail" which was a different option that would give the new railroad the best chance of becoming economically viable, even though it had the potential of eliminating competition in a number of major market areas.

Some of the eastern states were anxious to get their position on the record. A meeting was called on very short notice to be held in Philadelphia and only ten states were present. Clearly, this was not a quarum according to the groups bylaws. This, however, did not prevent the group from passing several "unanimous" resolutions related to industry structure.

Such attempts to promote state or regional interests were unusual. Pennsylvania introduced Governor Shapp's Rail Trust Fund proposal and wanted the Conference to endorse it.[7] However, they did not press the proposal when it appeared that such an endorsement was unlikely. The New England states favored the "Confac" concept; a consolidated facilities corporation which would take over the ownership of railroad right-of-way in the region and be responsible for its maintenance and rehabilitation. However, they were unable to get support for the concept outside of their region.

An Evaluation of the Conference and Its Early Activities

It is reasonable to ask what the Conference accomplished that would not have occurred in their absence. This is an impossible question to answer. It is possible to evaluate changes in legislation that were either initiated or supported by the Conference.

One such change was the provision of monies for state rail planning. The 3R Act required that each state in the region prepare a state rail plan. However, it did not provide any funds for this purpose. The Conference took the position that all federal-state transportation programs provide planning funds and such funds should also be provided in the case of the rail program. The Conference was successful in getting this into the 4R Act amendments of the reorganization act. It is possible that such funds would have been authorized without the Conference, but in this case it clearly deserves credit for the action taken.

Provisions of the 3R Act called for 70 percent federal and 30 percent state or local funding of subsidized operations. All members of the Conference supported a reduction in the 30 percent share. There was just about an even split of the group on whether the first year should be 100 percent federal, or 90 percent federal and 10 percent state or local. The 90/10 proponents believed that without some state or local financial contribution they would lack control over the program. As the act was amended, the first year was 100 percent federal, the second year was 90 percent federal and 10 percent state or local and so forth. Some credit must be given to the Conference for this change in the program, however, they were not alone in advocating such a change.

As an educational program the Conference and its sessions also deserve some recognition. The importance of coal and energy related lines, the concept of rail banking (analogous to land banking), costing concepts, and viability methodologies were given ample attention by the Conference to the benefit of all of its members. The group also had a role in correcting certain technical faults in the reorganization act which were overlooked by the law's original drafters.

From a policy perspective the Conference could have been a more useful organization. States were frequently represented by staff members that were far removed from the major rail policy makers in state government. These individuals were often unable to take a position that ran contrary to the majority.

Perhaps the major shortcoming of the Conference was its inability to influence the branch line viability methodology that was being developed by USRA. New York and Indiana had developed their own methods, however, the Conference, generally, was not really interested in such technical matters. Nevertheless, the adoption of a consistent methodology by all affected states would have resulted in more state input to that process than they had. It also could not have been ignored by the FRA and USRA if the Conference supported it.

The Conference also failed to develop methods that could have been utilized by the states in their state rail plans. For example, the development of measures for energy impacts, environmental impacts, social and non-railroad related economic impacts could have been developed by the Conference, but these were never discussed by the group to any significant extent. The reason for this is also related to the membership of the Conference, which consisted primarily of policy-makers, not planners or technicians.

In 1976 the Conference of States on Regional Rail Reorganization sought a permanent organizational affiliation with the American Association of State Highway and Transportation Officials (AASHTO). The name of the group was changed to the National Conference of State Rail Officials (NCSRO) and it became a division of AASHTO. Under the initial leadership of Cliff Elkins, and more recently William Druhan, NCSRO has become an information source and lobbying group for the states in rail matters. It appears to be very effective in that context.

USRA Technical Advisory Committee

In the late spring of 1974 USRA began offering technical sessions for selected representatives of each of the states affected by the reorganization. Although the state participants were referred to as the USRA Technical Advisory Committee, such a label was not applicable to the group's membership or its function. As was true of the Conference this group was also made up of state policy-makers who often had a difficult time comprehending technical or analytical methods, let alone offering advice on how these should be changed. Therefore, the sessions became primarily educational. On rare occasions advice would be offered by state attendees, and on still rarer occasions it was taken.

The precise motivation which led USRA to offer these sessions is not clear. If it was indeed the desire for advice or recommendations, the approach was wrong. There was rarely any preparation for such a session on the part of the states. The session would begin, an USRA staff member or consultant would explain the design of a particular piece of research for the *Preliminary System Plan*, and the presentation would close with a call for comments. In nearly every case the presenter and his or her staff would have put weeks of thinking into the research, and it would have been strange if the state representatives had found fault in the proposed work in the short time available.

If the sessions and participation were not as planned this apparently did not bother USRA which continued to have the group meet from July of 1974 until two weeks before the *Preliminary System Plan* was released in January of 1975. At the July meeting the major items of discussion were the research contracts awarded by USRA to several consulting firms for background and methodology development. Dr. Gerald K. Davies of the USRA office of strategic planning followed with a presentation of the methodology being developed by USRA and its consultants for assessing light density line viability. The conflict between the proposed USRA and RSPO methods was noted and the differences discussed.

Meetings which followed this session (about one every six weeks) included discussions by additional consultants as well as other presentations by the USRA staff. Paul Cruikshank, vice president for review and evaluation at USRA, presented material on Section 215 funds and their use; Russell Murphy, in charge of USRA's office of financial analysis, presented methods used to develop pro forma financial accounts for the new railroad (Conrail); Norbert Zucker of FRA discussed and answered questions regarding pending legislation; mainline planning and joint carrier coordination were presented by Gary Collins of USRA, and so on.

There were numerous questionable areas and conflicts frequently erupted between the states and USRA staff. In late summer of 1974 it became apparent to all of the states that the question of whether a line would go into Conrail would rest purely on economic viability considerations. The social and economic impacts were to be ignored by USRA. The agency interpreted the reorganization act as meaning that if such impacts were likely to occur then this was what the Title IV subsidy monies were provided for in the act. To reinforce this interpretation USRA distributed copies of a series of community impact manuals so that the states could utilize these in their subsidy evaluations.

The sessions were also used for the first distribution of the *PSP* findings. In November of 1974 most of the analyses of light density lines were completed and these were distributed to the states at that time. The strategic options for the new industry structure were also summarized and critiqued by USRA at these sessions.

Evaluating the USRA sessions as educational activities, they were successful. State planners and policy makers became quite familiar with USRA's planning process and the individuals in charge of the process. If this was all that was to occur, then the sessions were a success and only mislabelled.

The States: Positions, Plans, and Activities

Regardless of the consensus positions of the Conference of States on Regional Rail Reorganization, the states acted in an individual manner with regard to rail reorganization in general and the light-density lines program in particular. This could be expected since the factors motivating state concern included numerous local political considerations, the energy crisis, the unemployment situation, economic welfare of the state, and the potential social and economic impacts of abandonment.

In the pages that follow there are examinations of the manner in which the states reacted to the branch line problem. Some of these are more entensive than others for the simple reason that some states were more active than others. The chapter concludes with a summary of general factors that affected all the states.

Massachusetts

From the outset of the reorganization process Massachusetts made it clear that it would acquire the rail lines of interest to it. Legislation filed by Governor Michael Dukakis called for a state authorization of $10 million for acquisition and rehabilitation and one million dollars for operating costs.[8]

The Commonwealth of Massachusetts had been a leader of the New England states in favoring the Confac alternative. As previously noted, the "consolidated facilities" alternative called for government ownership of all right-of-way involved in the reorganization, and although it was not adopted by the federal government, it remained a popular idea in New England.

Peter Metz, an assistant secretary of transportation in the Massachusetts state government, was one of the most influential members of the

Conference of States on Regional Rail Reorganization. As a high level state official he was able to give his state's position on most issues. He also appeared to have a better liaison with the Massachusetts congressional delegation and was often able to get legislation altered during mark-up.

The USRA *Final System Plan* called for the exclusion of 147 miles of Massachusetts branch line from Conrail. The Commonwealth's state rail plan issued in December of 1975 called for the continued operation of 81.7 miles of track under subsidy.[9] Those lines that were not to be subsidized were to be acquired by the state and rail banked for use at some future time. With regard to the lines operated under subsidy, several of these were still assisted as late as the summer of 1982.

Rhode Island

Rhode Island did not appear to have a substantial branch line problem. *The Secretary's Report on Rail Service in the Midwest and Northeast Region* had identified about 25 miles of track as potentially excess in the state. Although this was not a large amount it nevertheless represented 17 percent of the state's rail system.[10] Although the potentially excess track of most states was generally greather than the "available for subsidy" lines in the *Final System Plan*, this was not the case in Rhode Island. The *FSP* identified 24 miles of instate line and 49 miles of interstate line (with Connecticut) as available for subsidy.[11]

Rhode Island was one of the three states (the others were Virginia and Ohio) that had a constitutional prohibition against subsidies to the private sector. The state did not have a problem with purchase of service agreements, and this was the direction its negotiations took with rail operators.

As a source of funding for their rail program the State had a $14 million bond issue that had been approved by the Rhode Island voters in June of 1975.[12] The state's rail plan called for state acquisition of two branch lines and the Providence and Worcester Railroad was to purchase another line. The lines would all be upgraded or rehabilitated with federal funds. Gerald L. Pieri, the state rail coordinator, stated "the Rhode Island plan should have the state out of the railroad business in about five years with one more mile of freight track than before the Penn Central collapse."[13]

Connecticut

The late governor of Connecticut, Ella T. Grasso, was concerned over what the rail reorganization would mean for that state. In January of 1976 she appointed a Rail Task Force to "advise the governor of Connecticut's rail needs." At the same time she stated "Our state is committed to the preservation and improvement of railroad service in Connecticut. Intelligent use of rail lines for freight and passenger service can help provide the transportation necessary to the efficient movement of people and goods throughout the state."[14] As the governor's statement implied Connecticut was concerned over the disappearance of rail branch line right-of-way; the assembling of right-of-way is a significant problem in the densely populated states of the East Coast. Therefore, the state wanted to acquire lines even though they had no intention of operating these lines in the foreseeable future.

Connecticut had already gone through the planning process when these statements were made. Its rail plan, submitted to FRA in 1975 (December), was considered one of the better plans at that time.

After conveyance Conrail was operating three lines for the state and the Providence and Worcester Railroad was operating one. These lines accounted for about 33 miles of track and provided service to 33 shippers and receivers. During the first four years of service the Connecticut program generated the cummulative program costs displayed in Table 7.1. As the table reveals the total project cost over the first four years was about $4.5 million. The table also reveals the extent of Connecticut's interest in rail acquisition and rail banking; slightly more than 40 percent of the program funds went into this area. An additional one million dollars was provided by FRA for the purchase of two lines which brought the total lines acquired to four and the total length to 65.2 miles. This total includes lines that had been abandoned as well as those under subsidy.

New York

The most impressive response to the rail reorganization by any state has to be that of New York. In 1974 the voters of that state passed a $250 million bond proposal for rail service preservation. In 1979 the voters again endorsed a bond proposal; this one was $500 million for energy conservation through improved transportation. In the second bond proposal, $400 million was designated for rail transportation.[15] To place the $650 million (available to rail) in the proper light it is worth noting that total federal authorizations in the local rail assistance area nationwide had only been $540 million.[16] Of course the state's essential rail service program and federal branchline assistance were only two of the six different state rail programs; the others focused on bridges, grade crossings, grade crossing elimination and capital programs.[17]

When the reorganization process began, 80 percent of New York's 5500 miles of rail were owned by bankrupt carriers. The FRA's orange line report designated 1875 miles of this total as "potentially excess." Later the *Final System Plan* designated about 1,000 miles of track as "available for subsidy." New York decided to take action on about 600 miles of the 1,000, which accounted for 99 percent of the traffic on these lines. Of this 600 miles New York allowed about 350 miles to be abandoned; approximately 175 miles were awarded to short line operators and about 50 miles

TABLE 7.1

Connecticut Rail Program: Cumulative Program Costs

1976-1980*

Program Area		Expenditure	% of Total
Operating Subsidies		$ 573,103	12.55
Lease Payments		586,196	12.84
Accelerated Maintenance		930,000	20.37
Bridge Maintenance		80,000	1.75
New Construction		220,000	4.82
Rehabilitation		325,000	7.12
Acquisition		1,851,708	40.55
	Total	$4,566,007**	100.00

*Source: U.S. Congress (House), "Local Rail Services Assistance Act
Authorization," Hearings before the Subcommittee on Commerce,
Transportation and Tourism of the Committee on Energy and Commerce, 97th
Congress, 1st session, Serial No. 97-23, March 17, 1981, pp. 45-46.
**The total does not include administrative and planning costs of the
Connecticut program over the four years.

were awarded to Class I carriers. In order to "save" this 225 miles, as well as to undertake other rail programs, the State of New York and others in the state or at the federal level spent in excess of $1 billion.[18]

As one would expect for this level of expenditure there have been significant spin-offs in the transport planning area. One of the early methods of analyzing branch line costs was attributable to New York.[19] This state was also, if not the only state, one of the few states to become concerned about mainline restructuring and planning and although its planners tried to get other states concerned in this area, they were never very successful at this.[20] The state's rail plan was praised by numerous individuals and groups for its "negotiated solution" to branch line problems. By this the planners simply meant the intense analysis of a branch line problem and solving that same problem through construction of new connections, identifying new operators, and so forth. While the approach taken might not have worked in other states, it was successful in New

York because of the very dense rail network that allowed such solutions to be feasible.

A strong critic of the FRA, USRA and their plans, New York became, in part, a defender of Conrail after conveyance took place. It continued to fault FRA for the manner in which it implemented the subsidy program and USRA for what it considered unmerited criticism of Conrail's early operations.

New Jersey

New Jersey's concerns in the reorganization process were similar to those of the other eastern states. It was more concerned about what the process would do to the state's rail passenger and commuter service than its freight service. It was also concerned over the potential abandonment of rail lines but not because of the loss of service as much as for the loss of right-of-way. As a result New Jersey was also interested in acquiring these right-of-way for future use.

The New Jersey rail plan stated: "It would not subsidize freight lines on a long term basis. Instead, it recommended . . . subsidy on 11 freight branches, provided that shippers along those lines were willing to form a 'shipper association' and put up the local matching funds. In two other cases the state itself agreed conditionally to put up the local funds."[21] The plan also included a recommendation that the state acquire several lines.

Due to the density of the rail network it was possible for New Jersey to undertake one of the most economical branch line programs of any state. For example, during the first year of subsidies New Jersey assisted 12 branch lines of 73.5 miles total length at a cost of 47,938 (not including the lease cost). During the period of April 1, 1976 to September 30, 1981, New Jersey acquired 48.5 miles of branch line for approximately $2.5 million, carried out rehabilitation projects for more than $2.2 million, paid leases of more than $300,000 and operating subsidies of $350,000. These are substantial outlays but comparatively reasonable given the scope of the state's program.[22]

Pennsylvania

The home state of Penn Central was covered with a dense network of branch lines which in many cases lacked sufficient traffic to merit their conveyance to Conrail. As a result it was not surprising that USRA's planners identified 1,281 miles of track in the state as "available for subsidy."[23]

Although the mileage involved was substantial, it was not unique. The unique thing about Pennsylvania was Milton Shapp, Governor of the state. For several years prior to the passage of the Regional Rail

Reorganization Act, Shapp had a notable interest in railroads. As early as 1962 when the boards of directors of the Pennsylvania Railroad and New York Central Railroad agreed to merge their roads to form the Penn Central, "Shapp mounted an offensive that never ceased until he was elected governor on November 3, 1970."[24] Daughen and Binzen, authors of the work *The Wreck of the Penn Central*, label Shapp simply as the "man against the merger."[25] They argue that Shapp used his opposition to the proposed merger to get publicity and media exposure during his brief campaign for the U.S. Senate in 1963. His campaign was unsuccessful, but he continued his attacks during his campaign for governor of the state in 1966. These attacks and the campaign were also unsuccessful with the merger being approved by the ICC on April 27, 1966 and Raymond Shafer being elected governor in November of that year.

Although some believe that Shapp's continuing criticism of the merger was due to certain individuals with rail connections opposing his 1966 election, it is doubtful that this was the case. It is probable that Shapp did "use" the merger for media exposure; he wouldn't be the first politician to do such a thing. But it seems there was more to the man than this. The "man against the merger" became the "man against the Penn Central" and then the "man against Conrail." This is magnifying a grudge into a vendetta unless there was more to Shapp's criticism than most are willing to give him credit for. The most plausible interpretation is that for political reasons Shapp opposed the merger, and the result of its consummation. Conrail, as the largest corporate "merger" in American business history, was simply more of the same. Some support for this view is in Shapp's statement that "Conrail is just phase two of the Penn Central merger, which I've been fighting for years. I assure you I intend to continue to fight until America has the rail service it needs and deserves."[26] In his defense it should be noted that most of the rhetorical criticism he expressed against the Penn Central merger turned out to be correct. Success has a tendency to make individuals believe they know what they're talking about even when this isn't the case. So Shapp became the rail expert and appeared at all the hearings offering his insight as well as his alternatives such as his rail trust fund.[27]

As could be expected Pennsylvania state government under the Shapp administration was active in the rail area. The Penn Central debacle and attempts to reorganize the shambles by USRA were of keen interest to the governor. During early meetings of the Conference of States on Regional Rail Reorganization, it was not uncommon for the state to be represented by the governor's office, the state planning and development unit, the public utility commission as well as the department of transportation. Coordination did not appear to exist.

Shapp was also active at the hearings held on the planning efforts of USRA. It is unfortunate that he made statements such as: "'Conrail' is indeed an appropriate name for this financial fantasy," because such statements tended to diffuse some very perceptive analysis made elsewhere.[28]

On the branch line issue Shapp noted that "in 1973 Penn Central tried to abandon 5,000 miles of branch lines and claimed it would save $20 million if allowed. This was the same year Penn Central had an operating loss of $189 million. Thus even by Penn Central's figures, branch lines accounted for less than a ninth of operating losses. Yet the idea that branch lines have been bleeding the railroad industry white persists, especially among those who seek simple explanations."[29] Even Shapp's proposed rail trust fund made considerable sense as a method of financing rail rehabilitation; it was properly criticized for not addressing the current problem. In other words the Shapp proposal offered a long term solution, but did not solve the bankruptcy problem in the Midwest and Northeast.

Although there is a temptation to view Shapp as more than just a politician, this would probably be erroneous. For example, at a time when he was talking of waste and rip-offs at public hearings he signed the "flagman alert liability bill" into law, which increased the crew size necessary for certain rail operations.[30] Shapp had vetoed the bill a year earlier on the grounds that it would unnecessarily increase rail payroll costs. His turnaround led the Philadelphia *Evening Bulletin* to editorialize ". . . there seems to be little question that political circumstances made it advantageous for Mr. Shapp to appease the United Transportation Union which backed the measure." They added, "Candidate Shapp is doing some political signaling on his own, waving his campaign pennant at union leaders and urging them to rally 'round."[31]

As the months passed it became evident that whether he liked it or not Conrail was going to come into existence. It was clear that the branch lines that Shapp had tried to retain would be lost if the state didn't act. On February 12, 1976, Shapp signed a rail bill that gave the state authority to subsidize rail freight lines.

Elaine King of Pennsylvania's Department of Transportation has summarized the activities of the state in the Local Rail Service Assistance program. She stated:

> As a result of the funding received through this program since April 1, 1976, the Pennsylvania Department of Transportation has rehabilitated 170 miles of track to Class I, rehabilitated 39 miles of track to Class II, constructed a connection between an LDL and a Conrail mainline thus eliminating eight miles of duplicate trackage, and constructed an intermodal transfer facility. In addition, we are continuing rail service through operating subsidies on 40 LDL's totaling 374 miles and serving 110 rail users. From April 1, 1976 through December 31, 1980, we have expended $14.3 million in federal funds provided through this program along with $2 million in state and local funds.[32]

This is a fair summary of the state's activities except to note that Pennsylvania was still subsidizing more than a dozen rail lines in September of 1982, a year after federal funds for this purpose had been withdrawn.

Ohio

Despite the active participation of Ohio in the early days of the rail reorganization in 1974, the state was very slow to move on the branch line problem. It was said that Governor Rhodes of Ohio was really Governor ROADS, which was an indication of the favored transport mode during his administration.

During most of the reorganization the State of Ohio maintained that it had a constitutional prohibition against participating in a rail subsidy program. A constitutional proposal on the Ohio ballot in November of 1975 to permit revenue bonds to be issued to provide railroad service went down to an overwhelming defeat.[33] Other states had constitutional problems but they had managed to work around them. Ohio seemed unwilling to do this. The specific prohibition was against the use of state funds for internal improvements owned by private corporations. Interestingly, the prohibition was added to the constitution in the middle of the 1800's after the use of state funds for railroad development nearly placed the state in bankruptcy. Ohio finally stated that it would not become an active participant in the program although they would pass the money through to shippers so long as they did not have to contribute a portion of the funds.

It was under pressure that the state actually went through the planning process and issued a branch line plan in December of 1975.[34] That plan was submitted to the Federal Railroad Administration and summarily rejected by that agency.[35] The rejection was a little too much for Judd Gould, an outreach attorney for the Office of the Public Counsel of the Rail Services Planning Office. The attorney granted an interview to an Associated Press reporter. "Gould said the rejection represents the latest failure by Ohio's state government to cope with the changing rail system." He went on to attack the governor, the legislature, the Ohio Department of Transportation, its rail planners, and the state's attorney general. Understandably, the State took offense at the criticism.[36]

This was not the only criticism directed toward the state. The fall of 1975 saw the creation of the Ohio Rail Transportation Authority (ORTA). Prior to that agency being created, the Ohio DOT had been in charge of rail planning and problems. ORTA's director, Graeme Mackeown, stated that "he had no idea what the department rail experts were doing because they would not talk to him." MacKeown further stated, ". . . I have to have some cooperation. I seem to be running into stone walls and I don't know why. I have no concept of what's happening or what's going on.

Those people won't deal with me."[37] What MacKeown didn't realize was that there was probably nothing going on at the Ohio DOT.

As late as February 13 representatives of FRA, USRA, and Conrail met with representatives of Ohio's state government and about one hundred shippers from that state in Columbus. The shippers of Ohio believed that their state government was working on the branch line problem for them, however, at the meeting state officials informed the shippers that they would have to negotiate independently with Conrail stating, once again, that they were constitutionally prohibited from doing so. The audience was shocked.

The Ohio congressional delegation had been active during the preparation of the 4R Act. There were three provisions in the act that would help Ohio. First, since it appeared that the state would be unable to negotiate with Conrail for reasons previously cited a provision was inserted in the law which designated the Secretary of the U.S. Department of Transportation, as contract negotiator for any state unable to do this.[38] FRA, as the representative of the Secretary, did not particularly care for the provision and they argued that ORTA could still negotiate on behalf of the state's shippers, which is what finally occurred.

A second provision sought to deal with the problem that the Erie-Lackawanna rail yard in Marion, Ohio, which employed 1,000 workers, would be closed down as well as certain port operations.[39] The provision allowed subsidies for a two year period after abandonment for "yards, shops, and docks." This provision was never implemented in Ohio. It would have paid the operating costs for the 1,000 Marion workers even if there was no work to do and since no trains were to use the yard this would have been the case. The workers were protected under the Title V labor protection provisions of the act (3R Act) although it is not apparent that the congressional delegation knew this.

A third provision of the 4R Act which was critical to the Ohio situation was the 100 percent federal branch line subsidy. Since Ohio could not subsidize the lines, the 100 percent subsidies were necessary for the start-up of the Ohio program. The fact that there was not a sufficient amount of time to negotiate with every shipper that desired subsidized rail service was also a factor.

As of 1982 ORTA had not funded any of the lines in that state; it has relied on local (shipper and community) sources for the matching share to meet federal entitlements. Ohio has also had numerous problems in its role as administrator of the program according to an audit report of the U.S. Department of Transportation's Office of Inspector General.[40]

Michigan

To the north of the country's manufacturing belt, Michigan is located in such a way as to make it inaccessible to major national markets at least in comparison with other states. Practically surrounded by water on the west, north and east it is connected to the rest of the nation on its southern border. To be sure it does not have the accessibility problems of Idaho or Maine, but the firm wishing access to a national market would find other states to be more attractive.

Certainly this perspective is a general one. There are areas of the state that are competitive in a locational context. Notably, that part of the state south of a line drawn from Grand Rapids to Saginaw has been and continues to be attractive. North of the line there is little economic activity of note: agriculture and lake-oriented tourism dominate the landscape. It would appear that this geography is not acceptable to the state and they continually talk about the economic development of the north as though this made some sort of sense.

Although these points may appear to be extraneous in the present context, they are not. Michigan's policy toward branch lines and the rail assistance program was in part determined by this "economic development" situation. The state believed that the lines had to be kept in place for future economic development. It is a well established fact that areas well endowed with resources and economic activity may be held back by poor transport facilities. However, the observation is not reflexive; the presence of transport in the absence of resources and activity will accomplish very little. Nevertheless, the lines had to be preserved in part for this future growth potential.

Also critical in the Michigan case was the unemployment situation at the time. It has been said that "as the auto industry goes, so goes the State of Michigan" and this statement is not incorrect. The early 1970's were not the best for the Detroit based auto industry; it was a time when foreign imports were capturing substantial parts of the national auto market. In addition to this problem, unemployment in the northern part of the state and in the Upper Peninsula was running 10 percent. It was believed that abandonment of rail lines would lead to further unemployment and, therefore, this was to be avoided.

The concerns for future economic development and the existing level of unemployment formed the basis for the state rail policy toward branch lines after a period of time. This was not the case initially.

Michigan was very active at the outset of the reorganization and planning effort. Although the state did have the political and economic problems noted, there was little or no reason to assume that this should impact the state's rail planning efforts. The result was a very clear policy report by Michigan that was praised for its objectivity.[41] Unfortunately, Governor Milliken did not perceive the railroads as having little impact on the state's problems nor did he feel that the report paid adequate attention to the unemployment situation. As a result the document was never really accepted as state policy. The preface to the report states:

It is intended that the material contained herein be used for planning and
discussion purposes *only*. This manual is considered to be a *preliminary*
appraisal of Michigan's railroad needs. It is not to be considered as
presenting state policy or positions regarding railroad property, routes, or
traffic. The *final report* when prepared will more specifically and adequately represent the State's position.[42]

Although some might call this statement a preface, it would perhaps be
better to label it a disclaimer. Following the release of the report there
were some internal shifts in the rail area personnel of Michigan's state
government; it is not certain whether these shifts were related to the
release of the report.

During the remainder of 1975 the state was busily engaged in the
planning process. The first Michigan rail plan was issued in December of
that year and it reflected a new "hang-tough" attitude and policy of the
state. "Of the 1,230 intrastate and interstate miles of bankrupt Penn
Central and Ann Arbor systems excluded from Conrail and directly
affecting Michigan, continued service is proposed for 1,099 miles."[43]
Retaining this much track would not be cheap. At the same time the plan
was submitted to the Federal Railroad Administration, the state asked the
FRA for $26.1 million "for track repairs and subsidies to salvage 1,060
miles of threatened rail lines."[44] Included in the plan were continued
operation of the entire Ann Arbor Railroad, the car ferries across Lake
Michigan, and numerous branch lines. A substantial portion of the
request was for the rehabilitation of track.

If there was any doubt that the car ferry would be supported, it was
eliminated with the passage of the 4R Act with its 100 percent federal
subsidies. Plans called for the state to continue ferry operations from
Frankfort, Michigan, to Kewaunee, Wisconsin, for one year. After that
time Michigan would share the local cost with Wisconsin according to
plans announced by Governor Milliken.[45]

Governor Milliken formally petitioned the USRA "for modification of
the final system plan to designate rail properties of the Ann Arbor
Railroad Co. to the State of Michigan."[46] At a meeting of the USRA Board
of Directors on February 20, 1976 the petition was accepted. Michigan
was conveyed the track and equipment necessary to continue to operate
the Ann Arbor, one of the seven bankrupt railroads under the reorganization act, for $521,482. Included in the agreement was a section of track
from Ann Arbor to Toledo, Ohio, which was to be conveyed to Conrail
according to the *Final System Plan* of the USRA.[47]

Edgerton (Bill) Bailey, who was then acting director of rail freight
programs in Michigan, noted that the Ann Arbor-Toledo stretch was
critical because it was the only profitable section of the Ann Arbor
system.[48] It was the state's intent to utilize profits from this section to
cross subsidize losses on the remainder of the system. Bailey further

noted that state acquisition "will add stability to the Ann Arbor system and encourage growth along the entire line."[49]

Michigan's rail plan was complex in terms of the number of different rail carriers that were to be involved in the operation of lines there under subsidy. Conrail was not expected to be one of the carriers. At the same time none of the other railroads were as organized as Conrail in the sense of having model contracts ready and so forth. Michigan was also under some pressure from USRA to find an operator for the Ann Arbor Railroad before that agreement could be finalized. As a result Conrail became the operator of nearly half of the 1,060 miles included in the state's assistance program.

Ignoring the various water operations Michigan's assistance program involved about 900 miles of rail line. Of this amount 161 miles have been transferred to operators that no longer receive financial aid from the state. The remainder, about 740 miles, continued to be operated under subsidy beyond the end of the federal operating assistance program.[50]

Indiana[51]

When the Regional Rail Reorganization Act was signed into law in January of 1974, Governor Otis Bowen of Indiana appointed a rail task force with the mission of determining the impact of the act on the state's economy. Although there were several agencies represented on the task force, the primary activity during the next two and one-half years was performed by William J. Watt of the Governor's Office, John Dring of the Public Service Commission, and the author from Indiana University. All of the research, analysis, and planning for the state in the rail area was performed by the Indiana University Center for Urban and Regional Analysis.

The Secretary of Transportation's report on *Rail Service in the Midwest and Northeast Region* identified 37 percent of Indiana's rail system as potentially excess. Later that spring USRA informed the state that they were analyzing 1300 miles of rail line in Indiana. The task force quickly acquired data from the Penn Central and conducted its own analysis of the lines identified by USRA. The task force planning report recommended that only about half (671 miles) of the 1300 miles of line should be included in Conrail and the remainder should be abandoned or operated under subsidy.[52]

Governor Bowen accepted the task force recommendations and informed the public of this. At this point the Governor became the polar opposite of Pennsylvania's Governor Milton Shapp. Bowen was in favor of the reorganization, a strong Conrail, and the abandonment of light-density lines in the belief that Indiana would benefit, or at least not be harmed, by these. In all cases the Governor was willing to accept the results of objective analysis over "political considerations."

While Bowen did not wholeheartedly accept USRA's preliminary plan he saw no clear alternative and therefore thought the country should move ahead. He stated:

> It is time that we face reality with respect to the problems of bankrupt railroads. I have some disagreements with the plan of the U.S. Railway Association. It proposes abandonments of some lines that I believe should be retained. I believe there is a need for modification of the system design. I believe there may be a need for modification of the financing, to give greater assurance of the ability of the new system. I believe that transitional programs—such as subsidies—need to be made more flexible.
>
> But I am opposed to delay and I am opposed to the notion that we are supposed to retain large numbers of lines that are heavy money losers.
>
> Every day that we delay the reorganization compounds our problems. Our shippers have been in "limbo" since the DOT report 18 months ago. They cannot plan for the future. Expansion plans are being deferred. Jobs are being lost.
>
> Delay will increase the cost of repairing the system. Delay will further dilute the economics of branch line operations. Delay will cost the taxpayer more than a million dollars a day because Congress pre-empted the normal processes and now must guarantee service in the interim.
>
> Several alternatives are being offered. Each has major flaws. I am not bound to the general planning approach of USRA but I haven't seen anything I like better.
>
> The eastern railroad system will not improve until we get the reorganization off dead center. I do not consider the USRA plan to be set in cement. As the years pass, change will be needed.
>
> We must go on with it. We must stop the accelerating deterioration of the systems. We must direct our money toward rebuilding, not continue to squander it to cover operating losses.[53]

When USRA's *Final System Plan* identified 734 miles for exclusion from Conrail the state's rail plan agreed with them on 48 percent of the mileage. The state intended to subsidize only 381 miles of branch line (this was later increased by the addition of another line), and the remaining 353 miles were abandoned. Conrail became the primary designated operator in the state's program although numerous short lines have been involved in the program as well.[54]

Although originally intended as a two year program by the state, this was difficult to sustain when 100 percent federal subsidies led off the program. The state was able to gradually drop lines and miles from the subsidy program over the period from 1976 to 1981. Beginning with 432 miles under subsidy in 1976, there were only 115 miles being assisted in 1981. The state also became involved in the rehabilitation of an Illinois Central Gulf Railroad line in the state during the period from 1979 to 1982. Including this latter project the price tag for Indiana's involvement in the program during the five years from 1976 to 1981 was substantial and estimated to be $23 million.[55]

Illinois

On the fringe of the reorganization region was the state of Illinois with ten percent of its rail lines owned by bankrupt carriers. The *Final System Plan* recommended that 309.7 of nearly 1300 miles of bankrupt line not be transferred to Conrail. Although a substantial amount of track, it was much lower than the 2600 miles identified in the secretary's report as "potentially excess."

Illinois held the view that the railroads were vital to the state's economic well-being. As a result the policy of the State was to retain service on every line. On February 20, 1976, Governor Dan Walker signed a freight assistance bill that would guarantee the continuation of service on lines designated as "available for subsidy" by USRA. This legislation, in conjunction with the federal subsidy program, resulted in no loss of rail service in Illinois.[56]

Clarification in the law and more precise measurement of the lines and locations of shippers resulted in about 247 miles of branch line in Illinois identified as "available for subsidy." This represented six lines composed of twelve segments. Two of these lines were operated by Conrail under subsidy from April of 1976 until November of 1977 at which time their operation was taken over by the Kankakee, Beaverville and Southern Railroad and the Wabash Valley Railroad, two new shortline railroads. Another line was operated by Conrail a month longer before being transferred to the Burlington Northern Railroad. Two other lines were also acquired by railroads in the region; one went to the Milwaukee Road and the other went to the Illinois Terminal Company. The last six line segments, known collectively as the Paris to Lawrenceville line, began operation under Conrail in April of 1976. The operation is notable for the difficulties that arose surrounding the line.

The problem line extended 63.4 miles from Paris to Lawrenceville, Illinois and had been part of the Cairo Branch of the Penn Central Transportation Company. This line, along with several others, connects the coal fields of southern Indiana and Illinois with the Chicago metropolitan region.

During the USRA planning process it was determined by the rail analysts that the line should be conveyed to Conrail only if the railroad could not obtain trackage rights over the parallel Louisville and Nashville Railroad (L & N) line through Indiana. The *Final System Plan* carried such a designation based primarily on the extremely poor physical condition of the line.[57]

As would be true of any state, the contract negotiators for Illinois (William Harsh and Kevin McCarthy) preferred the conveyance of the line to Conrail. Short of this they favored a contract with Conrail that would require that railroad as the operator of subsidized service on the line to continue using the line as the Penn Central had done. In other words, the coal traffic going to Chicago should continue to utilize the line. Pennsylvania and New Jersey also had routes with the possibility of such overhead traffic that could increase revenue and decrease subsidies and they shared the contract position of Illinois. Conrail found such a provision unacceptable.

When operations began on April 1, 1976, Conrail began utilizing the L & N line for which they had negotiated a trackage rights agreement on February 12, 1976.[58] This was irritating to Illinois since it meant that overhead traffic revenues would not be attributed to the line under subsidy. As a result the State of Illinois went to court and obtained a temporary restraining order in the federal district court for the eastern district of Illinois on August 5, 1976. On August 18 the same court granted a permanent injunction against Conrail operating over the L & N line since the trackage rights agreement was not obtained within the statutory 95 days allowed for negotiating such agreements in the 3R Act. The injunction prevented Conrail from continuing such alternate routing of coal without ICC approval. On the same day Conrail appealed to the Seventh Circuit Court of Appeals. Although Conrail had requested a stay of execution from the district court (which denied the request), it did not seek such relief from the appeals court.

During the appeal process Conrail and the L & N published a joint tariff on August 25 and 26 which permitted Conrail to operate over the alternate route through Indiana. The State of Illinois contested the tariff and requested the ICC to suspend the new tariff pending an investigation into the matter. The ICC refused to suspend the new tariff, but they did initiate an investigation into the situation.

On September 1, 1976, Illinois served an arbitration notice on Conrail under Article XII of its operating agreement (see Appendix B). The notice alleged that the diversion or reroute was in violation of the agreement. This was the proverbial "straw" for Conrail, and they sought injunctive relief from the Special Court created by the 3R Act to restrain Illinois from proceeding with its notice of arbitration, and to remove the injunction issued by the Illinois federal district court. At the same time Illinois asked the Special Court to dismiss Conrail's motion.

The Special Court considered the evidence before it and overruled the Illinois federal court, issued an injunction against Illinois proceeding with the arbitration, and refused Illinois' motion to dismiss. Its arguments were in essence that: the Special Court had exclusive jurisdiction in the matter; the trackage rights agreement between Conrail and the L & N was executed within the 95 days specified by the 3R Act (Illinois believed it was 96 days); and, Illinois was interferring with the implementation of the *Final System Plan.*

The Special Court gave Conrail a gentle smack on the hand when it stated:

> While Conrail's course of litigating the jurisdictional issue in another court rather than coming to us for an injunction is not to be commended and, we trust, will not be repeated, we must enforce what we take to be the will of Congress.[59]

Although Illinois lost its case, the implication of the loss were far greater than the case. What the Special Court was saying was that if anyone took legal action against implementation of the *Final System Plan* then the Special Court would halt that action through injunction.

There were several cases where Conrail could have utilized the Special Court to its advantage, but it did not. Whether this was due to ignorance or concerns over public reaction is not known.

Returning to the Illinois branch line program, the Paris to Lawrence-ville line was the last to be operated by Conrail under subsidy in that state. As was true of several other lines in the state rail program, its operation was later transferred to a short line railroad.

The Delmarva States

The Delmarva states of Delaware, Maryland, and Virginia all had one thing in common under the USRA *Final System Plan*. This was that practically the entire Penn Central operation in the peninsula area was not to be conveyed to Conrail, but instead was to be offered to the Southern Railway. Since all indications were that this transfer would go through, the states had very little interest in branch line subsidies initially.

The Southern, with the support of the Delmarva states, officially moved to acquire the entire Delmarva rail system. The railway's plan was to abandon seven branch lines and then put $30 million of rehabilitation funds into the remaining track and a float (ferry) operation. As noted in an earlier chapter the attempted acquisition quickly became ensnarled in labor disputes when the company's labor plans became known. Its intent was to transfer employees of the Penn Central, not needed for the operation, to other parts of its system. This could be tolerated by the labor unions. However, Southern intended to pay these former PC employees at Southern wage levels, which were lower than the PC wages. Because of this several unions refused to sign contracts with Southern, which obviously placed the entire acquisition in jeopardy.

Although Secretary of Transportation William S. Coleman attempted to resolve the dispute, he was unsuccessful. Southern dropped its plans to acquire the Delmarva lines and as a result the lines all became candidates for subsidy or abandonment. It was under these circumstances that

Virginia, Delaware and Maryland became involved in the branch line program.

This situation does not appear to be much different than the previously discussed Illinois case. That is, the action of the unions interferred with an USRA designation in the *Final System Plan*. As a result it seems strange that neither the Southern, nor USRA, nor any other party sought relief from the Special Court.

DELAWARE

When the *Final System Plan* was released in July of 1975, it did not create a great deal of concern in Delaware. For that matter even the Secretary's report on *Rail Service in the Midwest and Northeast Region*, which upset nearly everyone in that region, drew only about 17 witnesses to its hearings from Delaware. Returning to the *FSP* there were only about 20 miles of Delaware branch line listed as AVS (available for subsidy) and almost 16 miles of this was interstate line with Maryland. There were also 112 miles of intrastate and interstate lines that were offered to the Southern Railway, but in July of 1975 everyone believed this acquisition would go through.

By the winter this was no longer a certainty and the Delaware rail plan called for operating subsidies on about 25 miles of rail line that was to be offered to the Southern. The subsidies were fall-back positions in the event that the purchase fell through.

When the acquisition failed to materialize the state had Conrail operate 26.3 miles of branch line under subsidy. Conrail was also the operator of a water operation between Pigeon Point, Delaware and Carney's Point and Thompson's Point, New Jersey; this operation was known as the Pigeon Point Float.

MARYLAND

Maryland's initial rail plan was submitted to FRA in December of 1975 and called for a very minor role for the state in view of the proposed Southern acquisition. Collapse of the acquisition resulted in an amendment to the rail plan: the Maryland and Pennsylvania Railroad would operate one branch line in western Maryland; Conrail would operate several lines on the Delmarva peninsula; and, the Chessie would operate the Frederick branch.

When operations started Maryland was subsidizing 157.7 miles of track excluding the Pocomoke-Norfolk line. Of this mileage, 96.3 were operated by Conrail; 24.2 were operated by the Maryland and Pennsylvania; and, the Chessie operated 3.8 miles, while the Maryland and Delaware Railroad operated 33.4 miles. One year later Conrail's mileage had decreased to 5.6 miles and the Maryland and Delaware had increased to 124 miles with the others remaining about the same.[60]

VIRGINIA[61]

USRA's *Preliminary System Plan* had examined only two lines in Virginia. They concluded that one of the lines should be transferred to Conrail while the other line, known as the Pocomoke-Norfolk line, was to be transferred to a solvent railroad operating in the region.

USRA had determined that the Pocomoke line was unnecessary duplication of the lines going into Conrail and that the railroad would lose over $300 thousand a year on the operation. Since several railroads (Southern Railway, Seaboard Coast Line, and Richmond, Fredericksburg and Potomac Railroad) had expressed an interest in acquiring the line, this seemed like a reasonable option. When the *Final System Plan* designated the Southern Railway as the acquirer of the line, this was quite acceptable to the peninsula's shippers. But then those plans collapsed, and it appeared that subsidies might be necessary.

Virginia had made early contacts with the state negotiations group at Conrail. Although they were confident of a Southern acquisition they were not going to be caught without a back-up position. On several occasions Conrail had estimated the cost of operating the Pocomoke line (including the float operation) for Virginia's planners. However, Virginia had another problem that interferred with its subsidy plans.

As was true for Ohio and Rhode Island, Virginia had a constitution that prevented it from passing state or Federal money to a private sector industry. There were various ways of getting around this barrier and Virginia selected one of these. It created a regional transportation district commission, the Accomack-Northampton Transportation District Commission, which could receive federal subsidy monies via the Virginia Department of Highways and Transportation.

On March 27, 1976, negotiations were completed with Conrail to operate the line and the float for one year. A year later the operation was shifted over to the Virginia and Maryland Railroad for the land operation and a marine concern for the float operation across the Chesapeake.[62]

Robert Corder, Administrator of the Rail Division of Virginia's Department of Highways and Transportation, has stated that "through 1981 a total of approximately 9 million dollars (8 million in Federal funds) will have been spent for the provision of this rail service. Of this amount, approximately 2.3 million dollars has been provided for accelerated maintenance."[63]

Some Concluding Observations on the State Programs

These thirteen states were not the only states involved in the branch line program. The float operations on Lake Michigan crisscrossed the lake from Michigan to Wisconsin and the latter state had a role in assisting that operation. Maine, Vermont, and New Hampshire, although in the "region," had no bankrupt carriers that came under the reorganization act;

the Boston and Maine Railroad, though bankrupt, was attempting to reorganize independently of the new rail act. West Virginia was also in the region but it took no role in the early proceedings and later, following the failure of the Chessie to acquire certain lines, it became involved in a state owned short line railroad.

The state programs discussed in this chapter all qualified for assistance under section 402 of the 3R Act. There was also a national branch line program that stemmed from section 803 of the 4R Act. Surprisingly, the program never gained much of a foothold outside of the "rail reorganiza- tion region." This author knows of only two lines subsidized outside of the region; one was in Minnesota and the other was in Tennessee. The other states have sought to assist branch lines by rehabilitating them before service and traffic become negatively impacted by poor track conditions.

Although they were not mentioned in the discussion, there were several things that each of the states had to do as part of the reorganization and branch line planning process. All of the states had to prepare state rail plans and have these approved by the FRA. If they did not have state level legislation that permitted them to be involved in subsidizing rail- roads, then this had to be enacted. In a few cases there were legal problems surrounding the program because of a state's constitution. This also had to be resolved. Assuming these issues did not present barriers to the state's participation in the program, it was necessary to negotiate contracts for service with a railroad. In most cases this was Conrail. Access to the property required a lease with bankrupt rail estates and these were slow to be negotiated due to the valuation questions noted in chapter 6.

Although maintenance was to be part of the annual operating contract, many of the lines were in such poor condition, i.e., they were at less than FRA Class I safety standards, that special work had to be performed on them. This was handled by still another contract and referred to as "accelerated maintenance." Major rehabilitation of the lines beyond Class I was also covered by a contract for this purpose.

When everything was finalized, or slightly before that in some cases, the 4R Act was passed which amended the 3R Act in that it changed 70 percent federal funds, 30 percent state and local funds, to 100 percent federal funds for rail projects. There are probably some states that would say this legislative change had little or no impact on their program of projects; they should be viewed with some skepticism. It was practically impossible for a state to inform shippers that they were not going to receive subsidized service. This was particularly true when the cost of that service was to be borne entirely with federal funds. The political pressure at the state level was just too great. Therefore, the plans, projects, and contracts were generally revised following enactment of the 4R Act.

The point of this final section has been to note that the program was far more extensive and demanding of state resources than the individual state vignettes might suggest. The individual sketches sought to identify areas worthy of note and in the process played down the bureaucratic process that enabled these to occur.

Notes to Chapter 7

1. Letter from Martin D. Zell, Assistant Commissioner, New York State, to the author, June 24, 1974.

2. Present were: New Hampshire, New Jersey, Vermont, Massachusetts, Rhode Island, Connecticut, New York, Pennsylvania, West Virginia, Ohio, Michigan, Indiana, Illinois, Wisconsin. Absent were: Maine, Maryland, Delaware and Virginia.

3. These are the states noted in the previous footnote.

4. *By-laws of the Conference of States on Regional Rail Reorganization,* September 1974 (xerox).

5. See: ICC, RSPO, "Standards for Determining Rail Service Continuation Subsidies," *Federal Register,* Vol. 40, pp. 1624–1636, pp. 14186–14190.

6. USRA, *Preliminary System Plan, Vol. I, op. cit.,* pp. 251–258.

7. Milton J. Shapp, *et al., A United States Rail Trust Fund,* Harrisburg: Pennsylvania Department of Transportation, 1975.

8. Robert A. Jordan, "147 Miles of Mass. Track Cut in Penn Central Freight Plan," *Boston Sunday Globe,* Dec. 10, 1975.

9. The mileage was increased by 21.4 miles with passage of the 100 percent federal subsidies in the RRRRA. See: Thomas P. Southwick, "Subsidies Will Save Lines Excluded from Conrail," *Patriot Ledger,* (Quincy, Massachusetts), Feb. 10, 1976.

10. Rail Services Planning Office, *The Public Response to the Secretary of Transportation's Rail Services Report, Vol. I, New England States,* Washington, D.C.: Interstate Commerce Commission, August 1974, pp. 49–53.

11. Office of Public and Governmental Affairs, USRA, *News,* July 26, 1975.

12. Paul A. Kelly, "State Agrees to Acquire Pennsy Right of Way," *Providence Journal-Bulletin,* November 29, 1975.

13. John Kiffney, "Rail Service Plan Wins Praise," *Providence Journal,* February 4, 1976.

14. "Railroad Task Force Revived," *Hartford* (Connecticut) *Times,* January 21, 1976.

15. "Statement of John K. Lussi," in U.S. Congress (House), *Local Rail Service Assistance Act Authorization,* Hearing before the Subcommittee on Commerce, Transportation, and Tourism of the Committee on Energy and Commerce, 97th Congress, 1st Session, Serial No. 94–23, March 17, 1981, p. 103.

16. Not included here in the $650 million is a $30 million appropriation for rail assistance passed prior to the first bond issue. See: Benjamin Zodikoff, "New York State's Rail Assistance Programs," a paper presented at the AASHTO Annual Meeting, Birmingham, Alabama, November 16, 1976.

17. Louis Rossi, "New York State's Rail Programs," *AASHTO Quarterly,* Vol. 59, No. 2 (1980), p. 6.

18. "Statement of John K. Lussi," *op. cit.*

19. See: Northeast Rail Task Force, *Report on the Profitablity of New York State Branch Line Operations*, Albany, New York: New York State Department of Transportation, 1974.

20. For example, New York State Railroad Task Force, *Railroad Main Line System Planning and the Role of the Erie Lackawanna Main Line via Port Jervis*, Albany, New York: New York State Department of Transportation, July 1974.

21. Edward C. Burks, "New Rail Plan Drafted by State," *New York Times*, February 1, 1976.

22. "Letter of Melvin Lehr to William T. Druham," in *Local Rail Service Assistance Act Authorization*, *op. cit.*, pp. 34–35.

23. "FRA Authorizes Rail Subsidy Payments to Continue Post-April 1 Operations," *Traffic World*, April 5, 1976.

24. Joseph R. Daughen and Peter Binzen, *The Wreck of the Penn Central*, Boston: Little, Brown, and Co., 1971, p. 55.

25. *Ibid.*

26. "Shapp Attacks U.S. Railway Association's Plan," Press Release, Office of Governor, Commonwealth of Pennsylvania, March 25, 1975.

27. Milton J. Shapp, *et al.*, *A United States Rail Trust Fund*, *op. cit.*

28. "Shapp Attacks U.S. Railway Association Plan," *op. cit.*

29. *Ibid.*

30. "Shapp to Sign Flagman Alert Liability Bill," *Pittsburgh Press*, November 16, 1975.

31. Editorial, "Railroad Flagman Bill," *Evening Bulletin* (Philadelphia), December 10, 1975.

32. "Letter of Elaine King to William T. Druham," in *Local Rail Service Assistance Act Authorization*, *op. cit.* p. 92.

33. "Help for Ohio Railroads," *Youngstown* (Ohio) *Vindicator*, November 10, 1975.

34. Ohio Department of Transportation, *Phase II Ohio Branch Line Plan*, Columbus, Ohio, December 1975.

35. "Factories in Ohio Face Loss of Railroad Lines," *Youngstown* (Ohio) *Vindicator*, January 20, 1976.

36. *Ibid.*

37. "New Rail Agency Sidetracked, Executive Director Asserts," *Cleveland Plain Dealer*, April 7, 1976.

38. Section 402 (a), (3), Public Law 92–236, as amended.

39. Walter Trimble, "Rail Plan Watched Closely," *Columbus Dispatch*, January 30, 1976.

40. See: Office of Inspector General, *Report on Audit of Rail Service Assistance Program Accomplishments, Problems and Future Direction*, Washington, D.C.: U.S. Department of Transportation, Report No. AM-FR-1–015, September 9, 1981.

41. Michigan Department of State Highways and Transportation, *Michigan Railroad Needs: A Planning Report*, Lansing, Michigan, January 2, 1975.

42. *Ibid.*

43. Michigan Department of State Highways and Transportation, *Michigan Railroad Plan: Phase II*, Lansing, Michigan, December 9, 1975, p. iii.

44. "State Asks $26 Million Rail Aid," *Detroit Free Press*, December 11, 1975.

45. "U.S. Cash Will Save Rail Ferry," *Detroit Free Press*, February 5, 1976.

46. "USRA Accepts Ann Arbor Takeover but Rejects N & W Proposal in New England," *Traffic World*, March 1, 1976.

47. USRA, *Final System Plan, Vol. I*, op. cit. p. 282.

48. Hugh McDiarmid, "Milliken's Plan to Buy Railroad Picks Up Steam," *Detroit Free Press*, February 21, 1976.

49. *Ibid.*

50. "Statement of David S. Harrison," *Local Rail Service Assistance Act Authorization*, op. cit., pp. 110–113.

51. A review of the Indiana planning process is available in: William R. Black, "The Indiana Rail Plan: A Case Study," in James F. Runke and Norbert Y. Zucker (eds.) *Proceedings of the Regional Rail Planning Seminars Fall 1976*, Lexington, KY.: pp. 35–46; a thorough discussion of the actions of state government is available in William J. Watt, "Railroad Crisis," in his *Bowen: The Years as Governor*, Indianapoolis: Bierce Associates, 1981, pp. 135–147.

52. Governor's Rail Task Force, *USRA Segments in Indiana: State Analysis and Recommendations, Vol. 1 and 2*, Bloomington, Indiana: Center for Urban and Regional Analysis, Indiana University, August 20, 1974; also Vol. 3 and 4, February 1975.

53. William J. Watt, *op. cit.*, p. 142.

54. Division of Regional Transport Research, *Indiana State Rail Plan 1983 Update*, Bloomington, Ind., 1982.

55. Transportation Planning Office, *Indiana Transportation Fact Book*, Indianapolis, Indiana, 1982, pp. 86–87.

56. Illinois Department of Transportation, *Illinois Rail System Plan*, December 1975.

57. USRA, *Final System Plan, Vol. II*, op. cit., p. 67.

58. 423 F. Supp. 941 (1976).

59. 423 F. Supp. 950 (1976).

60. Maryland Department of Transportation, *Maryland State Rail Plan*, Baltimore-Washington International Airport, Maryland, August 1977.

61. A very good summary of Virginia's involvement in the reorganization see: Daniel C. Knudsen, "The Virginia Rail Subsidy Program: A Review," *Virginia Social Science Journal*, Vol. 16, No. 1 (1981), pp. 60–69.

62. Maryland Department of Transportation, *op. cit.*

63. "Letter of Robert Corder to William T. Druhan," *Local Rail Service Assistance Act Authorization*, pp. 99–100, *op. cit.*

Chapter 8

MAJOR ISSUES IN NEGOTIATIONS
BETWEEN CONRAIL AND THE STATES[1]

As noted in the previous chapter, the 3R Act required the states to prepare plans in order to identify the lines that would be supported through subsidy. Once these decisions were made the states had to negotiate operating agreements with Conrail or other railroads in the region to provide such subsidized service. The 4R Act extended the program to states outside the reorganization area and these states were also required to identify lines to be given operating assistance.

The entire area of negotiations between state agencies and railroads was relatively new, and in this chapter we will review the major issues that emerged during the negotiations between Conrail and the 13 states in which that railroad provided subsidized rail freight service. This chapter will also identify how most of the conflicts in these negotiations were resolved.[2] Before examining these points it is important to understand the environment within which the negotiations took place since this undoubtedly had an impact on the proceedings.

The Negotiating Environment

As the congressionally created successor to the eastern bankrupt railroads, Conrail was willing to provide service under the subsidy program. Although this may seem like a minor point, there was a genuine concern on the part of the states that the railroads would refuse to operate under subsidy. The Norfolk and Western Railway had expressed a preference not to operate under subsidy as early as the fall of 1975. The Chessie System saw hidden costs to them if they became involved in the program and as a result they were willing to look at specific situations only if they might prove profitable under their operation. Since these two major carriers were so opposed to the program this left a significant amount that would have to be served by Conrail. Therefore, there was a sigh of relief when Conrail announced they would operate under subsidy at a meeting of the Conference of States in Indianapolis in October 1975.[3]

Conrail was willing to be cooperative during the negotiations with the states. However, if the states asked for too much then the cooperative mood of the negotiations could, and often did, change dramatically. There was no way that Conrail could avoid operating on lines not to be conveyed to it. It could refuse to operate under the subsidy program leaving the states to petition for a directed service order from the Interstate Commerce Commission (ICC).[4] It is doubtful that the subsidy paid would have differed under the two approaches, however, the latter approach would not have placed any constraints on the railroad. It would have been free to simply set many of the factors negotiated with the states.

The states were in a weaker negotiating position. Their primary strength was in the possible use of a directed service order, and the potential negative image that this would give Conrail in the eyes of a Congress that still had to pass legislation if the conveyance was to occur. That piece of legislation was constantly being revised and it would have been possible for the states, collectively or individually, to change the legislation in several ways that could have been detrimental to the Conrail operation. If the states used the ICC mechanism, they would have virtually lost all control over the program since the directed service route would have resulted in the railroad reporting to the ICC.

Several of the states were reluctant to negotiate since they were uncertain as to the amount of funds that would be available to them. The 3R Act provided for 70 percent federal funds to be matched by 30 percent local or state funds. Proposed amendments to the act recommended that these shares be changed to 50-50 in one case and 100 percent federal monies in another case. It was the 100 percent that was subsequently included in the 4R Act amendments to the 3R Act. In addition several states had not had their state rail plans, which were required by the program, approved by the FRA. Such approval was necessary before the FRA would release any funds to a state for the program. Therefore, it was reasonable that the states were slow to actively negotiate in some cases.

In a sense it didn't matter when the negotiations started. Negotiations rarely end before deadlines in situations such as this. If these began in November or March they still would have concluded in time for the start-up of subsidized service on April 1.

Each of the contracts negotiated differed from the others and all of these differences are not worth discussing here. The major issues discussed below represent what could have become unpenetrable barriers with the potential of blocking the negotiations and preventing the execution of operating agreements between the states and Conrail. Conceivably, they could have halted the program before it began.

Specifying the Operating Plan and Rights

The states had the right to specify the base, or place from which the line or lines would be served, and the frequency of service on lines at the beginning of the program. They also wanted the flexibility of changing these during the term of the contract. Conrail initially resisted this flexibility since frequent changes could have resulted in their having significant operational problems. A compromise was finally reached which allowed the state to adopt on 120 days notice at least one change in service frequency per segment during the contract year.

Conrail retained the right to change the base of operations if this did not increase the cost of subsidy for a line. The states were given the right to reject any change in service frequency.

The Size of Crews

Crew size on the Conrail system as well as on the lines to be operated under subsidy was primarily four or five individuals. In most cases four-man crews were to be used, however, if a fireman were to bid to work the train as they have the right to do under collective bargaining agreements, then crew size would become five men. Firemen are actually apprentice engineers and their presence on a train is for instructional or training reasons; they are not necessary for the operation of the train.

Some states wanted two or three crew members working the subsidized branch lines. None of the states wanted more than a four-man crew. They argued that the training of engineers was the corporation's (Conrail's) responsibility not theirs, and that the fifth man should not appear on the subsidized branch lines.

The issue was actually more complex than this because the states believed that the branch lines being subsidized would become the primary employment area for the firemen. This concern might have had some merit if Conrail had control over where the firemen were utilized, however, they did not have this control.

Proposals were forwarded by the states calling for four crewmen on all trains, or Conrail's average crew size, on all branch lines. Conrail rejected these noting in the first case that the RSPO standards permitted payment of wages for the crew utilized, and in the second case that it would be almost impossible to calculate average crew size on the Conrail system in a manner that would be acceptable to all parties. The result of these negotiations was the states' acceptance of actual branch line crew costs. These latter figures would be auditable which satisfied most of the parties.

The irony of the situation was pointed out by a representative of Conrail's labor relations area during one of the negotiating sessions. He noted that whenever the railroads were able to keep crew size down during labor contract negotiations, the unions would simply go to the states and have their legislatures pass a law increasing crew size to the level that they failed to achieve during negotiations with railroad management. He added that the states had a financial interest in railroad crew size laws with the subsidy program and that they should realize this. Nevertheless, Pennsylvania, which had been a primary advocate of reduced crew size on the subsidized lines, passed a law during the negotiations which called for an extra crewman to be used during certain train operations.[5]

It is unfortunate that Conrail was not willing to negotiate with labor for reduced crew size on the branch lines they would be operating under subsidy. One reason for this was the massive amount of work that had to be accomplished in five months by the 170 individuals that made up Conrail's activation task force. The labor relations area had 11 individuals who had to reach agreements with more than 30 crafts covering more than 100,000 employees. Negotiating for reduced crews would have taken more time than was available. In addition there was a genuine fear that such negotiations could jeopardize other labor negotiations and eventually the conveyance of properties to Conrail.[6]

The problem of crew size could have been resolved by the unions. Representatives of the United Transportation Union actually sat in on some of the negotiating sessions between the states and Conrail. The railroad unions had the most to lose if a state decided that labor costs were simply too great to merit subsidizing a line. Nevertheless, they failed to come forward with a proposal that could have resolved the issue.

Maintenance and Rehabilitation Responsibilities

There were several issues that emerged during the negotiations in the general area of maintenance and rehabilitation. The issues included who would do this work and when, who would have the responsibility for requesting safety waivers if the track did not meet FRA Class I safety standards, and how much it would cost to maintain or rehabilitate the lines to be operated.

Conrail vacillated on the issue of who should control maintenance and rehabilitation. Initially they wanted complete control, then control of only maintenance, and finally they wanted the states to have the responsibility for these functions. The desire for complete control by Conrail was in the best interest of the taxpayers. It meant that Conrail would perform the work and in the process utilize rail labor and, therefore, decrease the drain on the 3R Act Title V labor protection monies which would have to be utilized if these employees were terminated or furloughed. The action was also motivated by the desire to keep the states from bidding-up the price of rail, ties, and rehabilitation equipment. At one point there was a genuine concern that sufficient ties and rail would not be available for Conrail's rehabilitation program.

After Conrail assessed the maintenance and rehabilitation needs that it had in relation to available supplies, manpower, and equipment it became evident that they might not be able to complete their own first year rehabilitation program. The states at the time believed that the condition of track on their branch lines was a major reason why the lines were not used by shippers. This point coupled with the 100 percent federally funded rehabilitation and maintenance resulted in the states being anxious to have work performed at the beginning of the program or at least during the first year. Conrail realized it could not guarantee that this work would be performed and became unwilling to enter into contracts that called for such work.

Maintenance did not appear to be the problem that rehabilitation was. As a result for a brief period of time the negotiations centered on Conrail having the responsibility for maintenance but the states having the responsibility for rehabilitation. Conrail's labor relations area found this unacceptable. If Conrail crews were to have the responsibility for maintenance, they should also have the rehabilitation work on these lines. Therefore, Conrail proposed an alternative solution: the states would have the *contractual responsibility* for both maintenance and rehabilitation.

Responsibility is the key to understanding this approach. If the states had the responsibility they could select anyone they wanted to perform the work, even Conrail. Under the agreement if Conrail was unable to do the work for one reason or another they could subcontract the project back to the state or to another party. The FRA noted that under the federal repayment plan the work had to be performed by a railroad and subcontracting by a railroad would satisfy that requirement.

Another issue in this area arose because Conrail was unwilling to initially accept the responsibility for requesting safety waivers for operations on some of the lines that would be in the subsidy program. From their point of view they did not have control of the monies to bring these lines up to FRA Class I standards and, while the states did have this control, not all of the states wanted to bring their lines up to that level. If Conrail accepted the safety waiver responsibility it might be subject to penalties if they failed to satisfy the conditions of the waivers.

When the FRA safety waiver order was issued on December 31, 1975, it noted that "In the event of any failure to comply with the terms and conditions of this waiver, FRA may, at any time, revoke the waiver or invoke the penalty provisions of 45 U.S.C. 438, or both."[7] Conrail met with representatives of FRA who were anxious to have Conrail apply for the waivers. FRA stated that they would consider the lack of state budgeted monies as a justifiable reason for the lines not being improved to a Class I level. In addition some states had plans for one year of service on a line and then abandonment. It would be a waste of the taxpayers money to bring the line to a Class I level so that it could be abandoned. Conrail finally accepted the responsibility for requesting the waivers.

The final issue in this area was the estimated cost of maintenance and rehabilitation. Although USRA had identified lines that did not meet Class I safety standards in the *Final System Plan*, it turned out these identifications were in most cases an estimate of track condition and not the result of a field survey using a rigorous methodology. Therefore, the USRA rehabilitation costs were at best an educated guess of track condition. The bankrupt railroads were also required to issue rehabilitation cost estimates as part of their discontinuance notices. Needless to say the estimates did not agree. Conrail accepted either estimate with the understanding that the states would be informed if the budgeted amount was not sufficient to carry out the intent of the state's planners.

Maintenance estimates also varied considerably. The RSPO standards specified that $1,000 per mile per year must be used as a minimum. Actually, this amount was to be used if the states and railroads could not agree on an alternative amount. It was clear to all parties that the $1,000 would barely pay for necessary track inspections. Conrail did not attempt to inflate the amount that the states wanted to put into maintenance; it did explain in each case what the states could expect to receive for various expenditure levels.

Liability and Risk

Liability was identified in the latter months of 1975 as a significant issue. If any issue had the potential of wrecking the subsidy program it was this one. Initially, all parties expected the states to insure the subsidized operations. Several short line insurance underwriters were contacted and asked to prepare estimates of what such insurance would cost. As the costs and the potential cash exposure below the deductible level became known, the states grew reluctant to move ahead.

Perhaps the liability issue was blown out of proportion, but this was not apparent at the time. The mileage to be operated under subsidy was by and large unsafe in that it did not meet FRA Class I safety standards. Hazardous materials, including toxic chemicals and munitions, were transported on the lines to be operated. It was a time of record level court settlements in liability cases and there was the possibility that one bad accident could destroy a community and in the process bankrupt a state.

The situation was not completely negative. Because the track was in such poor condition, trains had to go very slowly. Most severe rail accidents do not occur on branch lines with trains moving at less than ten mile per hour speeds. The hazardous materials were minimal in terms of the total traffic on these lines and insignificant in terms of the total traffic to be moved on the Conrail system. Nevertheless, there was the risk that a severe accident could occur.

In early December 1975, Conrail assumed that all losses resulting from freight claims, personal injury, or other accidents would be borne by the states as subsidizers. Conrail was unwilling to accept any of the risk or liability under the assumption that if the states did not wish to have service provided, Conrail would not incur any risk. If the states were willing to pay the premium Conrail was willing to acquire an insurance policy for the lines; Conrail had indicated at an earlier date that the states could participate in its catastrophe insurance at a very low rate. This insurance would have covered any accident with total claims between $2 million and $35 (later $50) million. The states found this unacceptable. They were concerned about the exposure to unlimited and repetitive losses of less than the $2 million level.

In January, Conrail offered to set up a fund to which the states could contribute an amount approximately equal to ten percent of the revenues on the lines being operated. This fund would be used to cover minor losses under the deductible amount in the event of a catastrophe. If the costs exceeded the fund, the states would have to compensate Conrail at the end of the subsidy year.

The states refused to accept this approach stating that the ten percent of revenues was too high. They believed that the most economical approach would be to spread the risk over all lines operated by Conrail. Although the states were correct on both points, Conrail was concerned that it would not have sufficient cash to cover claims and as a result had inflated the amount they expected to need to the ten percent of revenues figure.

Conrail did not know what the losses would be on the subsidized lines and it wanted to use the first year of the program to identify these. Merging all claims would obscure these losses and the second year of the program would begin with no better understanding of the problem than had existed prior to the beginning of the first year of service.

In mid-February the Conference of States presented a proposed solution to the liability problem.[8] Their proposal had the states contributing to Conrail's insurance costs, its expense of liabilities below the deductible level, and the administrative cost of the program. The contribution would be based on the avoidable costs of operating the subsidized service as compared to the total avoidable cost on the Conrail system. No special attempt would be made to identify the location of losses.

Conrail rejected the use of avoidable costs as the basis for the contribution noting that the entire definition of avoidable costs could be altered by the Rail Services Planning Office. The loss of information on the location of claims also disturbed the Conrail staff. However, the general approach was acceptable if these problems could be resolved to the satisfaction of each party. The states proposed that FRA could fund a study of the location of claims and the liability exposure on light-density lines. This was acceptable to Conrail and the FRA and left only the distribution mechanism to be resolved.

Conrail examined several indicators that could have been used to distribute the costs: train-miles, car-miles, train-hours, net ton-miles, and track-miles. Based on the standards and data in Table 8.1, these indicators yielded the following contributions: $1.235 million in train-mile costs; $100.8 thousand in car-mile costs; $2.096 million in train-hour

TABLE 8.1

INDICATORS AND DATA UTILIZED FOR

INSURANCE CALCULATIONS

Indicator or Data Item	Amount on Conrail System
Total Miles to be Operated Under Subsidy	3,000
Total Segments	200
Average Length (miles)	15
Miles Per Trip	30
Train Speed (MPH)	10
Trips Per Year Per Segment	104
Total Carloads in the Program	100,000
Cars Per Mile	35
Cars Per Segment	525
Annual On-Branch Train Miles Per Segment	3,120
Annual Loaded Car-Miles on Branch Per Segment	7,875
Annual Car-Miles on Branch Per Segment	15,750
Total Annual Car Miles	3,150,000
Annual Train Hours on Branch Per Segment	312
Total Annual Train-Hours	62,400
Tons Per Car	50
Annual Net Ton-Miles On-Branch Per Segment	393,750
Total Annual Net Ton-Miles	78,750,000

Source: Consolidated Rail Corporation, State Negotiations, 1976.

costs; $94.5 thousand in net ton-mile costs; and $25.884 million in track-mile costs. Of these the only reasonable values according to Conrail were those resulting from the use of train-mile costs or train-hour costs. The latter were not viewed by Conrail as a good measure because of the high number of hours spent on lines with low speeds, which would have have been the case with the subsidized lines. Train-miles, however, yielded a reasonable amount. The pro forma value of $1.98 per train mile and an administrative cost of seven percent ($.14 per train-mile) yielded a distribution mechanism of $2.12 per train-mile. This was proposed by Conrail and accepted by the states in March of 1976.

In the event that actual losses on the Conrail system had exceeded $2.12 a train-mile the states were to make up the difference. If the actual losses turned out to be less than this amount, the states were to receive a credit toward their second year insurance payment.

The negotiated solution to the liability problem was not the best that could have been achieved. The best approach would have involved contributing to an interstate insurance fund controlled by the states. Railroads would put in claims and the payment would come from the fund. It is doubtful that the states could ever agree on where the funds would be kept, let alone how they would contribute to them. The solution obtained was acceptable to all parties, however, as the states soon discovered, other railroads were unable to implement such a program. It was the size of Conrail that made the approach feasible; smaller railroads could not cover their losses for such a low amount.

Management Initiatives, Fees and Standards

As the 3R Act was originally passed, the avoidable costs of operation in excess of revenues on branch lines in the program were to be covered by a subsidy. Owners of the rail properties were to receive a return on investment, however, there was little or no incentive for railroads to provide service on these lines. The states, FRA and others began talking about the use of a management fee which would serve as a contribution to profit for operators in the summer of 1975.

Chapter 9 addresses the management fee question in considerable detail and it will not be discussed here as an issue. Suffice it to say that just as the states (with minor exceptions) were willing to give as large a management fee as the railroad wanted, Conrail was unwilling to even discuss standards or any fee system that would penalize the railroad. Conrail stated on numerous occasions that guarantees of a given level of service on branch lines in the program were probably discriminatory. The states did not press the point. The problem was finally resolved by the 4R Act which called for a management fee. The act stated that RSPO would set the fee level, but this was not before a considerable amount of negotiation on the issue.

Routing the Traffic and Segmentation

Conrail interpreted the local rail service continuation program in a literal sense as a program whereby shippers who would have lost rail service could have it continued. Some of the states wanted to utilize the branch lines for the movement of overhead traffic. In most cases Conrail rejected these proposals. There were several reasons. USRA had projected certain revenues for the Conrail system by assuming that traffic that had previously moved over bankrupt carriers' lines would move to the neareast point on the Conrail system. For example, USRA assumed that Ann Arbor Railroad traffic moving across Lake Michigan by ferry would no longer move in that manner, and Conrail would receive this traffic at Chicago. In another area USRA assumed that traffic coming from the southeast would not move over the Cape Charles, Virginia, ferry, but instead would move through Conrail's Potomac yards. If traffic moved overhead on these lines, it would not increase traffic on lines in the Conrail system, and at the same time the overhead revenue contribution to the line could make it appear viable. This latter point was another reason for rejecting the use of the branch line for special routings; the USRA line viability analysis had not considered overhead traffic, but had considered only locally originated and terminated traffic. In some cases Conrail agreed to the routing but most of these involved traffic coming onto the Conrail system. It was unwilling to consider situations where the traffic could move from the origin to the destination on other lines in the Conrail system unless it was to its financial advantage.

Segmentation, or the manner in which USRA had divided the bankrupt railroads into segments, also created problems related to the routing problems above. In many cases very long lines had been divided into segments in a uniform manner to facilitate analysis. This would have resulted in revenue originating on a subsidized line being credited to other parts of the same logical line and, in effect, would have given a double-counting of revenues. The states did not want any segmentation and the RSPO standards would have created an accounting nightmare for Conrail if they had received their wishes. Nevertheless, in certain cases it made considerable sense to consolidate several segments into a single segment and Conrail agreed to do this. It is for this reason that several of the branch lines discussed elsewhere are represented by several USRA numbers.

Cross-Subsidies, Excess Revenues and the Like

A cross-subsidy results when the profits from one operation are used to cover the losses of another operation. As it is used here, the states believed that the subsidized branch lines that turned out to be profitable should have those profits available for use in covering the losses on other lines and as such they supported the concept of cross-subsidies. At the same time Conrail believed that such profits or "excess revenues" as they were called should be retained by it. Taking a very close look at the statute Conrail argued that the phrase "the difference between revenue attributable to such properties and avoidable costs" is the literal and mathematical definition of excess revenue as well as subsidy and as such the operator was entitled to receive what the difference might be. The RSPO responded:

> In a literal and mathematical context conforming to the more normal case contemplated by the statute wherein the avoidable costs will exceed the attributable revenues, the excess revenues are a negative difference between these figures, and thus if Conrail's interpretation is correct, should be returned to the subsidizer.[9]

Although the RSPO did not accept Conrail's argument they did, more or less, allow Conrail to work out a solution to the problem with those states negotiating with it for continued rail service.

The states' position was based on an attempt to minimize the cost of the subsidy program or to increase the total number of lines that they could subsidize with their respective entitlements. Conrail opposed cross-subsidies for three reasons. First, it believed that if operation of the lines revealed that they were profitable then they should be placed in the Conrail system. Second, the states could eliminate the cost of subsidizing the lines by practicing deferred maintenance and generating apparent excess revenues or profits which could in turn be used to cover other costs of operations. Finally, it believed that if the states received the excess revenue and practiced cross-subsidization, they could extend the program forever which was not (at least originally) the intent of the Congress.

Conrail believed that it should be able to retain excess revenues to cover costs that were not covered by the RSPO standards. For example, those standards allowed one half of one percent of revenues as an administrative fee for the program's railroads. Assuming $30 million in revenue meant that the administrative cost allowed for the program would be $150,000. This would not even cover the accounting cost of the 3,000 miles expected to be operated by the Conrail system under subsidy.

The FRA informed Conrail that revenues generated by a federal program must be utilized by the program. Conrail responded by proposing a series of interest bearing escrow accounts into which excess revenues could be placed.

The first escrow account was identified as a *maintenance and rehabilitation account*. If at the end of the first year of operation a line generated excess revenues then an amount, not to exceed what would be necessary to perform any maintenance and/or rehabilitation that might be necessary on the line during a second year, was to be deposited in this account. If the excess revenues were not sufficient for this purpose, they could be placed in the account and supplemented with funds from other sources. If the excess revenues exceeded what was necessary for maintenance and rehabilitation during the second year, then the excess could be placed in an acquisition account.

The *acquisition account* as the name implies was to be utilized for the purchase of profitable lines by Conrail. Obviously a line would have to be in very good physical condition from a maintenance and rehabilitation standpoint in order for the funds to be placed in this account. In addition the line would have to be able to cover on an annual basis the total costs of operation before Conrail would consider acquisition. When the monies in the acquisition account were equal to the fair market value of the property, Conrail would consider the line for acquisition.

Some of the states intended to be involved in the subsidy program for only a short period of time, e.g., one or two years. They did not intend to carry out massive maintenance or rehabilitation programs on the lines. It would have made very little sense to place these funds in the two previous accounts, and therefore, the funds were placed in the *interim account.* Funds remained in the interim account until such time as the line was abandoned or the subsidy terminated. When this occurred the monies in the account were transferred to the acquisition account having the largest proportion of fair market value for a line. If this transfer exceeded the funds necessary to acquire the latter line, the excess was to go to the next line segment acquisition account under the same criterion.

Conrail opposed state proposals that would have transferred funds from one line to another line except in the case of the interim account noted above. The states also proposed that the excess revenues could be utilized to cover operating subsidies, however, Conrail also refused to consider this. Some states had obviously designated Conrail to perform the service on their lines because of the inability to work out details with a preferred carrier by conveyance day when the program was to begin. These states proposed that funds in the accounts could be transferred to another railroad at a later date. Conrail refused to consider this proposal.

In the event of termination of service by the subsidizing state, the federal government, or any other party, Conrail proposed that it would combine all funds in all accounts for that subsidizer and utilize the funds to acquire a line segment or portion of a line segment in the state's operating agreement with Conrail.

The states and FRA accepted the excess revenue proposal of Conrail after minor modifications. All parties were satisfied with the approach. The states did not want to see Conrail retain a windfall profit from the program, and they were successful. FRA wanted to see the excess revenues go back into the federal program area that generated them and they were successful. Conrail had two goals: (1) prohibiting the use of funds for cross subsidy, and (2) providing a mechanism for getting profitable lines into the Conrail system when they were identified. They were also successful in obtaining these goals.

Of the various issues raised during the negotiations, the treatment of excess revenues was probably the closest to being a ghost or non-issue. Not more than six or eight of the 150 lines operated by Conrail generated excess revenues of any significant amount. Nevertheless, all parties to the negotiations gave the issue more attention than it deserved.

A Policy Recommendation

These were the major issues in the negotiations between Conrail and the 13 states in the Midwest and Northeast under the local rail service continuation program of the 3R Act of 1973. Other issues were also involved but these were minor in comparison with those discussed above, and generally affected only a few states. Some of the issues should have been addressed by the Congress in amendments to the original legislation. This was particularly true of crew size and other related labor issues. However, the legislation did not really take a hard line with labor and labor practices; it is doubtful that such issues will ever be resolved in that quarter.

The liability issue and its significance was not apparant until relatively late in the reorganization process. It was also an issue that should have been resolved by the Congress, but it was not. The most desirable approach would have been a fund set up under the administration of FRA. All states could have contributed a portion of their entitlement to the fund which could have then been used to cover claims and losses on the lines operated under subsidy. Since this did not occur the states and taxpayers had to pay a considerably higher cost for insurance than should have been necessary.

Although a legislative solution should have been sought for the labor and liability issues, the other issues were and in the future should remain the subject of negotiations between the states and the railroads they designate to provide rail service.

NOTES TO CHAPTER 8

1. An earlier version of this chapter appeared as the author's "Negotiations for Local Rail Service Continuation: The Major Issues," in *Traffic Quarterly*, 31, No. 3 (1977), pp. 455–469.

2. The states where Conrail was asked to operate under subsidy were: Massachusetts, Rhode Island, Connecticut, New York, New Jersey, Pennsylvania, Delaware, Maryland, Virginia, Ohio, Michigan, Indiana, and Illinois. Also effected by the act were Vermont, New Hampshire, Maine, the District of Columbia and portions of contiguous states.

3. This was the Conference of States for Regional Rail Reorganization that was discussed in chapter 7.

4. The directed rail service capability was given to the ICC in Section 304(d)(3) of the 3R Act as amended.

5. This act, the "Flagman Alert Liability Act," was signed into law by Governor Shapp of Pennsylvania in December of 1975.

6. The capability of labor to jeopardize the start-up of Conrail is aptly illustrated by the inability of the Southern Railroad and the Chessie System to participate in the USRA reorganization plan due to their failure to reach agreements with certain labor unions.

7. Federal Railroad Administration, Penn Central Transportation Company, Supplemental Report and Order, Docket No. RST-1, Waiver Petition No. 17, December 31, 1975.

8. *Insurance Proposal Between Conrail and the Conference of States*, prepared for the Conference of States by L. E. Peabody and Associates, Inc., February 17, 1976.

9. Interstate Commerce Commission, "Rail Service Continuation Subsidies: Standards for Determination," *Federal Register*, March 26, 1976, p. 12837.

Chapter 9

THE ISSUE OF MANAGEMENT FEES FOR
SUBSIDIZED SERVICE: A CASE STUDY[1]

The major issues during the negotiations between Conrail and the states were summarized in the previous chapter. Each issue was far more complex than the discussion would suggest. To illustrate this point as well as to discuss one of the more important of these issues in the detail it deserves, this chapter will examine the issue of management fees.

Under Section 304 (c)(2) of the 3R Act operators of subsidized rail freight service were entitled to receive:

> . . . the difference between the revenue attributable to such rail properties and the avoidable costs of providing service on such rail properties . . .[2]

During the first year of subsidized service the railroads operating under subsidy received this difference but they also received management fees that were in excess of two million dollars.[3] This chapter will examine how this originally breakeven situation resulted in a contribution to rail profits.

The nature of the management fee was not clearly understood in 1975 and 1976 and is still unclear to some writers and legislators who confuse the management fee with a reasonable return on value.[4] A reasonable return on value, as that phrase is generally used, is a rental or lease value payable to the owner of property used. In this case that would be the estates of the several railroads that went bankrupt. The management fee is paid to the operator of a service that uses facilities which it does not own or in which it has no capital investment. This would be any of the so-called designated operators (railroads) that performed subsidized service in the Midwest and Northeast states. If a railroad retained ownership of a rail line and the equipment necessary to serve that line, and if it performed subsidized service, then under the legislation it was entitled to receive a reasonable return on value, but it would not receive a management fee.

In addition to examining how the management fee developed, this chapter will examine the rationale for its inclusion in the legislation and program, the positions of affected parties, and the alternatives considered in its development. A summary and some observations on the practice of using management fees in rail subsidy programs conclude the chapter.

Background of the Issue

By the summer of 1975 the bulk of the federal rail reorganization planning was completed and the attention of the states, railroads, and federal agencies was focused on the development of operating agreements or contracts for the provision of subsidized service. In order to facilitate the development of these agreements, the FRA created an "Advisory Task Force on Title IV Program."[5] The group was composed of representatives from the FRA (6), USRA (3), RSPO (6), profitable (solvent) railroads (4), bankrupt railroads (5), and the states (6).

The states affected by the planning and program were at best skeptical regarding the quality of service that could be expected on lines to be operated under subsidy. They knew in many cases the same crews would be providing the local rail service. RSPO had developed subsidy cost standards which were viewed at the time as strict; they were neither generous nor fully compensatory to an operator.[6] Such a situation was hardly conducive to the development of better quality service. Hearings held on the national rail plans had made it clear that at least part of the reason for low traffic levels on so many local branch lines was attributable to the low quality of service.[7] The subsidy program created by the 3R Act and the RSPO standards did not provide a mechanism for changing this situation. For these reasons the states began to talk about and propose the use of management incentives in the agreements that were to be drawn up between the railroads and states.

The Incentive Proposals

At one of the first meetings of the FRA advisory task force, a representative from the State of Indiana proposed a management incentive formula. It was:

$$MI = .10 \ SYR + .25 \ (SYR\text{-}BYR) - .25 \ (SYC\text{-}BYC)$$

where:

MI = the management incentive,
SYR = subsidy year branch line revenues,
BYR = base year branch line revenues,
SYC = subsidy year avoidable costs on the branch lines, and
BYC = the base year avoidable costs on the branch lines.[8]

Later (October 10, 1975) when the FRA sent out "model" contracts drafted by RSPO and USRA to those affected by the program, similar incentive formulations appeared. The RSPO contract stated:

In addition to the subsidy payment defined above, the subsidizer agrees to

pay the operating railroad for the purpose of encouraging management
initiative on the part of the operating railroad an amount equal to ____
percent of the revenue attributable to the subject rail properties, such
amount not to be less than $ _____ or more than $ _____ in any subsidy
year.

The USRA model was more flexible and stated:

In addition to the Administrative Fee of .5% of the branch revenues, and
for the purpose of encouraging rairoad management initiatives, the State
agrees to pay the railroad an amount equal to:
A. $ _____ per carload, or;
B. $ _____ per period (month, year), or;
C. A sliding scale amount based on the efficiency of service as measured
   by $11
       95% or better target accomplishment for projected "time spent
       serving the branch," provided that the average time per car on the
       branch does not exceed 5% of the base year estimate.
D. Other methods.[9]

Additional model contracts were sent to affected parties in December
of 1975. FRA noted on each contract:

costs such as management fees which a subsidizer desires to include in an
operating agreement but which are not covered by the standards must be
paid entirely by the state or local subsidizing body and cannot be included
in the non-federal share.

This is a clear statement of the situation at the time: the states wanted the
provision, but the FRA, as financial administrator of the program, was not
going to encourage its use. The position of the FRA was very reasonable.
The fee was not viewed as an avoidable cost by the RSPO standards and,
therefore, it could not be allowed as a reimbursable cost if the states
elected to use it. At the same time, the incentive formulations could
confuse any forecast of the funds that would be necessary for a given
state's program.

The Position of Conrail

It is notable that by the end of 1975 instead of a management initiative
or management incentive, the references were to management fees. The
change from incentives to fees grew out of the negotiations between
Conrail and the states. Conrail was unwilling to accept the concept of a
management incentive because most of these would have involved the
possibility of penalty provisions. As is apparent from the examples cited
there were bonus provisions for improved service, but there were also

direct and indirect penalty clauses that would have reduced the amount Conrail would receive if the service quality decreased.

Conrail wanted a fee primarily because: (1) it saw costs in the operation of subsidized service that were not recoverable under the standards issued by the RSPO and although these were not that significant for one or two branch lines, they could be substantial for the 2500 to 3000 miles that Conrail expected it might have to operate; (2) it believed, perhaps naively, that a contribution to profit would increase the incentive for better performance by the crews serving the lines; and not unrelated to the first point, (3) it believed that the corporation had to be made "whole," i.e., services were not to be performed if they were not completely compensatory. Conrail did not take this last position lightly, but viewed it as a statutory requirement based on the legislation which had created it. That legislation had identified Conrail as a for-profit corporation, and as such, it was unwilling to accept a contract provision that could negatively impact the corporation's future financial viability. As a result of those beliefs, the earliest Conrail contracts included provisions for a management fee, and its level was set at 10% of the revenue attributable to the branch line.

Involvement by the Congress

Although some of the states reacted negatively to the 10% proposal, it was not a surprise to them. As early as the spring of 1975, the states affected by the 3R Act, notably the Conference of States, had identified the lack of a branch line management function in the bankrupt roads as a primary reason for the light-density line problem being as significant as it was. Such a function would have, in the eyes of the states, identified problems of poor track condition or decreasing traffic and attempted to remedy these prior to any need for abandonment. At a meeting of the Conference of States held at Philadelphia in April of 1975, the group passed a resolution requiring Conrail to create a branch line management function, and added that ". . . the cost of this management function should be borne by the branch lines."[10]

In July of 1975, Peter Metz, who was then assistant secretary of transportation for Massachusetts, testified on behalf of the Conference of States before the U.S. Senate. He proposed:

. . . that Conrail be required to establish a branch line management function to give explicit attention to the operation and marketing of branch line services for branch lines either included in the final system plan and those operated under subsidy. We are willing to have the cost of this market (sic) function borne by the branch lines.[11]

The Congress then responded.

Before the end of September, Senator Kennedy of Massachusetts introduced a bill that would have created such a branch line function within Conrail. The bill (S. 2368) called for "the cost of this management function to be allocated to the avoidable costs of operating the branch lines,"[12] which was in essence the proposal of the Conference of States.

In October, Senator Hartke of Indiana introduced legislation (S. 2520) that bypassed the proposed branch line management function. It stated that the operator of subsidized rail service would receive" . . . the difference between revenues attributable to such properties and the avoidable costs of providing service on such rail properties together with a management fee determined by the Secretary . . ."[13] This bill was the administration's solution to the problem of branch lines. There was to be no legislated branch line management function in Conrail and although the bill yielded on the management fee it placed the determination of its value in FRA, which would have acted for the Secretary of Transportation in the matter.

There was another reason why the administration and Congress wanted to incorporate a management fee into the program. The general consensus was that the 3R Act (Section 304 (c)) placed a legal obligation only on Conrail to provide subsidized branch line service. Other solvent railroads that were not in reorganization would have had no legal reason to participate in the program. This was recognized by the Office of Public Counsel when it stated in October of 1975:

> Therefore, the solvents cannot be expected to participate in the subsidy program unless they are specifically required to do so and unless they are paid a reasonable profit for their efforts.[14]

Since there were numerous cases where railroads other than Conrail could provide more economical service to local branch lines, it was considered important to obtain their participation and it was believed that the management fee would accomplish this.

A month later, Senator Kennedy amended his bill (S. 2368) to include the management fee language of the Hartke bill. The amendment also called for something that Conrail's management dreaded: the transfer to Conrail of all lines to be operated under subsidy.[15] If the Senator from Massachusetts was attempting to get things moving, he was successful. Placing the lines in Conrail would have reversed one of the most visible outcomes of nearly two years of planning. A comprehensive piece of legislation (S. 2718) was introduced by Senator Hartke within the week and within two weeks it had passed the Senate.[16] In another week the House passed its version, and a week later on December 19, 1975 the House agreed to the conference report on S. 2718, clearing the measure for the President.[17] After several delays the Rail Revitalization and

Regulatory Reform Act, Public Law 94-210, later dubbed the 4R Act, was signed into law by Gerald Ford on February 5, 1976.[18]

The new law did not convey the branch lines to Conrail, but the explicit branch line management function was also lost in the legislative process. The management fee language remained except that the level of the fee was to be determined by the RSPO, not the FRA. More specifically the new law amended Title III of the 3R Act. Section 304 (d)(1)(C) of the amended law now stated that the railroad offering subsidized rail service shall . . .

> be entitled to receive, from the person offering such payment, the differ-
> ence between revenue attributable to such properties and the avoidable
> costs of providing service on such rail properties, together with a reasonable
> management fee, as determined by the Office.

Before moving on it should be noted that an attempt was made in 1976 to create a separate organization area within Conrail that would have performed the management functions desired by the states. This area, to be known as State Rail Programs, was to have a negotiating, accounting, and planning role as well as economic analysis and engineering capabilities.[19] It was also to have a field staff in regular communication with the main office to ensure that all was functioning as intended on the local level. It was expected that 31 to 40 individuals (excluding secretarial staff) would be necessary for the anticipated functions and this was viewed as excessive by Conrail's management. Subsequently, such an area was created within Conrail. It became known as Regional Market Development and after a few years it was larger than the area originally proposed.

Management Fees and the RSPO Standards

RSPO had the problem of determining standards for "a reasonable management fee." It issued a notice and order on the fee in late February of 1976.[20] Based on its internal review, the RSPO had concluded that the management fee should be a function of the revenues attributable to the branch line. They believed that this would provide an incentive to the operator to increase revenues on the line. In determining the numerical value of the fee it was noted that the net income of all Class I railroads (before federal income taxes) averaged 4.34 percent of operating revenues, and that the expected performance of Conrail over its first ten years would yield a value of 4.68 percent of revenues. The agency concluded that a reasonable management fee would be 4.5 percent of the revenues attributable to the branch line.

There was one complicating factor and this was that some of the lines operated under subsidy might actually be profitable. USRA's planning might have been very good, but no one thought it was perfect. If such profits, which were referred to as "excess revenues," occurred, RSPO believed it would be inappropriate for the operator of subsidized service to retain these profits, and receive a management fee, for this would result in a "windfall gain without any related risk." RSPO proposed that the operator select to receive the "excess revenues" or the fee, but not both.

The railroads and states reacted to a call for comments on the proposed statement.[21] The Association of American Railroads proposed a 20 percent of revenue figure, while Conrail, the Chessie, and Southern Railway argued for no less than 10 percent. The railroads based their arguments either on the fact that the RSPO average of 4.5 percent was not representative since it was calculated during a period when 20 percent of the national rail system was in bankruptcy, or on earlier ICC action under the 3R Act regarding directed service provisions of Section 601 (e). RSPO did not respond to the former point. With regard to directed service, Conrail noted that when directed service was ordered over parts of the Lehigh and New England Railway Company the ICC had permitted 6 percent of revenues and fully allocated costs; 10 percent with avoidable costs seemed comparable.[22] RSPO did not agree with the argument presented.

The states' responses found the 4.5 percent of revenues acceptable, but argued for incentive formulations in the future. Pennsylvania's response suggested a base fee of 2.5 percent of revenue plus an incentive formulation of two-thirds of any savings resulting from time saved in serving the branch line and twenty percent of any additional revenue resulting from new users of the line.[23] Although the Pennsylvania proposal was a reasonable formulation that would not have necessarily penalized the operator, RSPO believed the 4.5 percent figure was generally better and it elected to use this as a base figure allowing negotiations to modify it.

All parties responding to the call for comments believed the "either-or" situation of the fee or excess revenues was unacceptable. This was the case primarily because an alternative had already been negotiated between Conrail and the states (as discussed in chapter 8) that would apply such excess revenues to the maintenance and rehabilitation of the line. As a result the RSPO dropped its proposal for excess revenues.

As noted above, RSPO was anxious that the parties negotiate any resonable fee mechanism. This was reflected in the wording of the final standard:

> Four and one-half percent of the total annual revenues attributable to the branch . . . shall be paid to the railroad as a reasonable management fee. If the railroad and the person offering the subsidy agree to an additional fee designed as an incentive to maximize revenues, minimize expenses, promote efficient service or otherwise achieve public interest objectives, the railroad shall be paid such a fee as determined in accordance with such agreement.[24]

During the life of the operating assistance program the standard did not change substantially although clarifications of the standard were issued by RSPO. It stated that the 4.5 percent was a bottom or base value; an operator of subsidized service should not receive less than that amount.[25] Also, in the case of short line railroads, it noted that the 4.5 percent fee was probably not a sufficient contribution to profit.[26] Although RSPO was apparently willing to approve any value derived through negotiations between an operator and a subsidizer, the author knows of no case where incentive formulations were used. In addition, the 4.5 percent of revenue management fee appears to have been the standard fee value utilized in the subsidy program although there were some exceptions that went as high as ten percent.

Summary and Some Observations

The Conference of States for Regional Rail Reorganization believed that a major reason for unprofitable branch lines was the lack of a clear railroad management function devoted to such lines. It also believed that a properly structured management incentive scheme could be used to build traffic on the lines to be operated under subsidy. Federal legislation was introduced to create a branch line management function in Conrail; however, it was apparently lost during the legislative process. Management incentives turned into management fees that provided no real incentive to build traffic on branch lines under subsidy as compared to lines owned by the railroad. On the surface the situation was rather negative.

On the positive side Conrail did create and staff an area concerned with the light-density traffic lines that it owned or was operating under subsidy. Also, the RSPO standards remained flexible enough to permit the use of incentive formulations for the management fee. But what did the experience show us and what have we learned from the use of the fee and creation of the special function within Conrail to solve the problem of unviable branch lines? Five observations are possible.

1. A management fee, or contribution to profit, was seen as necessary for the involvement of Conrail, the Chessie, and the Norfolk and Western (N&W) in the subsidy program. Actually, Conrail had little choice in the matter at the time. The fee was not a sufficient inducement for the Chessie or the N&W to become involved. One Chessie official noted that the accounting system for tracking of subsidy costs would easily absorb any management fee it would receive. In one case known to the author the Chessie provided service to a "subsidized" line at no cost to the state. It believed its losses would be less under such free service than its losses resulting from involvement with the program.

2. If the management fee was expected to help generate traffic on lines under subsidy, then it was apparently unsuccessful based on research discussed in the following chapter. One of the studies noted that "in general traffic trends for the eighty-five lines examined . . . are stable to negative with a small minority reflecting growth."[27] Seventy percent of the lines operated had fewer than 34 carloads per mile according to that study; the USRA cut-off between viable and unviable lines was between 90 to 100 carloads per mile.

3. The flexibility of the RSPO with regard to the management fee, while desirable, resulted in the creation of numerous short line railroads that would have most likely failed in the absence of the subsidy program. The short lines created to serve the lines had nearly all of their costs identified as "avoidable," and they were guaranteed in some cases management fees as high as ten percent of revenues, which would be real profit in such cases. Under such situations there is little incentive to make the lines viable even if this was possible; success is guaranteed for the operator.

4. Although a railroad might negotiate an agreement with a state, as Conrail did with 13 states, the intentions of the negotiators do not appear to be generally transferable to the parties they represent. Shippers rarely lived up to the promises they made to states regarding future traffic, and branch line crews did not necessarily deliver the level of service envisioned by the railroad negotiators.

5. In the Conrail case the management fee did contribute to the profitability of the railroad, but it is doubtful that even half of the two million dollars it received annually would be profit due to the branch line management function it created.

NOTES TO CHAPTER 9

1. An earlier version of this chapter appeared as the author's "On the Development of Management Fees for Subsidized Rail Service," *Transportation Journal*, 18, No. 4 (1979), pp. 20–27.

2. The 3R Act was amended by the 4R Act in February of 1976. One of the amendments was the addition of section 304 (d)(1)(C) which called for the explicit payment of a management fee. The amendment was in response to an item negotiated by the parties involved prior to the law's enactment.

3. The two million dollar estimate is based on an expansion of the .5% administrative fee of $230,000 forecasted near the end of the third quarter of the first year of subsidized service by the RSPO; see, Interstate Commerce Commis-

sion, "Rail Service Continuation Subsidies: Standards for Determination," *Federal Register*, Vol. 41, No. 246, December 21, 1976, p. 55689.

4. See for example: M.J. Hirschey. "Rail Service Subsidies—A Critical Analysis of the Program," *Quarterly Review of Economics and Business*, Vol. 18, No. 2, 1978, pp. 41–53.

5. Title IV was that portion of the 3R Act concerned with rail freight subsidies.

6. The RSPO Standards in effect at the time were: Interstate Commerce Commission, "Standards for Determining Rail Service Continuation Subsidies," *Federal Register*, Vol. 40, No. 5, pp. 1624-1636, and Vol. 40, No. 61, pp. 14186–14190, of 1975.

7. See: Interstate Commerce Commission, *The Public Response to the Secretary of Transportation's Rail Services Report, Vol. I, New England States, Vol. II, Middle Atlantic States, and Vol. III, Midwestern States*, (Washington, D.C.: U.S.G.P.O., 1974); and, *Evaluation of the U.S. Railway Association's Preliminary System Plan* (Washington, D.C.: U.S.G.P.O.), 1975.

8. Formulated by Bruce W. Pigozzi, Assistant Director of the Indiana State Rail Plan, August 1975.

9. USRA's rationale for part C of this model is not clear; however, it would appear that the intent was to ensure that service would not "slow down" on subsidized lines. Such a slow down could have significantly increased operating costs and as a result subsidies.

10. Conference of States for Regional Rail Reorganization, *Resolutions of the Philadelphia Meeting*, April 1975, p. 6.

11. U.S. Congress, Senate Committee on Commerce, *Railroads—1975, Part 2*, Hearings, 94th Congress, 1st Session, 1975, p. 770.

12. 121 *Congressional Record* 94, September 17, 1975.

13. This is not unusual since Secretary of Transportation Coleman had sent the bill to the Senate for introduction.

14. Office of Public Counsel, Rail Services Planning Office, *Memorandum: Legal and Operational Problems of Title IV Subsidy Program of the Regional Rail Reorganization Act of 1973 (P.L. 93–236)*, (Washington, D.C.: Interstate Commerce Commission, October 20, 1975), p. 5.

15. 121 *Congressional Record* 94, November 18, 1975.

16. 121 *Congressional Record* 94, December 4, 1975.

17. The measure passed the House with 205 votes in favor and 150 votes against it. See: 121 *Congressional Record*, 94, December 19, 1975.

18. The delays were due in part to the fear of a pocket veto over the Christmas recess initially. Later Secretary Coleman stated that the President would veto the measure and certain changes were made in the bill to make it more acceptable.

19. William R. Black, internal memorandum to Leo F. Mullin, Activation Task Force, Consolidated Rail Corporation, March 15, 1976.

20. Interstate Commerce Commission, "Rail Service Continuation Subsidies: Standards for Determination," *Federal Register*, Vol. 41, No. 39, February 26, 1976, pp. 8468–8469.

21. *Ibid., Federal Register*, Vol. 41, No. 60, March 26, 1976, pp. 12836–12838.

22. *A Submission of the Consolidated Rail Corporation in the Matter of Standards for Determining Rail Service Continuation Subsidies*, Ex Parte No. 293 (Sub. No. 2), March 12, 1976, p. 5.

23. See note 17, p. 12836.

24. *Ibid.*, p. 12838.

25. Interstate Commerce Commission, "Rail Service Continuation Subsidies: Standards for Determination," *Federal Register*, Vol. 41, No. 165, August 24, 1976, pp. 35730–35733.

26. *Ibid.*, *Federal Register*, Vol. 41, No. 246, December 21, 1976, pp. 55686–55694.

27. William R. Black. "Local Rail Service Assistance: Objectives and Initial Trends," *Transportation Research A*, Vol. 13A, 1979, pp. 351–360.

Chapter 10

THE PROGRAM: AN ASSESSMENT
OF TRENDS

With the agreements in place between the states and Conrail the new railroad began operations on April 1, 1976. Critics of the reorganization were quick to point out the appropriateness of Conrail starting-up on "April Fool's Day." The news media gave considerable attention to the new railroad and waited for something newsworthy to report, but the transition went very smoothly and without the chaos that many had predicted.

In the freight subsidy program there was little out of the ordinary. A few branch lines did not receive service because local rail management thought the lines had been abandoned by the *Final System Plan*. This was easily corrected and the program got underway.

In this chapter we will examine the successes and failures of the program in light of the objectives set for the program and traffic on the lines involved. Two time series analyses are involved in this comparison. The first involves branch line operations after the first 29 months of service; it covers the period from April 1, 1976 to September of 1978. Shortly after this (November of 1978) the Local Rail Service Assistance Act was enacted. The second time series incorporates the first and examines the program from its origin in April of 1976 through April of 1982. Before we begin these examinations let us first re-examine the reasons for creating the program as identified by the Congress as well as the perceived objectives of the program as viewed by the states.

Branch Line Subsidies: The Congressional Rationale

The Congress stated their rationale for creating the branch line subsidy program in Section 401 of the 3R Act. They stated:

(1) The Nation is facing an energy shortage of acute proportions in the next decade.
(2) Railroads are one of the most energy efficient modes of transportation for the movement of passengers and freight and cause the least amount of pollution.
(3) Abandonment, termination, or substantial reduction of rail service in any locality will adversely affect the Nation's long term and im-

mediate goals with respect to energy conservation and environmental protection.

(4) Under certain circumstances the cost to the taxpayers of rail service continuation subsidies would be less than the cost of abandonment of rail service in terms of lost jobs, energy shortages, and degradation of the environment.

These "findings" are conjectural by and large except for the fourth point that "under certain circumstances the cost to the taxpayers of . . ." the subsidies would ". . . be less than the cost of abandonment of rail services in terms of lost jobs, energy shortages and degradation of the environment." This is perhaps the strongest rationale offered for the program and unfortunately it was faulty, but this was not apparent at the time.

Hearings held on the rail crisis (as it was called) in 1973 convinced members of Congress that there was a community impact problem and that problem was the potential impact of abandonment on employment. In the absence of war nothing appears to be more sacred to the electorate than employment. Anything that might increase unemployment must be attacked head-on. Members of Congress also realized it would be difficult to explain why they had voted to remove rail service from their home districts. The solution was simple; they had only to keep the local branch lines in place, but this would have cost the railroad money. So a program of subsidies was created so that the railroad would not be burdened by operation of these unprofitable local branch lines. Just as important was the fact that branch line abandonment was seen as an unacceptable and unpopular action and a subsidy program would essentially allow local areas to make the uneasy decision of whether to continue a line in service or abandon it.

As an aside one might raise the question of why Conrail was created. There was certainly nothing in the local rail service assistance area that required the formation of Conrail. It probably didn't have to be created, but the Congress balked at the idea of giving funds directly to the bankrupt roads. Conrail was created because it was "different;" it was not one of the bankrupt roads, but it wasn't a private sector railroad either. It was viewed as part of a solution as opposed to part of a problem.

If we look at Conrail in 1976 it was little more than the bankrupt estates pumped up with federal funds. Employees had come primarily from the bankrupt roads. Conrail moved into the offices vacated by the Penn Central in Philadelphia. The rolling stock was that of the prior bankrupt roads and even today some of it has not been painted. Even the rail network was the same. Admittedly, it might have been difficult working out agreements with labor for several railroads, but it could have been done. Funds could have gone to each of the bankrupt roads with instructions from USRA as to what was to be done with the funds. It was simpler dealing with one road as opposed to seven or more, but it was not necessary. It was more palatable to the average informed citizen to believe that something new such as Conrail was being created to solve the problem.

State Objectives for the Program

Although the states shared the same energy, environmental and employment concerns expressed by the Congress, they had other considerations that necessitated their involvement with the program. The states had always had an explicit concern for the impact of rail abandonment on their communities. They saw the removal of rail service as a catalyst for the closure of grain elevators, coal mines, industrial plants, and the like, and a subsequent reduction in local income due to increases in unemployment.

State officials argued that the termination of rail service would divert rail traffic to a highway system that they already lacked the resources to maintain. Of particular concern were the heavy loads that would increase the amount and frequency of highway and bridge maintenance.

Some state planners expressed the view that removal of rail service would effectively terminate any chance the communities ever had of seeing substantial economic growth in the future. The fact that in most cases the areas lacked the resources that would move by rail did not appear to matter in this reasoning. Also unimportant was the fact that the areas had had rail service for more than one hundred years and they had not experienced rapid growth at any time during that period. Nevertheless, planners believed the lines had to be preserved for future welfare and this was the rationale, in some cases, for their involvement with the program.

At several of the meetings of state rail planners and officials the question came up of the representativeness and accuracy of the data being utilized by the United States Railway Association in its planning efforts. Many believed that these data, which would determine whether a line would be retained or abandoned, were erroneous. As their rationale for this position they noted that the year utilized (1973) for most analysis was not a typical year. On some lines in the East it is clear that 1973 may not have been a "typical" year since Hurricane Agnes washed out several rail lines during 1972. As for the data being erroneous this was documented elsewhere. Based on research undertaken since 1975 it does not appear that the data were that poor. But at the time several states decided to subsidize lines for the sole purpose of clarifying the data question for the lines of concern.

Some states were uncertain as to the importance of the local rail services that were to be abandoned. These states participated in the program in order to provide a transitional period for firms to alter their production locations or the mode of transport that they used for their shipments.

As a final rationale for participation in the program some states believed that they could through subsidy, and in conjunction with existing state commerce and development agencies, make certain lines viable. If there was not sufficient traffic on a line the state agencies noted would have rail using industries locate on the line and as a result increase carloadings and the line's viability. The states believed that this was a reasonable strategy that they could successfully implement.

Of the various objectives and rationales for program involvement, most states followed two or more of those discussed above. It is doubtful if any single state followed all of these.

The Meaning of Traffic Levels

In order to evaluate the meaning of different traffic levels it is beneficial to have certain benchmarks for comparative purposes. That is, if we know that a given branch line has twenty carloads of traffic per mile on an annual basis, this does not necessarily mean a great deal unless we know the minimal number of carloads per mile that are necessary for profitable operation. Fortunately, there are some standard "carload per mile" benchmarks that may be utilized for comparative purposes. These are the Interstate Commerce Commission (ICC) "34 carload rule" and the Department of Transportation (DOT) upper criterion level of 70 carloads per mile.

In 1972 the ICC issued a standard that was referred to as the "34 carload rule."[1] This standard was part of a regulation that gave railroads permission to abandon any rail line if traffic on that line was less than 34 carloads per mile provided there were no public objections to the abandonment and if the requirements of the public convenience and necessity were minimal. When it was issued the rule caused considerable objections from shipper and labor groups as well as state officials. Injunctive relief was sought and received by the Congress of Railway Unions and the Commonwealth of Pennsylvania against utilization of the rule, but the U.S. Supreme Court later upheld the ICC standard. However, by that time the local rail service assistance program was in place and the rule was never applied. Nevertheless, it remains a reasonable standard for comparative purposes.

The DOT upper criterion level of 70 carloads per mile stems from the report prepared for that agency by R.L. Banks.[2] That report, as was noted in chapter 4, basically upheld the ICC's 34 carload rule and went on to state that profitable operations began at about 70 carloads per mile. The range from 34 to 70 is apparently a gray area where, depending on the traffic mix, profit or losses may occur. In the discussion later we will refer to the 34 and 70 carload per mile benchmarks in order to interpret the traffic levels found.

Rail Traffic Data and Methodology

When the rail freight subsidy program began in April of 1976 there where 6,000 miles of track eligible for subsidies in the Northeast and Midwest. States and shippers had requested the operation of 3,100 route miles of this total under subsidy arrangements. Initially, the bulk of this mileage (2,500 route miles or 140 rail line segments) was operated by Conrail with short line railroads offering service on a few lines as well. The federal program continued for 66 months until October of 1981 although some states continued their participation until October of 1982.

The two analyses, one reviewed and the other undertaken here, examine traffic on up to 90 different branch lines that had subsidized rail freight service from Conrail for at least 24 months of the period from April 1976 to October of 1982. For these 90 branch lines data were available on the length of each line and their monthly traffic (in carloads) for up to 72 months of service. Aggregation of the traffic yields carloads per year and division by branch line length yields carloads per mile.

Each analysis utilized two different approaches to examine the extent to which the program's performance satisfied its initial objectives. First, linear time series analysis was performed on monthly carload data for each line. Of the possible outcomes, i.e., a significant positive trend, a significant negative trend, and a non-significant trend, the presence of a positive trend will generally be viewed as satisfying most of the program objectives. That is, a positive growth trend would indicate: (1) local areas were not losing traffic, (2) traffic was not being diverted to highways, (3) future economic growth would not be inhibited, and (4) the states were able to generate traffic on the lines. It should be noted that this is a conservative approach to examining these questions in that only monthly carloads during service are represented in the time series; if the line was served for only 48 months and then abandoned, the analyses include only the 48 months of service.

The second approach used to examine the objectives involved comparisons of the average carloads per mile between each pair of years of subsidized rail service. For these comparisons Sandler's A statistic for correlated samples was utilized.[3] Such a test statistic supplements the findings of the trend analyses and, in addition, enables us to determine if rail traffic, in the aggregate, significantly changed over the period from 1973 through 1981.

The First Study

In 1978 this writer undertook an analysis of 85 of the 95 rail segments operated by Conrail from April 1, 1976 to August 31, 1978.[4] The ten lines deleted represented lines which had changed considerably over the subsidy period.[5] The lines included represented 1167.2 route miles or nearly 95 percent of the Conrail program as of August 31, 1978. A similar

amount of track was operated by short line railroads; they were not
included in the study due to a lack of comparable data.

Using regression techniques a linear trend was fitted to the 29 months
of operating data for each of the 85 lines. The dependent variable was
carloads per month as compiled from the waybills for the lines in
question, and the independent variable was time in months as measured
from 1 to 29. A linear model of the form

$$CL_i = a + b\,T$$

where CL_i = the monthly carloads for some line i,
a = the intercept value for the carloads per month axis,
b = the regression coefficient indicating whether traffic is increasing $(+)$
or decreasing $(-)$ over time, and T = time in months, where T = 1,
2, . . . 29.

In order to have models that are comparable from one line to the next it
is necessary to standardize the models in order to eliminate variations due
to length. This was accomplished by dividing the dependent variable as
well as the *a* and *b* parameters by the length of the line to yield a model of
carloads per unit length per month. This may be represented by

$$CL_i d_i^{-1} = a d_i^{-1} + b d_i^{-1}\,T$$

where d_i = the length of the rail line and the other values are as
previously defined. Let us briefly examine the results of fitting the above
model to the 85 lines.

Eight of the trend lines fitted had statistically significant positive
growth rates. Twenty-eight of the lines displayed a statistically significant
negative trend or decreasing traffic over time. Traffic levels on the
remaining forty-nine lines were not significantly related to time.

With regard to the forty-nine lines which did not display a significant
trend, their median carloads per mile was 19, considerably under the ICC
standard. The negative and positive subgroups of the forty-nine lines had
median carload per mile figures of 18 and 26 respectively. Some of the
lines in this group, although not linearly related to time, did have strong
twelve month cyclical components. In such cases the carloads per mile
figure is the crucial factor in determining viability.

In general one must say that the traffic trends and levels for the 85 lines
examined in 1978 were stable to negative with a very small minority
reflecting growth. Traffic levels in general were lower than they were in
1973. Seventy percent of the lines had carloads per mile that were below
the ICC standard, while only twelve percent had traffic above the DOT
upper criterion of financial viability.

With certain qualifications the research concluded that the program
was not being used as a two-year transitional program leading to abandonment. In addition, states had not been successful at building traffic on the
lines; they had been unable to maintain initial levels. Finally, although

traffic levels did not change significantly over time, they did decrease slightly from year to year.

States argued that they had not had sufficient time to build traffic or that the lines had been in such poor condition that this inhibited use of the rail by shippers. These factors had resulted in the relatively poor showing for the lines in question. By 1982 the states had sufficient time to build traffic on the lines and to have the lines rehabilitated. It was for these reasons that a more extensive study over a longer period of time was undertaken.

A Second Study

The second analysis involved an examination of 90 rail segments located in 12 states and representing 1,214.2 route miles of subsidized service (see Table 10.1). All of these line segments were operated by Conrail and

TABLE 10.1

SUMMARY STATISTICS FOR LINES EXAMINED

State	Lines in Study	Length (miles)
Connecticut	3	16.4
Delaware	1	16.5
Illinois	1	63.4
Indiana	5	78.1
Maryland	1	5.6
Massachusetts	5	84.9
Michigan	5	111.8
New Jersey	7	37.6
New York	19	428.7
Ohio	9	93.6
Pennsylvania	33	268.3
Rhode Island	1	9.3
Totals	90	1214.2

Source: Compiled or calculated by the author from monthly and quarterly reports of the Consolidated Rail Corporation.

the sample represents about one-half of the maximum mileage in the
Conrail program, but probably eighty percent of the traffic handled by
that road as part of the program. The actual lines examined, their
identification number based on the United States Railway Association
(USRA), their endpoints and mileposts are given in Table 10.2.[6]

Annual carloads per mile for the 1973 USRA planning year and each

TABLE 10.2

LINE IDENTIFICATION

State	USRA Line No.	Subsidy Points and Mileposts
Connecticut	47	Wethersfield (7.0) - Rocky Hill (10.2)
	50	Hartford (2.0) - Griffins (8.7)
	55/54	Avon (9.7) - Simsbury (16.2)
Delaware	159/160/161	Georgetown (24.3) - Lewes (38.0) and Lewes Beach (0.0) - (2.4)
Illinois	605a/b/606	Paris (38.2) - Lawrenceville (101.0)
Indiana	418	LaGrange (137.4) - Michigan State Line (146.7)
	523	Anderson (127.0) - Frankton (133.4)
	554	Hunter (130.8) - Maxwell (116.5)
	571/571a	Valley Junction, O. (17.8) - Brookville (43.9)
	633a	Cambridge City (136.2) - Charlottesville (158.0)
Maryland	676	Salisbury (40.8) - Hebron (35.2)
Massachusetts	8	Palmer (1.6) - Old Furnace - South Barre (25.0)
	13	South Sudbury (4.8) - Chelmsford (24.4)
	17	North Abington (0.0) - West Hanover (3.6)
	21/22	E. Sandwich (7.5) - Hyannis (24.3) and Yarmouth (0.0) - S. Dennis (5.6)
	23/24	Buzzards Bay (0.3) - Falmouth (13.8)
Michigan	451	Grand Rapids (88.1) - Varmontville (46.0)
	456/457/458	Sturgis (150.4) - Nottawa (157.9)
	456a/457/458	Wasepi (159.5) - Mendon (164.1)
	466	Kalamazoo (145.0) - Dowagiac (178.6)
	467	Buchanan (200.8) - Indiana State Line (222.8)
New Jersey	123/124/124a	Farmingdale (8.3) - Freehold (12.7)
	1104	Matawan (10.9) - Morganville (14.1)
	1105	Bradley Beach (29.0) - Bay Head Junction (38.0)
	1107	Kenvil (22.0) - Bartley Road (15.3)
	1206	Bloomfield (10.0) - West Orange (12.7)
	1800	McKee City (53.1) - Pleasantville (56.9)
	1808	Palermo (59.6) - Ocean City (66.4)
New York	66c	Wassaic (81.8) - Millertown (94.8)
	81	S. Amsterdam (165.9) - S. Fort Plain (194.5)
	87	Malone (0.0) - Canadian Border (10.3)
	98	Canadiaqua (75.8) - Victor (84.5)
	102	Hannibal (34.2) - Wallington (62.2)
	103/104	Wallington (62.2) - Webster (84.8)
	105/107	Charlotte (96.0) - Model City (168.5)
	108	Newark (18.3) - Sodus Point (33.4)
	109/110	Newark (0.2) - Marion (8.9)

TABLE 10.2 (continued)

New York	233/234	Bellona (46.3) - Seneca Castle (4.9) and Canadaigua Track at Stanley (52.2 - 52.8)
	249	Mayville (64.8) - Corry (93.5)
	1003/1002	Owego (288.0) - Dryden (321.2)
	1002	Cortland Secondary at Cortland (67.8 - 70.8)
	1022	Geneva (344.5) - Victor (371.0)
	1023/1024	Niagara Junction (436.3) - Batavia (410.9)
	1240	Batavia (388.8) - LeRoy (378.6)
	1242	Depew Junction (385.6) - Lancaster (382.5)
	1246	BC Junction (2.7) - Gowanda (33.5)
	1250	Salamanca (414.0) - Cattaraugus (428.1)
Ohio	371	Minerva (4.5) - Magnolia (15.3)
	477a	Hamilton Park Industrial at Columbus (138.0-139.0)
	478	Howard (89.9) - Holmesville (54.6)
	516	Spring Valley (57.8) - Roxanna (63.4)
	525	Lebanon (25.5) - Hageman (31.4)
	527/528	Hempstead (7.0) - Centerville (11.0)
	536/537	Yellow Springs (7.5) - Springfield (19.3)
	643	Genoa (281.5) - Lindsey (273.0)
	1263	Marion (305.1) - Richwood (319.4)
Pennsylvania	135	Allen Lane (0.0) - East Lane (1.4)
	177	Pomeroy (0.0) - Buck Run (3.5)
	180/181	At Lebanon (0.0-1.2) and 2.1 - 21.7)
	196/197	Reading (61.1) - Hamburg-Auburn (86.0)
	203	Mechanicsburg (9.5) - Dillsburg (16.4)
	206	Marion (59.1) - Mercersburg (72.7)
	208	Yeagertown (4.0) - Reedsville (5.8)
	252	Warren (66.5) - Kane (92.5)
	257	Brookville (0.0 - 1.3)
	260a	Warren (54.8) - N. Warren (51.3)
	303	Price Run Branch near Dixonville (V.S. 0 & 00 - V.S. 25 & 26)
	331	Hempfield Jct. (0.0) - Herminie (8.8)
	344	Bridgeville (1.0) - Sygan (1.4)
	651	Falls Creek (27.1) - Minns Coal (22.6)
	663	Connellsville (28.1) - Mt. Braddock (31.7)
	903	Wayne Jct. (5.6) - Germantown (6.8)
	904	Cheltenham Jct. (9.6) - Newtown (26.4)
	905	Lansdale (Fortuna) (1.5) - Doylestown (10.1)
	906	Emmaus Jct. (38.2) - E. Greenville (22.6)
	906a	Oaks (1.5) - Collegeville (5.9)
	909	Pottstown (0.0) - Boyertown (9.1)
	910	Topton (0.2) - Kutztown (4.4)
	915	Lebanon (0.0) - Suedburg (18.3)
	916	Manheim (0.4) - Myers Propane (1.0)
	921	Bear Run Jct. - Frackville (8.7-9.6) and (0.0-2.9)
	923	E. Mahonoy Jct. (103.6) - Ringtown (124.0)
	925	Tremont (29.6) - Pine Grove (23.0)
	935	Lansdale (1.2) - Norristown (9.7)
	1007	Laurel Jct. (157.5) - Skytop Coal (162.7)
	1009	Nesquehoning (0.0) - Tazanend (16.7)
	1012	Franklin Branch-Crossing with Nanticoke Branch (1.0) Crossing with TR 309 (1.4)
	1228	Hicks Ferry (170.0) - Berwick (177.0)
	1229	Old Line Jct. (155.0) - Foster (157.8) and Nicholson (152.1)
Rhode Island	28	Portsmouth (21.5) - Newport (30.5)

Source: See Table 10.1

year of subsidized service are given in Table 10.3 along with the length of each of the segments analyzed. An asterisk in this table simply means that the branch line did not receive service for all twelve months of the year. Excluding these non-service years and the planning year data, there are 399 years of rail service represented by the data. Of these 72.5% of the annual traffic figures were less than the ICC standard of 34 carloads per

TABLE 10.3

LINE SEGMENT LENGTHS AND ANNUAL CARLOADS PER MILE

USRA Line Number	Length (miles)	1973	1976	Annual Carloads Per Mile				
				1977	1978	1979	1980	1981
47	3.2	22.5	21.3	17.2	17.5	18.8	25.3	31.9
50	6.7	47.9	70.7	60.8	62.2	39.5	31.7	14.4
55/54	6.5	15.6	5.6	4.0	4.1	7.3	3.0	*
159/160/161	16.5	17.4	12.0	10.0	12.1	11.6	12.0	5.6
605a/b/606	63.4	60.7	37.4	45.7	44.6	35.1	24.7	*
418	9.0	48.4	13.8	8.4	6.3	*	*	*
523	6.4	9.0	39.0	67.9	129.8	192.0	*	*
554	14.7	7.0	24.1	29.9	20.2	8.7	*	*
571/571a	26.2	39.0	30.4	29.3	11.4	*	*	*
633a	21.8	5.6	5.3	3.9	1.1	.7	.2	*
676	5.6	155.3	109.2	68.5	39.1	39.4	22.5	*
8	25.0	16.8	7.7	9.0	8.8	*	*	*
13	20.0	13.6	21.1	16.0	13.9	11.7	9.6	10.2
17	3.6	168.0	136.6	148.3	165.0	139.4	86.3	68.0
21/22	22.4	65.3	46.0	45.0	46.4	42.0	30.9	19.0
23/24	13.5	16.4	17.3	20.4	19.7	13.0	21.7	11.8
451	42.1	9.9	6.8	6.4	7.8	*	*	*
456/457/458	7.5	.6	4.0	4.4	7.7	3.3	4.0	*
456a/457/458	6.6	14.2	16.0	16.0	10.3	6.0	5.6	3.4
466	33.6	9.0	7.0	7.5	9.1	*	*	*
467	22.0	.7	4.5	.5	1.5	*	*	*
123/124/124a	5.2	15.0	7.6	0.0	.5	*	*	*
1104	3.2	24.6	5.0	3.4	7.8	13.1	26.2	*
1105	9.0	51.6	41.3	15.5	18.2	27.3	28.3	*
1107	6.9	25.6	1.4	7.6	6.9	12.6	4.4	*
1206	2.7	101.1	130.3	35.5	70.3	39.6	29.6	*
1800	3.8	21.3	7.3	7.8	5.7	9.7	7.6	*
1808	6.8	17.0	4.7	5.1	4.8	5.0	*	*
66c	13.2	58.3	30.9	26.6	19.6	14.3	*	*
81	29.5	54.4	32.5	23.9	22.9	16.9	11.5	*
87	10.3	46.7	41.4	30.3	27.2	25.5	*	*
98	8.5	28.3	19.2	18.3	*	*	*	*
102	28.0	27.8	15.8	19.2	18.6	*	*	*
103/104	22.6	45.0	44.6	42.5	44.6	*	*	*
105/107	72.5	15.0	8.0	6.5	*	*	*	*
108	14.6	5.4	11.8	5.4	13.8	*	*	*
109/110	8.9	54.8	29.2	27.8	8.5	*	*	*
233/234	41.6	4.9	3.8	2.9	3.3	2.4	1.9	*
249	28.7	14.4	19.4	23.1	*	*	*	*
1003/1002	34.2	63.9	38.8	37.4	32.3	*	*	*
1002	4.0	48.2	28.0	45.0	35.2	25.2	*	*
1022	26.5	25.6	16.6	20.0	28.0	*	*	*
1023/1024	27.0	11.8	10.6	1.5	*	*	*	*
1240	11.0	44.2	40.7	14.0	11.4	16.5	*	*
1242	3.0	108.0	79.3	95.3	107.6	123.0	*	*

TABLE 10.3 (continued)

1250	14.2	29.1	17.1	20.8	*	*	*	*
371	10.8	75.7	31.2	31.6	28.9	34.6	28.5	*
477a	1.0	71.0	91.0	155.0	172.0	109.0	41.0	*
478	35.3	24.8	18.9	18.9	15.8	*	*	*
516	2.0	39.5	39.0	49.5	43.5	46.5	52.5	*
525	5.9	53.2	28.9	24.4	19.6	20.8	15.5	10.0
527/528	4.0	187.5	77.7	120.7	119.0	51.0	68.0	*
536/537	11.8	41.6	28.8	21.0	17.2	13.9	12.2	*
643	8.5	35.6	18.9	23.1	18.3	9.8	8.1	*
1263	14.3	43.3	24.7	23.1	31.3	20.6	7.5	*
135	1.4	35.7	57.8	57.8	*	*	*	*
177	3.5	85.1	38.5	36.2	34.5	32.5	*	*
180/181	1.5	NR	222.6	170.6	165.3	194.6	106.6	*
196/197	24.9	44.3	19.4	43.9	43.2	6.0	6.0	4.6
203	6.9	32.1	9.8	6.8	5.0	*	*	*
206	13.6	21.2	18.4	11.1	6.7	0.0	4.6	*
208	1.8	115.0	96.1	82.2	81.1	63.8	50.0	*
252	26.0	11.3	4.7	4.1	3.9	4.6	3.8	*
257	1.3	32.3	10.0	6.1	4.6	*	*	*
260a	3.5	41.7	40.0	22.2	28.5	32.2	28.2	6.8
303	.5	50.0	28.0	14.0	14.0	12.0	16.0	*
331	8.8	22.3	29.4	30.9	27.5	20.7	14.5	*
344	.4	17.5	77.5	260.0	395.0	65.0	182.5	*
651	4.6	136.3	257.3	231.3	325.6	556.7	*	*
663	4.2	2.8	8.3	9.5	5.4	7.8	8.5	*
903	1.4	101.4	62.1	29.2	12.1	24.2	103.5	130.7
904	16.8	7.2	8.2	11.7	6.7	7.9	2.4	*
905	8.6	49.8	55.9	49.3	38.8	43.0	15.5	13.7
906	15.6	53.5	25.4	32.1	28.4	30.6	29.6	32.6
906a	4.4	21.3	6.8	8.8	6.8	6.3	*	*
909	9.1	116.2	51.8	46.9	39.4	31.6	27.2	22.4
910	4.2	97.1	44.5	25.4	22.1	14.5	29.5	57.1
915	18.3	7.6	12.9	14.5	14.4	16.0	16.5	*
916	.6	70.0	421.6	18.3	35.0	38.3	*	*
921	4.0	86.5	69.2	60.2	74.2	38.7	26.5	*
923	20.8	5.2	4.8	5.7	10.3	6.2	5.0	*
925	6.6	38.3	4.0	9.0	.3	*	*	*
935	8.5	17.6	17.1	14.5	10.1	5.4	4.5	3.6
1007	16.7	NR	*	1.7	2.9	*	*	*
1009	16.7	29.2	19.2	13.2	9.7	8.2	13.0	12.3
1012	.4	265.0	175.0	272.5	247.5	192.5	62.5	5.0
1228	7.0	NR	16.5	9.8	21.2	5.8	2.5	4.2
1229	5.7	41.2	17.3	15.6	14.3	20.1	*	*
28	9.3	17.9	3.9	3.3	4.7	*	*	*

Source: See Table 10.1; NR = no record

mile. An additional 16.3% were less than the DOT upper criterion of 70 carloads per mile for profitable service. Finally, 11.5% of the values were in excess of the 70 carload per mile rule of thumb. As is apparent from these summary statistics these are clearly light-density lines.

Turning to the research question of interest here, simple linear regression models were fitted to the monthly carloads per mile and time as defined in the earlier study (see Table 10.4). Assuming that the provision of subsidies resulted in the growth of traffic then the trend for these

TABLE 10.4

LINEAR MODELS OF CARLOADS PER MILE PER MONTH

USRA #	N	r	a	b
47	72	.287	1.343	.012
50	72	-.807*	6.656	-.076
55/54	60	-.090	.461	-.001
159/160	72	-.080	1.012	-.003
605a/605b/606	60	-.274	3.930	-.026
418	36	-.663*	1.311	-.027
523	48	.585*	.625	.390
554	60	-.162	2.353	-.027
571/571a	36	-.703*	3.423	-.078
633a	60	-.445*	.449	-.008
676	60	-.780*	.892	-.139
8	36	.112	.668	.002
13	72	-.700*	1.695	-.015
17	72	-.587*	14.444	-.113
21/22	72	-.624*	4.602	-.038
23/24	72	-.144	1.770	-.008
451	36	.192	.517	.003
456/457/458	60	.002	.386	.001
456a/457/458	60	-.334*	1.697	-.025
466	36	.151	.577	.004
467	36	-.464*	.395	-.011
123/124/124a	36	-.332	.653	-.023
1104	60	.463*	-.218	.037
1105	60	-.147	2.588	-.013
1107	60	.246	.318	.007
1206	60	-.524*	9.259	-.137
1800	60	.028	.631	.001
1808	48	.073	.456	.003
66c	48	-.727*	2.985	-.044
81	60	-.751*	2.902	-.036
87	48	-.476*	3.379	-.032
98	24	-.215	1.753	-.014
102	36	.115	1.389	.005
103/104	36	.140	3.438	.012
105/107	24	-.291	.731	-.010
108	36	.016	.842	.001
109/110	36	-.458*	3.607	-.097
233/234	60	-.344*	.360	-.004
249	24	.137	1.648	.010
1003/1002	36	-.354	3.509	-.027
1002	48	-.133	3.100	-.013
1022	36	.538*	.774	.055
1023	24	-.471	1.422	-.073
1240	48	-.366	3.054	-.055
1242	48	.556*	5.967	.100
1246	48	-.363	2.447	-.026
1250	24	.281	1.366	.018
371	60	-.125	2.806	-.007
477a	60	-.306	12.900	-.110
478a	36	-.384	1.745	-.008
516	60	.021	3.700	.004
525	72	-.531*	2.508	-.024
527/528	60	-.321	9.325	-.067
536/537	60	-.374*	2.381	-.027
643	60	-.435*	2.141	-.027
1263	60	-.386*	2.594	-.027
135	24	-.067	5.071	-.021

TABLE 10.4 (continued)

177	48	-.230	3.286	-.014
180/181	60	-.198	17.733	-.080
196/197	72	-.577*	3.309	-.044
203	36	-.564*	.956	-.019
206	60	-.507*	1.507	-.027
208	60	-.501*	8.500	-.072
252	60	-.170	.396	-.001
257	60	-.334*	.846	-.015
260a	72	-.410*	3.200	-.029
303	60	-.242	2.000	-.020
331	60	-.542*	3.023	-.032
344	60	.007	16.000	.008
651	48	.393*	14.630	.570
663	60	-.009	.667	-.000
903	72	.405*	1.000	.107
904	60	-.407*	.946	-.011
905	72	-.747*	5.279	-.062
906	72	.263	2.186	.008
906a	48	-.128	.750	-.007
909	72	-.657*	4.659	-.044
910	72	.140	2.238	.012
915	60	.065	1.148	.003
916	48	-.310	27.000	-.666
921	60	-.534*	6.775	.075
923	60	.010	.529	.000
925	36	-.069	.469	-.005
935	72	-.713*	1.506	-.020
1007	36	.473*	-.066	.011
1009	72	-.324*	1.341	-.008
1012	72	-.550*	24.750	-.325
1228	72	-.344*	1.600	-.021
1229	48	.035	1.351	.002
28	36	.143	.258	.004

models should be positive. In fact only about 8% of the line segments have positive trends that were statistically significant at the .01 level of significance. At the same time 39% of the line segments displayed a significant trend in the negative direction. Ignoring statistical significance and simply evaluating the signs of each model we find that 62 of the 90 segments are negative and 28 are positive. Although the evidence is not conclusive we can state the lines losing traffic exceeded those gaining traffic by a two to one margin.

Examining the linear models developed the a intercept represents the carloads per month per mile one month prior to the initiation of service. Under the 34 carload rule this figure would have to be 2.83 in order to be at about 34 carloads per mile prior to the initiation of service. For the 70 carload criterion the a intercept would have to be at about 5.83. Of the seven models having significant positive growth rates only two (1242 and 651) had a value above the 2.83 value; these lines also exceeded the 5.83 value.

The b coefficient reflects the monthly rate of growth in carloads per mile per month. For the 90 models developed the highest rate of growth was .570 or a little more than a half a carload per month for each mile of track. The average rate of growth for those lines with significant positive trends was .0496 or an annual rate of growth of slightly more than one-half carload per mile. These findings regarding the parameters of the linear models support the previously stated finding that the lines do not appear to have gained much traffic over the 24 to 72 months of rail service and that the subsidies offered do not appear to have made any of the lines profitable.

Moving away from the line specific models it is reasonable to ask whether these findings are confirmed by macro comparisons of the rail lines. Specifically, what is the difference in traffic levels for each pair of years for which service was available? Using the previously noted A statistic we find that none of the year to year changes have been statistically significant at the .01 level. Perhaps the most interesting aspect of these comparisons is reflected in the carload per mile figures (average carloads in Table 10.5). The average of this value from 1976 to

TABLE 10.5

ANNUAL SUMMARY STATISTICS

Year	Total Miles	Number of Branchlines	Average Length	Total Carloads	Average Carloads	A Statistic
1973	1195.60	88	13.58	38,473	32.17	
						.593
1976	1197.10	89	13.45	27,687	23.12	
						1.187
1977	1213.80	90	13.48	26,750	22.03	
						.680
1978	1061.50	84	12.63	24,338	22.92	
						1.075
1979	687.50	65	10.57	16,650	24.21	
						1.299
1980	568.90	51	11.15	8,766	15.40	
						.724
1981	198.30	20	9.91	3,075	15.50	

Source: See Table 10.1

1979 reflects the fact that for those lines in the analysis there was a tendency for traffic to stay at practically the same level. This is most notable in the years 1976, 1977 and 1978, since there were few changes in the number of line segments in those years. This is significant and implies that public subsidies may be utilized to hold traffic at a given level. At the same time it must be recognized that this was not one of the objectives of the program.

With regard to the objectives of the program as identified at the outset of this chapter, it is possible to make a few observations. First, the analysis clearly indicates that the states were unable to build traffic on the lines to profitable levels. It may also indicate that the states never seriously tried to do this, but they nevertheless professed such an intent early in the planning process. Second, the data that were utilized during the planning process may have been erroneous, but this analysis suggests that actual traffic levels were even lower than USRA's 1973 planning data. Third, there is very little here to indicate that the states used the program as a transitional program leading to abandonment. Traffic volume tended to remain at relatively high levels for too long a period for this to have been the case. Fourth, there has been no analysis of the impact of rail abandonment on the highway sector here. As previously noted there was a belief that diversion of rail traffic to the highways would significantly increase financial needs in the latter sector. Other research has tended to suggest this would not occur. It is apparent that the total volume of traffic being discussed here is so small that it would have little impact when spread across the Midwest and Northeast. Finally, the mutual concerns of current community impacts of abandonment and the future impact of such abandonments on growth needs to be addressed. It seems apparent that these impacts could be extremely negative in the presence of high traffic volume and significant numbers of rail users, but if these existed in the first place then the line would not have been under consideration for possible abandonment. Future growth may be affected in those localities that have lost rail service, but once again these areas were already witnessing a downturn in local economic conditions. It is very difficult to separate cause from effect in these situations, but it seems logical, based on the traffic levels under discussion, that the loss of rail traffic was the result of a depressed economy.

A Final Comment

Although in 1976 some rail planners and policy makers believed that subsidies could be utilized to stimulate traffic growth, another group believed this would not occur and that nothing could prevent the lines from losing traffic. Considering the data and analyses undertaken here, it would appear that the major finding is that the expenditure of large amounts of public funds to stimulate growth will probably, in the aggregate, fail to accomplish this goal. If the concern is with the maintenance of given traffic levels, then the use of public monies may be successful at this task over a short term of three or four years. It does not seem that it is even possible to maintain traffic beyond a four year period, but this may be a reflection of decreasing public support for the lines and the program.

Notes to Chapter 10

1. Interstate Commerce Commission, Ex Parte No. 274 (Sub. No. 1), *Abandonment of Railroad Lines*, Effective January 18, 1972.

2. R.L. Banks and Associates, *Development of an Economic Abstraction of Light Density Rail Line Operations*, prepared for the Federal Railroad Administration under contract DOT-FRZ-0020, 1973.

3. J. Sandler, "A Test of the Significance of the Difference Between the Means of Correlated Measures, Based on a Simplification of Student's t," *British Journal of Psychology*, Vol. 46, 1955, pp. 225–226.

4. The analysis was published as: William R. Black, "Local Rail Services Assistance: Objectives and Initial Trends," *Transportation Research A*, Vol. 13A, 1979, pp. 351–360.

5. The lines deleted were USRA Nos. 950 (a float operation) and lines 633a, 33, 119, 1104, 123, 137a, 180/181, 1007, 1228 and 1035. More information on these lines may be found in USRA's *Final System Plan*, Vol. II, 1975.

6. Further information on the lines included in the analysis may also be found in USRA's *Final System Plan*, Vol. II, 1975.

Chapter 11

CORRECTING THE DEFICIENCIES

In April of 1978 a little more than two years after the beginning of the rail freight subsidy program, Senator Howard Cannon of Nevada introduced Senate bill 2981, which at the time was dubbed the "Railroad Amendments Act of 1978." According to the Senate report that accompanied the bill, the proposed legislation was to correct several key deficiencies in the existing local rail service assistance program. It stated:

> . . . funds presently are only provided to States for those lines authorized for abandonment by the Final System Plan or for which the ICC has determined the public convenience and necessity no longer require operation. Consequently, lines which may serve no valid transportation purpose and which should no longer be in the rail system are being maintained with Federal funds. In addition, operating subsidy assistance which was intended to be short term and transitional in nature is being viewed by some states as long term and developmental. Service on lines which, from an economic standpoint, would have been discontinued after a brief period is being supported. In some cases, such lines are even being rehabilitated under the program. Many States are therefore using scarce resources to attempt to restore these worst and least needed lines to financial viability. Yet rehabilitation costs for many of these lines are excessive due to years of deferred maintenance. The potential for returning these lines to profitability is exceedingly slim or nonexistent.[1]

The report goes on to state:

> As a result of these conditions, Federal funds are being spent under the current law to attempt to salvage the worst lines in the railroad system, at high cost, and with little, if any potential for success. At the same time, more important and valuable lines owned by the railroads continue to deteriorate for lack of private investment because the return on such an investment is too low to attract private capital.[2]

As is apparent from these two passages the Senate was aware of the waste occurring in the operating assistance area. It was also in favor of correcting branch line problems before lines were abandoned. However, it would be erroneous to infer that a pre-abandonment assistance program (as it was called) stemmed from failure of the existing operating assistance program. The proposed bill (S. 2981) was introduced in April, the second anniversary of the subsidy program; it is unlikely that the Congress had more than a year and one-half of operating data to evaluate at that time. The more probable source of the pre-abandonment program was the rail industry.

Local Rail Service Assistance Act of 1978

Although the Congress recognized the problems in the operating assistance area and the need for a pre-abandonment program, the manner in which it addressed these is somewhat questionable. While one would expect a cancellation of the former with the creation of the latter, this was not what occurred. Instead, the Local Rail Service Assistance Act of 1978, as signed by President Carter on November 8 of that year, broadened the federal assistance area.[3]

The new law provided financial assistance for rehabilitating branch lines of profitable railroads carrying less than three million (and with the Secretary's permission less than five million) gross tons of freight per mile each year. It was thought that in certain cases deferred maintenance had caused the line's costs to increase and that the revenues of some lines could no longer cover these costs. Funding of the new program was to be accomplished through an 80-20 federal-local cost sharing ratio.

For the branch line operating assistance program, the legislation provided federal assistance for an additional three years (until September 30, 1981). The cost sharing in this latter case was 80-20 for the first and second year and 70-30 for the third year.

The law also enabled states to establish or continue to maintain their light-density rail freight program. For this purpose a state could use $100,000 or five percent of its allocation (whichever was greater) each fiscal year for this purpose. although the law had other provisions relating to rate flexibility, power of the ICC to order railroads to install "safe and adequate facilities and equipment" and other provisions, the powers previously noted were the ones that had the greatest impact on light-density lines.

With regard to funds for the program, no new monies were authorized. Instead funds previously authorized for the Department of Transportation Act in the 3R and 4R Acts were carried over for this law. For 1979 this was $67 million. Of this amount the legislation authorized two-thirds of the funds for rehabilitation of operating lines and the remaining one-third for operating assistance.[4]

Given the Senate's report that "federal funds are being spent under the current law to attempt to salvage the worst lines," one cannot help wondering what would have happened to a program assisting mediocre lines. A ten year extension of the program would not have been unlikely.

Returning to the legislation the act also incorporated a requirement that the state rail plans must include, as soon as practicable "a methodology for determining the ratio of benefits to costs of projects which are proposed to be initiated" in the following four areas:

(1) the cost of acquiring, by purchase, lease, or in such other manner as the State considers appropriate, a line of railroad or other rail properties, or any interest therein to maintain existing or provide for future rail service;

(2) the cost of rehabilitating and improving rail properties on a line of railroad to the extent necessary to permit adequate and efficient rail freight service on such line;

(3) the cost of reducing the costs of lost rail service in a manner less expensive than continuing rail service; and

(4) the cost of constructing rail or rail related facilities (including new connections between two or more existing lines of railroad, intermodal freight terminals, sidings, and relocation of existing lines) for the purpose of improving the quality and efficiency of rail freight service.[5]

These four classes of projects were referred to as acquisition, rehabilitation, substitute service, and new construction. Obviously missing from this list was operating assistance, which although it was to continue for three more years, was not to be subjected to any objective analysis. When asked about this an FRA staff member confided that they realized that operating subsidies could not be objectively justified on any of the lines being assisted.

The net effect of the light-density line changes induced by the Local Rail Service Assistance Act was minor. Operating subsidies continued with only minor changes. The other project areas had implicitly been in existence prior to the act so there was little change in that area. Perhaps the major change was in the allocation procedure for entitlement funds. Restricting only a third of the funds to previously abandoned lines and two-thirds to lines not yet abandoned shifted most of the funds out of the Midwest and Northeast reorganization region into the Plains states where several railroads were facing bankruptcy. This had the effect of reducing the size of the program in the reorganization region.

Related to this change in entitlements was the program change whereby program funds could be utilized for rehabilitation assistance on lines of profitable railroads. This had been the need identified outside the reorganization region for more than two years and the legislation certainly responded to it.[6]

The Staggers Rail Act of 1980

The program was left alone for the next two years or so as the Congress grappled with deregulation proposals for all of the major transport modes including railroads. The result in the rail area was the Staggers Rail Act of 1980,[7] which was signed into law on October 14 of that year.

The provisions of this act did not directly affect the branch line program. However, there were several provisions that affected the branch lines of profitable railroads. First, carriers were given authorization to apply a surcharge to any joint rate that did not yield 110 percent of variable costs (i.e., Rail Form A costs). The surcharge could be large enough to cover all costs of service on lines carrying gross ton-miles of less than 3 million per mile.

Second, the Staggers Rail Act altered certain timing aspects of the abandonment process. Unprotested abandonments were to be granted by the ICC in 75 days from the date of application. Abandonments that were protested but not investigated were to be permitted 120 days after the date the railroad applied for abandonment. In the case of abandonments that were protested and investigated, a final decision had to be handed down within 255 days. The law also specified that the effective date of a permitted abandonment had to be within 330 days. These represented significant improvements in a process that was historically slow for the rail industry.

Third, the legislation incorporated the "feeder railroad development program." Under this program a "financially responsible person" (excluding Class I and Class II rail carriers) could acquire a rail line with a traffic density of less than 3 million gross ton-miles per mile per year after an ICC finding that: the existing carrier refused to provide adequate service; existing service was inadequate for shippers; sale of the line would not adversely affect the existing carrier; and, the sale would result in better transportation service. The program, which was to last three years, required that payment for a line must be net liquidation value or going concern value (whichever was greater).

After the three years any rail line can be acquired in this manner regardless of density. The ICC can also require the sale of a line proposed for abandonment. In this case, if the buyer of such a line stops service then the seller may repurchase the line at the original selling price plus interest.[8]

As is evident from this summary the Staggers Rail Act came close to the branch line issue, but did not really address it. The feeder line program set up by the act has not attracted much attention or action. Abandonments also did not change substantially with the new provisions. The third area addressed, the use of surcharges, has been used to a considerable extent to increase revenues on low density lines.

Omnibus Economic Reconciliation Act of 1981[9]

Hidden away as Section 1131 of the Omnibus Economic Reconciliation Act of 1981 were provisions pertaining to Conrail; these were subtitled the "Northeast Rail Services Act of 1981" (otherwise known as NERSA). Based on what was assessed as unsatisfactory performance, the act sought to remove the federal obligation to subsidize Conrail's passenger and freight services, as well as provide for the return of the railroad to the private sector. The law also provided Conrail with the opportunity to become profitable. Most of its provisions have little to do with the topic of interest here—branch lines and programs affecting branch lines—but one section did.

Section 1156 amended Section 308 of the 3R Act and allowed Conrail to expeditiously abandon lines. The law stated that:

> Any application for abandonment that is filed by the Corporation under this section before December 1, 1981, shall be granted by the Commission within 90 days after the date such application is filed unless, within such 90 day period, an offer of financial assistance is made . . ."

Another provision stated:

> The Corporation may, prior to November 1, 1983, file with the Commission a notice of insufficient revenues for any line which is part of the system of the Corporation . . . At any time after the 90 day period beginning with the filing of (that) notice . . . the Corporation may file for the abandonment for such line . . . (which) shall be granted by the Commission within 90 days after the date (of) such application . . . unless . . . an offer of financial assistance is made . . .

Quickly labeled as the "90 day window" and the "180 day window" these provisions generated immediate concern on the part of the states. Under the provisions Conrail could abandon its entire operation in selected states. However, this would have been folly for the railroad. Instead, Conrail's planners initially identified about 2630 route miles of track (see Table 11.1) and later "sought permission to abandon 363 line segments in eleven states totalling 2,614 route miles. Permission was granted in 1981 to abandon 20 of these line segments . . ."[10] and the remainder followed in 1982. The irony of this action is that after the states fought for eight years to retain or continue service on similar light-density lines, these 2,614 miles were dropped without a significant murmur.

Another provision of the Omnibus Economic Reconciliation Act (though not part of NERSA) concerned the branch line operating subsidy program. Section 1192 simply amended the five categories of possible assistance to four categories deleting operating subsidies in the process to make this law compatible with provisions of the Local Rail Service Assistance Act of 1978. This part of the law took effect October 1, 1982, although subsidized service had ended in October 1981. Also altered by the act was the level of federal funds which had been 80 percent and now

TABLE 11.1

"DECEMBER 1" CONRAIL LINE ABANDONMENTS

State	No. of Lines	Route Miles
Connecticut	0	0
Massachusetts	16	103.5
Rhode Island	0	0
Delaware	4	15.2
Maryland	2	24.1
Illinois	14	305.0
Indiana	26	324.0
Michigan	15	159.5
New Jersey	47	157.4
New York	54	426.1
Ohio	52	398.9
Pennsylvania	136	715.8
West Virginia	1	.7
Totals	367	2630.2

Source: Regional Market Development, Consolidated Rail Corporation, December 1, 1981

would be 70 percent in all programs retained. In effect, even if the states or shippers were interested in short term financial aid in the form of operating assistance, the federal program was no longer in existence.

In 1976 the local rail service program had budget authorization in excess of one-half billion dollars. In 1978 the program merited its own legislation: the Local Rail Service Assistance Act. Major deregulation movements in 1980 left the program alone. And in the fall of 1981 the program of operating assistance died and the remaining program areas shrunk considerably. What happened?

Causes of Change

The answer to this question is "the Reagan Administration." Whether one identifies President Ronald Reagan, David Stockman (the head of the

Office of Management and Budget), Drew Lewis (Secretary of Transportation), or Robert Blanchette (Administrator of the Federal Railroad Administration) is a moot point. The administration sought to reduce the scale or eliminate numerous federal programs in an attempt to get control of a budget that was out of control. The legislation that indirectly put the finishing touches on operating assistance by not renewing it was the Omnibus Economic Reconciliation Act.

It is doubtful that most members of the administration were even aware of the program. The same cannot be said of Robert Blanchette. As the newly appointed administrator of the Federal Railroad Administration, Blanchette should have been very familiar with the Local Rail Service Assistance Act. Although he was new to FRA he was certainly not new to railroads and their problems. From 1963 to 1968 he had served as general counsel of the New York, New Haven and Hartford Railroad. During 1969 and 1970 Blanchette served as executive director of a railroad industry task force established to study the nation's rail problems; the group was America's Sound Transportation Review Organization, otherwise known as ASTRO. From 1970 to 1978 he had been with the Penn Central Transportation Company where he held the position of counsel for that bankrupt carrier. Prior to his appointment in January of 1981 as FRA administrator, Blanchette had been practicing law in Washington, D.C.[11] So Blanchette's background, particularly his background at the Penn Central during the reorganization, should have made him familiar with the program. If he was familiar with the program, and some might doubt this based on his statements, he certainly didn't care for it.[12] But then there was very little indication that he approved of any action taken by the government to resolve the Penn Central bankruptcy problem in the mid-1970's.[13]

So it is not surprising that Blanchette was selected as administrator of an agency where numerous programs had begun during the '70's. And it was also not surprising when he testified before Representative James J. Florio's House committee that the local rail subsidy program

> . . . has produced mixed results. The initial subsidies were intended to be an interim measure while lone range plans were developed. Instead, more than 2,000 miles of the 3,000 miles originally subsidized were still in the program as of September 30, 1980. Subsidized operations have been discontinued generally where shippers or local communities were unwilling to contribute at least a portion of the non-Federal share of the subsidy.[14]

His statement continued,

> As it evolved, the program developed major deficiencies. They include using grant funds for long term operating subsidies, using Federal funds to solve isolated transportation issues appropriately within the local domain of

the states, and allocating funds by a formula which made them available to areas without serious rail problems.[15]

Blanchette concluded,

> In light of the history of the Local Rail Service Assistance program, and the existence of programs targeted at specific problems, we believe that the Local Rail Services Program has served its purposes and should be terminated.[16]

The Congress accepted most of the wishes of the Administration and cut the program funds significantly. The appropriation in FY 1981 had been $80 million and in FY 1982 this was reduced to $35 million. It was this high only because of commitments from previous years in the form of continuing projects.

During the 1983 appropriations hearings the Administration requested $20 million in funding for the program. The late Adam Benjamin, Representative from Indiana, chaired the hearings and he queried Mr. Blanchette, "Last year you proposed no funding for the local rail service assistance program. Why have you changed your mind and requested $20 million for this program in fiscal year 1983?" Blanchette responded, "Our conclusion was that there were some States that were in the last year of a 3-year program and that there were some expectations that had been generated, whether legally sound or not. So we concluded that we ought to get the last-phase funding in, and it is our judgement that $20 million will do it."[17]

When Representative Conte of Massachusetts asked a similar question of the FRA, the response came back as follows:

> Recent legislation and policy initiative by the Federal Government have resulted in new economic and financial tools for the railroad industry. These include greater freedom to negotiate higher rates or withdraw from serving uneconomic rail lines. Additionally, over the past several years, the more serious rail service problems have been resolved and the states have become proficient at solving problems associated with service on light density rail lines. Consistent with the diminishing problem, $20 million was included in the Administration's budget for fiscal year 1983 to accommodate the orderly close of the LRSA program. Under Section 5 of the Department of Transportation Act, $362 million is authorized to be appropriated for LRSA purposes; there is no termination date. Through fiscal year 1982, $250.8 million has been appropriated. The Administration does not intend to seek budget authority after fiscal year 1983 for this program.[18]

Of course most of the justification for eliminating the program is sheer jibberish. The "recent legislation," presumably the Staggers Rail Act of 1980, had not significantly touched the branch line question. There was indeed "greater freedom . . . to withdraw from serving uneconomic lines," but this would seem to argue for retaining the program. States may "have become proficient at solving problems associated with service on light density rail lines," but they had not figured out how to do this at zero cost. And as far as there being a "diminishing problem" Conrail had just finished abandoning nearly 3,000 miles of track prior to the hearings in 1982. So clearly the justification offered by the FRA was nonsense. It was an attempt to demonstrate that the program was not needed by an administration that didn't care if it was needed or not. The administration was merely trying to control the level of the budget and whether the program served a useful function did not matter.

This is not to say that the program lacked faults. It clearly had enough of these as the Senate had identified in 1978, but "correcting deficiencies" did not mean that the program had to be eliminated. Such a proposal was far from constructive.

NOTES TO CHAPTER 11

1. U.S. Congress .Senate., *Local Rail Services Act of 1978*, Senate Report No. 95–1159, 95th Congress, 2nd Session, Calendar No. 1082, August 25, 1978, p. 5.

2. *Ibid.*

3. Public Law 95–607.

4. For a summary of the legislation see: "Expanded Aid to Local Freight Rail Lines Enacted," *Congressional Quarterly*, Nov. 18, 1978, pp. 3317–3318.

5. 49, USC, 1654 (f), (1), (2), (3), (4),

6. The need had been identified during the Regional Rail Planning Seminars of the Federal Railroad Administration and the Council of State Governments in the fall of 1976. See: James F. Runke and Norbert Y. Zucker, *Proceedings of the Regional Rail Planning Seminars*, Lexington, KY: The Council of State Governments, 1977.

7. Public Law 96–448.

8. An excellent summary of the basic provisions of the Staggers Rail Act of 1980 may be found in: Association of American Railroads, *Rail News Update*, Washington, DC, No. 2308, October 29, 1980.

9. Public Law 97–35.

10. United States Railway Association, *1981 Conrail Performance Review*, Washington, DC (1982), p. 42.

11. U.S. Congress .Senate. *Department of Transportation and Related Agencies Appropriation for Fiscal Year 1982*. Hearings before a Subcommittee of the Committee on Appropriations, 97th Congress, First Session, Part 1, Washington, DC, pp. 766–767.

12. The administrator appeared to believe all branch lines of Conrail were covered by the program. See: *Ibid.*, p. 802.

13. See his testimony before Senator Hartke's Subcommittee in U.S. Congress .Senate., *Railroads 1975*, Hearings before the Subcommittee on Surface Transportation of the Committee on Commerce, 94th Congress, 1st Session, Serial No. 94–31, Part 4, 1975, pp. 1411–1451.

14. U.S. Congress .House., *Local Rail Services Assistance Act Authorization*, Hearings before the Subcommittee on Commerce, Transportation and Tourism of the Committee on Energy and Commerce, 97th Congress, 1st Session, Serial No. 97–23, 1981, p. 8.

15. *Ibid.*, p. 9.

16. *Ibid.*, p. 12.

17. U.S. Congress .House., *Department of Transportation and Related Agencies Approfor 1983*. Hearings before the Subcommittee of the Committee on Appropriations, 97th Congress, 2nd Session, Part 5, 1982, p. 387.

18. *Ibid.*, p. 452.

Chapter 12

EVALUATIONS AND PROBLEMS
WITH THE PROGRAM

One of the program assessments noted in chapter 10 was completed in the fall of 1978 and subsequently appeared as a research paper.[1] As such, the assessment was one of the earliest evaluations of the local rail service assistance program. Among the findings of that early study were the following:

1. the program is not being used to fund a two-year transitional phase leading to abandonment; and,
2. states have not been able to build traffic on the lines; actually they were not able to maintain the initial low levels.[2]

These findings are not particularly damning and since only 29 months of operations were involved in that early study there was every probability that the program would be turned around.

There were three other evaluations completed prior to this study: one by an analyst of the Congressional Research Service;[3] the second by a consulting firm under contract to the Federal Railroad Administration;[4] and, the third by the U.S. Department of Transportation's Office of Inspector General.[5] This chapter will summarize the major findings and problems noted by these evaluations as well as identify other problems that developed with the assistance program.

CONGRESSIONAL RESEARCH SERVICE STUDY

John W. Fischer, a transport economics analyst with the Congressional Research Service completed the first evaluation of the program.[6] Evaluation may be the wrong label to attach to this early report completed in February of 1980, for the author intended only to catalog "a selected sample of . . . state actions and identify the direction in which the states were moving."[7]

Following an introductory overview, Fischer reviews the abandonment issue, the role of the 3R and 4R Acts and the Local Rail Service Assistance Act. He then proceeds to examine the rail programs of Florida, Tennessee, California, South Dakota, Pennsylvania, Michigan, and Illinois. Of these states only the last three are in the reorganization region and as a result they were the states where operating assistance had been the common form of assistance. Of the remaining four states only Tennessee had provided operating assistance and this involved only one line.

The brief reports on state programs were generally positive in tone. This is to be expected since the report is based primarily on telephone conversations with state planners and copies of state rail plans.

Fischer concluded that the continuing subsidy for operation of branch lines no longer seemed to be the best solution in most parts of the country. He attributed its continued existence in the Northeast and Midwest (in 1980) to the scale of the problem created by the massive railroad reorganization in those areas.

Short lines, which were once viewed as the solution for continued service, were no longer viewed in that manner according to Fischer. There are many different factors, including timing and sound management, that must come together in order to have a viable short line.

Rehabilitation of rail lines was seen by Fischer as the most desirable alternative for a state rail assistance program. He noted that several states believed that the weight limit of three million gross ton-miles was restrictive and they would rather see the weight increased. Actually, the Secretary of Transportation did have the discretionary authority to permit projects on track carrying up to five million gross ton miles; a fact which Fischer does not appear aware of.

Comment

It is true that short lines are not usually the answer to the continuation of branch line rail service. The same must also be said of long term rail service operating subsidies in a general sense. As for the rehabilitation of rail lines, as popular as the idea was (and is), it does not appear that this offers a permanent solution. There are few cases where rehabilitation will generate the traffic levels expected or necessary in order to rehabilitate the line the next time around. Also, if lines carry more than 3 million gross ton-miles annually one should ask why the revenues attributable to the lines are not sufficient to cover its own rehabilitation costs.

ERNST & WHINNEY EVALUATION

In the fall of 1978 FRA's Office of State Assistance Programs, then directed by Madeline S. Bloom, initiated a comprehensive evaluation of the effectiveness of the Local Rail Service Assistance Program. The evaluation was performed by the consulting firm of Ernst & Whinney (E&W).[8] In addition to the evaluation E&W was to develop a framework for continuing evaluation and an appropriate system of financial management and control for the program at the state and federal level. Although these latter elements are notable, the evaluation of the program is of primary interest here.

E&W reached several conclusions in the final report completed in January of 1980 and these appear below.[9]

1. The program has been a major factor in the development of effective statewide planning.

There can be little doubt that this was the case. Prior to the existence of the program only two or three states had a rail planning component to their state level transport planning. It is not readily apparent what would become of this rail planning function if federal planning funds were stopped. Based on the experience with other programs at the state level it is likely that rail planning would cease if not assisted by federal planning funds.

2. The expenditure of program funds, one measure of program performance, is steadily increasing in terms of the state ability to obligate appropriated funds.

There is some question as to whether expenditure of program funds is a valid measure of program performance in this writer's viewpoint. Programs for which the demand for funds decrease over time are exceedingly rare.

3. The program has been effective in many cases in reducing the adverse impacts of rail service abandonments.

This is true but as E&W note only 31 of 186 operating assistance projects has ended by 1980 and therefore it is questionable as to whether this objective was sought by very many states.

4. Because of its relative scope and size the program effect on the overall rail system or railroad financial viability is negligible though it may well contribute to the financial viability of certain rail systems.

Since not more than 7,000 miles of track have been affected by the program for all types of projects, its impact on a 180,000 mile national rail system has been negligible. Even the 3,000 or so miles of line operated at one time by Conrail was a small part of that railroad's total operations and revenues.

5. The maintenance or stimulation of community economic well-being is an objective that the program has been able to achieve in most cases and has the potential for substantial achievement.

There is some question as to whether this has been achieved at all in the operating assistance case although E&W saw considerable evidence of this in the pre-abandonment case. While there is reason to concur in this latter case, it is probable that pouring funds into any local industry would have had the same effect.

6. Although the contribution of rights of way preservation to overall program success has been limited, the program has allowed significant rail banking.

This has been the case particularly in the coastal states of the Northeast.
    With regard to other aspects of their report that focus on financial management and control, E&W note:

7. The complexity of the financial management requirements involved in program participation is such that, to some extent, each state has had problems identifying, understanding and complying with all the requirements in an adequate manner.

This does seem to have become a problem with the program.

8. Whereas the existing financial management requirements are largely adequate, the performance of most program participants can be improved by further explanation and clarification of the requirements.

Elimination of some of the requirements might also have been considered.
    The E&W report was a significant step forward in the evaluation of the LRSA program. It identified problems with the program and often suggested solutions for these. Nevertheless, there is some question as to whether E&W ever really came to grips with many elements of the program and as the comments in this summary note there was an apparent desire on the part of the E&W firm to identify positive attributes of the program in the report summary.
    There is also some question as to whether participants in the program (the states and the FRA) should have set the objectives of the program as noted by E&W (see Table 12.1). Title IV of the 3R Act states that the Local Rail Services program was created because:
    The Congress finds and declares that—
    (1) The Nation is facing an energy shortage of acute proportions in the next decade.
    (2) Railroads are one of the most energy-efficient modes of transportation for the movement of passengers and freight and cause the least amount of pollution.
    (3) Abandonment, termination, or substantial reduction of rail

TABLE 12.1

SUMMARY OF OVERALL STATE OBJECTIVES[a],[b]

Objectives	% of all states[c]
Minimize Adverse Community Impacts of Rail Service Abandonment	76
Promote Rail System Financial Viability	67
Maintain and/or Stimulate Community Economic Well-Being	85
Preserve Essential Rights-of-way for Transportation Uses	54
Provide for Safe Rail Transportation Service	28
Promote Private and Public Cooperation in Rail Freight Transportation Service	72
Insure Cost Effective Public Investments	20
Promote Natural Resource Efficiency	61
Develop a Balanced Transportation System	63
Acquire Rail Right-of-way for Alternative Uses	9
Improve Rail Service	30
Establish Rail Transportation Planning and Research Capability	67

[a] Source: Ernst and Whinney, Evaluation of State Rail Assistance Program...p. III-7.

[b] Based on State Rail Plans and Planning Work Statements.

[c] This information is based on State Rail Plans on file with FRA as of November 1978. Therefore, only 14 of the 803 states are represented in this sample.

service in any locality will adversely affect the Nation's long-term and immediate goals with respect to energy conservation and environmental protection.

(4) Under certain circumstances the cost to the taxpayers of rail service continuation subsidies would be less than the cost of abandonment of rail service in terms of lost jobs, energy shortages, and degradation of the environment.

It would appear that the primary goals of the program are contained in the fourth finding which suggests that lines should be subsidized if the costs of those subsidies are less than the costs resulting from abandonment. These latter costs are defined as employment costs, energy costs and environmental costs. E&W did not examine the extent to which the program addressed any of these areas, but rather accepted the goals as redefined in the state rail plans. As a result only a few of the reasons for creating the program were evaluated in the report.

REPORT OF THE OFFICE OF INSPECTOR GENERAL

The third major evaluation was undertaken by the Office of Inspector General (OIG) of the U.S. Department of Transportation in 1981.[10] It was actually an audit evaluation that had as its objective an evaluation of the "accomplishments, and the efficiency and effectiveness of the FRA and State agencies administration of the program."[11] Although this would appear to be a general audit, it examined the program as implemented through short lines, as opposed to Class I carriers such as Conrail. Nine lines (eight of them short lines) were examined in three states (Ohio, Pennsylvania, and Illinois).

In their report the OIG noted that the Office of Management and Budget (OMB) review of the DOT/FRA 1981 and 1982 budgets recommended that the program be terminated stating that most of the program objectives had been met. Considering the 3,000 miles of Conrail line yet to be abandoned at the time this makes little sense; there was still a need for some kind of program. It would appear that the report sought to defend the OMB recommendations without a clear understanding that operating assistance was scheduled to end less than a month after the release of its final report. The OIG also did not appear to be very familiar with the program.

The OIG report began by noting that "although Ernst and Whinney did a thorough review of the Program and made many recommendations for improvement, neither FRA nor the States took sufficient action on the report."[12] The report then proceeded to identify problems and make recommendations in three areas: the future direction of federal support, excess funding, and unreasonable costs.

Future Direction of Federal Support

The OIG concluded that the program had not been successful in making the lines assisted viable and as a result it was unsuccessful in providing long term transportation service to affected communities. Based on its analysis the OIG believed that the program should be eliminated. In the event that the program continued the report recommended that:

　　a. Legislation be initiated that provided more rigid eligibility
　　　　criteria for lines.

b. Limitations be placed on the assistance for clearly unprofitable operations and that short term funding should concentrate on substitute service.

c. Federal assistance be awarded only if accurate and complete cost/benefit analyses had been completed.[13]

Excess Funding

OIG believed that the FRA had to improve its financial management of the rail assistance program. It noted that states were overfunded; FRA funded projects that were never completed; the agency was carrying-over large amounts of funds; and, FRA was obligating most of the program funds in the last quarter of the year. Most of these faults were attributed to the untimely submission and review of state rail plans. Recommendations on excess funding were directed primarily at tightening up the requirements related to the submission and content of state rail plans.

Unreasonable Costs

It was in the cost area that the OIG raised the greatest number of specific questions. They faulted the states for: (1) leasing locomotives that could have been purchased for one-half the cost; (2) leasing rail cars for which the leasing costs exceeded car revenues (by nearly $500,000); (3) paying management fees in excess of fees permitted under RSPO standards; (4) payment of incentive fees even though financial aspects of the operation were not improved; (5) contracting for excess termination costs; and, (6) the unreasonable level of salary charges.

There followed a series of recommendations on how to avoid such problems in the future. These recommendations involved primarily examining each item in terms of costing principles, OMB leasing requirements, or RSPO standards. It was also suggested that all states should establish adequate accounting systems and budget revision procedures.

Commentary

The OIG report is without doubt one of the most scathing evaluations of the program. After each of these groups of critical comments the FRA was given the opportunity to respond. In each case it was noted that the FRA agreed with the criticisms; this is difficult to believe in all cases.

Examining the first series of recommendations it is clear that federal legislation would be necessary in order to make the eligibility criteria for funding tougher, or more limited, or to otherwise make the funds available only after certain requirements had been met. These are hardly criticisms of the FRA or the states since neither was in a position to change this factor. From the outset the various pieces of legislation produced made it clear that the Congress viewed the program as an entitlement program, i.e., each state was entitled to a certain amount of funds. As it was FRA had been criticized more than once for placing certain requirements on the states in order for them to receive funds.

The second set of criticisms are not well-founded either. The criticisms were directed at carry-overs in funds from year to year; the legislation had been worded ". . . such sums as are appropriated are authorized to remain available until expended." As a result carry-overs were to be expected and of no significance. Awarding grants in the last quarter of the fiscal year was another criticism that mattered little since the states could just as easily apply for the same funds in the first quarter of the following fiscal year. As for the criticism that certain projects were never completed, this is to be expected in view of significant variation in the amount of annual allocations for each state.

In the third area the ignorance of the OIG reached its peak. Regarding the leasing as opposed to purchasing locomotives this would be prudent for a program of indefinite length. The operating assistance program could have ended at any time and a lease arrangement would be proper in that situation. It is apparent that the OIG did not understand that the RSPO standards represented a floor as opposed to a ceiling on management fees and incentive fees. FRA had disagreed with RSPO on this matter several times, however they were not successful in getting RSPO to change the standards. It seems clear that the OIG criticism of the states or FRA on this matter lacked a foundation. The termination cost issue was also an empty criticism since such costs would have to withstand an audit to be allowable. Regarding the rail car leasing and unreasonable salary criticisms little can be offered in the way of justification for these. They would appear to have been unwise business decisions.

To those not familiar with the program, the OIG report would appear to be confirmation of the OMB position that the program should have been terminated. Upon closer examination the report offers criticism with some substance only in cases under congressional control. Critical comments of the FRA or the states do not appear to be well-founded or valid. The data presented were also questionable since in two cases the data were allegedly based on five year averages and the short lines to which the data referred had not been in existence for five years at the time of the report.[14] There is also some question as to whether the program audit should have been based exclusively on short lines; only one Conrail line was examined, but that railroad operated more than two thirds of the subsidized lines.

This does not mean that the program was without faults, but it does imply that such superficial examinations would not identify the bulk of these. In the following section there is a presentation of the salient problems that existed with the program. If the program is reinstituted at some future time perhaps these shortcomings will be corrected.

MORE PROBLEMS WITH THE PROGRAM

As it was established the rail freight assistance program of the 3R Act had numerous problems. The recognition of these problems in several cases may be due to the excellence of hindsight, but there are several other problems that were recognized as the program developed. In some cases these may have been noted in passing during the evaluation summaries earlier in this chapter and they deserve and are given more attention here. Others have not been noted before, but they certainly merit discussion.

Lowest Cost to the Taxpayers

It is always possible to have a dozen different interpretations as to the intent of Congress. However, one phrase in Title IV of the 3R Act states that "Under certain circumstances the cost to the taxpayers of rail service continuation subsidies would be less than the cost of abandonment of rail service . . ."[15] Implied in this statement is (1) the concern that the cost to the taxpayers should be kept as low as possible, and (2) subsidies should be offered only in those cases where the subsidies exceeded this value, then the societal cost would be less if the abandonment were allowed to occur.

This is almost a form of benefit cost analysis for the subsidy program, but such an analysis was never required for that program. It is also clear that there was no conscious attempt to keep the program cost at a minimum.

The Labor Question

For several years the Florida East Coast Railroad has been operating its trains with two crew members.[16] There was absolutely no reason for believing that any larger crew would have been necessary on the branch lines. The unwillingness of Conrail, or the Congress for that matter, to address the crew size problem was unfortunate. Early research indicated the possibility of up to 10% savings in cost per branch line per crew member, but this apparently was not sufficient to prompt action.[17] Given the unwillingness of the Congress to address the labor issue in the Delmarva case, it is understandable why they were reluctant to attack what must have been viewed as a minor point. The hesitance of the Congress is baffling in this case unless they believe that the railroads still employ 30 out of every thousand members of the labor force as they did in 1929. Today this figure is more like four out of every thousand so that rail labor is no longer the political force that it once was. It is true that each of those members is represented by a union and this may provide at least some basis for the congressional behavior.

Lines in the National Interest

It should be recognized that there are certain rail lines that are of national interest and the preservation of these should hardly fall on local areas or states. During the reorganization there were numerous cases of lines that had a military value. They might have been the only lines in an area capable of carrying "high and wide" loads such as tanks, missles, and so forth, or they might have been lines that provided rail access to military depots or testing facilities. Although some work has been done in this area it does not appear that the federal government is willing to accept sole responsibility for these lines even though their importance transcends local interests.[18]

This is also the case with low-density branch lines in coal mining regions of the nation. The traffic density may be the specific result of a federal policy regarding the environmental quality of this fuel. At the same time an energy crisis may precipitate a change in federal policy. Although it is of little interest here whether such policy changes could occur, it is of interest to ask whether the states or federal government should maintain (or bank) such lines in the interim.

It would be possible to go on and offer additional illustrations but this is not necessary. The point is that the national or federal importance of some branch lines far exceeds their local value, however, this is not well understood at the federal level. For example, the OMB as part of their justification for eliminating the program noted: "This action returns to States and localities a program whose benefits are primarily local."[19] It is clear that at least the OMB does not have a firm grasp of this problem.

Costing Concepts

There are many different costing approaches that could be utilized in the rail planning area. Avoidable costs appeared early in the reorganization effort and managed to get adopted by USRA and others. It was intended to represent the costs that could be "avoided" if a particular line were discontinued. To some extent the concept is accurate. However, let us assume that several thousand dollars were to be spent rehabilitating or maintaining a rail line and in reality the railroad had no intention of making this expenditure, but instead intended to practice deferred maintenance. The result is that using an avoidable cost argument the line might have been abandoned based on a savings that the railroad would receive even if the line were not abandoned.

It was argued in 1974 and 1975 that avoidable cost was "the way to go" for subsidies. For example, the salary of a railroad's president would not be avoided if a branch line were abandoned and therefore, that salary was not an avoidable cost. But what about the Conrail situation where that chief executive had to give some attention to the 3,000 miles of branch line being served under subsidy? Certainly that railroad could have utilized attention in other areas. However, costs of that type were not permitted and as a result Conrail could argue convincingly on numerous occasions that it was not being "made whole" under the subsidy program. In other words the avoidable cost approach had meaning perhaps in the single line case, but not in the case where one railroad provided nearly all the subsidized service.

Another approach to costing would have been fully-allocated average cost, as opposed to avoidable cost. This might have covered some problem situations in the subsidy program, but it would not have helped at all in the planning or rationalization area since in most cases the average costs would not have been recovered on abandonment.

There were others who advocated the use of marginal costs. This had considerable attraction in what was called the "off-branch cost" controversy. It was argued by some state officials that the marginal cost of handling a carload of goods after it left a branch line was practically zero for the railroad. There can be little doubt that this was correct and most federal rail planners agreed. However, they raised the point that the marginal cost would not be zero for 20 carloads and therefore if marginal cost was used a very sophisticated measure of this cost would be necessary. Perhaps such a measure of marginal costs could have been operationalized, but this never occurred. It would have improved the costing in the one area noted and this was overlooked by federal planners.

The major approaches to the question of costing were viewed as all-or-nothing propositions, when a combination of several different costing approaches should have been tried. This would have resolved some of the logical problems that developed using "avoidable costs." It is hoped that more attention will be devoted to this problem in the future.

Origins and Destinations

A fact that was extremely significant in all reorganization planning, but which was not discussed at all, was the inherent double-counting in the method of analysis selected by USRA. As an illustration of this take the case of two branch lines, *a* and *b*, having low traffic density and therefore under analysis for possible abandonment. Let us assume that all goods shipped from *a* go to *b* and all goods shipped from *b* go to *a*. We will relax this assumption momentarily. Under the methodology developed by USRA the revenue of all goods received and shipped on the line would establish "the revenue attributable to the line." Therefore, if this revenue value for line *a* is X dollars, the revenue value for line *b* is also X dollars. In other words the revenues of the originating line and terminating line are being counted and as a result the revenues are double-counted. The same applies for costs.

Now it is unlikely that two lines would interact exclusively with each other in this manner, but a certain amount of such interaction is likely for all lines. The methods developed by USRA and RSPO fail to treat this situation.

One other point that seemed not well understood regarding origins and destinations is worth a comment. There were numerous branch lines that received traffic from origins outside the reorganization region. These originating areas were for all practical purposes ignored. For example, shipments of lumber from a line in Oregon may have been destined for one of the light- density lines under analysis. Yet in no case (known to this writer) did the RSPO inform these shippers of the pending termination or seek their views on the matter.

Violations of the Interstate Commerce Act

As the states in the reorganization region began designating Conrail as operator on just about every line it became evident that legal questions were taking a back seat to expediency. The law in question, the Interstate Commerce Act, states in Section 5 (15)

> . . . it shall be unlawful for any carrier . . . to own, lease, operate, control, or have an interest . . . in any common carrier by water . . . with which such carrier aforesaid does or may compete for traffic.

Under the subsidy program Conrail was placed in such situations of having to operate water routes that were in competition with itself in Michigan, Virgnia, and Delaware. The FRA should not have agreed to fund these, and the ICC should not have accepted Conrail as the designated operator. As in many regulatory cases the question of legality becomes an issue only if someone objects to the specific situation or issue. No one objected and as a result no action was taken. At the same time the subsidizers noted criticized Conrail for not using the water routes as much as they could. It was not in Conrail's economic interest to use the routes involving the water movement.

Extended Subsidy Period

As originally conceived in the 3R Act the rail continuation program was intended to be a two year program to mitigate the impacts of abandon-ment or allow for a shift to an alternate mode of transport. This was more than a sufficient amount of time to accomplish either of these objectives. Extending the subsidy period beyond the two years made little sense. The fact that this occurred in the 4R Act prior to the beginning of the 3R Act program suggests there was no empirical basis for the change.

There is some indication that the states believed they could accomplish additional objectives (e.g., return the lines to viability) if they had more time. Experience has shown this belief was erroneous.

Rehabilitation of Lines Under Subsidy

Another catch-22 situation evolved over the question of whether subsidized light-density lines should be rehabilitated. Since most of the lines were less than FRA Class I (which would have allowed 10 mph operating speeds), it was unsafe to operate the lines unless they were repaired, but if the lines were to be abandoned after the subsidy period such rehabilitation would be a waste of money. In some ways this was the most difficult decision that FRA had to make since they were the administrators of both the rehabilitation funds and rail safety.

The decision was made to allow a sufficient amount of investment in the lines to allow them to be operated at a safe speed of 10 miles per hour or FRA Class I. For reasons most likely of a political origin, the decision was made to refer to this activity as "accelerated maintenance" instead of rehabilitation. Rehabilitation is the word commonly used to describe the activity, however use of public monies for "rehabilitation" of lines that were to be abandoned was more than most people could easily accept. As a result there was much accelerated maintenance, but no rehabilitation.

Congress soon got word of this and numerous officials of the FRA were asked to explain what was going on in the rehabilitation area during appropriation hearings. They did explain and the procedure continued. Today with many of these lines abandoned, it would appear that the taxpayers have had to pick up the tab for some very expensive rail service.

The Alternate Mode Question

At the outset of the subsidy program there was a great amount of research underway to evaluate the best course of action to take for providing continued transportation service to those shippers having a genuine need for it. At the time several planners and researchers believed that the rail subsidy program was not a panacea. They saw cases where motor carriers could offer service at a lower cost, with less energy utilization and less pollution.

The legislation had left the door open for using motor carriers, but it was closed by the Federal Railroad Administration. In their defense it should be noted that they were having a difficult enough time just getting the rail subsidy program started and to develop another type of subsidy program would have brought their activity to a halt. At the same time it is doubtful that the states would have been anxious to have two subsidy programs to start-up at the same time. Nevertheless, there can be little doubt that such a program would have had considerable merit and would have saved the taxpayers of the country a great deal.

Should the FRA have been expected to develop a motor carrier program? The agency is part of the U.S. Department of Transportation which implies the existence of some type of intermodal cooperation and coordination. However the implication may be more apparent than real. The FRA has a set of programs to administer as does the Federal Highway Administration and other DOT transportation agencies. There does not appear to be any high level of cooperation when it comes to the administration of programs or the development of rules and regulations. Certainly, the agencies cooperate if mandated to do so in legislation, but if the latter fails to require this then it does not occur.

The first year after enactment of the 3R Act went by, then the second, and then a third. Shortly after the beginning of the fourth year in 1978 the FRA announced that it would revise its rules and regulations, and it specifically called for comments on the alternate mode or substitute service question. FRA had funded a small highway project outside the Northeast in Minnesota, which was the first indication that the rail freight subsidy program could have an intermodal dimension. Now they were following that action with the possibility of still another subsidy program.

The advance rulemaking notice acknowledged that the 4R Act states that:

> The Secretary shall, in accordance with this section provide financial assistance to states for rail freight assistance programs that are designed to cover—. . . (4) The cost of reducing the costs of lost rail service in a manner less expensive than continuing rail service.[20]

This was seen by FRA as having two components: relocation of shippers and operating subsidies for use of non-rail freight transportation. In the relocation area comments were requested on the following questions:

1. Should relocation of shippers be considered substitute service assistance?
2. If relocation is included as substitute service assistance what should such assistance consist of?
3. What should be allowed as proper relocation costs? If necessary explain the methods of arriving at such costs?
4. What eligibility criteria should govern receipt of relocation assistance? To what extent should such assistance be limited by shipper location, duration of use, and traffic density?
5. To what extent are administrative problems foreseen as a result of such assistance?[21]

In the non-rail freight subsidy area they raised five additional questions.

1. Should such operating subsidies be considered substitute service assistance?

2. If such subsidies are to be provided, what geographic or modal requirements should be considered?
3. What should be considered proper allowable costs? If necessary explain the methods of arriving at such costs. Suggest methods for determining substitute service costs.
4. What eligibility criteria should govern receipt of such assistance? To what extent should such assistance be limited by shipper location, duration of use, and traffic density?
5. To what extent are any administrative problems foreseen as a result of such assistance?[22]

The agency allowed 30 days for the return of comments.

According to FRA docket records only two responses were received: one from Agrico, an agricultural products corporation, and one from the Minnesota Department of Transportation. These responses suggested approaches that could be taken in setting up a relocation and/or alternate mode assistance program. In their next publication on the question the FRA noted:

> The very few comments received did not reflect a clear consensus regarding the need for operating subsidies for non-rail freight transportation as a substitute service alternative. In light of the broadened eligibility and formula changes embodied in the 1978 Act, it is FRA's view that the scope of the substitute assistance should be limited to permanent transportation solutions, which foster long term viability, such as the construction of alternate facilities or relocation of shippers. Accordingly, nonrail operating subsidies are not eligible to be funded with substitute service assistance.[23]

Although the responses were minimal Agrico did suggest the use of a transfer facility and trucking. Minnesota's DOT went so far as to suggest the allowable costs for an alternate mode should be the difference between the rail cost and the least cost alternative transportation to existing major markets or terminals. So it appears that there was a consensus although the response was minimal.

It is easy to find fault with the FRA for their decision. Their rationalization above for doing nothing in face of the 1978 legislation fails to recognize that that piece of legislation extended the subsidy program until 1981; that was hardly a permanent solution.

But the FRA is not alone when one questions the failure to act. The states should also share a large part of the blame for their near apathetic response to the questions raised. Exactly why the states failed to come forth with a strong position on these questions may never be known. It is reasonable to conjecture that neither FRA nor the states wanted to have the responsibility of administering a non-rail program. In the state case more than three years had been spent in creating and staffing rail planning and administrative agencies; this was required by the Congress and the FRA. These agencies were, by and large, staffed by "new people." The original state people were on loan from other planning agencies, utility commissions, governor's offices, universities, and the like. They were not rail advocates although it may be said that they were transport advocates. The new people worked for the rail agency or division and they had a vested interest in a strong state rail program. It is now apparent that the states' rail agencies had about as much interest in cooperating with a motor carrier program as the FRA had in such a program.

A Pre-abandonment Program

A major change in the Local Rail Service Assistance Act of 1978 was the provision of grants for rail lines that needed an infusion of funds to continue operating. The law essentially applied to lines that carried less than 3 million gross tons of freight per mile per year although some exceptions to this standard were permitted (with approval of the Secretary) for lines handling up to 5 million gross tons. The basic premise here was that lines carrying more than these amounts should have been generating sufficient profits to cover the necessary upgrading. The legislation set aside two-thirds of all authorized funds for such deteriorated lines and established an 80-20 federal-local cost-sharing ratio for such improvements.

On the surface a program aimed at preventing the abandonment of branch lines through rehabilitation had considerable appeal. Such a program had been requested for at least two years.[24] Everyone believed that it made more sense to keep lines in the system, as opposed to maintaining lines that had been abandoned. At the same time it is difficult to rationalize the existence of such a program aimed at the utilization of public monies for assisting the operations of otherwise profitable railroads. Apparently, no one had given much thought to this logical question.

The pre-abandonment program began but there were few takers at the outset. It was the railroads that took the initiative in most cases. The states by and large did not even have access to the type of data that would enable them to identify whether a line had less than or more than the criterion number of gross tons per mile. If they had such data, they did not necessarily know the lines were in such poor condition. So the initial activity taking place in the rail sector is not surprising, but this had the capability of introducing additional problems as well. These multiple problems are aptly illustrated by the case of a branch line in the state of Indiana.

In September of 1977 the Illinois Central Gulf Railroad Company (ICG) petitioned the ICC for permission to abandon their line from Switz City to Indianapolis including a branch line near Bloomington. The lines in question had a total length of 97.26 miles. In August of 1978 the ICC ruled that the petition was denied stating that the line generated sufficient revenue to cover its operating and maintenance costs.

In the spring of 1979 the ICG approached the State of Indiana requesting funds for upgrading the line under provisions of the Local Rail Service Assistance Act of 1978. The program was new and there were no examples to look at to determine whether the line was or was not a reasonable candidate for the pre-abandonment program. The State's Public Service Commission was fairly sure that it did not want to use its funds for such a program. As a result, its willingness to move ahead was conditioned on the ICG supplying the local (20%) share. In other words the state would act as a broker in getting the railroad together with the FRA to make investments in the line.

One of the other provisions of the 1978 Act was the requirement that the pre-abandonment projects would have to be subjected to a benefit-cost analysis by the state. This is where the problem began. The State of Indiana contracted with Indiana University to develop a set of benefit cost procedures for project analysis and to apply that methodology to the ICG line.

Those familiar with benefit cost analysis understand that this methodology involves the comparison of alternatives. One alternative might be the abandonment of the line under analysis and therefore the comparison is with what will occur if the line is abandoned. It may also be that a very feasible alternative involves the comparison of the benefits and costs of the proposed project with the benefits and costs of performing the same work on another line that could perform essentially the same function. In an objective analysis the project yielding the highest ratio of benefits to costs (i.e., B/C) would be selected.

The university conducted such an analysis and concluded that there was an alternative project on a line of the Consolidated Rail Corporation that yielded a significantly higher benefit-cost ratio. Actually, the benefits of the proposed Conrail project were not that different but its cost was less than $200,000 and involved the construction of a switch in comparison to the $7 million upgrading of 95 miles of the ICG line. Practically, all traffic would have been retained under the Conrail alternative. The university forwarded its recommendations to the State.

The State in turn contacted Conrail and informed them of the results of their analysis and the potential project in Indiana. That railroad responded that they had no interest in the project which would have resulted in a substantial increase in traffic over their Evansville to Indianapolis line. It was later disclosed that Conrail was concerned that it would lose a substantial amount of interline traffic which it received from the ICG at Effingham, Illinois, if it went along with the alternative project and, therefore, it indicated no interest in the proposal.

Although this should have ended the entire discussion the State of

Indiana was receiving a substantial amount of pressure from the FRA to move ahead with the ICG project and that is what happened. They submitted the necessary paperwork and benefit-cost analysis. Also appended was the Conrail rejection of interest in the State's first alternative. FRA approved the project application and the taxpayers lost a few million dollars in comparison to the Conrail solution initially identified.

The problems with the pre-abandonment program are evident in this actual case study. Some of the problems are related to the benefit-cost analysis and these are discussed in more detail later. It is apparent that the projects selected for funding may not represent the best investment of public monies since some railroads are not even interested in the program. It is difficult to view corporate benefits as public benefits as the methods developed by the FRA require. If the program is a grant program for railroads in marginal financial condition then the FRA should say so and deal directly with the roads of interest. State involvement does not do anything to improve the program, and as it currently stands, such involvement is unnecessary.

Benefit-Cost Analysis

There is a certain amount of irony in the fact that the Local Rail Service Assistance Act of 1978 set in place the requirement for benefit-cost analyses of all state rail projects except subsidy projects. Why the subsidy projects were ignored was a mystery at the time since experience had indicated that this was the area of greatest need for a rigorous evaluation methodology. In addition, it was difficult to rank a series of capital and subsidy projects that did not utilize the same evaluation technique. This latter problem was recognized in the initial "Benefit-Cost Guidelines" prepared by the Transportation System Center for the Federal Railroad Administration in 1979.[25] The initial and revised guidelines incorporate discussions of benefit-cost analysis applied to subsidy projects, while noting that such analyses are not required, but useful for project selection. Such analyses are required for substitute service projects, acquisition projects and rehabilitation and new construction projects, whether these latter two occur on subsidized or non-subsidized lines.

As previously noted the State of Indiana began the development of its own benefit-cost analysis methodology in 1979 for use with subsidy and rehabilitation projects; these were the only programs in which the State expected to be involved. It is quite probable that new construction projects could be examined with the rehabilitation model should such projects be identified in the future. Substitute service, in its form at the time, did not appear to be a viable alternative and methods were not developed for that program. Acquisition of rail lines was contrary to existing state policy at the time so this area was also excluded.

The benefit-cost model developed for subsidy decisions is described in considerable detail elsewhere, but the general components of the model are worth noting.[26] Benefits in the subsidy case are essentially costs that will be incurred if the rail line under analysis is abandoned. These include a labor cost impact term, a motor carrier cost term, and an annualized new facilities cost term. The sum of these terms is diminished by the current on-branch rail operating cost and a discounted salvage value for the line. The numerator resulting from these operations is then divided by the estimated subsidy to yield the benefit-cost ratio.

The rehabilitation model is much simpler conceptually. In this case the benefits are the annual savings in railroad operating costs which result from implementing the project. Rehabilitation cost over the life of the project is converted to an annual capital cost to form the denominator of the model. This model was admittedly influenced by the specific project under analysis in the state of Indiana. That project involved up-grading a non-subsidized line, which was about 95 miles long, from FRA Class I (10 mph) to FRA Class II (25 mph). As a result the model is not as general as it could be and other components might be necessary to evaluate other rehabilitation projects.

The results of applying these two models in Indiana may be of interest. With regard to the subsidy model, nine lines were analyzed. Eight of the lines yielded benefit-cost ratios which were negative. The lines were subsidized; subsidies ranged from $232 to $1420 per carload.[27] The line for which the benefit-cost ratio was positive and in excess of unity (actually, the value was 40.2) received a subsidy of nine dollars per carload. As noted earlier the result of applying the rehabilitation model to the non-subsidized 95 mile line was a benefit-cost ratio in excess of unity, and that project has since been completed.

Similar methods are available in the "Benefit-Cost Guidelines" prepared for the Federal Railroad Administration.[28] These guidelines are far more ambitious an undertaking than the Indiana models. Beginning on a theoretical level the authors proceed to develop operational models which are consistent with the theory on which they are based. When the models derived are applied to reasonable hypothetical situations, each of the projects—acquisition, new construction, substitute service, and subsidy—is rejected. Only the hypothetical situation for the rehabilitation project yields a benefit-cost ratio in excess of unity and this ratio results from the assumption that a steel fabrication plant will locate on this line if it is upgraded. Even the FRA is entitled to certain illusions.

These models, as well as the Indiana models, appear to be robust. Undesirable projects are identified by the appropriate benefit-cost models as such. This does not mean that we have developed the most appropriate methods. Indeed, there are some very serious philosophical, conceptual, and measurement considerations which have been bypassed in getting to this state of the art. Let us examine some of these.

Returning to the non-subsidized line rehabilitation project in Indiana, it is notable that upgrading the line from Class I to Class II generated rail operating cost savings that were significant enough to yield a benefit-cost ratio in excess of unity. Others have noted that in this case the public benefits exceed the public project costs. This raises the question of exactly what are the public benefits? Generally, in the rehabilitation case they would be composed of reduced transportation costs, consumer (shipper) surplus and producer (carrier) surplus. However, in the Indiana case consumer and producer surpluses were ignored since they accrue primarily from the generation of new traffic which was not assumed to result from this project. In effect, the Indiana project was justified because its savings to the rail corporation exceeded its public cost. It is possible to view these savings in an abstract sense and state that any good or service produced with fewer resources yields a social or public benefit, but this would be true of any firm that was able to find a cheaper method of producing its product. Since total project cost is synonomous with public cost the same results would have been obtained by the railroad in its own corporate planning division. In other words, a project that is worth undertaking from a private or corporate perspective is being funded primarily with public funds.

Although the logical conclusion at this point is to fault the Indiana model for rehabilitation, this would be incorrect. The Indiana model yields a more conservative (lower) ratio than any other rehabilitation model proposed or in use; these latter methods would also support a decision to fund the project. In fact any project submitted which is worth funding from a corporate perspective will be worth funding from a public perspective with public funds.

This seems likely to be a situation that will reoccur whenever rehabilitation projects are examined on other non-subsidized lines. Whether new traffic in the form of consumer and producer surplus would be sufficient to merit such projects is doubtful simply because there would have to be very significant increases in traffic before this term was large enough to yield, by itself, a positive ratio. As a result some serious consideration should be given to deleting the benefit cost analysis requirement for rehabilitation and new construction projects on non-subsidized lines. It would make considerably more sense to have a capital grant program for railroads administered directly by the FRA without a state level benefit cost analysis being required.

There should also be more consideration given to the reasonableness of benefit-cost ratios which are based primarily on the assumption or forecast of increases in rail traffic. It is very unlikely that an industry needing reliable rail transportation and service would locate on a marginal line. Indeed, railroads would and should try to steer such traffic generators to their better lines. As for existing shippers and their estimates of future traffic, one can only say that these have not been very reliable in the past. All to often the expected traffic increases that should result from a given project do not materialize and the project may not be justifiable based on savings in transport cost, or other criteria dependent on the type of project.

Another aspect of benefit-cost analysis in the rehabilitation area that needs to be given a little more thought is the use of opportunity costs of crew labor as opposed to their actual wages. The opportunity cost in this case does not bear any similarity to actual crew wages, which are a function of labor negotiations, work rules, and arbitraries. Utilization of opportunity costs may lead us to the conclusion that reducing the time necessary to serve a branch line from 7 hours to 5 hours will result in savings in labor costs, when in reality these savings may not be real.

In most cases it would appear that in order for there to be savings in labor costs from upgrading lines, there must be a reduction in the actual number of crews or crew members utilized to serve the line. Although it is possible to envision a case where a crew, while not released, does have additional time because of a line improvement. This crew could in theory be utilized elsewhere, however, this would not appear to be the common case. A natural inference that can be drawn from the need to reduce crews is that the lines to be rehabilitated will have to be rather long (probably fifty miles in length or more) in order for this to occur.

In the area of substitute service and subsidy there is another significant problem that was not considered. As an illustration consider the case where a line is under analysis for the purpose of determining whether it should receive a subsidy or be abandoned. A benefit-cost analysis is performed and let us say that the ratio obtained is too small to justify subsidizing the line. This could occur in cases where the motor carrier operating costs for serving shippers along a rail line are similar to the railroad operating costs for the same service, which is not uncommon for light-density rail lines. The decision is made not to subsidize the rail service. What has not been considered is the fact that the motor carrier costs to the shipper may not only be greater than the cost of the previous rail service, but may also be more than the rail user is able to pay for transportation service. In this case it would be desirable to subsidize the shipper for motor carrier costs in excess of the previous rail costs to the nearest rail line where it is possible to receive service. Unfortunately, motor carrier costs were never recognized as an allowable substitute service, and therefore it was not possible to subsidize the shipper for these additional costs. As a result, the states, in attempting to mitigate the impacts of abandonment on shippers, subsidized the less efficient and more expensive rail operations.

Essentially the same situation occurs under substitute service projects that are eligible for financial assistance. One such project would be the resurfacing of a road so that it could bear the weight of heavier trucks necessary to serve rail shippers that are about to lose rail service. The fact that the motor carriers may actually cost the shippers more than the previous rail service does not seem to be considered.

Future use of these methods may disturb planners, researchers and economic analysts. They may be disturbed at the thought of estimating demand curves for firms that are not yet in existence, or forecasting shippers' responses to changes in rail costs. They may also dislike the use of shadow prices. However, these are attitudinal problems and there is no sound reason for objecting to some of these if it is possible to obtain reasonable estimates of their values *a priori* the analysis.

It should be noted that there does not appear to be anything of a significant methodological nature wrong with the existing federal "Guidelines for Benefit-Cost Analysis" and this section has not sought to critique them. The guidelines represent a skillful translation from textbook theory to practice. Individuals might argue whether a particular item should be measured in a certain way, and this type of dialogue seems to be desirable, but the basic structure of the methods derived appears to be quite reasonable given the theory.

Whether the theory that we have been using is appropriate for the analysis of all projects appears to be doubtful. As previously noted, there is something very annoying about the use of benefit-cost analysis for rehabilitation or new construction projects on non-subsidized lines as mandated by the Congress. If we examine the benefit-cost analysis literature we find the method has been used to: locate airports, evaluate transit proposals, identify highway projects, evaluate water resource projects, assess the safety benefits of highway improvements; the list goes on and on. all of these projects have one thing in common: they examine the *public* benefits and *public* costs of *public* projects that will remain under *public* control. It is not surprising to find that the methods are very popular in analyzing proposed rail projects in Great Britain, but there is a fundamental difference between that rail system and the U.S. rail system. Any benefits from projects on a nationalized rail system or on subsidized lines are indeed public benefits, and it is in this light that we must ask whether some of the U.S. projects are yielding public benefits or private benefits. From this perspective it is apparent that the only types of rail projects in this country that appear to be consistent with benefit-cost theory are those on subsidized lines. Major rehabilitation or new construction projects on non-subsidized lines of private rail corporations are not appropriate candidates for benefit-cost analyses by the public sector.

Allocating Fault

Each of the three major evaluations noted at the outset of this chapter examined different aspects of the Local Rail Service Assistance Program. The Congressional Research Service (CRS) study looked at the state activities in relation to the program and found little to fault in that area. Ernst and Whinney had a different mission: to evaluate the effectiveness of the program and to help set up a financial management and control system. Unfortunately, they sought to define effectiveness as the states defined it. As a result what they evaluated and analyzed was not the effectiveness of the program created by Congress, but rather the effectiveness of the program as implemented by the states and FRA. Had the transition from idea to program been accurate this distinction would have been unimportant, but the program did not necessarily reflect the will of Congress. Finally, the Office of Inspector General (OIG) of the U.S. DOT looked at the program. If the CRS study could see only roses, the OIG report saw only thorns. The FRA was the focus of severe criticism which it simply accepted in most cases. Charges levelled against the states almost implied criminal behavior, but the only thing criminal was the OIG's ignorance of the program and the law. This does not mean that the program was without problems; it had its share of these. But for some reason these studies did not identify them.

This chapter has examined some of these problems. Although there has been no explicit attempt to identify the agency responsible for each problem or problem area, such an identification will be presented here. The reader should be aware that to a certain extent all of the principals share responsibility for certain faults. Nevertheless, an attempt is made here to identify the major unit responsible for each problem. The units considered here are the Congress, the FRA, the USRA, and (collectively) the states.

Of the various problems noted in this chapter the Congress must share the major responsibility for (1) extension of the subsidy period to more than two years even before the program had begun; (2) creation of the pre-abandonment program; and (3) violations of the Interstate Commerce Act when sections of that law could have easily been amended.

USRA appears to have been primarily responsible for failure to view "national interest" lines as a federal responsibility. They also should have devoted more attention to different costing systems and the double-counting inherent in the costing system utilized although these were not major program flaws.

The failure to obtain agreements with labor that crew size on light-density lines that were to be subsidized should be treated as a special case must be shared by Congress, the FRA, and perhaps more than any other unit, Conrail. There was a fear that such action could lead to labor refusing to participate in the reorganization. Congress could have re-solved the issue legislatively, but it was too busy making concessions to labor in the retirement area. The FRA kept at arms length whenever such questions arose. Conrail saw only the Southern-Delmarva problem and the possibility of a major strike. So the crew issue was ignored and subsidies increased accordingly.

The problems of the program attributable solely to the FRA are not as numerous as one might imagine. The major problem was the failure of the FRA to make approval of light-density line subsidy projects contingent on the completion of a favorable benefit cost analysis. While it is true that the Congress did not require this in the 1978 amendments, there can be little doubt that FRA had substantial influence on that legislation. As a result the failure to keep down program costs is also, in part, due to the FRA. Related to this is the nature of benefit-cost analysis and whether it should have been operationalized as it was by FRA.

Other problems are attributable to the FRA and/or the states. The rehabilitation of most light-density lines was a waste of the taxpayers' money. To some extent the FRA tried to avoid this expenditure at the outset but later gave in to state requests. The failure to adequately consider alternate modes is due to the FRA's delay in addressing the problem. By the time the issue was raised the states had a vested interest in rail programs so that a potentially more efficient assistance program never materialized.

NOTES TO CHAPTER 12

1. William R. Black, "Local Rail Service Assistance: Objectives and Initial Trends," *Transportation Research*, Vol. 13A (1979), pp. 351–360.

2. *Ibid.*, p. 359.

3. John W. Fischer, *Local Rail Service: The State Experience*, Congressional Research Service, Report No. 80–22 E, February 1, 1980.

4. Ernst & Whinney, *Evaluation of the State Rail Assistance Program: Findings and Guidelines for Program Evaluation and Management*, prepared for the Office of State Assistance Programs, Federal Railroad Administration, U.S. Department of Transportation, January 1980.

5. Office of Inspector General, *Report on Audit of Rail Service Assistance Program Accomplishments, Problems and Future Direction*, Washington, D.C.: U.S. Department of Transportation, Report Number AM-FR-1-015, September 9, 1981.

6. *Op. cit.*

7. *Ibid.*, p. i.

8. *Op. cit.*

9. *Ibid.*, pp. iii–v.

10. *Op. cit.*

11. *Ibid.*, p. i.

12. *Ibid.*, p. 1.

13. *Ibid.*, p. 2

14. The OIG report notes that data for two short lines cover a five year period. These were the Spencerville and Elgin Railroad, formed in February 1979, and the Western Ohio Railroad, formed in March of 1977. The report was released in

September of 1981 and it may take six months or more to settle divisions. As a result it is unlikely that more than two or four years were available for the study.

15. Public Law 93–236, Sec. 401 (a)(4).

16. W. L. Thornton, *How to Deal with the Railroad Crisis: An Open Letter to Congress.* St. Augustine, Florida: Florida East Coast Railway Company, June 1975.

17. William R. Black and James F. Runke, *The States and Rail Preservation: Alternative Strategies*, Lexington, KY: The Council of State Governments, 1975, pp. 83–84.

18. See for example, H. Duke Niebur, "Railroads for National Defense," in James F. Runke and Norbert Y. Zucker (eds.), *Proceedings of the Regional Rail Planning Seminars Fall 1976*, Lexington, KY: The Council of State Governments, 1977, pp. 73–75.

19. Office of Management and Budget, *Additional Details on Budget Savings, Fiscal Year 1982, Budget Revisions*, Washington, DC: Executive Office of the President, Office of Management and Budget, April 1981, p. 276.

20. Public Law 94–210, Section 803.

21. Federal Railroad Administration, "Substitute Service Assistance," *Federal Register*, Vol. 43, January 6, 1978, p. 1108.

22. *Ibid.*

23. Federal Railroad Administration, "Assistance to States for Local Rail Service," *Federal Register*, Vol. 44, No. 170, August 30, 1979, pp. 51126–51127.

24. This need was noted repeatedly across the country during the Regional Rail Planning Seminars in the Fall of 1976 that were sponsored by the FRA.

25. Office of State Assistance Programs, Federal Railroad Administration. *Benefit-Cost Guideliens, Rail Branch Line Continuation Assistance Programs*, April 1979.

26. W. R. Black, S. D. Eisenach, and D. C. Knudsen. *Illinois Central Gulf Indianapolis District Rehabilitation Program and Cost Estimate - The State's Benefit-Cost Analysis.* Indianapolis: Public Service Commission of Indiana, July 1979; see also their: *Indiana's Local Rail Service Assistance Program—The State's Benefit-Cost Analysis.* Indianapolis: Public Service Commission of Indiana, August 1979; and, W. R. Black, S. D. Eisenach, D. C. Knudsen, and J. C. Robbins. *A Manual for State Benefit-Cost Analysis of Railroad Projects.* Indianapolis: Public Service Commission of Indiana, September 1979.

27. *Indiana's Local Rail Service Assistance Program . . . op. cit.*

28. *Op. cit.*

Chapter 13

THE PROGRAM: A FINANCIAL
ASSESSMENT AND SOME ANSWERS

Although enacted with the 3R Act in January of 1974, the rail freight subsidy program did not become operational until April of 1976. During the five and one-half years of its existence there was a substantial amount of federal and state money expended on the program. In this chapter the amount of this investment, as reflected in annual appropriations at the federal level and approximate matching shares at the state or local level, will be examined.

There were numerous questions of a planning or policy nature that existed in 1974 regarding a rail branch line assistance program. At the time no one knew the answer to these questions and it seems worthwhile to determine to what extent these questions can now be answered based on the experience of the program. Among the questions that were of interest are the following.

1. Will the provision of financial assistance to keep a line in operation be sufficient to allow that line to return to viability?

2. Is identifying a branch line as a potential candidate for abandonment sufficient to "kill" its chances of becoming viable?

3. Given that a branch line is to be served by a designated operator, will the lowest cost operator be a short line railroad or a Class I carrier?

4. Does the abandonment of a branch line result in the cessation or decrease of economic growth for the area served by the line?

5. Is a branch line assistance program necessary in order to avoid substantial increases in unemployment after abandonment?

6. Are railroads the most energy efficient mode for serving areas of light traffic density? Are they the most efficient on environmental grounds?

7. Does abandonment of a rail line result in significant negative highway impacts as that traffic is moved by motor carriers?

8. Does rehabilitation of a line result in its becoming viable?

To a greater or lesser extent each of these questions will be answered in this chapter. However, let us begin with a summary of the financial aspects of the program.

Funding of the Subsidy Program

The 3R Act authorized $180 million for the rail freight assistance program in the Northeast and Midwest. This was followed in 1976 by the 4R Act and its authorization of $360 million for a national rail freight assistance program. Of this total authorization of $540 million, appropriations through fiscal year 1983 used nearly $475 million as reflected in Table 13.1. The table reveals several interesting points regarding funding of the program. First, the initial funding for the program was very ambitious and these funds continued to grow until fiscal year 1982. Second, funding dropped off substantially as the Reagan administration attempted to phase out the program. The bulk of these latter funds were for multi-year commitments due to prior years' obligations. Third, although the 803 program for states outside the Midwest and Northeast developed slowly, the total funds allocated to its states exceeded the allocations of the 402 program. Fourth, the program has had some problems with carryovers that have prompted some FRA officials to demand that the states apply for program funds.

In addition to these federal funds one must also consider the state or local share since these were matching funds after the first year of assistance. Assuming that this share averaged about 20% this would represent a program of $675 million with $135 million coming from non-federal sources. However, this is only the proverbial tip of the iceberg since programs in New York and Michigan, for example, had state funds far in excess of their federal allocations.

There were also cases where other federal programs supplied monies for acquisition of lines. The Economic Development Administration and the Department of Housing and Urban Development assisted local areas with such funds. In addition, several of the regional commissions of the Economic Development Administration spent millions of dollars for planning research and rehabilitation projects.

Given these various sources of funds it is quite likely that an accurate account of funds spent on the program will never be known. It appears very probable that the program managed to consume well over one billion dollars over the few years of its existence.

From Subsidy to Viability

A major assumption of the original (3R Act) subsidy program was that given a subsidy it would be possible to build traffic on a branch line to profitable levels. The background of this logic was that there was a significant amount of traffic that had left the railroad because of poor service and if good service was provided this would draw the rail patrons

TABLE 13.1

LOCAL RAIL SERVICE ASSISTANCE FUNDING

Fiscal Year	Appropriation	Carryover	Total Available	Allocation (and Carryover) 402 States	Allocation (and Carryover) 803 States
1976	$53,750,000	-0-	$53,750,000	$48,750,000	$ 5,000,000
1977	$70,000,000	$ 8,851,205	$78,851,205	$63,250,000	$ 6,750,000
1978	$67,000,000	$ 8,675,840	$75,675,840	($3,851,205)[a]	($ 5,000,000)
				$52,000,000	$15,000,000
				($ 5,725,288)	($ 2,950,552)
1979	$69,000,000	$18,681,998	$87,681,998	$55,818,756	$31,863,242
1980	$80,000,000	$10,508,478	$90,508,478	$36,462,750	$54,045,728
1981	$80,000,000	$ 7,436,684	$87,436,684	$31,185,744	$56,250,940
1982	$35,000,000	N.A.	$35,000,000	$11,085,685	$23,914,315
1983	$20,000,000	N.A.	$20,000,000	$ 5,657,981	$14,342,019

Source: Appropriations Hearings of the U.S. Department of Transportation and the Office of State Assistance, Federal Railroad Administration.

[a] Carryovers were identifiable for 1977 and 1978 by program. After this they became a single program and the distinction here between the 402 and 803 programs is only for illustration of the division of funds between states.

back to the branch line. To be sure this was not the only logic behind the subsidy program; there was a desire to mitigate the impacts of abandonment by allowing rail users and others time to adjust to the loss of rail service. But for many policy makers and planners there was this wishful thinking that it was possible to turn the entire picture around through operating assistance. Unfortunately, it just didn't happen.

Of all the lines available for subsidy that were indeed subsidized only a handful became viable. These may just as easily be regarded as errors on the part of USRA's planners. Even assuming some of the latter, the accuracy of USRA's light-density line analysis is very impressive.

If we consider the operating subsidy program solely as a program to make unprofitable branch lines profitable, then we must conclude that it was a dismal failure on the whole. The program did find a few lines that were to be abandoned erroneously, however, it is debatable whether the cost of this finding was merited.

The "Kiss of Death" Syndrome

State planners expressed concern very early in the reorganization effort that identifying a line as "under study," or "potentially excess," or any similar euphemism circulating at the time, was sufficient to give it what one planner referred to as the "kiss of death." He argued that shippers would begin to look at alternative modes for moving their freight and even if the line was not in that poor of condition in terms of traffic before such a designation, the designation would be sufficient to destroy the line's viability.

It is difficult to say if this syndrome is more apparent than real even today. There is no clear evidence that identifying a line as under study ruins the future viability of the line. USRA identified the lines that it had under study and analysis in the summer of 1974 more than a year before the appearance of the *Final System Plan*. To be sure many of the lines were not conveyed to Conrail, but many of the lines were conveyed to the new railroad. Therefore, this approach to the question does not give a definitive answer.

Examining a sample of lines abandoned by Conrail under provisions of the Northeast Rail Services Act is also ambiguous. Several lines abandoned under that act were noted as under study in USRA's *Preliminary System Plan*. In 1975 and 1976 the lines had been conveyed to Conrail for operational or profitability reasons. After five years the lines were either no longer necessary or unprofitable and abandonment was sought. It is doubtful that the designation of the lines as "under subsidy" was the catalyst for their eventual abandonment. There were a large number of other lines also "under study" at the time that were conveyed to Conrail and remain as part of that rail system today.

Even if all of the lines studied by USRA had since been dropped or

abandoned by USRA or Conrail this would not necessarily prove the case
in question. It must be remembered that the bases for identification of
lines for study by USRA in 1974 were:
1. Those lines of bankrupt carriers identified by the DOT report
   as potentially excess,
2. Those identified by bankrupt carriers for possible abandonment,
3. Those identified by USRA and its consultants as requiring
   study.[1]
Of these sources the bulk of the lines came from the first group and it will
be recalled from chapter 4 that the major criterion used in the DOT
report was a simple (carload) traffic cut-off. Given the economic environment from 1976 to 1981 it is surprising that any line that was weak in 1976
is still part of Conrail.

In effect, it is not possible to say that this "kiss of death" syndrome is
real. It does seem clear that identifying a line that is profitable, and
recognized as such, as under study will do little to harm it. Alternatively,
the same designation for a marginal line may have positive or negative
effects depending on the reaction of the line's rail users. Finally, identifying very light density lines as under study will probably do such lines
considerable harm, but then so will a host of other factors.

The Lowest Subsidy Cost: Short Lines or Class I Carriers?

As the operating assistance program began there was a flurry of activity
as state officials and planners sought operators for their branch lines.
There was a sincere belief that operations by Conrail would mean only
more of the same poor service the lines had seen under the Penn Central
and other bankrupt roads. The belief was not completely unreasonable
since it was very likely that the employees at the branch line level would
be the same ones that had worked for the bankrupts. The states in several
cases wanted operators that they thought would be more responsive to
local situations and try to stimulate new traffic from the local area. In
addition, Conrail was allowed certain costs by the RSPO standards that
were not allowable for short line railroads, e.g., off-branch costs, and the
states in many cases wanted to avoid these charges.

The fact that certain costs were not allowed or even relevant in the
short line case, plus their perceived lower labor cost, gave many the
impression that short line railroads were the best operators for the lines.
However, there were an equal number of negative factors. The short lines
that were created to serve branch lines under subsidy could literally view
every cost as an avoidable cost including several administrative costs not
allowed of larger Class I roads. In addition, most short lines had as their
revenue approximately ten to twenty percent of the total revenue that

originated or terminated on the line. This value resulted from agreements with connecting carriers regarding the division of revenues.[2] While perhaps an impressive amount from many points of view for moving traffic generally only a few miles, the Conrail lines were able to attribute all revenues from traffic originating or terminating on the branch line to that line. In other words the Conrail operated lines may have had to cover their off-branch costs, but they had from five to ten times more costs that could be covered before a subsidy would have to be paid.

Although there were several positive points for Class I operators, there were also numerous points for operations by short lines. As a result there was no clear answer to the question of which of the two would represent the lowest subsidy operator. Let us examine this question in more detail.

The problem is not as easy to examine as one would assume. One major difficulty is the lack of data for examining the question. Using several different sources it was possible to compile similar information for a set of 15 short line railroads (Table 13.2) and 29 branch lines operated by Conrail (Table 13.3). Each of these 44 lines received funds from the local rail service assistance program.

Examining the tables it can be seen that most of the data presented are very skewed statistically. The basic problem with the short lines are some extreme subsidy values that inflate the average subsidy. Nevertheless, the average annual subsidy per mile for short lines is $12,442, which is higher than Conrail's value of $10,233. Examining a non-parametric median annual subsidy per mile yields a value of $9,351 for short lines and $8,506 for Conrail.

If we use the means to set up a value for classifying lines as short line operated or Conrail operated on the basis of subsidy cost (as is done in two-group discriminant analysis), we find that the optimal score is a subsidy of $11,337. Using this value we would correctly classify only 6 of 15 short lines and 20 of the 29 branch lines for a total of 26 out of 44; this results in less than 60% accuracy.

There are problems with trying to make too much of this analysis. Other things being equal, the short line costs should be greater than the Conrail costs since they were allowed to include more avoidable costs. This is true even considering the off-branch costs previously noted. This was found to be the case in both the analysis of the mean and median average subsidy per mile per year. But both of these data sets may be biased. First, some of the short line data are from a report of the Office of the Inspector General (OIG) of the U.S. Department of Transportation, and the OIG viewed the charges as excessive.[3] Second, most of the Conrail branch line costs are from state rail plans and, while accurate, one must recognize the fact that some states put far more money into this program than others, i.e., the states determined the frequency of service, amount of maintenance, and so on. The notable case of this was New York which spent significantly more per mile of branch line than other states

TABLE 13.2

SUBSIDIZED LINES OPERATED BY SHORT LINE RAILROADS

USRA No.	State	Railroad	Length (miles)	Years of Data	Subsidy[a] Average
401	Indiana	Hillsdale County Railroad	19.1	3	$ 6,079
571	Indiana	Indiana and Ohio Railroad	26.2	3	$ 6,538
589/590	Indiana	Madison Railway	25.8	3	$15,899
577a	Illinois	Kankakee, Beaverville, and Southern Railroad	27.0	3	$19,485[b]
609	Illinois	Wabash Valley Railroad	75.0	3	$22,321[b]
454/454a/461/470	Michigan	Michigan Northern Railway	244.8	3	$ 9,351
398/402/692a/693a	Michigan	Hillsdale County Railroad (part)	39.2	3	$12,006
440/440b	Michigan	Detroit and Mackinac Railway	105.6	3	$10,341
89a	New York	Ogdensburg Bridge and Port Authority	20.8	1	$ 2,979
1239	New York	Bath and Hammondsport Railroad	22.1	1	$ 5,171
533/534/534a/535 1261 ----	Ohio	Spencerville and Eastern Railroad	37.0	5	$ 5,302[b]
	Ohio	Western Ohio Railway	5.3	5	$34,075[b]
184	Pennsylvania	Lykens Valley Railroad	9.9	2	$27,225[b]
----	Pennsylvania	Maryland and Pennsylvania Railroad (part)	5.9	3	$ 5,220[b]
907/939	Pennsylvania	Octoraro Railway	22.0	3	$ 4,639[b]

[a] Based on state rail plans unless otherwise noted. This is the average annual subsidy per mile of track.

[b] Average subsidy based on: Office of Inspector General, Report on Audit of Rail Service Assistance Program Accomplishments, Problems and Future Direction, Washington, D.C.: U.S. Department of Transportation, Report AM-FR-1-015, September 9, 1981.

did due to transportation bond funds, the value of which exceeded the federal program funds. Since both of these data problems would increase the averages, it is possible that they have little impact on the analysis.

Subject to the considerations noted above, we may conclude that the short line railroads under the program tended to have higher average subsidies than the Conrail operated branch lines. However, this difference is not very great.

The Question of Economic Growth

For many years there has been a "clear" link between railroads and economic growth; the former was necessary to obtain the latter. Exactly where these ideas originated is not clear but they possibly go back to the late 1800's when public officials sought to rationalize grants from the federal government to the railroads being constructed at the time.

In point of fact there is a clear link between economic development and transport availability. That is, given an area whose development is being held back by the lack of transport or poor transport, then the provision of transport may stimulate development. In the absence of some developable resource or industry the provision of transport will not result in growth.

By and large if a branch line is about to be abandoned this implies that the area it serves does not have developable resources or activities remaining. In any event there is not sufficient local traffic to support the line and withdrawal of the line is just one more step in a sequence of events leading to a depressed local economy. In effect, removal of the branch line is not the cause of the loss of economic growth, it is a consequence. In the regional reorganization area of the Midwest and Northeast most of the lines under analysis had been in place for more than one hundred years and to argue that their removal (due to little or no traffic) would hurt the local economy was nonsense.

A related but slightly different question revolved around the case of future development. There was always a potential shipper that was considering the branch line as a probable site for this or that activity which would stimulate future rail traffic. While there may have been some substance to these claims in a few cases, this would hardly justify retention of a branch line. It would make far more sense to locate on a viable branch line and, in the process, make that line stronger economically.

In addition to the above points, there is no body of research that would substantiate the belief that abandonment of a rail branch line has a significant economic impact on the regional economy in which it is located. If we examine the specific question of "what are the impacts of abandonment?" there are essentially two classes of literature. The first seeks to answer the question in an *a priori* sense: "what will be the

TABLE 13.3

SUBSIDIZED LINES OPERATED BY THE CONSOLIDATED RAIL CORPORATION

USRA No.	State	Line Limits	Length (miles)	Years of Data	Subsidy[a] Average
47	Connecticut	Wethersfield - Rocky Hill	3.2	5	$13,867
50	Connecticut	Hartford - Griffins	6.7	5	$13,985
55/54	Connecticut	Avon - Simsbury	6.5	5	$ 8,804
523	Indiana	Anderson - Frankton	5.8	3	$27,207
554	Indiana	Hunter - Maxwell	14.3	3	$10,591
464/465	Michigan	Richland - Doster Tee	15.4	2	$ 4,527
456/457/458	Michigan	Sturgis - Nottawa	8.1	3	$ 4,647
451/452/453	Michigan	Vermontville - Grand Rapids	42.0	3	$ 7,041
456/457/458	Michigan	Wasepi - Mendon	4.6	3	$ 8,048
1104	New Jersey	Matawan - Morganville	3.2	1	$ 828
1107	New Jersey	Bartley - Ferremont	6.7	1	$ 5,564
1206	New Jersey	Bloomfield - West Orange	2.7	1	$ 5,160
1800	New Jersey	McKee City - Pleasantville	3.8	1	$ 2,886

66c	New York	Wassaic - Millertown	13.2	1	$20,756
81	New York	South Amsterdam - South Fort Plain	29.5	1	$17,414
87	New York	Malone Industrial Track	10.3	1	$ 7,063
98	New York	Canandaigua - Victor	8.5	1	$ 8,784
102/103	New York	Charlotte - Oswego	66.4	1	$ 3,727
108	New York	Newark - Sodus Point	14.6	1	$ 7,472
109	New York	Marion Industrial Park	8.9	1	$11,439
233	New York	Bellona - Seneca Castle	10.8	1	$10,736
249	New York	Mayville - Corry	22.6	1	$10,116
1002a	New York	At Cortland	4.0	1	$23,404
1022	New York	Geneva - Victor	26.5	1	$ 8,506
1023	New York	Niagara Junction - Batavia	27.0	1	$ 4,168
1240	New York	Batavia - LeRoy	11.0	1	$ 2,941
1242	New York	Depew - Lancaster	3.0	1	$17,986
1246	New York	Buffalo Creek Junction - Gowanda	30.4	1	$22,379
1250	New York	Salamanca - Cattaraugus	14.2	1	$ 6,779

a This is an average annual subsidy per mile of track as derived from the state rail plans.

impacts of abandoning a given branch line?" In this area the works of CONSAD,[4] Fergurson,[5] Humphrey,[6] Jack Faucett Associates,[7] RSPO,[8] and the FRA[9] are notable. This question and the approaches developed are of interest to the planner or forecaster concerned with future events and impacts. It would be desirable to have these methods based on empirical case studies of actual impact situations, but this does not appear to be the case. As such, this literature is not particularly of interest in the present context since we are more concerned with what actually occurred.

The second body of literature seeks to answer the question: "what were the impacts of abandoning the rail line?" In this case the approach is *ex post facto* and the answers may be found by analyzing data on what impacts have occurred since abandonment. There is far less literature in this area. The near classical work in this area is the *Retrospective Rail Line Abandonment Study* of Simat, Hellison, and Eichner that was prepared in 1973.[10] That study found that a number of abandonments had significant impacts on individual protestants and communities and that these impacts could have been expected based on pre-abandonment hearings testimony. A follow-up study had similar findings.[11]

Another study which appeared nearly a decade earlier was the *Rutland Railroad Study*.[12] That study sought to examine the economic impact of discontinuing the Rutland Railroad in 1962. The study documented significant negative railroad employment impacts (although no shipper employment impacts), an increase in transport costs, and a minimal positive impact on trucking. It is doubtful that one should attempt to generalize the findings of the Rutland study to light-density lines in view of the fact that the Rutland Railroad was 331 miles in length. But the fact that the impacts of abandoning this entire system were practically negligible should not be overlooked.

In addition to these two studies the work of Bunker,[13] and Bunker and Hill,[14] as well as case studies of Due[15] are notable. There do not appear to have been any large scale retrospective studies completed of lines which were not conveyed to Conrail by USRA or of lines initially subsidized and later terminated by the subsidizers. A couple of small scale studies have appeared in state rail plans. In a New York study it was noted that

> A total of 23 shippers on seven (7) lines were surveyed; two of which originally stated in 1975 that they would go out of business, and two others which stated that they would relocate out-of-state. Results showed that one (1) shipper ceased operations and one other located out-of-state, but for reasons other than the loss of direct rail service; eight (8) others switched to trucking; nine (9) utilized team track facilities and three (3) relocated on a viable line within the state. The only impact reported was that of slightly higher transportation costs.[16]

An Indiana study examined eight lines abandoned under the provisions of NERSA. It stated

. . . it is quite clear that most of the lines examined had insignificant quantities of freight. As a result the impacts of abandonment were, for the most part, quite negligible. In a few cases, the abandonment has proven to be beneficial to former users. The abandonment created a situation which forced the user to examine alternative shipping and marketing strategies with the result that those firms are now shipping their commodities at a lower cost than before.[17]

Synthesizing, it can be stated that most of the studies that have forecasted regional gloom and doom as a result of branch line abandonments have little basis in fact. It is evident that harm would result only from excessive dependence on rail transport and such dependence would usually generate sufficient traffic to maintain the viability of the line.

The Impact on Employment

Related to the general question of economic growth was the question of whether the loss of rail service would significantly increase unemployment. Although a localized problem in the early 1970's when Michigan's auto industry was beginning to feel the impact of foreign competition, the problem grew during the decade. From the outset of the reorganization planning Michigan feared that the loss of rail service would lead to the loss of jobs. There was no firm empirical basis for this belief, it just seemed logical to state officials. However, the loss of rail service results primarily in the loss of rail employment as the Rutland study had shown and the 3R Act certainly provided for that eventuality.

As for other losses in employment these were certainly possible, but not in the number that would have created concern. If the shippers or receivers were small or had little use for the rail service, they obviously would generate little rail traffic in relation to their total operation. If they generated little rail traffic they would hardly be crippled by suddenly having to use an alternate mode of transportation. Therefore, large amounts of unemployment resulting from abandonment would be very unlikely.

If a firm's cost structure was such that it could not withstand an increase in transport costs, then in all probability it had far more problems with its location, scale of production, and level of technology, i.e., the loss of rail service would be a minor problem. Yet it is possible that the loss of rail service might become the proverbial straw in some cases, but such a loss, or any other single factor, can not be considered the cause in such a case.

Energy and the Environment

In many ways the rail industry is guilty of doing too good a job of promoting itself. Industry spokesmen have told us for the last two decades that railroads pollute the environment less than other modes and, more recently, that they utilize less energy. Data were presented and we were all convinced of these efficiencies. Whether shippers really cared enough about this to change their distribution patterns is debatable. It is difficult to envision the board of directors of any major corporation deciding to ship by rail because it results in less atmospheric pollution. Indeed, the image of such a discussion during a corporate board meeting is the stuff of comedy. So it is doubtful that the industry gained any new traffic from such promotions.

Those who apparently did listen to the energy and environmental efficiency arguments were the community leaders, mayors, planners, policy makers, and others who testified at the national hearings on the *Secretary's Report* and the USRA plans. There was even the occasional shipper that offered such arguments in his testimony.

The industry found itself in the rather unique position of saying, "Yes, we are more energy efficient and we do pollute less than motor carriers," and then came the hard part, "but not all the time." Was nothing sacred? Of course the industry had been talking about long hauls of 300 to 3,000 miles when they made their efficiency statements. There was nothing efficient about a locomotive serving a ten mile branch line three times a week for a carload or two of traffic per week. Add to this the operating speeds, which were generally less than ten miles per hour, and any discussion of efficiency seems woefully out of place.

Although some planners recognized the limitations of the railroads' statements, others did not. There have been several comparative studies of energy efficiency for different transport modes, but it does not appear that this question has been analyzed in detail.[18] Given that most short (under twenty miles) branch lines do not permit locomotives to reach optimal operating speeds, it is ludicrous to argue for rail service retention on these grounds unless there are anomalous circumstances.

Although this discussion has focused on energy efficiency the same general conclusions pertain to environmental efficiency since the bulk of the environmental damage is due to air pollution which results from the consumption of fuels for energy.

Negative Highway Impacts

At the beginning of the reorganization planning effort it was feared that the diversion of the projected rail traffic from abandoned lines to the U.S. highway system would result in the distruction of the latter. At no point was a significant amount of rail traffic being discussed. The highway system would be able to handle the additional volume in nearly all cases without significant highway impacts of a negative nature.

Once again there is surprisingly little research on this question. One notable study that did appear in the last few years was based on research undertaken by Purnell.[19] Purnell did a detailed engineering analysis of two branch lines in Indiana that had relatively high traffic levels, but no direct access to an Interstate highway. In the case of the first line, he concluded that a state highway parallel to the branch line was sufficient to accommodate the additional truck traffic that would be generated by rail abandonment without major expenditures. In the second case, a highway resurfacing investment of about $150,00 would be necessary. This latter figure is very small in comparison to the operating subsidy the line has been receiving annually.

In general it would appear that branch line abandonments do not generate sufficient motor carrier traffic to damage existing highways. Although there may be exceptions to this statement, it would appear that this is the expected situation and cases of significant negative impacts on highways should be regarded as the exceptions.

Rehabilitation to Viability

Very early in the planning process it was believed that a major cause for the unprofitable status of many rail lines was the failure of the railroads to maintain the track. To some, the lines were subsidy candidates because of corporate decisions to defer maintenance. There was some logic to this position and it went basically like this: the line is in poor condition necessitating reduced operating speeds for trains serving the lines. Due to the reduced operating speeds it is necessary to have greater crew costs for serving the line. Ergo, rehabilitate the lines, increase the speeds, reduce labor costs and make the line viable.

The problem with this logic is that rehabilitation of the line does not have a significant impact on total operating costs. It has no impact on off-branch costs. It does not have an appreciable effect on fuel costs or car costs. It may only affect on-branch labor costs when the lines are of considerable length, have had significant crew costs, and experienced significant increases in operating speeds. These circumstances usually do not occur in the light-density line case. As a result we can conclude that rehabilitation would not have a significant impact on line viability. But the logic was not so clear in 1975 and 1976.

Based on the experience of the local rail service assistance program we can conclude that the logic is correct. Since only a handful of lines are what could be construed as viable and nearly all lines received some type of rehabilitation (or accelerated maintenance), we can state that empirically there is little basis for the rehabilitation to viability position.

Approaching the problem in a different manner, Friedlaender and Spady have stated:

> A . . . policy that is likely to be unsuccessful is the rehabilitation of low density branchline track. As we have seen, the total effect of capital misallocations is small, and low density branchline service is at least as labor

intensive as other service; thus the savings on branchline track rehabilitation are likely to be small.[20]

As for the few lines that were rehabilitated and are now viable, it is reasonable to conclude that these lines were very close to viability and similar results could have been obtained by other cost saving measures.

A Concluding Note

There is a tendency for evaluations of this type to suggest that the federal program has been a waste of the taxpayer's money. Afterall, the program did manage to use nearly a billion dollars of the taxpayers' funds. It saved a few lines but it is probable that the lines saved may have been analytical errors by USRA planners. So was the program a waste?

The program did enable us to answer or at least clarify a number of different research questions that have been reviewed in this chapter. In some cases we are still unable to definitely answer certain questions and the FRA and ICC should seek to undertake research in these areas while the data are still available. In other cases the answers obtained seem readily apparent today, but this was not the case in 1974. Whether this is sufficient success for the program is debatable, but we must not lose sight of the fact that the primary goal of the program was to mitigate the impacts of rail abandonment and the program must be viewed as a success in this light. Exactly how the program could have been restructured to accomplish the same end more efficiently is the question addressed in the following chapter.

NOTES TO CHAPTER 13

1. USRA, *Preliminary System Plan*, op. cit. Vol. II, p. 336.

2. J.E. Musslewhite, "Divisions for Short Line Railroads," Consolidated Rail Corporation, internal memorandum, July 1976.

3. Office of Inspector General, *Report on Audit of Rail Service Assistance Program Accomplishments, Problems, and Future Direction*, Washington, DC: U.S. Department of Transportation, Report AM-FR-1-015, September 9, 1981.

4. CONSAD Research Corporation, *Analysis of Community Impacts Resulting from the Loss of Rail Service*, Four Volumes, for the United States Railway Association, Pittsburgh, October 18, 1974.

5. Allen R. Ferguson, Norman H. Jones, Jr., Barry I. Slavsky, Lawrence H. Reece II, Stanley Rothenberg and Frances Topping, *Community Impacts of Abandonment of Railroad Service*, Public Interest Economics Center, Washington, DC, November 20, 1974.

6. Thomas J. Humphrey, *Framework for Predicting External Impacts of Railroad Abandonments*, Massachusetts Institute of Technology, Department of Civil Engineering, Transportation Systems Division, Cambridge, 1975.

7. Jack Faucett Associates, Inc., *Potential Economic Impact of Termination of Rail Service to Twelve Selected Communities*, Chevy Chase, Md., for U.S. Department of Transportation, Office of the Secretary, December 1973.

8. Rail Services Planning Office, *Guide for Evaluating the Community Impact of Rail Service Discontinuance*, Interstate Commerce Commission, Washington, DC, January 10, 1975.

9. Federal Railroad Administration, *Rail Planning Manual*, Two Volumes, U.S. Department of Transportation, Washington, DC, July 1978.

10. Simat, Helliesen and Eichner, Inc., *Retrospective Rail Lines Abandonment Study* (Revised), Boston, submitted to the U.S. Department of Transportation, Office of the Secretary, 1973.

11. Simat, Helliesen and Eichner, Inc., *Additional Retrospective Rail Line Abandonment Studies*, Boston, submitted to the U.S. Department of Transportation, Office of the Secretary and the Federal Railroad Administration, March 1975.

12. Boston University Bureau of Business, "The Economic Impact of Discontinuance of the Rutland Railway," in *Studies on the Economic Impact of Railway Abandonment and Service Discontinuance*, United States Department of Commerce, Transportation Research, Washington, June 1965.

13. Arvin R. Bunker, *Impact of Rail Line Abandonment on Agricultural Production and Associated Grain Marketing and Fertilizer Supply Firms*, Department of Agricultural Economics, Ph.D. Thesis, University of Illinois at Urban-Champaign, 1975.

14. A.R. Bunker and L.D. Hill, "Impact of Rail Abandonment on Agricultural Production and Associated Grain Marketing and Fertilizer Supply Firms," *Illinois Agricultural Economics*, Vol. 15, No. 1, 1975, pp. 12-20.

15. See for example, John F. Due, *A Case Study of the Effects of the Abandonment of a Railway Line—Sherman and Wasco Counties, Oregon*, Transportation Research Paper #5, and his, *Long Term Impact of Abandonment of Railway Lines*, Transportation Research Paper #7, College of Commerce and Business Administration, University of Illinois at Urbana-Champaign, September 1974 and June 1975.

16. *New York State Rail Plan Annual Update*, Rail Division, New York State Department of Transportation, Albany, August 1978, p. I-5.

17. The Division of Regional Transport Research, *Indiana Rail Plan 1983 Update*, Department of Geography, Indiana University, August 1982, p. 54.

18. Some examples are: Nigel Seymer, "Intermodal Comparisons of Energy Intensiveness in Long-Distance Transport," *Transportation Research*, Vol. 10, 1976, pp. 275–279; John B. Hopkins, A.T. Newfell, and Morrin Hazel, "Fuel Consumption in Rail Freight Service," presented at the 56th annual meeting of the Transportation Research Board, 1977; and Edward K. Morlok, "An Engineering Analysis and Comparison of Railroad and Truck Line-Haul Work (Energy) Requirements," presented at the 56th Annual Meeting of the Transportation Research Board, 1976.

19. Lynn O. Purnell, *A Methodology for Evaluating the Impact of Railroad Abandonment on Rural Highways*, School of Civil Engineering, Purdue University, Joint Highway Research Project, JHRP–76–4, 1976.

20. Ann F. Friedlaender and Richard H. Spady, *Freight Transport Regulation*, Cambridge, MA: The MIT Press, p. 163.

Chapter 14

SOME CONCLUDING THOUGHTS AND POLICY RECOMMENDATIONS

In reviewing this program there are several observations that come to mind that have only been referred to in passing. These observations will be given further attention here. In addition, this volume is filled with implicit and in some cases explicit policy recommendations regarding the design of a local rail service assistance program. In this chapter these recommendations and the attributes of what could be called a model program of operating assistance at the federal and state levels are presented. Let us begin with the observations.

What's in a Name?

Initially the talk was of "subsidies for light-density rail lines." Later it became "local rail service assistance." Some called it a "freight assistance program." But none of these labels seem to adequately capture the essence of the program. What did the program do? In most cases profitable Class I rail carriers provided rail service on lines of low traffic density for which the railroad received payment; this payment was to cover costs in excess of revenues. There is no doubt of this fact, but there is some question as to exactly what was being subsidized.

In other words were the railroads offering the service being subsidized or were the rail users along the line being subsidized so that they could use an uneconomical transport service? All indications are that in reality the later was occurring.

In another context we frequently hear discussions in the urban transit area regarding operating assistance for public transit properties. Such payments are necessary because it is considered desirable in a social welfare sense to keep fares low so that transit users will not have to bear the burden of full cost. The rail freight situation is really no different than the transit case: the railroad is not being subsidized, it is the rail user that is being subsidized. In a majority of the cases the railroads offering the service would probably have been pleased to stop the service; newly created short line railroads are the only operators that depended on the service. In each case the operator received a payment for offering an uneconomical service that in most cases was unable to cover its costs.

The fact that the transit property or the railroad receives such "subsidies" as opposed to the users should not confuse the issue. It is far more economical and administratively neater to give the eventual receiver the subsidy rather than each transit rider or rail user. But policy makers should not be confused as to who was being subsidized. The primary beneficiaries of the local rail service operating assistance program were the rail users. These were, in several cases, major corporations that clearly could afford a few more dollars of shipping costs. This point was never dwelt upon by policy makers because unlike the popular support that transit receives for the provision of its service for the old, the poor, and the handicapped, it is difficult to support a program that subsidizes the transportation costs of corporations that might be enjoying record profits.

Is a Program Needed?

It is very easy to conclude that an assistance program that kept rail service in place for a period of time is unnecessary. More than likely this would be the wrong conclusion to reach. There are cases where the loss of rail service creates significant short-term hardships for shippers and receivers, and it is probable that an assistance program may be of value in these cases. The type of program necessary for this purpose would not have to be for more than one or two years. Even then such a program would have to be structured somewhat differently than the local rail service assistance program was.

Whether there is a need for a long term assistance program of the type most states were operating is debatable on philosophical grounds. However, motor carrier deregulation and other factors have dealt a significant blow to that industry as well as to rural areas having low traffic density. With regard to the latter it is difficult to say how long these rural areas will continue receiving service. This is a relevant factor because it has always been assumed that the loss of rail service will be met by the use of motor carriers. Apparently, this is not necessarily so.

It is possible to take a laissez faire attitude and argue that if the traffic volume is sufficient, then service will be provided. But what if traffic is never that great? In that case the shipper must either have his own fleet of motor carriers or relocate to an area that has transport available.

The general tendency in this country has been to try to hold regional economies in place as evinced by the numerous federally funded regional commissions that exist in depressed areas, e.g., the Appalachian Regional Commission, the New England Regional Commission, and so forth. However, support for these endeavors also seems destined to decrease under the Reagan administration. This would imply that it is far more likely that the future will see corporate policy being utilized to resolve long term problems of this nature rather than public policy.

As the nation moved away from operating assistance in this program area, it moved toward what has been called the pre-abandonment program. Realizing that a lot of public funds were being wasted many state policy makers actively lobbied for such a program. The rationale was why wait for a line to lose traffic due to poor maintenance, rehabilitate the line now. The program was very popular with a few railroads.

It was noted in an earlier chapter that this program has a few problems. This is clearly a rail subsidy program in that railroads receive federal and state or local funds for track rehabilitation. The lines that receive the funds must have limited traffic, but they may be profitable lines. It is not unheard of to give public monies to for-profit corporations, but it is a little unusual to provide such monies to private and profitable corporations. The railroads that have utilized the pre-abandonment program are profitable and hardly on the brink of financial disaster. Should public monies be spent in such a fashion?

To the extent that nearly every transport mode in the U.S. is subsidized today, it is reasonable, in the interest of equity, to provide some subsidies to railroads. Unlike motor carriers, river and waterway carriers, and air carriers, the railroads own their right-of-way and related facilities. As a result indirect government subsidies in the right-of-way are not possible for railroads, even though such subsidies are common for its two major competitors: highways for motor carriers and river and channel improvements for waterborne carriers. Until such indirect subsidies are removed it is reasonable to subsidize railroads.

The exact form the subsidy should take is difficult to identify. It could be a tax credit program or a program similar to the pre-abandonment program. In the event of the latter it seems reasonable that a federal program that involves the FRA and the railroads is sufficient. In other words it makes little sense to have the states involved in this process as a contributor or planner.

A Recommended Operating Assistance Program

In the belief that a program of some sort is necessary for shippers that may lose rail service, it is reasonable to identify the major attributes of such a program. The proposed program is similar to the proposals incorporated in the 3R Act although there are some significant differences. Let us examine the major attributes of this proposed program.

MODAL TEST

Any branch line about to be abandoned should be a candidate for a transport service continuation subsidy. That subsidy would not necessarily provide for continued rail service; it might provide for service by a motor carrier. In order to determine which mode would be provided with a subsidy the rail user would have to supply information on its current rail freight cost and the cost of substitute service by motor carriers, and the rail carrier would have to supply information regarding the estimated cost of subsidized service. Subsidized rail service would be provided in the event the estimated rail subsidy was less than the additional cost (motor carrier costs less rail costs) of using motor carriers. If this was not the case then the motor carrier would be assisted, but only the additional cost of using this mode.

LENGTH OF ASSISTANCE

In no case should the length of assisted service exceed two years. The proposed program is intended to mitigate the impacts of abandonment, not prevent them entirely. In view of the short amount of time within which abandonments can occur today, it is not unreasonable to provide for a transitional period of one or two years. Shippers and receivers would be entitled to the second year of assistance only if there were no declines in traffic during the first year. In other words some shippers might try to build traffic to profitable levels and if this can be accomplished it should not be discouraged. In the event that aid is provided for motor carrier service, then one year of assistance would be the limit.

FUNDING MECHANISM

It is believed that the proposed program should be funded by the federal government and shippers and receivers. In this arrangement the federal share would be seventy percent and the rail users share would be thirty percent. Obviously missing is a state share and if a state felt compelled to get involved they could always pass legislation that would enable them to pay part of the rail user share. This is not recommended.

Based on past experience it is possible for a shipper to make a rail line viable by simply using the line more. That is, it may be that a firm currently uses rail for 10% of its shipments, and it might be possible for the shipper to increase this rail modal share to 20% with only a slight increase in cost. The firm will not even evaluate this option if they have others paying the subsidy for them. The thirty percent share should at least get such shippers to evaluate their options.

OPERATORS OF SERVICE

It is believed that all rail service under an assistance program should be provided by existing rail carriers. Since the program envisioned here is only of two years duration, it would make little sense to start new short line railroads for such a brief period. In addition, short lines tend to bring with them a vested interest in continuation of the program since it guarantees a profit for such operators.

UPGRADING OF LINES

The reorganization of railroads in the Northeast and Midwest was an anomalous situation in terms of the massive amounts of track that were receiving rail service under safety waivers granted by the FRA. As a result many miles of subsidized line' had to have funds invested in them in order that they could safely receive rail service. Recall that this activity, which would have normally been referred to as rehabilitation, was referred to as accelerated maintenance in the 3R program. It is doubtful that such a situation of massive amounts of poor track will reoccur. It is not impossible.

Assuming the lines are at Class I FRA safety standards, it does not make sense to upgrade most short branch lines to Class II. In addition, since the proposed program is of such a brief duration, such an investment would make very little sense. Of course the lines should receive regular maintenance, although it would be difficult to justify normalized maintenance for such lines.

Other Programs?

When the local rail service assistance program was expanded to include the rehabilitation or pre-abandonment program, there were also other programs for acquisition, new construction, and substitute service. It seems that there is a need for these programs, but not as great a need as might be assumed. Acquisition monies should be available for those cases where it appears that a particularly vital right-of-way might disappear, or where a right-of-way might easily be used for a rail transit line, or similar purpose. It should be apparent that whether we are talking about a rail transit line, a bike path, a hiking trail, or similar use, there are generally funds available for such acquisitions and the rail program funds if used at all, would be used only as an interim measure.

New construction seems to be the responsibility of the railroad but there are occasions when a number of rail users on a line to be abandoned can be connected to a different line which is to be retained and in the process save the rail service for these shippers and receivers. Such projects should be approved only if they result in viable operations in a profit sense.

Substitute service is probably worth funding on a temporary basis as noted under the bimodal program discussed earlier. Whether funds should be provided for motor carrier terminals or loading facilities is doubtful. It is unlikely that the cost of such facilities will be prohibitive for shippers and if it is the service will probably not be viable. So beyond a temporary shipper motor carrier subsidy this is probably not worth pursuing.

A FINAL COMMENT

A little more than five years after the beginning of subsidized rail service the Local Rail Service Assistance Program that permitted such subsidies came to an end. Created under the 3R Act the program actually made some sense as a method of mitigating the impacts of abandonment. But, as is true of most regional legislation, it was politically necessary to address the problem beyond the region. As a result the program began to take on different dimensions that were at best not well thought out. There continues to be a need for the type of program recommended here. It is hoped that such a need will be recognized.

APPENDICES

APPENDIX A
Lines Assisted by the Program

The lines that are listed on the following pages represent those lines that were assisted by the states and federal government at the outset of the operating assistance program. The lines listed here were all served by the Consolidated Rail Corporation at least at the time the program began. Those lines that were operated by other railroads at the beginning of the program appear in the text as Table 6.2.

The railroad (RR) given in the following list was the owner of the line at the beginning of the program; some of these lines were later acquired by states and others. The railroads represented are the Penn Central (PC), Reading (RDG), Erie Lackawanna (EL), Ann Arbor (AA), Central of New Jersey (CNJ), Pennsylvania-Reading Seashore Lines (PRSL), Lehigh Valley (LV).

USRA LINE NO.	STATE	SUBSIDY POINTS	RR	LENGTH
47	CT	Wethersfield (7.0) - Rocky Hill (10.2)	PC	3.2
50	CT	Hartford (2.0) - Griffins (8.7)	PC	6.7
55/54	CT	Avon (9.4) - Simsbury (16.2)	PC	6.8
159/160/ 161	DE	Georgetown (23.9) - Lewes (38.0) and Lewes Beach (0.0 - 2.4)	PC	16.5
907a	DE	Elsmere Jct. (2.9) - Pa/Del State Line (12.7)	RDG	9.8
950	DE	Pigeon Point, Del. to Carney's Point to Thompson's Point, N.J. (float)		14.0
415	IL	Matteson (24.8) - Frankfort (33.2)	PC	8.4
577a	IL	Kankakee (246.3) - Sheldon (219.4)	PC	26.9
605a/605b/ 606	IL	Paris (37.6) - Lawrenceville (101.0)	PC	63.4
607a	IL	Olmstead (245.3) - Cairo (255.0)	PC	9.7
609	IL	Paris (22.5) - Decatur (95.5)	PC	73.0
399	IN	Goshen (0.7) - Shipshewana (16.7)	PC	16.0

418	IN	Kendallville (121.0) - Mich. State Line (145.8)	PC	24.8
419	IN	Mexico (14.2) to Roann (27.2) via N. Manchester	PC	22.7
423	IN	Logansport (115.9) - Lucerne (124.5)	PC	8.6
429	IN	Decatur (70.4) - Portland (42.6)	PC	27.8
523	IN	Anderson (127.0) - Frankton (132.6)	PC	5.6
554	IN	Hunter (131.2) - Maxwell (118.0)	PC	13.2
554a	IN	Wilkinson (109.0) - New Castle (96.9)	PC	12.1
554b	IN	New Castle (95.3) - Lynn (68.8)	PC	26.5
571/571a	IN	Valley Jct., O. (17.7) - Brookville (43.9)	PC	26.2
579a/578	IN	Emporia (173.5) - Carthage (193.5)	PC	20.0
582	IN	Columbus (3.8) - Clifford (7.0)	PC	3.2
589/590	IN	North Vernon (19.1) - Madison (44.9)	PC	25.8
1261/1262	IN	Decatur (96.9) - N. Judson (199.4)	EL	102.5
148	MD	Massey (9.2) - Centerville (35.1)	PC	25.9
149/147	MD	Townsend, Del. (0.0) - Chestertown (20.4) via Massey (0.0 - 9.2)	PC	29.6
169/150	MD	Clayton, Del. (0.0) - Easton (45.3) and Queen Anne (0.0) - Denton (8.8)	PC	54.1
168/152	MD	Seaford, Del. (2.3) - Cambridge (32.9) and Hurlock (16.6) - Preston (10.0)	PC	37.2
676	MD	Salisbury (40.8) - Hebron (35.2)	PC	5.6
8	MA	Palmer (0.0) - Old Furnace - South Barre (25.0)	PC	25.0
13	MA	South Sudbury (4.0) - Chelmsford (24.4)	PC	20.4
17	MA	North Abington (0.0) - West Hanover (3.6)	PC	3.6
21/22	MA	E. Sandwich (7.5) - Hyannis (24.3) and Yarmouth (0.0) - S. Dennis (5.6)	PC	22.4
23/24	MA	Buzzards Bay (0.3) - Falmouth (13.8)	PC	13.5
392a/393	MI	Lenawee (324.5) - Adrian (333.6)	PC	9.1
394	MI	Grosvenor (0.0) - Morenci (18.6)	PC	18.6
444/444a/ 445/438/ 438a	MI	Millington (79.6) - Munger (101.1) and Caro Jct. (0.0) - Colling (22.2)	PC	43.7
451	MI	Grand Rapids (88.1) - Vermontville (46.4)	PC	41.7

455a	MI	Owosso (63.6) - Swan Creek (91.8)	PC	28.2
456/457/ 458	MI	Sturgis (150.4) - Nottawa (157.9)	PC	7.5
456a/457/ 458	MI	Vicksburg (171.9) - Mendon (164.1)	PC	7.8
464/465	MI	Parchment (42.3) - Richland Jct. (35.0) and Richland (0.0) - Doster (8.1)	PC	15.4
466	MI	Kalamazoo (145.0) - Dowagiac (178.6)	PC	33.6
467	MI	Buchanan (200.8) - Indiana State Line (222.8)	PC	22.0
1300/1301	MI	Entire Ann Arbor Railroad System, Toledo (0.0) - Frankfort (292.0) and Frankfort - Kewaunee, Wis. (float)	AA	292.0
119	NJ	Monmouth Jct. (2.7) - Rocky Hill (6.3)	PC	3.6
123/124/ 124a	NJ	Farmingdale (8.3) - Freehold (13.5)	PC	5.2
1104	NJ	Matawan (10.9) - Morganville (14.1)	CNJ	3.2
1105	NJ	Bradley Beach (29.0) - Bayhead Jct. (38.0)	CNJ	9.0
1106	NJ	Toms River (47.4) - Pinewald (51.5)	CNJ	4.1
1107	NJ	High Bridge (0.0) - plus 300 feet	CNJ	.1
1204	NJ	Millington (30.0) - Gladstone (42.3)	EL	12.3
1206	NJ	Bloomfield (10.0) - West Orange (12.7)	EL	2.7
1800	NJ	McKee City (53.1) - Pleasantville (56.9)	PRSL	3.8
1807	NJ	Haddonfield (6.1) - Lucaston (13.6)	PRSL	7.5
1808	NJ	Palermo (59.6) - Ocean City (66.4)	PRSL	6.8
66c	NY	Wassaic (81.6) - Millerton (94.8)	PC	13.2
80	NY	Camden (22.9) - McConnellsville (27.4)	PC	4.5
81	NY	S. Amsterdam (165.0) - S. Fort Plain (194.5)	PC	29.5
85	NY	Vernon (246.3) - Oneida Castle (251.9)	PC	5.6
86	NY	E. Syracuse (5.8) - Fayetteville (9.9)	PC	4.1
87	NY	Malone (0.0) - Canadian border (10.3)	PC	10.3
90	NY	Emeryville (8.0) - Edwards (13.9)	PC	5.9
98	NY	Canandaigua (76.0) - Victor (84.5)	PC	8.5
100/101	NY	Akron Jct. (17.9) - Transit Road (26.5)	PC	8.6
102	NY	Oswego (26.6) - Wallington (62.2)	PC	35.6

103/104	NY	Wallington (62.2) - Windsor Beach (93.0)	PC	30.8
105/107	NY	Charlotte (95.6) - Model City (168.5)	PC	72.9
108	NY	Newark (18.8) - Sodus Point (33.4)	PC	14.6
109/110	NY	Neward (0.0) - Marion (8.9)	PC	8.9
137	NY	Kingston (2.9) - Bloomville (86.6)	PC	83.7
137a	NY	Kingston Point (0.0) - Kingston (2.9)	PC	2.9
233/234	NY	Bellona (46.3) - Seneca Castle (4.9) and Canandaigua Trk. at Stanley (52.2-52.8)	PC	11.4
249	NY	Maybille (65.1) - Corry (93.8)	PC	28.7
260	NY	Falconer (33.4) - Frewsburg (37.1)	PC	3.7
1003/1002	NY	Owego (289.6) - Mead (339.3) and Freeville (59.8) - East Ithaca (50.4)	LV	59.1
1002	NY	Cortland Secondary at Cortland (67.8-71.8)	LV	4.0
1020	NY	Van Etten Jct. (285.8) - Odessa (302.2)	LV	16.4
1022	NY	Geneva (344.5) - Victor (372.0)	LV	27.5
1023/1024	NY	Niagara Jct. (438.0) - Batavia (411.0)	LV	27.0
1221	NY	Crawford (0.0) - Pine Bush (10.0)	EL	10.0
1240	NY	Batavia (388.8) - LeRoy (379.8)	EL	9.0
1242	NY	Depew Jct. (385.5) - Lancaster (382.5)	EL	3.0
1246	NY	BC Jct. (2.7) - Gowanda (33.1)	EL	30.4
1250	NY	Salamanca (413.9) - Cattaraugus (428.1)	EL	14.2
371	OH	Minerva (4.5) - Magnolia (15.3)	PC	10.8
477a	OH	Hamilton Parker Industrial Track at Columbus (138.0-139.0)	PC	1.0
478	OH	Howard (89.9) - Holmesville (54.6)	PC	35.3
516	OH	Spring Valley (61.4) - Roxanna (63.4)	PC	2.0
525	OH	Lebanon (25.5) - Hageman (31.4)	PC	5.9
527/528	OH	Hempstead (7.0) - Lytle (16.0)	PC	9.0
531/531a/ 532	OH	Van Wert (102.0) - North Paulding (80.5)	PC	21.5
533/534/ 534a/535	OH	Van Wert (104.2) - Rockford (118.7)	PC	14.5
536/537	OH	Yellow Springs (7.5) - Springfield (19.3)	PC	11.8
643	OH	Genoa (281.5) - Lindsey (273.0)	PC	8.5
714	OH	Ashtabula (124.3) - Rock Creek (109.4)	PC	14.9

1260/1261	OH	Lima (54.3) - Elgin (72.0)	EL	17.7
1263	OH	Marion (305.1) - Richwood (319.4)	EL	14.3
1264	OH	Peoria (330.3) - Broadway (328.5)	EL	1.8
135	PA	Allen Lane (0.0) - East Lane (1.4)	EL	1.4
177	PA	Pomeroy (0.0) - Buck Run (3.7)	PC	3.7
180/181	PA	At Lebanon (0.0-1.2), 21.4-21.7)	PC	1.5
196/197b	PA	Reading (60.4) - Hamburg-Auburn (85.0)	PC	24.6
203	PA	Mechanicsburg (8.9) - Dillsburg (16.4)	PC	7.5
206	PA	Marion (59.1) - Mercersburg (72.7)	PC	13.6
208	PA	Yeagertown (3.9) - Reedsville (5.8)	PC	1.9
250	PA	Corry (95.0) - Spartansburg (102.5)	PC	7.5
252	PA	Warren (66.5) - Kane (92.5)	PC	26.0
257	PA	Brookville (0.0-1.4)	PC	1.4
260a	PA	Warren (51.3) - N. Warren (54.1)	PC	2.8
303	PA	Price Run Branch near Dixonville (V.S. 0 - 00, V.S. 25 - 26)	PC	.5
331	PA	Hempfield Jct. (0.0) - Herminie (8.9)	PC	8.9
344	PA	Bridgeville (0.9) - Sygan (1.4)	PC	.5
360	PA	Jamestown (90.5) - Westford (97.6)	PC	7.1
651	PA	Falls Creek (22.5) - Minns Coal (27.3)	PC	4.8
663	PA	Connellsville (27.5) - Mt. Braddock (31.7)	PC	4.2
903	PA	Wayne Jct. (5.1) - Germantown (7.0)	RDG	1.9
904	PA	Cheltenham Jct. (9.6) - Newtown (26.4)	RDG	16.8
905	PA	Lansdale (Fortuna) (1.5) - Dylestown (10.0)	RDG	8.5
906	PA	Emmaus Jct. (38.6) - E. Greenville (23.0)	RDG	15.6
906a	PA	Oaks (1.5) - Collegeville (6.0)	RDG	4.5
907	PA	Modena (30.2) - Pa./Del. State Line (12.7)	RDG	17.5
908	PA	Elverson (0.0) - Warwick (0.4)	RDG	.4
909	PA	Pottstown (0.0) - Boyertown (9.0)	RDG	9.0
910	PA	Topton (0.0) - Kutztown (4.4)	RDG	4.4
912	PA	Carlisle Jct. (7.8) - Gettysburg (31.2)	RDG	23.4
915	PA	Lebanon (0.0) - Suedburg (18.5)	RDG	18.5

916	PA	Manheim (0.0) - Myers Propane (0.7)	RDG	.7
921	PA	Bear Run Jct.-Frackville (8.7-9.9,0.0-2.9)	RDG	4.1
923	PA	Haucks (105.4) - Ringtown (123.0)	RDG	17.6
925	PA	Tremont (23.0) - Pine Grove (29.6)	RDG	6.6
935	PA	Lansdale (1.5) - Norristown (9.0)	RDG	7.5
1007	PA	Laurel Jct. (157.5) - Skytop Coal Co. (162.7)	LV	5.2
1008	PA	Delano (158.4) - Shenandoah (165.5)	LV	7.1
1009	PA	Nesquehoning (0.0) - Tamanend (16.7)	LV	16.7
1012	PA	Franklin Branch - Nanticoke Branch (174.0-175.0, VS 0.0 - 45+89.6)	LV	1.9
1228	PA	Hicks Ferry (170.0) - Berwick (177.0)	EL	7.0
1229	PA	Old Line Jct. (155.0) - Foster (157.8) and Nicholson (152.1)	EL	5.7
1256	PA	Wheatland (4.4) - Pulaski (12.0)	EL	7.6
1256a	PA	New Castle (19.3) - Fleming Steel (18.0)	EL	1.3
28	RI	Portsmouth (21.2) - Newport (30.5)	PC	9.3
166/165	VA	Pocomoke, Md. (31.5) - Cape Charles (95.0) and Little Creek (6.7) - Norfolk (0.0) float	PC	96.2

APPENDIX B
The CRC-State Contract

CONSOLIDATED RAIL CORPORATION

OPERATING AGREEMENT

UNDER

RAIL SERVICE CONTINUATION SUBSIDY

WITH

[   ]

Model Agreement   23 March 1976

OPERATING AGREEMENT
UNDER
RAIL SERVICE CONTINUATION SUBSIDY

OPERATING AGREEMENT
UNDER
RAIL SERVICE CONTINUATION SUBSIDY

THIS AGREEMENT made and entered into this   day of March, 1976, by and between CONSOLIDATED RAIL CORPORATION ("ConRail"), a Delaware corporation organized pursuant to the Regional Rail Reorganization Act of 1973, with principal offices at 1818 Market Street, Philadelphia, Pennsylvania 19103, and

("Subsidizer").

WHEREAS, Subsidizer has offered a subsidy to ConRail to conduct a rail freight service operation on certain rail facilities identified herein in order to prevent discontinuance of service previously provided; and

WHEREAS, ConRail is willing to provide this public service on the basis of compensation defined herein; and

WHEREAS, the owners of the rail facilities have or will have leased or otherwise made such facilities available to the Subsidizer for operations hereunder;

NOW, THEREFORE, the parties do hereby mutually agree that ConRail shall perform rail freight services and shall be compensated by the Subsidizer therefor as follows:

ARTICLE ONE - DEFINITIONS

Section 101. Definitions. The following words and phrases shall have the following meanings ascribed to them unless the context clearly determines otherwise:

"costs of providing service" means and shall include all costs of providing service as are defined and included in the RSPO Standards as reimbursable to the operator.

"crew" means the individual train and engine personnel employed to perform the rail freight service described in Attachment 2 hereto.

"maintenance" means the normal and regular work required to keep a rail facility in the condition necessary to continuously perform the level of rail freight service required by this Agreement.

"RRRA" means the Regional Rail Reorganization Act of 1973, Public Law 93236 (87 Stat. 985), as amended.

"RRRRA" means the Railroad Revitalization and Regulatory Reform Act of 1976, Public Law 94210 (90 Stat. 31), as amended.

"RSPO Standards" means those standards promulgated by the Rail Services Planning Office of the Interstate Commerce Commission, entitled "Standards for Determining Rail Service Continuation Subsidies" (49 CFR 1125, as amended).

"rail facility and rail facilities" collectively means the track, bridges, signals, switches, structures and related railroad transportation property located on the one or more segments over which rail freight service is to be provided pursuant to this Agreement, as more fully described in Attachment 1, which identifies each segment by mileage, associated facilities, ownership, and bases of operation.

"rail freight service" means that service to be provided by ConRail pursuant to this Agreement, as more fully described in the "Local Freight Service Characteristics" in Attachment 2 hereto.

"rehabilitation" means the work required in addition to maintenance, including capital improvements, to improve or upgrade the condition of a rail facility.

"segment" means a section of a railroad line that is not designated to ConRail in the Final System Plan and that is the subject of a notice in writing of intent to discontinue service under Section 304(a) of the RRRA and/or notice of intent to abandon rail properties under Section 304(b) of the RRRA, as to which Subsidizer has or will have acquired the rights of use for the service hereunder, all as more fully described in Attachment 1. All segments so identified are herein from time to time collectively referred to as "rail facilities".

"subsidy year" means the twelve month period beginning with the effective date hereof as defined in Section 1701 below.

"total liability costs" means and shall include only the freight portion of the following Interstate Commerce Commission accounts: 274 (Injuries - Maintenance of Way), 275 (Insurance - Maintenance of Way), 332 (Injuries - Maintenance

of Equipment), 333 (Insurance - Maintenance of Equipment), 357
(Insurance - Traffic), 414 (Insurance - Transportation), 415
(Clearing Wrecks), 416 (Damage to Property), 417 (Damage to
Livestock), 418 (Loss and Damage - Freight), 420 (Injuries -
Transportation), and 455 (Insurance - General).

ARTICLE TWO - OPERATING PLAN

Section 201. Provision of Service. ConRail
agrees to provide a rail freight service on each segment of
the rail facilities identified in Attachment 1 hereto which
service is more fully described as to operations, equipment
and frequency in Attachment 2 hereto entitled "Local Freight
Service Characteristics". The provision of the service
described in Attachment 2 may be subject to modifications
pursuant to negotiations under applicable collective bargaining
agreements. ConRail, on reasonable notice to Subsidizer,
may in the interest of greater efficiency from time to time
change the base of operations, service frequency or other
aspects of the service and appropriately adjust the costs of
providing the rail freight service. The Subsidizer may
reject changes in the base of operations which would result
in an increase in the subsidy for the segment, or any change
in service frequency. The Subsidizer may propose and ConRail
will adopt at least one change in the service frequency per
segment during the subsidy year. Such a proposal by the
Subsidizer must be made at least 120 days prior to its taking
effect.

Section 202. Operational Rights. Subsidizer has
assembled, or prior to the effective date hereof will have
assembled, the rail facilities described in detail on Attachment
1 hereto from the owners thereof and hereby assigns to
ConRail all necessary rights and licenses to enter upon and

operate the rail freight service on the effective date
hereof. The rights herein granted to ConRail are for the
provision of rail freight service including picking up and
setting out cars for the use of shippers. ConRail assumes
no obligations other than stated herein except as expressly
provided in the RRRA and assumes no obligations with respect
to rail services previously operated by any railroad. All
rail facilities remain the property of the present respective
owners or their successors, subject to contracts with Subsidizer.
ConRail shall not be held liable for normal wear and tear of
such property used in the normal course of railroad business.

   Section 203. Force Majeure; Excuse. (a) The
parties hereto will be excused from performance of any of
their respective obligations hereunder where such performance
is prevented by any event beyond their respective control,
which shall include, without limitation, any actions of
any federal, state or local agency or instrumentality; acts
of God; strikes or other labor troubles; explosions, fires,
or vandalism.

   (b) ConRail will not incur liability for any
failure to perform the rail freight service if such failure
is the result of any condition of any of the rail facilities
including, without limitation, any condition attributable to
maintenance which existed on the effective date of this
Agreement, until a reasonable time has elapsed for the
performance of any maintenance or rehabilitation which
ConRail has agreed to perform.

   ARTICLE THREE - MANAGEMENT AND CONTROL
   Section 301. Control. ConRail shall have exclusive control in the management and operation of the rail

freight service, including the dispatching of trains,
assignment of available cars in good order, assignment of
crews, and assignment and utilization of power. ConRail
will endeavor to provide such service in an efficient manner.

Section 302. Operating Rules and Regulations.
ConRail shall have exclusive authority to promulgate and
adopt rules and regulations for the operation of the rail
freight service.

Section 303. Crew Size. ConRail shall determine
the size of each crew not inconsistent with nor more than
required by applicable collective bargaining agreements and
state law. Negotiations with the labor unions for adjustments in crew size are the responsibility of ConRail; however,
Subsidizer will be notified of, and may have its representative
present to observe, the negotiations.

Section 304. Joint Use of Facilities. In the
event joint use of any segment is contemplated by the parties,
the terms of any such joint use shall have the prior approval
of ConRail, which prior approval shall not be unreasonably
withheld.

ARTICLE FOUR - MAINTENANCE

Section 401. Responsibility. Subsidizer shall
be responsible for providing all maintenance on the rail
facilities and shall maintain the rail facilities at a
satisfactory level to permit operation of the rail freight
service in compliance with Federal Railroad Administration
(FRA) Class I safety standards or pursuant to any safety
waiver issued in relation to any segment of the facilities.

Section 402. Cost Estimates. Included in Attachment
3 hereto are the estimates of Subsidizer of the cost of

maintenance, which estimates shall be subject to ConRail's
review.

Section 403. Safety Waivers. ConRail shall be
responsible for requesting safety waivers, or transfers of
such waivers, if FRA Class I standards are not met. ConRail
shall conduct routine inspections of the rail facilities
regardless of the party contractually responsible for
maintenance. If ConRail deems maintenance inadequate in any
respect, whether or not contained in the estimates referred
to in Section 402 above, it will notify Subsidizer of such
deficiency. If Subsidizer fails to correct such deficiency
within a reasonable time, ConRail shall perform the maintenance
it deems necessary and Subsidizer shall bear the cost in
accordance with the RSPO standards.

Section 404. Maintenance Contractor. Subsidizer
may select others to provide the maintenance required hereunder
or may contract with ConRail to provide, or arrange for the
provision of, the agreed upon maintenance by so indicating
on Attachment 3 hereto. The party undertaking the performance
of the maintenance shall schedule maintenance work so as to
interfere minimally with the rail freight service.

ARTICLE FIVE - REHABILITATION

Section 501. Rehabilitation Program. Included in
Attachment 3 hereto are the cost estimates of the Subsidizer
setting forth any rehabilitation of rail facilities which in
the opinion of the Subsidizer should be performed to bring
the rail facilities to a satisfactory level to permit operation
of the rail freight service. The Subsidizer shall perform
the scheduled rehabilitation, subject to ConRail's prior

approval of the scheduling of work to avoid interference
with the rail freight service, which approval shall not
be unreasonably withheld. The Subsidizer may contract
separately with ConRail or a third party for performance of
such rehabilitation. Work not performed by ConRail will be
inspected by ConRail on notice of completion and either
accepted as complete or rejected with specification of the
reason for rejection.

ARTICLE SIX - LIABILITY

Section 601. ConRail's Liability. When any loss,
damage, destruction, injury or death occurs as a result of
the management, control, use, or operation by ConRail of
rail freight service and the rail facilities appertaining
thereto, ConRail hereby agrees to indemnify and hold harmless
the Subsidizer, or the Trustees or owners of the rail facilities,
or any or all of them, from any such loss or liability
including all related costs and counsel fees, unless such
loss, damage, destruction, injury or death occurs as a
result of maintenance or rehabilitation neither undertaken
by ConRail nor approved on completion by ConRail.

Section 602. Insurance. In consideration of
ConRail's assumption of all liabilities arising from its
operations, as provided in Section 601 above, Subsidizer agrees
to pay its designated share of: (1) ConRail's cost of insurance
acquired to protect against all such assumed risks of
liabilities, (2) the expense of liabilities below the
deductible limits of such insurance policies, and (3) an
amount equal to seven percent of the expense of insurance
policies and liabilities below the deductible limits of
such insurance policies. The designated share shall be
computed at the end of the subsidy year by applying a ratio

to the freight train-miles generated on the rail facilities where
the numerator of the ratio is 1.07 times ConRail's total liability
costs, and the denominator is ConRail's total freight train-
miles operated.

Section 603. Subsidizer's Liabilities. In the
event Subsidizer elects to perform maintenance or rehabilitation
through its own employees or those of a government agency or
department, or elects to engage a third party independent
contractor for such purpose, Subsidizer shall be responsible
for any loss or liability incurred by ConRail by reason of
the work so performed or omitted and Subsidizer shall indemnify
and hold harmless and defend ConRail from any such claim,
loss or liability asserted against it by any third party;
provided, however, that if ConRail approves maintenance or
rehabilitation conducted by or through Subsidizer upon its
completion, such claim, loss, or liability shall be assumed
by ConRail pursuant to Section 601 above.

ARTICLE SEVEN - SUBSIDY PAYMENTS

Section 701. Compensation. As to each segment
over which the rail freight service is operated ConRail
shall receive a rail continuation subsidy payment equal to
the costs of providing service less ConRail revenues which
are each attributable to the segment, all as more fully
defined in the RSPO Standards.

Section 702. Payment Schedule. Payments due
ConRail hereunder shall be made on or before the fifteenth
day of the first and each succeeding month by the Subsidizer
to ConRail in monthly installments per estimates submitted
pursuant hereto. If the estimated subsidy payments do not
conform to the actual results of operations during the
subsidy year, any deficiency shall be paid to ConRail within

thirty (30) days following delivery of the Annual Report.
Excess payments shall be placed in a special interest-
bearing escrow account and made available to the Subsidizer
as a credit in the next year of operation. All lease,
return on value and other payments for rail facilities shall
be the sole and direct responsibility of the Subsidizer who
shall indemnify and hold ConRail harmless from any claim by
the Trustees or owners of rail facilities arising under the
terms of related lease agreements. In the event, however,
that the estimated revenues attributable to the rail facilities
exceed the estimated costs of providing service for those
facilities, ConRail will upon written notification act as
Subsidizer's agent for the purpose of making lease payments
to the Trustee or owner of the rail facilities.

Section 703. Federal Reimbursement. It is understood and agreed by the parties hereto that the promises to
pay contained herein are conditioned upon the availability and
receipt by the Subsidizer of Federal appropriations for the
purposes contemplated in this Agreement.

Section 704. Excess Revenues. Excess revenues
occur when a segment produces more revenue than is necessary
to cover all avoidable costs, including any tax payments or
other payments related to rental of property from the
Trustee or owner thereof. These revenues may be placed in
three different types of interest bearing escrow accounts.

(a) The first escrow account to receive excess
revenues will be the maintenance and rehabilitation account.
Funds in this account will be used for maintenance and/or
rehabilitation during the year following the year in which
they were generated. Any funds remaining in this account at
the end of a year beyond those necessary for maintenance

and/or rehabilitation shall be placed in an acquisition account.

(b) Excess revenues may be placed in the acquisition account at the end of the first year after the funds were generated. The acquisition account will be utilized in the acquisition of profitable segments by ConRail. The segment must be in good condition from a maintenance and rehabilitation standpoint in order for funds to be placed in this account. ConRail will not utilize these funds for acquisition unless the segment is able to cover all costs and the account is capable of meeting the fair market value of the property.

(c) The interim account shall be established in those circumstances where the Subsidizer has offered a subsidy for a segment which they desire to utilize for only a short time, and the segment generates excess revenues either during its being phased out, or due to a very low budget for maintenance and rehabilitation. The excess revenues will be placed in the interim account until such time as the segment is abandoned. Upon abandonment the funds in an interim account will be transferred to the acquisition account having the greatest proportion of the fair market value of its property. Should such a transfer produce an excess of the funds necessary to acquire the latter segment, that excess shall be placed in the next acquisition account under the same criterion. Funds will not be transferred from the maintenance and rehabilitation account of one segment to the same account of another segment. No escrow accounts will be utilized to cover operating subsidies. No funds in any escrow account will be transferred to another railroad for acquisition or any other purposes.

(d) If a Subsidizer withdraws from subsidizing segments, or a segment where there is only one, or if the

subsidy program terminates for some reason, ConRail will
utilize funds remaining in all of the escrow accounts to
acquire a segment or portion of a segment which is involved
in the program described in this Agreement.

(e) In the event that there is no property which
may be acquired, funds remaining in the escrow accounts may
be utilized for any purpose consistent with the objectives of
the Federal Railroad Administration rail service continuation
program under the RRRA.

ARTICLE EIGHT - ESTIMATED REVENUES AND OPERATING COSTS

Section 801. Estimated Revenues. The estimated
operating revenue required by Section 702 above is as
indicated on Attachment 3 hereto as "Estimate of ConRail
Revenue".

Section 802. Estimated Operating Costs. The
estimated costs required by Section 702 above are set forth
in Attachment 3 hereto.

ARTICLE NINE - MANAGEMENT FEE

Section 901. Management Fee. In addition to an
Administration Fee of 0.5% of the ConRail segment revenues,
and for the purpose of encouraging railroad management
initiative, the Subsidizer agrees to pay ConRail a management
fee on each segment in an amount equal to 4.5% of ConRail
segment revenues.

ARTICLE TEN - FREIGHT CHARGES AND ADJUSTMENTS

Section 1001. Freight Charges. ConRail will on
the effective date hereof adopt all the applicable tariffs
and divisions of any predecessor carrier or carriers which
had previously served the rail facilities for the local rail
freight service described in Attachment 2 hereto.

Section 1002. Changes. ConRail may from time to time seek changes in tariffs, rates and divisions. Any proposed changes will be submitted to the appropriate regulatory authorities. The Subsidizer shall have the right to propose new tariffs to ConRail applicable to the rail facilities, and ConRail shall use its best efforts to implement the proposed tariffs provided such proposals are consistent with the economic objectives of ConRail.

ARTICLE ELEVEN - ACCOUNTING REPORTS

Section 1101. Record Keeping. ConRail will keep accounting records in accordance with the RSPO Standards.

Section 1102. Report Schedule. A quarterly report of revenues and costs of providing service will be issued to the Subsidizer within ninety (90) days after each three months of continuous operation under this Agreement. An annual report will be issued to the Subsidizer within ninety (90) days following the end of the subsidy year.

Section 1103. Audit and Inspection. Upon reasonable notice, ConRail will allow the auditors of the Subsidizer or of any governmental agency having jurisdiction over ConRail, to audit all the records of ConRail that were used to determine the revenues and costs related to the rail continuation subsidy. All such records will be kept for a period of at least four years after the issuance of the annual report for the related year, and any such records that are the subject of an auditing dispute shall be kept for the term of that dispute. ConRail will also allow inspection of the rail facilities and the equipment used thereon by the authorized agents of the Subsidizer upon reasonable notice. ConRail shall require such agents to execute an instrument releasing

ConRail from liability for any injury or death that may result from any cause during such inspections, except that ConRail shall be liable for injury or death resulting to any agent from the operation of rail freight service.

ARTICLE TWELVE - ARBITRATION

Section 1201. <u>General</u>. In the event of any disagreement between the parties concerning the construction of this Agreement or the performance by either party hereunder, the parties shall submit such disagreement to arbitration pursuant to the procedures set forth in this Article.

Section 1202. <u>Procedures for Arbitration</u>.

(a) The party desiring arbitration shall give notice to that effect to the other party identifying the matter in issue and shall designate an individual as an arbitrator. Within fifteen (15) days thereafter, the other party shall, by written notice to the original party, appoint a second arbitrator. The arbitrators so appointed shall, within fifteen (15) days after the second arbitrator is appointed, appoint a third arbitrator, and the three arbitrators shall determine the matter within sixty (60) days of the appointment of the third arbitrator. If a second arbitrator shall not have been appointed as aforesaid, the first arbitrator shall proceed to determine the matter within sixty (60) days of the failure to so appoint a second arbitrator. If the two arbitrators appointed by the parties are unable to agree upon the appointment of a third arbitrator as aforesaid, either party may request the appointment of a third arbitrator by the President of the American Arbitration Association. If any arbitrator shall decline or fail to act, the party originally having chosen such arbitrator, or the President,

as the case may be, shall appoint another to act in his
place.

(b)   Except as otherwise provided herein, the
arbitrators shall arbitrate the issue in accordance with the
rules and procedures of the American Arbitration Association.

(c)   The determination of the majority of the
arbitrators or of the sole arbitrator, as the case may be,
shall be final and conclusive between and upon the parties
and judgment upon the same may be entered in any court
having jurisdiction thereof.

(d)   The arbitrators or the sole arbitrator shall
give written notice to the party stating their determination
and shall furnish to each party a copy of such determination
signed by the arbitrators.   The expenses of arbitration,
except for payment of each respective party's counsel fees
and fees of experts, shall be borne by the parties as directed
by the arbitrators as part of their determination.

Section 1203.   Conduct Pending Decision.   When a
question has been submitted to arbitration, pending the
decision, the rail freight service and payments under this
Agreement shall be transacted in the manner in which they
were transacted prior to the submission of the question to
arbitration.

ARTICLE THIRTEEN - CONTRACT TERM, RENEWAL AND RENEGOTIATION

Section 1301.   Term.   This Agreement shall be in
effect for one (1) full year from the effective date hereof
as determined by Section 1701 below, subject to the termination
provisions of Article Fourteen hereof regarding defaults.

Section 1302.   Renewal of Agreement.   Subsidizer
shall notify ConRail by certified mail forty-five (45) days
in advance of the beginning of the second year of operation

hereunder that the Subsidizer wishes to continue the service for one additional year. The terms of this Agreement shall however be open to renegotiation at the option of either party.

Section 1303. <u>Renegotiation</u>. Thirty (30) days after written notice by either party, or at the end of the subsidy year, whichever first occurs, the terms of this Agreement may be opened for renegotiation but rail service shall continue under the terms of this Agreement. The effective date of contract modifications shall be mutually agreed to, but no sooner than the first practical date by which ConRail can adjust its accounting records.

Each party shall bear its own expenses of renegotiation if the Agreement is opened for purposes of renewal, by expiration, or by mutual request, otherwise the party requesting negotiation shall bear all reasonable costs of the renegotiation.

ARTICLE FOURTEEN - <u>TERMINATION AND CANCELLATION</u>

Section 1401. <u>Termination for Money Default</u>. In the event of any failure on the part of either party to perform its obligations regarding payments of cost of providing service, including but not limited to transmittal of scheduled contractual payments under this Agreement, and the continuance by such party in such default for a period of ten (10) days, the other party shall have the right, at its option, after first giving twenty (20) days' written notice thereof by certified mail to the party in default and notwithstanding any waiver by the party giving notice of any prior breach thereof, to terminate this Agreement and the exercise of such right shall not impair any other rights of the party giving notice under this Agreement or any rights of action against the defaulting party for the recovery of damages; provided, however, that default with respect to matters which a party shall, in good faith, have submitted to arbitration hereunder, shall not, until five (5) days further default by such party after final decision of the arbitrators, be cause for termination.

Section 1402. Termination for Non-Money Default. In the event of any substantial failure on the part of either party to perform its obligations (under this Agreement), other than payments for costs of providing service, and the continuance by such party in such default for a period of sixty (60) days, the other party shall have the right at its option, after first giving thirty (30) days' written notice thereof by certified mail to the party in default and not-withstanding any waiver by the party giving notice of any prior breach thereof, to terminate this Agreement and the exercise of such right shall not impair any other rights of the party giving notice under this Agreement or any rights of action against the defaulting party for the recovery of damages; provided, however, that default with respect of matters which a party shall, in good faith, have submitted to arbitration hereunder, shall not until thirty (30) days further default by such party after final decision of the arbitrators, be cause for forfeiture as aforesaid.

Section 1403. Subsidizer's Termination. Subsidizer may terminate this Agreement on thirty (30) days notice.

Section 1404. Expenses of Termination. Expenses of termination shall be a cost of providing service. ConRail shall mitigate the cost of termination to the extent possible. The cost of the termination of crews and other personnel employed for the performance of the rail freight service shall be covered by Title V of the RRRA if applicable and if

funds are available thereunder for such purpose, if not,
such costs shall be reimbursable costs of termination hereunder.

Section 1405. Cancellation. This agreement may
be cancelled without cost or liability to either party and
at the option of either party at any time prior to the
initiation of the rail freight service in the event that:

(a)   the presently existing provisions of the RRRA
which authorized inter alia the formation of ConRail, and/or
the Final System Plan issued pursuant thereto have been
substantially adversely modified, amended or affected by
legislative or judicial action prior to the effective date
hereof;

(b)   orders of the Special Court and the reorganizing
railroads district courts directing the conveyance of assets
designated in the present Final System Plan to ConRail have
not become final and non-appealable before such conveyance
date; and

(c)   ConRail has not received funding substantially
as contemplated by the present Final System Plan before the
conveyance date.

ARTICLE FIFTEEN - REPRESENTATIONS AND WARRANTIES

Section 1501. ConRail. ConRail represents and
warrants the following:

(a)   ConRail is a corporation duly organized,
validly existing and in good standing under the laws of the
State of Delaware, and is duly qualified to do business in
each jurisdiction where the ownership of its real property
requires such qualification;

(b)   ConRail has the full power and authority to

enter into this Agreement and to carry out the functions
which it has undertaken in this Agreement;

(c) All corporate and other proceedings required
to be taken by or on the part of ConRail to authorize ConRail
to enter into this Agreement and perform the rail freight
service have been duly taken; and

(d) The execution of this Agreement and the
operation of the rail freight service will not violate any
statute, rule, regulation, order, writ, injunction or decree
of any court, administrative agency or governmental body.

Section 1502. The Subsidizer. The Subsidizer
represents and warrants the following:

(a) The Subsidizer is duly organized, validly
existing and in good standing under the laws of its domicile;

(b) The Subsidizer has the power and authority to
enter into this Agreement and to carry out its obligations
under this Agreement;

(c) The entering into and performance of this
Agreement on the part of the Subsidizer does not violate any
statute, rule, regulation, order, writ, injunction or
decree of any court, administrative agency or governmental
body;

(d) The Subsidizer has duly and validly acquired
or will acquire the rights to use the rail facilities on the
segments in accordance with Section 304(c) of the RRRA or
through acquisition and has made or will have made those
rights available to ConRail without charge prior to the commencement of the rail freight service specified herein. Copies
of the agreements between owners of the segments comprising
the Rail Facilities and the Subsidizer regarding these
rights will be furnished;

(e) Funds for the payment of the subsidy required
by the Agreement will be obtained or have been authorized
and appropriated to the Subsidizer.

ARTICLE SIXTEEN - GENERAL PROVISIONS

Section 1601. Captions. The captions used in
this Agreement are used for convenience and identification
purposes only and do not form a part of the Agreement.

Section 1602. Entire Agreement. This Agreement
and the Attachments annexed hereto and integrated herewith
contain the entire agreement of the parties and supersede any and
all prior agreements or oral understandings between the
parties.

Section 1603. Amendment. No term or provision of
this Agreement may be changed, waived, discharged or terminated
orally, but only by an instrument in writing signed by the
party against which the enforcement of the change, waiver,
discharge or termination is sought; provided however that
when an emergency situation arises, such as a change in
service frequency or emergency rehabilitation, changes in
this contract may be made orally by authorized representatives of both parties by mutual agreement subject to
immediate confirmation by telegram or other delivered writing.

Section 1604. Choice of Law. This Agreement
shall in all respects be governed by the laws of _____

_____

Section 1605. Notices. Any notice required under
this Agreement may be sent to the parties at the addresses
set forth at the beginning hereof, unless such parties shall
have informed the other party in writing of any change in
that address.

Except as provided in Section 1603 above, all notices, requests, demands and other communications hereunder shall be in writing and shall be deemed to have been duly given if delivered or mailed by certified mail, postage prepaid, to the addresses herein designated or at such other address as may be designated in writing by notice similarly given.

Section 1606. Governmental Approval. Whenever an action of one of the parties is required by the Agreement which action is subject to the approval or consent of a governmental agency, the requirement of this Agreement shall be deemed satisfied if the party has applied for that approval and uses and continues to use its best efforts to obtain such approval or consent without delay.

In the event of termination of this Agreement by reason of the default of Subsidizer, ConRail shall not be required to obtain the consent of any regulatory authority to abandon or discontinue all or any portion of the rail freight service.

Section 1607. Severability. If any term, covenant, condition or provision (or part thereof) of this Agreement or the application thereof to any party or circumstance shall, at any time or to any extent, be invalid or unenforceable, the remainder of this Agreement or the application of such term or provision (or remainder thereof) to parties or circumstances other than those as to which it is held invalid or unenforceable, shall not be affected thereby, and each term, covenant, condition and provision of this Agreement shall be valid and be enforced to the fullest extent permitted by law.

Section 1608. Anti-Discrimination Clause. In

connection with the performance of rail freight services under this agreement, ConRail agrees to comply with the provisions of any state law relating to Anti-Discrimination, comply with the Federal Civil Rights Act of 1964 (78 Stat. 252) and applicable anti-discrimination provisions of the RRRA and the RRRRA.

ARTICLE SEVENTEEN - EFFECTIVE DATE

Section 1701. Effective Date. This Agreement shall become effective on the date on which conveyance pursuant to the Final System Plan becomes effective. The date of such conveyance shall be termed the "Effective Date".

IN WITNESS WHEREOF, the parties hereto have caused this Agreement to be executed and attested by their duly authorized officers on the date and year first above written.

CONSOLIDATED RAIL CORPORATION

ATTEST:

By:_____ (SEAL)

_____

(Subsidizer)

ATTEST:

By:_____ (SEAL)

_____

APPENDIX C
The Penn Central Model Lease

AGREEMENT FOR USE

OF RAIL PROPERTIES

between

Robert W. Blanchette, Richard C. Bond, and
John H. McArthur, Trustees of the property
of Penn Central Transportation Company

and

(_____ state _____)

TABLE OF CONTENTS

AGREEMENT FOR USE OF RAIL PROPERTIES

Agreement, dated as of April 1, 1976, by and between Robert W. Blanchette, Richard C. Bond and John H. McArthur, as Trustees of the Property of Penn Central Transportation Company, Debtor, a railroad corporation in reorganization under Section 77 of Bankruptcy Act and not individually (the Trustees) and _____(the Subsidizer).

WHEREAS, this Agreement results from an offer by the Subsidizer of a "rail service continuation payment" in accordance with Section 304(c) (2)(A) of the Regional Rail Reorganization Act of 1973, as amended, 87 Stat. 985 (1974) (codified in scattered sections of 45 USCA), (hereinafter referred to as the "Act").

WHEREAS, the offer of payment was made in order to maintain rail service over certain rail lines located in the State of _____ which are under the ownership or control of said Trustees, as more specifically defined in ARTICLE I hereof:

WHEREAS, the parties hereto have not been able to reach agreement on a fair and reasonable rental or return on the value of the Trustees' properties and the annual charges in the amount set forth herein is the basis for a charge for the use of such properties, which the Trustees are compelled to make available for subsidy operation by reason of the Act; and

WHEREAS, the Trustees do not agree that such charges constitute a reasonable return on the value of said properties and the Trustees therefore have represented to the Subsidizer that the taking and use of their property for operation under Section 304 of the Act, 90 Stat. 133 (1976), 45 USCA Sec. 744 (1976) for the charges herein provided, constitutes a taking of property of the Trustees without just compensation in contravention of the Constitution of the United States of America and that the Trustees expressly reserve the right to pursue any and all remedies available to them to recover the right to pursue any and all remedies available to them to recover from the United States of America or any of its instrumentalities and agencies, except the Subsidizer, a fair and reasonable compensation for such taking and use of its properties;

NOW, THEREFORE, in consideration of the mutual promises contained herein, the parties hereto, with the intention of being bound hereby, agree as follows:

ARTICLE I.   The Properties

The Trustees hereby agree that subject to the provisions of this Agreement, including, but without limitation, the provisions of ARTICLE VII herein, the Subsidizer is permitted the exclusive use of the following rail facilities for railroad operation. These lines, facilities, buildings and appurtenances thereto shall be referred to herein both collectively and individually as the Properties.

USRA Line No.	Terminal Points From	To	Mileposts From	To	Route Miles

ARTICLE II.   Payments

A. Right-of-Way and Track Facilities

The Subsidizer shall pay for usage of main track, sidings, yards, buildings, enginehouses, signal systems and other necessary track facilities on the Properties the sum of $206.25 per month per route mile of line. Such payments to be made on the 15th day of each month for the preceding calendar month, except that the payment due for the period from April 1, 1976 through the end of the calendar month next preceding the date of execution of this Agreement shall be made within sixty (60) days after the date of approval of this Agreement by the United States District Court for the Eastern District of Pennsylvania.

B. Taxes and Assessments

1. Except with respect to such property or facilities as to which the Trustees retain profits or rents thereon pursuant to ARTICLE VII. B. herein which are payable to the Trustees by others than the Subsidizer, in which event there shall be a pro-rating (where appropriate) of the taxes and/or utility, or other expenses, the Subsidizer shall also pay so long as this Agreement continues in effect, any and all taxes, assessments, sewer rentals, service charges and special assessments for public improvements and other governmental impositions and charges that shall, during the term of this Agreement, be charged, levied, assessed, imposed or become due and payable, with respect to the Properties or any part thereof, or any improvements thereon, under or by virtue of all present or future laws, ordinances, rules or regulations of any Federal, State, County, or municipal government and of all other governmental authorities whatsoever (all of which shall hereafter be referred to as "Taxes") and of sewer rents and charges for water, gas, electricity, and other utility services, furnished to the Properties or the occupants thereof during the term of this Agreement (hereinafter referred to as "Utility Expenses"). The Subsidizer agrees that the Trustees may, with the consent of the Subsidizer, or at the termination of this Agreement or in the event of a tax sale, (unless the subsidizer defends against the same), at the option of the Trustees, make direct payments of any and all bills for the aforesaid charges, and in the case of such payment, the Subsidizer shall repay the same to Trustees.

2. The Subsidizer shall have the right to contest all taxes and utility expenses by legal proceedings, or in such other manner as it may deem suitable.

3. Trustees covenant and agree that if there shall be any refunds or rebates received on account of the taxes or utility expenses paid during the term of this Agreement by the Subsidizer under the provisions of this Agreement, such refund or rebate shall belong to the Subsidizer. Trustees will, upon the request of the Subsidizer, sign any receipts which may be necessary to secure the payment of any such refund or rebate. In the event that Trustees fail to pay over to the Subsidizer such refund or rebate, Trustees specifically authorize the Subsidizer to deduct the amount of said refund or rebate from the next payment due.

C. Joint Facility Agreements, Trackage Rights, Etc.

Subsidizer hereby agrees to reimburse Trustees for all charges
incurred and all costs chargeable during the term of this
Agreement pursuant to any Joint Facility and/or Trackage Rights
Agreements, etc., appurtenant to the lines and facilities
operated. In return for this, Subsidizer shall succeed to all
rights of the Trustees thereunder.

D. Federal Funding

It is understood and agreed by the parties hereto that the promises to pay contained herein are conditional upon the availability and receipt by the Subsidizer of Federal appropriations
for the purposes herein comtemplated. Provided, however, that
failure to make cash payments when due, regardless of cause,
shall constitute a default under Article XV herein.

ARTICLE III.   Non-Prejudicial Effect Of Payments

Because of the exigencies created by the Act the parties have agreed
to the payments set forth in ARTICLE II, above, for an interim
period constituting the term of this Agreement.
The acceptance of any agreed-upon payments for the use of the
Properties is for the sole purpose of assuring continued rail service and is not to be construed by any person as an admission or
agreement by the Trustees that the payments imply a valuation that
is sufficient to satisfy the constitutional minimum which the
Trustees should receive for the use of the Properties.

In keeping with the provisions of Section 304(d)(4) of the Act, the
providing of Federal financial assistance is not to be construed as
an admission, agreement or acquiescence by the Trustees or by the
Federal Railroad Administration (FRA), the United States Department
of Transportation (DOT), or the United States as to the value of the
Properties, or as to an appropriate theory of valuation for rail
properties in general. The payments prescribed herein for the use
of the Properties shall be of no precedential effect whatsoever, and
no one of the Trustees, the Subsidizer, the United States or any
other person or entity will attempt to use the level of these
payments or the method by which they were derived or any payments
made upon the exercise of the right first refusal contained in
ARTICLE VII herein in any litigation between the Trustees and the
United States or any other person or entity involving the
Constitutional minimum which the Trustees should receive for the
Properties or other rail properties.

ARTICLE IV.   Determination of Payments To Be Made During
                 Extensions Or Renewals

In the determination of the amount of payments to be made upon any
extensions or renewals hereof, unless after negotiations the parties
are able to agree on the basis or the amount of such future
payments, either party may, during or after the term of this
Agreement, seek a determination of the payments to which the owners
are entitled before an appropriate forum. The parties agree that
the payments made hereunder are not relevant evidence of the value
of the Properties.

In addition, in determining the amount of such payments, no value shall be ascribed to any improvements or replacements made pursuant to ARTICLE V herein either to increase or decrease the payments to be made and the Properties shall be valued as if such improvements or replacements had not been made. Provided, however, if the Subsidizer has not maintained the Properties in accordance with ARTICLE XII herein, no reduction in value shall be permitted for the condition of the Properties. Provided, further, however, if the Properties are leased to a party other than the Subsidizer, the Subsidizer may request that any additional value of the Properties attributable to the aforesaid improvements or replacements be considered in the establishment of fair rental values for the Properties, in which event, an aliquot share of the rentals so determined shall be paid to the Subsidizer either in the form of a credit toward other sums owed by the Subsidizer to the Trustees or in cash.

ARTICLE V.   Improvements, Title, Proceeds From Sales or Lease

The Subsidizer shall have the right to make, at its own expense, improvements for railroad purposes on the Properties during the term of this Agreement subject to the following terms and conditions:

A. Any and all replacements installed by the Subsidizer shall be the property of the Subsidizer and the net salvage value of any improvement made by the Subsidizer in excess of the net salvage value of the asset it improves shall belong to the Subsidizer.

B. Where such improvement requires or involves the replacement of an asset in place as of the date of this Agreement, at the option of the Subsidizer, either the salvaged material shall be made available to the Trustees for disposition by them, or the net salvage value of the replaced asset shall be paid over to the Trustees for disposition in accordance with applicable orders of the United States District Court for the Eastern District of Pennsylvania.

C. Upon the authorized termination of railroad service and subsequent disposal of the Properties:

1. If the Properties are sold with rail facilities intact to other than the Subsidizer, the Subsidizer shall join in executing any documents necessary to effect such sale and shall receive payment from the net proceeds, (either in the form of a credit toward other sums owed by the Subsidizer to the Trustees or in cash), of the aliquot share of such net proceeds attributable to: a. the net salvage value of improvements made by it in excess of the net salvage of the assets improved; and b. the net salvage value of any replacements made by the Subsidizer where the Trustees have received the net salvage value of the asset replaced as set forth in ARTICLE V. B., above.

2. Unless the Subsidizer purchases the Properties during the term, the Trustees may, unless otherwise prohibited by law, dispose of the rail assets and the right-of-way separately. In which event, upon notice of the Trustees' intent to dispose of the rail assets separately, the Subsidizer may, at its option, and upon notice to the Trustees, either remove the assets solely belonging to the Subsidizer or request the Trustees to dispose of such assets together with assets on the Properties belonging

solely to the Trustees and assets belonging jointly to the
Trustees and the Subsidizer. The Subsidizer shall have
sixty (60) days after receipt of the above Trustees' notice
in which to elect which option to pursue.

    a. If the Subsidizer requests the Trustees to dispose
of rail assets belonging solely to the Subsidizer
together with Trustees' assets and jointly owned
assets, the Subdidizer shall join in executing any
documents necessary to effect such disposal and shall
be paid from the net proceeds resulting therefrom
(either in the form of a credit towards other sums owed
by the Subsidizer to the Trustees or in cash) the aliquot share of such net proceeds attributable to:

    i. the net salvage value of improvements made by it in
excess of the net salvage value of the assets improved;
and

    ii. the net salvage value of any replacements made by
the Subsidizer where the Trustees have received the net
salvage value of the asset replaced as set forth in
ARTICLE V. B., above.

b. If the Subsidizer elects to remove assets belonging
solely to the Subsidizer:

    i. The Subsidizer shall remove them within sixty (60)
days of giving notice of such election to the Trustees
or within any shorter time that the Trustees are obli-
gated to remove all such rail assets because of the
sale of the underlying Properties. If the underlying
Properties are not sold prior to removal of rail assets
solely owned by the Trustees and jointly owned rail
assets, storage charges may be assessed by the Trustees
against the Subsidizer for any Subsidizer-owned assets
remaining after the above sixty-day period (or after
removal and/or sale of all other rail assets, whichever
occurs later).

    ii. The Subsidizer shall join in executing any docu-
ments necessary to effect the disposal of any jointly
owned assets and shall receive from the net proceeds
therefrom, (either in the form of a credit towards
other sums owed by the Subsidizer to the Trustees or in
cash) the aliquot share of such net proceeds attributable to the net salvage value of improvements made by
it in excess of the net salvage value of the assets
improved.

    iii. In the event any replacement or improvement made
by the Subsidizer (and owned by the Subsidizer as set
forth in this ARTICLE V) has a cost of removal greater
than the salvage value of such replacement or improvement upon removal by the Trustees after providing the
Subsidizer an opportunity to remove same as set forth
in this ARTICLE V, the Subsidizer shall pay to the
Trustees such excess cost of removal.

D. The Subsidizer shall notify the Trustees in writing of any
and all improvements or replacements made pursuant to this
Agreement and shall keep all necessary property account and
provide copies of all plans, costs, lists of materials used and

any other data required or necessary to establish the extent of
any joint ownership of improvements as described above,
ownership of replacements as described above and the respective
values thereof. The Subsidizer shall also keep a complete
accounting of any and all assets removed from the Properties
and sold and the values received therefor. The Trustees shall
have the right, upon reasonable notice and during normal business hours to inspect and audit the Subsidizer's books,
accounts and records pertaining to the Properties. Such right
of inspection and audit shall continue for a period of three
years beyond the termination of the Agreement.

ARTICLE VI.   Sidetracks

A. From time to time, the Subsidizer or an industry may wish
to establish or relocate sidetracks on the Properties. Plans
for such proposed sidetracks shall be submitted to the Trustees
for their approval, which approval shall not unreasonably be
withheld. Grounds for disapproval shall be limited to: (a)
failure to comply with the Trustees' engineering standards; or,
(b) the proposed sidetrack would interfere with the sale of the
Properties or other rights therein as contemplated in ARTICLE
VII herein.

B. For the purpose of establishing guidelines for the determination of whether a proposed sidetrack interferes with
possible sale of the Properties or other rights therein as contemplated in ARTICLE VII herein, it is agreed that, in general,
where the property line of the Properties is more than twenty
(20) feet beyond the limits of the outside rail, any use of
this additional property by the Subsidizer or an industry must
be by a lease or purchase of an easement. If rental is
charged, or an easement sold, to permit construction of a
sidetrack, such sidetracks constructed on property leased by an
industry, or on property over which such industry has purchased
an easement, shall be the property of such industry.

C. In addition to the charges and taxes to be paid for the use
of Properties as provided in ARTICLE II herein, it is agreed
that there will be added thereto the cost of any sidetrack
refunds the Trustees may be compelled to pay, after duly
defending the action, by the final judgement of any court of
competent jurisdiction arising by reason of freight moved to
and from the sidetracks of shippers on the Properties during
the terms of this Agreement.

ARTICLE VII.   Sales, Leases, etc. and Other Uses of the
                 Properties; Reserved Rights

A. Sales, Leases, etc.

   1. It is understood and agreed that during the term of
   this Agreement or during any period of time thereafter that
   the Properties are continued in operation under the subsidy
   program as required by the Act, the Trustees shall not sell
   or lease all or part of the Properties rights to any longitudinal occupancies for pipe lines, power lines, energy
   corridors, or the commercial development of air, sub-
   terranean, or surface rights or grant easements with
   respect to any of the foregoing without first giving the
   Subsidizer notice in writing that either or both the
   Properties and the aforesaid rights or any portion thereof,

are offered for sale to the Subsidizer at the price or prices stated in said notice. The Subsidizer shall have a period of ninety (90) days after receipt of said notice to purchase or lease either or both the Properties and the aforesaid rights or the portion thereof or acquire easements with respect thereto at the price or prices stated in said notice.

2. In the event the Subsidizer fails to purchase or lease either or both the Properties or the aforesaid rights, or any portion thereof as offered in said notice or easements with respect thereto, within said ninety (90) day period at the price or prices stated in the aforesaid notice, the Trustees shall have the right to sell or lease either or both the Properties and the aforesaid rights, or any portion thereof as offered in said notice, or grant easements with respect thereto, to any person or persons, without further notice to the Subsidizer, at a price not less than the price stated in the aforesaid notice to the Subsidizer, provided, however, such sale, lease or easement with respect to the same shall be subject to the Subsidizer's right to continue its use of the Properties under and pursuant to the terms of this Agreement or during any period thereafter in which the operation of the Properties is continued under the subsidy program as required by the Act.

3. It is also understood and agreed that the Trustees shall not sell or lease the Properties or the aforesaid rights, or grant easements with respect thereto, at a price less than the price stated in the aforesaid notice to the Subsidizer without giving the Subsidizer notice in writing of the price at which all or part of the Properties or the aforesaid rights, or easements with respect thereto, are offered for sale. The Subsidizer shall have a period of sixty (60) days after receipt of said notice to purchase or lease either or both the Properties and the aforesaid rights, or the portions thereof offered for sale, or acquire easements with respect thereto, at the price or prices stated in said notice.

4. In the event the Subsidizer fails to purchase or lease either or both the Properties or the aforesaid rights or any portion thereof as offered in said notice, or acquire easements with respect thereto, within said sixty (60) day period at the price or prices stated in said notice, the Trustees shall have the right to sell or lease either or both the Properties and the aforesaid rights or any portion thereof as offered in said notice, or grant easements with respect thereto to any person or persons, without further notice to the Subsidizer, provided, however, such sale, lease or easement with respect to the same shall be subject to the Subsidizer's right to continue its use of the Properties under and pursuant to the terms of this Agreement or during any period thereafter in which the operation of the Properties is continued under the subsidy program as required by the Act.

5. Notwithstanding any other provision in this ARTICLE to the contrary, the Trustees may at any time sell or lease all or any part of the Properties and/or the aforesaid rights with the written consent of the Subsidizer.

B. Rights Reserved by Trustees

The Trustees reserve the exclusive right, title and interest,
including the right to collect the same, in and to the rents,
profits and income payable or resulting from any and all
existing easements, licenses, privileges and rights granted to
others for the use of the Properties including, but without
limitation of the foregoing, leases of property or facilities,
rights of way, longitudinal occupancies or crossings of the
Properties for high power and other wire lines, water, sewer,
gas, oil, coal slurry or other pipe lines, drilling or mining
for gas, oil, coal or other minerals; provided, however, taxes
or utility expenses attributable to such uses and occupancies
will be pro-rated with the subsidizer as provided in ARTICLE II
herein.

ARTICLE VIII.   Indemnification and Insurance

A. The Subsidizer agrees to include in its operating agreement
with its Operator a provision requiring the Operator to indemnify and insure both the Trustees and Subsidizer from and
against any loss, damage, destruction, injury or death which
occurs as a result of the management, control, use or operations of the Operator of rail freight services and rail freight
facilities appertaining thereto and to indemnify and hold the
Subsidizer and the Trustees or owners of the rail facilities
harmless from any such loss or liability including all related
costs and counsel fees, unless such loss, damage, destruction,
injury or death occurs as a result of maintenance or rehabilitation performed after the effective date, which was neither
undertaken by the Operator nor approved on completion by the
Operator.

B. The Subsidizer shall require its Operator to have the
Trustees named as an additional party insured under the
Operator's policy or policies of insurance and furnish the
Trustees with a certificate of insurance on or before the date
of execution of this Agreement. The policies shall be endorsed
to provide that such policy or policies shall not be canceled,
changed or modified without sixty (60) days prior written
notice to the Trustees.

C. Subsidizer shall also furnish the Trustees on or before the
date of execution of this Agreement with a certified copy of
its agreement with its Operator containing the provision set
forth in (A.) above.

D. Subsidizer's full compliance with the provisions of this
ARTICLE VIII shall absolve Subsidizer from any liability for
such injury or damage upon acceptance by the Trustees of said
Indemnification Agreement which acceptance is given contem-
poraneously with the execution of this Agreement by the
Trustees.

ARTICLE IX.   Unconditional Obligation To Make Payments
                 in Cash

The Subsidizer hereby acknowledges that under the Act and the Grant
Agreement between the Subsidizer and the Secretary of Transportation
of the United States, acting by and through the Federal Railroad

Administrator (Administrator), the Subsidizer is not entitled to a
grant of funds or to initiate cash drawdowns against any letter of
credit issued by the Administrator to fund payments to the Trustees
for a reasonable return on the value of the Properties unless such
funds are paid to the Trustees in accordance with the Terms and provisions of Section 110 of the aforementioned Grant Agreement. A
copy of said Section 110 is attached hereto as Appendix A.
Subsidizer, therefore, expressly covenants and agrees that all
payments due the Trustees here under shall be paid in cash when due
and disbursed to the Trustees by the Subsidizer forthwith upon
receipt from the Administrator in accordance with the Grant
Agreement and shall not be withheld for any reason whatsoever and
shall not be subjected to any set-offs or counterclaims based upon
claims of any kind or nature whatsoever, including, but without
limitation, claims for taxes or any governmental claims, assessments
or charges asserted by Subsidizer against the Trustees.

ARTICLE X.   Condition of Roadbed, Track, Structure and
               Facilities, Warranties

The Trustees specifically make no warranties concerning the condition of the roadbed, track, structures or other rail facilities,
(such as communication and signal facilities) and on the Properties,
either as complying with any track standards of the Federal Railroad
Administration or with respect to fitness for purpose and the
Subsidizer accepts them "as is".

ARTICLE XI.   Compliance With Statutes and Regulations

    A. Subsidizer agrees to require its Operator to conform to all
    Federal and State statutes and regulatory requirements and
    orders relating to rail services performed on the Properties
    and to hold the Trustees harmless against all costs of
    compliance or penalties or other liabilities for damages or
    other consequences for any failure to adhere to such statutes
    or regulatory requirements.

    B. Subsidizer specifically acknowledges that certain
    "Supplemental Report and Order" dated December 31, 1975, in
    "Federal Railroad Administration Docket No. RST-1, Waiver
    Petition No. 17 Penn Central Transportation Company" and that
    compliance therewith is covered by this covenant.

ARTICLE XII.   Subsidizer's Maintenance Obligation

Subsidizer shall have the sole obligation to maintain the Properties
during the term of the lease and shall return the premises to
Trustees at the end of the term in as good condition as received,
reasonable wear and tear expected.

ARTICLE XIII. Force Majeure

    A. In the event of some occurrence which may be deemed "Force
    Majeure" such as flood, tropical storm, hurricane, etc., which
    results in rendering the Properties inoperable as a railroad
    without major reconstruction, Subsidizer may, at its option:
    (a) repair the Properties to render them operable; or, (b) ter-
    minate this Agreement without placing the premises in as good
    and complete condition as received as required by ARTICLE XII

above. Provided, however, if the Subsidizer elects option (b)
herein, and if, as a result of such Force Majeure, any bridges,
rail, other track material, ties, ballast, etc., or any portion
thereof, contained in the Properties, are deposited in rivers,
streams, or watercourses or on the property of another, the
Subsidizer agrees, at no cost to the Trustees, to remove any
such bridges, etc., from any such rivers, streams, watercourses
or property of another and place such items on the right-of-way
of the Properties for subsequent disposal by the Trustees.

    B. It is understood and agreed by the parties hereto that the
promises to place bridges, etc. on the Trustees' rights-of-way,
pursuant to option (b) set forth in A. above, are conditioned
upon the availability and receipt by the Subsidizer, of Federal
appropriations, under any program, which may be used for the
purpose contemplated.

ARTICLE XIV.   Conditions Precedent

This Agreement will become effective as of the date first set forth
above upon:

    A. Approval of the United States District Court for the
Eastern District of Pennsylvania (Court). The Trustees hereby
agree to submit the Agreement for such approval promptly upon
execution; and

    B. Approval by the Federal Railroad Administration for funding
pursuant to Title IV of the Regional Rail Reorganization Act of
1973, as amended.

    (Subsidizer may, at its discretion, waive this condition B.)

    C. Subsidizer shall have furnished the Trustees evidence
satisfactory to the Trustees that Subsidizer has a duly executed operating agreement with its Operating Railroad containing the indemnity and insurance provisions referred to in
ARTICLE VIII above.

    D. The Subsidizer shall have delivered to the Trustees the
certificate of insurance referred to in ARTICLE VIII above.

ARTICLE XV.   Default

    The following are events of default by Subsidizer:

    A. Failure to make payments in cash when due;

    B. Bankruptcy of Subsidizer;

    C. Failure to procure and keep in effect the indemnification
agreement and insurance pursuant to ARTICLE VIII herein.

ARTICLE XVI.   Term

This Agreement shall commence on the date above written and shall
terminate on March 31, 1978 unless sooner terminated pursuant to
ARTICLE XVII herein.

ARTICLE XVII.   Termination

A. By Subsidizer

Subsidizer may terminate this Agreement in whole, or with respect to any segment or part thereof, prior to the end of the term upon thirty (30) days' written notice to the Trustees.

B. By Trustees

The Trustees may terminate this Agreement upon any default by Subsidizer as set forth in ARTICLE XV. herein by giving Subsidizer thirty (30) days' written notice. Provided, however, that if subsidizer cures such default within such 30 days, such termination shall not be effective.

ARTICLE XVIII.   Waiver

Failure of any of the parties to assert any right or declare any default hereunder shall not act as a waiver of such right or default and shall not preclude such assertion or declaration at a later date or upon a recurrence of violation of such rights or event of default. Insofar as legally possible, Subsidizer also waives any and all rights it may have pursuant to any statutes restricting the contractual rights and remedies of the Trustees.

ARTICLE XIX.   Expiration; Releases

Upon expiration of the Agreement, the Subsidizer shall provide releases of any and all liens and encumbrances including, but without limitation, tax liens and mechanics liens, etc., which have or may have attached to the Properties as a result of Subsidizer's operations or other activities, notwithstanding Subsidizer's rights under subdivision 2 ARTICLE II. B. herein.

ARTICLE XX.   Assignment

This Agreement or any right hereunder may be assigned by the Subsidizer with the written consent of the Trustees, which consent shall not be unreasonably withheld.

ARTICLE XXI.   Condemnation

If the Properties, or any part thereof, is taken by eminent domain, this Agreement shall not expire, but the payment shall be appropriately adjusted as of that date to reflect the value, as of the date of commencement hereof of the portion of the Properties not taken. The Trustees shall have the right to receive any and all proceeds of such award except for the proceeds attributable to such assets to which the Subsidizer has title pursuant to ARTICLE V hereof.

ARTICLE XXII.   Quiet Enjoyment

Subsidizer, upon making the monthly payments prescribed herein and all other sums and charges to be paid by it as herein provided, and observing and keeping all covenants, warranties, agreements and conditions of this Agreement on its part to be kept, shall quietly have and enjoy the Properties during the term of this Agreement or any extensions thereof, without hindrance or molestation by the Trustees, their agents or employees.

ARTICLE XXIII.   Governing Law

This Agreement and the performance thereof shall be governed, interpreted, construed and regulated by the laws of the State of
_____.

ARTICLE XXIV.   Subordination

This Agreement is subordinate to all Federal laws, and, except as provided in ARTICLE V herein, to all liens, mortgages and other encumbrances existing on the property as of the date of its execution.

ARTICLE XXV.   Required Standard Clauses

The Trustees agree to comply with the terms of the state and federal required standard clauses attached hereto as Appendix B and made a part hereof.

ARTICLE XXVI.   Notices

Any request, demand, authorization, direction, notice, consent, waiver or other document provided or permitted by this Agreement to be made upon, given or furnished to, or filed with one party by the other party shall be in writing and shall be delivered by hand or by registered or certified mail with return receipt requested, postage prepaid, in an envelope addressed as follows:

If to Trustees: E.L. Claypole
                   Penn Central Transportation Company
                   Suite 2900
                   1700 Market Street
                   Philadelphia, PA 19103

APPENDIX D
The Regional Rail
Reorganization Act of 1973

Public Law 93-236
93rd Congress, H. R. 9142
January 2, 1974

𝔄n 𝔄ct

87 STAT. 985

To authorize and direct the maintenance of adequate and efficient rail services in the Midwest and Northeast region of the United States, and for other purposes.

Be it enacted by the Senate and House of Representatives of the United States of America in Congress assembled, That this Act, divided into titles and sections according to the following table of contents, may be cited as the "Regional Rail Reorganization Act of 1973".

Regional Rail Reorganization Act of 1973.

TABLE OF CONTENTS

87 STAT. 986

DECLARATION OF POLICY

Sec. 101. (a) Findings.—The Congress finds and declares that—

(1) Essential rail service in the midwest and northeast region of the United States is provided by railroads which are today insolvent and attempting to undergo reorganization under the Bankruptcy Act.

30 Stat. 544.
11 USC 1 note.

(2) This essential rail service is threatened with cessation or significant curtailment because of the inability of the trustees of such railroads to formulate acceptable plans of reorganization. This rail service is operated over rail properties which were acquired for a public use, but which have been permitted to deteriorate and now require extensive rehabilitation and modernization.

(3) The public convenience and necessity require adequate and efficient rail service in this region and throughout the Nation to meet the needs of commerce, the national defense, the environment, and the service requirements of passengers, United States mail, shippers, States and their political subdivisions, and consumers.

(4) Continuation and improvement of essential rail service in this region is also necessary to preserve and maintain adequate national rail services and an efficient national rail transportation system.

(5) Rail service and rail transportation offer economic and environmental advantages with respect to land use, air pollution, noise levels, energy efficiency and conservation, resource allocation, safety, and cost per ton-mile of movement to such extent that the preservation and maintenance of adequate and efficient rail service is in the national interest.

(6) These needs cannot be met without substantial action by the Federal Government.

(b) Purposes.—It is therefore declared to be the purpose of Congress in this Act to provide for—

(1) the identification of a rail service system in the midwest and northeast region which is adequate to meet the needs and service requirements of this region and of the national rail transportation system;

(2) the reorganization of railroads in this region into an economically viable system capable of providing adequate and efficient rail service to the region;

(3) the establishment of the United States Railway Association, with enumerated powers and responsibilities;

(4) the establishment of the Consolidated Rail Corporation, with enumerated powers and responsibilities;

(5) assistance to States and local and regional transportation authorities for continuation of local rail services threatened with cessation; and

(6) necessary Federal financial assistance at the lowest possible cost to the general taxpayer.

DEFINITIONS

Sec. 102. As used in this Act, unless the context otherwise requires—

(1) "Association" means the United States Railway Association, established under section 201 of this Act;

(2) "Commission" means the Interstate Commerce Commission;

(3) "Corporation" means the Consolidated Rail Corporation required to be established under section 301 of this Act;

87 STAT. 987

(4) "effective date of the final system plan" means the date on which the final system plan or any revised final system plan is deemed approved by Congress, in accordance with section 208 of this Act;

(5) "employee stock ownership plan" means a technique of corporate finance that uses a stock bonus trust or a company stock money purchase pension trust which qualifies under section 401 (a) of the Internal Revenue Code of 1954 (26 U.S.C. 401(a)) in connection with the financing of corporate improvements, transfers in the ownership of corporate assets, and other capital requirements of a corporation and which is designed to build beneficial equity ownership of shares in the employer corporation into its employees substantially in proportion to their relative incomes, without requiring any cash outlay, any reduction in pay or other employee benefits, or the surrender of any other rights on the part of such employees. 68A Stat. 134; 76 Stat. 809.

(6) "final system plan" means the plan of reorganization for the restructure, rehabilitation, and modernization of railroads in reorganization prepared pursuant to section 206 and approved pursuant to section 208 of this Act;

(7) "includes" and variants thereof should be read as if the phrase "but is not limited to" were also set forth;

(8) "Office" means the Rail Services Planning Office established under section 205 of this Act;

(9) "profitable railroad" means a railroad which is not a railroad in reorganization. The term does not include the Corporation, the National Railroad Passenger Corporation, or a railroad leased, operated, or controlled by a railroad in reorganization in the region;

(10) "rail properties" means assets or rights owned, leased, or otherwise controlled by a railroad which are used or useful in rail transportation service; except that the term, when used in conjunction with the phase "railroads leased, operated, or controlled by a railroad in reorganization", shall not include assets or rights owned, leased, or otherwise controlled by a Class I railroad which is not wholly owned, operated, or leased by a railroad in reorganization but is controlled by a railroad in reorganization;

(11) "railroad" means a common carrier by railroad as defined in section 1(3) of part I of the Interstate Commerce Act (49 U.S.C. 1(3)). The term includes the Corporation and the National Railroad Passenger Corporation; 41 Stat. 474.

(12) "railroad in reorganization" means a railroad which is subject to a bankruptcy proceeding and which has not been determined by a court to be reorganizable or not subject to reorganization pursuant to this Act as prescribed in section 207(b) of this Act. A "bankruptcy proceeding" includes a proceeding pursuant to section 77 of the Bankruptcy Act (11 U.S.C. 205) and an equity receivership or equivalent proceeding; 49 Stat. 911; 76 Stat. 572.

(13) "Region" means the States of Maine, New Hampshire, Vermont, Massachusetts, Connecticut, Rhode Island, New York, New Jersey, Pennsylvania, Delaware, Maryland, Virginia, West Virginia, Ohio, Indiana, Michigan, and Illinois; the District of Columbia; and those portions of contiguous States in which are located rail properties owned or operated by railroads doing business primarily in the aforementioned jurisdictions (as determined by the Commission by order);

(14) "Secretary" means the Secretary of Transportation or his delegate, unless the context indicates otherwise; and

(15) "State" means any State or the District of Columbia.

87 STAT. 988

TITLE II—UNITED STATES RAILWAY ASSOCIATION

FORMATION AND STRUCTURE

SEC. 201. (a) ESTABLISHMENT.—There is established, in accordance with the provisions of this section, an incorporated nonprofit association to be known as the United States Railway Association.

(b) ADMINISTRATION.—The Association shall be directed by a Board of Directors. The individuals designated, pursuant to subsection (d) (2) of this section, as the Government members of such Board shall be deemed the incorporators of the Association and shall take whatever steps are necessary to establish the Association, including filing of articles of incorporation, and serving as an acting Board of Directors for a period of not more than 45 days after the date of incorporation of the Association.

(c) STATUS.—The Association shall be a government corporation of the District of Columbia subject, to the extent not inconsistent with this title, to the District of Columbia Nonprofit Corporation Act (D.C. Code, sec. 29–1001 et seq.). Except as otherwise provided, employees of the Association shall not be deemed employees of the Federal Government. The Association shall have succession until dissolved by Act of Congress, shall maintain its principal office in the District of Columbia, and shall be deemed to be a resident of the District of Columbia with respect to venue in any legal proceeding.

76 Stat. 265.

(d) BOARD OF DIRECTORS.—The Board of Directors of the Association shall consist of 11 individuals, as follows:

(1) the Chairman, a qualified individual who shall be appointed by the President, by and with the advice and consent of the Senate;

(2) three Government members, who shall be the Secretary, the Chairman of the Commission, and the Secretary of the Treasury, or their duly authorized representatives; and

(3) seven nongovernment members, who shall be appointed by the President, by and with the advice and consent of the Senate, on the following basis—

(A) one to be selected from a list of qualified individuals recommended by the Association of American Railroads or its successor who are representatives of profitable railroads;

(B) one to be selected from a list of qualified individuals recommended by the American Federation of Labor and Congress of Industrial Organizations or its successor who are representative of railroad labor;

(C) one to be selected from a list of qualified individuals recommended by the National Governors Conference;

(D) one to be selected from a list of qualified individuals recommended by the National League of Cities and Conference of Mayors;

(E) two to be selected from lists of qualified individuals recommended by shippers and organizations representative of significant shipping interests including small shippers;

(F) one to be selected from lists of qualified individuals recommended by financial institutions, the financial community, and recognized financial leaders.

As used in this paragraph, a list of qualified individuals shall consist of not less than three individuals.

Except for the members appointed under paragraphs (1) and (3) (A), (B), (E), and (F), no member of the Board may have any employment or other direct financial relationship with any railroad.

Compensation.

A member of the Board who is not otherwise an employee of the Fed-

87 STAT. 989

eral Government may receive $300 per diem when engaged in the actual performance of his duties plus reimbursement for travel, subsistence, and other necessary expenses incurred in the performance of such duties.

(e) TERMS OF OFFICE.—The terms of office of the nongovernment members of the Board of Directors of the Association first taking office shall expire as designated by the President at the time of nomination—two at the end of the second year; two at the end of the fourth year; and three at the end of the sixth year. The term of office of the Chairman of such Board shall be 6 years. Successors to members of such Board shall be appointed in the same manner as the original members and, except in the case of government members, shall have terms of office expiring 6 years from the date of expiration of the terms for which their predecessors were appointed. Any individual appointed to fill a vacancy occurring prior to the expiration of any term of office shall be appointed for the remainder of that term.

(f) QUORUM.—Beginning 45 days after the date of incorporation of the Association, six members of the Board, including three of the nongovernment members, shall constitute a quorum for the transaction of any function of the Association.

(g) PRESIDENT.—The Board of Directors of the Association, upon the recommendation of the Secretary, shall appoint a qualified individual to serve as the President of the Association at the pleasure of the Board. The President of the Association, subject to the direction of the Board, shall manage and supervise the affairs of the Association.

(h) EXECUTIVE COMMITTEE.—The Board of Directors of the Association shall have an executive committee which shall consist of the Chairman of the Board, the Secretary, the Chairman of the Commission, and two other members who shall be selected by the members of the Board.

(i) MISCELLANEOUS.—(1) The Association shall have a seal which shall be judicially recognized.

(2) The Administrator of General Services shall furnish the Association with such offices, equipment, supplies, and services as he is authorized to furnish to any other agency or instrumentality of the United States.

(3) The Secretary is authorized to transfer to the Association or the Corporation rights in intellectual property which are directly related to the conduct of the functions of the Association or the Corporation, to the extent that the Federal Government has such rights and to the extent that transfer is necessary to carry out the purposes of this Act.

(j) USE OF NAMES.—No person, except the Association, shall hereafter use the words "United States Railway Association" as a name for any business purpose. No person, except the corporation directed to be established under section 301 of this Act, shall hereafter use the words "Consolidated Rail Corporation" as a name for any business purpose. Violations of these provisions may be enjoined by any court of general jurisdiction in an action commenced by the Association or the Corporation. In any such action, the Association or the Corporation Penalty. may recover any actual damages flowing from such violation, and, in addition, shall be entitled to punitive damages (regardless of the existence or nonexistence of actual damage) in an amount not to exceed $100 for each day during which such violation was committed. The district courts of the United States shall have jurisdiction over actions brought under this subsection, without regard to the amount in controversy or the citizenship of the parties.

87 STAT. 990

GENERAL POWERS AND DUTIES OF THE ASSOCIATION

Sec. 202. (a) General.—To carry out the purposes of this Act, the Association is authorized to—

(1) engage in the preparation and implementation of the final system plan;

Post, p. 1000.

(2) issue obligations under section 210 of this title and make loans under section 211 of this title;

(3) provide assistance to States and local or regional transportation authorities in accordance with section 403 of this Act;

(4) sue and be sued, complain and defend, in the name of the Association and through its own attorneys; adopt, amend, and repeal bylaws governing the operation of the Association and such rules and regulations as are necessary to carry out the authority granted under this Act; conduct its affairs, carry on operations, and maintain offices;

(5) appoint, fix the compensation, and assign the duties of such attorneys, agents, consultants, and other full- and part-time employees as it deems necessary or appropriate; except that (1) no officer of the Association, including the Chairman, may receive compensation at a rate in excess of that prescribed for level I of the Executive Schedule under section 5312 of title 5, United States

80 Stat. 460;
84 Stat. 776.

Code; and (2) no individual may hold a position in violation of regulations which the Secretary shall establish to avoid conflicts of interest and to protect the interests of the public;

(6) acquire and hold such real and personal property as it deems necessary or appropriate in the exercise of its responsibilities under this Act, and to dispose of any such property held by it;

(7) consult with the Secretary of the Army and the Chief of Engineers and request the assistance of the Corps of Engineers, and the Secretary of the Army may direct the Corps of Engineers to cooperate fully with the Association, the Corporation, or any entity designated in accordance with section 206(c)(1)(C) in order to carry out the purposes of this Act;

(8) consult on an ongoing basis with the Chairman of the Federal Trade Commission and the Attorney General to assess the possible anticompetitive effects of various proposals and to negotiate provisions which would, to the greatest extent practicable in accordance with the purposes of this Act and the goal set forth in section 206(a)(5) of this title, alleviate any such anticompetitive effects;

(9) consult with representatives of science, industry, agriculture, labor, environmental protection and consumer organizations, and other groups, as it deems advisable; and

(10) enter into, without regard to section 3709 of the Revised Statutes of the United States (41 U.S.C. 5), such contracts, leases, cooperative agreements, or other transactions as may be necessary in the conduct of its functions and duties with any person (including a government entity).

(b) Duties.—In addition to its duties and responsibilities under other provisions of this Act, the Association shall—

(1) prepare a survey of existing rail services in the region, including patterns of traffic movement; traffic density over identified lines; pertinent costs and revenues of lines; and plant, equipment, and facilities (includng yards and terminals);

Study.

(2) prepare an economic and operational study and analysis of present and future rail service needs in the region; the nature and volume of the traffic in the region now being moved by rail or

87 STAT. 991

likely to be moved by rail in the future; the extent to which available alternative modes of transportation could move such traffic as is now carried by railroads in reorganization; the relative economic, social, and environmental costs that would be involved in the use of such available alternative modes, including energy resource costs; and the competitive or other effects on profitable railroads;

(3) prepare a study of rail passenger services in the region, in terms of scope and quality;

(4) consider the views of the Office and of all government officials and persons who submit views, reports, or testimony under section 205(d)(1) of this title or in the course of proceedings conducted by the Office; Post, p. 994.

(5) consider methods of achieving economies in the cost of rail system operations in the region including consolidation, pooling, and joint use or operation of lines, facilities, and operating equipment; relocation; rehabilitation and modernization of equipment, track, and other facilities; and abandonment of lines consistent with meeting needs and service requirements; together with the anticipated economic, social, and environmental costs and benefits of each such method;

(6) consider the effect on railroad employees of any restructuring of rail services in the region;

(7) make available to the Secretary, the Director of the Office and appropriate committees of the Congress all studies, data, and other information acquired or developed by the Association.

(c) INVESTMENT OF FUNDS.—Uncommitted funds of the Association shall be kept in cash on hand or on deposit, or invested in obligations of the United States or guaranteed thereby, or in obligations, participations, or other investments which are lawful investments for fiduciary, trust, or public funds.

(d) EXEMPTION FROM TAXATION.—The Association, including its franchise, capital reserves, surplus, security holdings, and income shall be exempt from all taxation now or hereafter imposed by the United States, any commonwealth, territory, dependency, or possession thereof, or by any State or political subdivision thereof, except that any real property of the Association shall be subject to taxation to the same extent according to its value as other real property is taxed.

(e) ANNUAL REPORT.—The Association shall transmit to the Congress and the President, not later than 90 days after the end of each fiscal year, a comprehensive and detailed report on all activities of the Association during the preceding fiscal year. Each such report shall include (1) the Association's statement of specific and detailed objectives for the activities and programs conducted and assisted under this Act; (2) statements of the Association's conclusions as to the effectiveness of such activities and programs in meeting the stated objectives and the purposes of this Act, measured through the end of the preceding fiscal year; (3) recommendations with respect to any legislation or administrative action which the Association deems necessary or desirable; (4) a statistical compilation of the obligations issued and loans made under this Act; (5) a summary of outstanding problems confronting the Association, in order of priority; (6) all other information required to be submitted to the Congress pursuant to any other provision of this Act; and (7) the Association's projections and plans for its activities and programs during the next fiscal year. Report to Congress and President.

(f) BUDGET.—The receipts and disbursements of the Association (other than administrative expenses referred to in subsection (g) of

87 STAT. 992

this section) in the discharge of its functions shall not be included in the totals of the budget of the United States Government, and shall be exempt from any annual expenditure and net lending (budget outlays) limitations imposed on a budget of the United States Government.

Budget transmittal to Congress.

The Chairman of the Association shall transmit annually to the Congress a budget for program activities and for administrative expenses of the Association. The Chairman shall report annually to the Congress the amount of net lending of the Association, which would be included in the totals of the budgets of the United States Government, if the Association's activities were not excluded from those totals as a result of this section.

(g) ACCOUNTABILITY.—(1) Section 201 of the Government Corporation Control Act (31 U.S.C. 856) is amended by striking out "and" at the end of clause (6) and by inserting immediately before the period at the end thereof the following: ", (8) the United States Railway Association".

70 Stat. 667;
85 Stat. 37.

(2) The Chairman of the Association shall transmit annually to the Office of Management and Budget a budget for administrative expenses of the Association. Whenever the Association submits any budget estimate or request to the Office of Management and Budget, it shall concurrently transmit a copy of the estimate or request to the Congress. Within budgetary constraints of the Congress, the maximum feasible and prudent budgetary flexibility shall be provided to the Association to permit effective operations.

Budget transmittal to Office of Management and Budget and Congress.

ACCESS TO INFORMATION

SEC. 203. (a) PLANNING.—Each railroad operating in the region shall provide such relevant information as may be requested by the Secretary, the Office, or the Association in connection with the performance of their respective functions under any provision of this Act. No information may be requested under this subsection after the effective date of the final system plan.

Recordkeeping.

(b) OTHER.—Each railroad or other person or government entity seeking financial assistance from the Association shall maintain and make available such records, make and submit such reports, and provide such data, materials, or other relevant information as may be requested by the Association.

(c) ENFORCEMENT.—Where authorized under subsection (a) or (b) of this section and upon presenting appropriate credentials and a written notice of inspection authority, any officer or employee duly designated by the Secretary, the Office, or the Association may, at reasonable times, inspect records, papers, processes, rolling stock, systems, equipment, or facilities and may, in furtherance of their respective functions under this Act, hold such hearings, sit and act at such times and places, administer such oaths, and require by subpoena or other order the attendance and testimony of such witnesses and the production of such information as is deemed advisable. Subpoenas shall be issued under the signature of the Secretary, the Director of the Office, or the Chairman or President of the Association and may be served by any duly designated individual. In case of contumacy or refusal to obey such a subpoena or order by any person who resides, is found, or transacts business within the jurisdiction of any district court of the United States, such district court shall, upon petition, have jurisdiction to issue to such person an order requiring him to comply forthwith. Failure to obey such an order is punishable by such court as a contempt of court.

(d) CONGRESS.—Nothing in this section shall authorize the withholding of information from any duly authorized committee of the Congress.

87 STAT. 993

REPORT

SEC. 204. (a) PREPARATION.—Within 30 days after the date of enactment of this Act, the Secretary shall prepare a comprehensive report containing his conclusions and recommendations with respect to the geographic zones within the region in and between which rail service should be provided and the criteria upon which such conclusions and recommendations are based. The Secretary may use as a basis for the identification of such geographic zones the standard metropolitan statistical areas, groups of such areas, counties, or groups of counties having similar economic characteristics such as mining, manufacturing, or farming.

(b) SUBMISSION.—The Secretary shall submit the report required by subsection (a) of this section to the Office, the Association, the Governor and public utilities commission of each State studied in the report, local governments, consumer organizations, environmental groups, the public, and the Congress. The Secretary shall further cause a copy of the report to be published in the Federal Register.

Publication in Federal Register.

RAIL SERVICES PLANNING OFFICE

SEC. 205. (a) ESTABLISHMENT.—There is established, on the date of enactment of this Act, a new Office in the Commission to be known as the Rail Services Planning Office. The Office shall function continuously pursuant to the provisions of this Act, and shall cease to exist 5 years after the date of enactment of this Act. The Office shall be administered by a director.

(b) DIRECTOR.—The Director of the Office shall be appointed by the Chairman of the Commission with the concurrence of 5 members of the Commission. The Director of the Office shall administer and be responsible for the discharge of the functions and duties of the Office from the date he takes office unless removed for cause by the Commission. He shall be compensated at a rate to be set by the Chairman of the Commission without regard to the provisions of title 5, United States Code, governing appointments in the competitive service, classification, and General Schedule pay rates, but at a rate not in excess of the maximum rate for GS–18 of the General Schedule under section 5332 of such title.

5 USC 5332 note.

(c) POWERS.—The Director of the Office is subject to the direction of, and shall report to, such member of the Commission as the Chairman thereof shall designate. The Chairman may designate himself as that member. Such Director is authorized, with the concurrence of such member or (in case of disagreement) the Chairman of the Commission, to—

(1) appoint, fix the compensation, and assign the duties of employees of the Office without regard to the provisions of title 5, United States Code, governing appointments in the competitive service, and to procure temporary and intermittent services to the same extent as is authorized under section 3109 of title 5, United States Code, but at rates not to exceed $250 a day for qualified experts. Each department, agency, and instrumentality of the executive branch of the Federal Government and each independent regulatory agency of the United States is authorized and shall give careful consideration to a request to furnish to the Director of the Office, upon written request, on a reimbursable basis or otherwise, such assistance as the Director deems necessary to carry out the functions and duties of the Office. Such assistance includes transfer of personnel with their consent and without prejudice to their position and rating; and

80 Stat. 416.

87 STAT. 994

Contract author-
ity.
(2) enter into, without regard to section 3709 of the Revised Statutes of the United States (41 U.S.C. 5), such contracts, leases, cooperative agreements, or other transactions as may be necessary in the conduct of the functions and duties of the Office, with any person (including a government entity).

(d) DUTIES.—In addition to its duties, and responsibilities under other provisions of this Act, the Office shall—

(1) study and evaluate the Secretary's report on rail services in the region required under section 204(a) of this Act and submit its report thereon to the Association within 120 days after the date of enactment of this Act. The Office shall also solicit, study, and evaluate the views with respect to present and future rail service needs of the region from Governors of States within the region; mayors and chief executives of political subdivisions within such States; shippers; the Secretary of Defense; manufacturers, wholesalers, and retailers within the region; consumers of goods and products shipped by rail; and all other interested persons. The Office shall conduct public hearings to solicit comments

Public hearings.
on such report and to receive such views;

(2) employ and utilize the services of attorneys and such other personnel as may be required in order properly to protect the interests of those communities and users of rail service which, for whatever reason, such as their size or location, might not otherwise be adequately represented in the course of the hearings and evaluations which the Office is required to conduct and perform under other provisions of this Act;

(3) within 180 days after the date of enactment of this Act, determine and publish standards for determining the "revenue attributable to the rail properties", the "avoidable costs of providing service", and "a reasonable return on the value", as those phrases are used in section 304 of this Act, after a proceeding in accordance with the provisions of section 553 of title 5, United

80 Stat. 383.
States Code; and

(4) assist States and local and regional transportation agencies in making determinations whether to provide rail service continuation subsidies to maintain in operation particular rail properties by establishing criteria for determining whether particular rail properties are suitable for rail service continuation subsidies. Such criteria should include the following considerations: Rail properties are suitable if the cost of the required subsidy for such properties per year to the taxpayers is less than the cost of termination of rail service over such properties measured by increased fuel consumption and operational costs for alternative modes of transportation; the cost to the gross national product in terms of reduced output of goods and services; the cost of relocating or assisting through unemployment, retraining, and welfare benefits to individuals and firms adversely affected thereby; and the cost to the environment measured by damage caused by increased pollution.

FINAL SYSTEM PLAN

SEC. 206. (a) GOALS.—The final system plan shall be formulated in such a way as to effectuate the following goals:

(1) the creation, through a process of reorganization, of a financially self-sustaining rail service system in the region;

(2) the establishment and maintenance of a rail service system adequate to meet the rail transportation needs and service requirements of the region;

87 STAT. 995

(3) the establishment of improved high-speed rail passenger service, consonant with the recommendations of the Secretary in his report of September 1971, entitled "Recommendations for Northeast Corridor Transportation";

(4) the preservation, to the extent consistent with other goals, of existing patterns of service by railroads (including short-line and terminal railroads), and of existing railroad trackage in areas in which fossil fuel natural resources are located, and the utilization of those modes of transportation in the region which require the smallest amount of scarce energy resources and which can most efficiently transport energy resources;

(5) the retention and promotion of competition in the provision of rail and other transportation services in the region;

(6) the attainment and maintenance of any environmental standards, particularly the applicable national ambient air quality standards and plans established under the Clean Air Act Amendments of 1970, taking into consideration the environmental impact of alternative choices of action; 84 Stat. 1676. 42 USC 1857b note.

(7) the movement of passengers and freight in rail transportation in the region in the most efficient manner consistent with safe operation, including the requirements of commuter and intercity rail passenger service; the extent to which there should be coordination with the National Railroad Passenger Corporation and similar entities; and the identification of all short-to-medium distance corridors in densely populated areas in which the major upgrading of rail lines for high-speed passenger operation would return substantial public benefits; and

(8) the minimization of job losses and associated increases in unemployment and community benefit costs in areas in the region presently served by rail service.

(b) FACTORS.—The final system plan shall be based upon due consideration of all factors relevant to the realization of the goals set forth in subsection (a) of this section. Such factors include the need for and the cost of rehabilitation and modernization of track, equipment, and other facilities; methods of achieving economies in the cost of rail operations in the region; means of achieving rationalization of rail services and the rail service system in the region; marketing studies; the impact on railroad employees; consumer needs; traffic analyses; financial studies; and any other factors identified by the Association under section 202(b) of this title or in the report of the Secretary required under section 204(a) of this title. Ante, p. 990.

(c) DESIGNATIONS.—The final system plan shall designate—

(1) which rail properties of railroads in reorganization in the region or of railroads leased, operated, or controlled by any railroad in reorganization in the region—

(A) shall be transferred to the Corporation;

(B) shall be offered for sale to a profitable railroad operating in the region and, if such offer is accepted, operated by such railroad; the plan shall designate what additions shall be made to the designation under subparagraph (A) of this paragraph in the event such profitable railroad fails to accept such offer;

(C) shall be purchased, leased, or otherwise acquired from the Corporation by the National Railroad Passenger Corporation in accordance with the exercise of its option under section 601(d) of this Act for improvement to achieve the goal set forth in subsection (a)(3) of this section;

87 STAT. 996

(D) may be purchased or leased from the Corporation by a State or a local or regional transportation authority to meet the needs of commuter and intercity rail passenger service; and

(E) if not otherwise required to be operated by the Corporation, a government entity, or a responsible person, are suitable for use for other public purposes, including highways, other forms of transportation, conservation, energy transmission, education or health care facilities, or recreation. In carrying out this subparagraph, the Association shall solicit the views and recommendations of the Secretary, the Secretary of the Interior, the Administrator of the Environmental Protection Agency, and other agencies of the Federal Government and of the States and political subdivisions thereof within the region, and the general public; and

(2) which rail properties of profitable railroads operating in the region may be offered for sale to the Corporation or to other profitable railroads operating in the region subject to paragraphs (3) and (4) of subsection (d) of this section.

(d) TRANSFERS.—All transfers or conveyances pursuant to the final system plan shall be made in accordance with, and subject to, the following principles:

(1) All rail properties to be transferred to the Corporation by a profitable railroad, by trustees of a railroad in reorganization, or by any railroad leased, operated, or controlled by a railroad in reorganization in the region, shall be transferred in exchange for stock and other securities of the Corporation (including obligations of the Association) and the other benefits accruing to such railroad by reason of such transfer.

(2) All rail properties to be conveyed to a profitable railroad operating in the region by trustees of a railroad in reorganization, or by any railroad leased, operated, or controlled by a railroad in reorganization in the region, shall be conveyed in exchange for compensation from the profitable railroad.

(3) Notwithstanding any other provision of this Act, no acquisition under this Act shall be made by any profitable railroad operating in the region without a determination with respect to each such transaction and all such transactions cumulatively (A) by the Association, upon adoption and release of the preliminary system plan, that such acquisition or acquisitions will not materially impair the profitability of any other profitable railroad operating in the region or of the Corporation, and (B) by the Commission, which shall be made within 90 days after adoption and release by the Association of the preliminary system plan, that such acquisition or acquisitions will be in full accord and comply with the provisions and standards of section 5 of part I

62 Stat. 472.

of the Interstate Commerce Act (49 U.S.C. 5). The determination by the Association shall not be reviewable in any court. The determination by the Commission shall not be reviewable in any court.

(4) Where the final system plan designates specified rail properties of a railroad in reorganization in the region, or of a railroad leased, operated, or controlled by a railroad in reorganization in the region, to be offered for sale to and operated by a profitable railroad operating in the region, such designation shall terminate 30 days after the effective date of the final system plan unless, prior to such date, such profitable railroad has notified the Association in writing of its acceptance of such offer. Where the final

system plan designates specified rail properties of a profitable railroad operating in the region as authorized to be offered for sale or lease to the Corporation or to other profitable railroads operating in the region, such designation and authorization shall terminate 60 days after the effective date of the final system plan unless, prior to such date, a binding agreement with respect to such properties has been entered into and concluded.

(5) All properties sold by the Corporation pursuant to sections 206(c)(1)(C) and 601(d) of this Act shall be transferred at a value related to the value received for the transfer to the Corporation of such properties.

(e) CORPORATION FEATURES.—The final system plan shall set forth—

(1) pro forma earnings for the Corporation, as reasonably projected and considering the additions or changes in the designation of rail properties to be operated by the Corporation which may be made under subsection (d)(4) of this section;

(2) the capital structure of the Corporation, based on the pro forma earnings of the Corporation as set forth, including such debt capitalization as shall be reasonably deemed to conform to the requirements of the public interest with respect to railroad debt securities, including the adequacy of coverage of fixed charges; and

(3) the manner in which employee stock ownership plans may, to the extent practicable, be utilized for meeting the capitalization requirements of the Corporation, taking into account (A) the relative cost savings compared to conventional methods of corporate finance; (B) the labor cost savings; (C) the potential for minimizing strikes and producing more harmonious relations between labor organizations and railway management; (D) the projected employee dividend incomes; (E) the impact on quality of service and prices to railway users; and (F) the promotion of the objectives of this Act of creating a financially self-sustaining railway system in the region which also meets the service needs of the region and the Nation.

(f) VALUE.—The final system plan shall designate the value of all rail properties to be transferred under the final system plan and the value of the securities and other benefits to be received for transferring those rail properties to the Corporation in accordance with the final system plan.

(g) OTHER PROVISIONS.—The final system plan may recommend arrangements among various railroads for joint use or operation of rail properties on a shared ownership, cooperative, pooled, or condominium-type basis, subject to such terms and conditions as may be specified in the final system plan. The final system plan shall also make such designations as are determined to be necessary in accordance with the provisions of section 402 or 403 of this Act.

(h) OBLIGATIONAL AUTHORITY.—The final system plan shall recommend the amount of obligations of the Association which are necessary to enable it to implement the final system plan.

(i) TERMS AND CONDITIONS FOR SECURITIES.—The final system plan may include terms and conditions for any securities to be issued by the Corporation in exchange for the conveyance of rail properties under the final system plan which in the judgement of the Association will minimize any actual or potential debt burden on the Corporation. Any such terms and conditions for securities of the Corporation which purport to directly obligate the Association shall not become effective without affirmative approval, with or without modification by a joint resolution of the Congress.

87 STAT. 998

ADOPTION OF FINAL SYSTEM PLAN

SEC. 207. (a) PRELIMINARY SYSTEM PLAN.—(1) Within 300 days after the date of enactment of this Act, the Association shall adopt and release a preliminary system plan prepared by it on the basis of reports and other information submitted to it by the Secretary, the Office, and interested persons in accordance with this Act and on the basis of its own investigations, consultations, research, evaluation, and analysis pursuant to this Act. Copies of the preliminary system plan shall be transmitted by the Association to the Secretary, the Office, the Governor and public utility commission of each State in the region, the Congress, each court having jurisdiction over a railroad in reorganization in the region, the special court, and interested persons, and a copy shall be published in the Federal Register. The Association shall invite and afford interested persons an opportunity to submit comments on the preliminary system plan to the Association within 60 days after the date of its release.

Copies, transmittal to Congress.

Publication in Federal Register.

Public hearings.

(2) The Office is authorized and directed to hold public hearings on the preliminary system plan and to make available to the Association a summary and analysis of the evidence received in the course of such proceedings, together with its critique and evaluation of the preliminary system plan, not later than 60 days after the date of release of such plan.

(b) APPROVAL.—Within 120 days after the date of enactment of this Act each United States district court or other court having jurisdiction over a railroad in reorganization shall decide whether the railroad is reorganizable on an income basis within a reasonable time under section 77 of the Bankruptcy Act (11 U.S.C. 205) and that the public interest would be better served by continuing the present reorganization proceedings than by a reorganization under this Act. Within 60 days after the submission of the report by the Office, under section 205(d)(1) of this title, on the Secretary's report on rail services in the region, each United States district court or other court having jurisdiction over a railroad in reorganization shall decide whether or not such railroad shall be reorganized by means of transferring some of its rail properties to the Corporation pursuant to the provisions of this Act. Because of the strong public interest in the continuance of rail transportation in the region pursuant to a system plan devised under the provisions of this Act, each such court shall order that the reorganization be proceeded with pursuant to this Act unless it (1) has found that the railroad is reorganizable on an income basis within a reasonable time under section 77 of the Bankruptcy Act (11 U.S.C. 205) and that the public interest would be better served by such a reorganization than by a reorganization under this Act, or (2) finds that this Act does not provide a process which would be fair and equitable to the estate of the railroad in reorganization in which case it shall dismiss the reorganization proceeding. If a court does not enter an order or make a finding as required by this subsection, the reorganization shall be proceeded with pursuant to this Act. An appeal from an order made under this section may be made only to the special court. Appeal to the special court shall be taken within 10 days following entry of an order pursuant to this subsection, and the special court shall complete its review and render its decision within 80 days after such appeal is taken. There shall be no review of the decision of the special court.

49 Stat. 911;
76 Stat. 572.

(c) ADOPTION.—Within 420 days after the date of enactment of this Act, the executive committee of the Association shall prepare and submit a final system plan for the approval of the Board of Directors of the Association. A copy of such submission shall be simultaneously

87 STAT. 999

presented to the Commission. The submission shall reflect evaluation of all responses and summaries of responses received, testimony at any public hearings, and the results of additional study and review. Within 30 days thereafter, the Board of Directors of the Association shall by a majority vote of all its members approve a final system plan which meets all of the requirements of section 206 of this title. *Ante*, p. 994.

(d) REVIEW OF COMMISSION.—Within 30 days following the adoption of the final system plan by the Association under subsection (c) of this section and the submission of such plan to Congress under section 208(a) of this title, the Commission shall submit to the Congress an evaluation of the final system plan delivered to both Houses of Congress. Plan evaluation, submittal to Congress.

REVIEW BY CONGRESS

SEC. 208. (a) GENERAL.—The Board of Directors of the Association shall deliver the final system plan adopted by the Association to both Houses of Congress and to the Committee on Interstate and Foreign Commerce of the House of Representatives and the Committee on Commerce of the Senate. The final system plan shall be deemed approved at the end of the first period of 60 calendar days of continuous session of Congress after such date of transmittal unless either the House of Representatives or the Senate passes a resolution during such period stating that it does not favor the final system plan.

(b) REVISED PLAN.—If either the House or the Senate passes a resolution of disapproval under subsection (a) of this section, the Association, with the cooperation and assistance of the Secretary and the Office, shall prepare, determine, and adopt a revised final system plan. Each such revised plan shall be submitted to Congress for review pursuant to subsection (a) of this section.

(c) COMPUTATION.—For purposes of this section—

(1) continuity of session of Congress is broken only by an adjournment sine die; and

(2) the days on which either House is not in session because of an adjournment of more than 3 days to a day certain are excluded in the computation of the 60-day period.

JUDICIAL REVIEW

SEC. 209. (a) GENERAL.—Notwithstanding any other provision of law, the final system plan which is adopted by the Association and which becomes effective after review by the Congress is not subject to review by any court except in accordance with this section. After the final system plan becomes effective under section 208 of this title, it may be reviewed with respect to matters concerning the value of the rail properties to be conveyed under the plan and the value of the consideration to be received for such properties.

(b) SPECIAL COURT.—Within 30 days after the date of enactment of this Act, the Association shall make application to the judicial panel on multi-district litigation authorized by section 1407 of title 28, United States Code, for the consolidation in a single, three-judge district court of the United States of all judicial proceedings with respect to the final system plan. Within 30 days after such application is received, the panel shall make the consolidation in a district court (cited herein as the "special court") which the panel determines to be convenient to the parties and the one most likely to be able to conduct any proceedings under this section with the least delay and the greatest possible fairness and ability. Such proceedings shall be conducted by the special court which shall be composed of three Federal judges who shall be selected by the panel, except that none of the judges selected

82 Stat. 109.

87 STAT, 1000

49 Stat. 911;
76 Stat. 572.

may be a judge assigned to a proceeding involving any railroad in reorganization in the region under section 77 of the Bankruptcy Act (11 U.S.C. 205). The special court is authorized to exercise the powers of a district judge in any judicial district with respect to such proceedings and such powers shall include those of a reorganization court. The special court shall have the power to order the conveyance of rail properties of railroads leased, operated, or controlled by a railroad in reorganization in the region. The panel may issue rules for the conduct of its functions under this subsection. No determination by the panel under this subsection may be reviewed in any court.

(c) DELIVERY OF PLAN TO SPECIAL COURT.—Within 90 days after its effective date, the Association shall deliver a certified copy of the final system plan to the special court and shall certify to the special court—

(1) which rail properties of the respective railroads in reorganization in the region and of any railroad leased, operated, or controlled by such railroads in reorganization are to be transferred to the Corporation, in accordance with the final system plan;

(2) which rail properties of the respective railroads in reorganization in the region or railroads leased, operated, or controlled by such railroads in reorganization are to be conveyed to profitable railroads, in accordance with the final system plan;

(3) the amount, terms, and value of the securities of the Corporation (including any obligations of the Association) to be exchanged for those rail properties to be transferred to the Corporation pursuant to the final system plan, and as indicated in paragraph (1) of this subsection; and

(4) that the transfer of rail properties in exchange for securities of the Corporation (including any obligations of the Association) and other benefits is fair and equitable and in the public interest.

(d) BANKRUPTCY COURTS.—Within 90 days after its effective date, the Association shall deliver a certified copy of the final system plan to each district court of the United States or any other court having jurisdiction over a railroad in reorganization in the region and shall certify to each such court—

(1) which rail properties of that railroad in reorganization are to be transferred to the Corporation under the final system plan; and

(2) which rail properties of that railroad in reorganization, if any, are to be conveyed to profitable railroads operating in the region, under the final system plan.

OBLIGATIONS OF THE ASSOCIATION

SEC. 210. (a) GENERAL.—To carry out the purposes of this Act, the Association is authorized to issue bonds, debentures, trust certificates, securities, or other obligations (herein cited as "obligations") in accordance with this section. Such obligations shall have such maturities and bear such rate or rates of interest as are determined by the Association with the approval of the Secretary of the Treasury. Such obligations shall be redeemable at the option of the Association prior to maturity in the manner stipulated in each such obligation, and may be purchased by the Association in the open market at a price which is reasonable.

(b) MAXIMUM OBLIGATIONAL AUTHORITY.—Except as otherwise provided in the last sentence of this subsection, the aggregate amount of obligations of the Association issued under this section which may be outstanding at any one time shall not exceed $1,500,000,000 of which the aggregate amount issued to the Corporation shall not exceed

87 STAT. 1001

$1,000,000,000. Of the aggregate amount of obligations issued to the Corporation by the Association, not less than $500,000,000 shall be available solely for the rehabilitation and modernization of rail properties acquired by the Corporation under this Act and not disposed of by the Corporation pursuant to section 206(c) (1) (C) of this Act. Any modification to the limitations set forth in this subsection shall be made by joint resolution adopted by the Congress.

(c) GUARANTEES.—The Secretary shall guarantee the payment of principal and interest on all obligations issued by the Association in accordance with this Act and which the Association requests be guaranteed.

(d) VALIDITY.—No obligation issued by the Association under this section shall be terminated, canceled, or otherwise revoked, except in accordance with lawful terms and conditions prescribed by the Association. Such an obligation shall be conclusive evidence that it is in compliance with this section, has been approved, and is legal as to principal, interest, and other terms. An obligation of the Association shall be valid and incontestable in the hands of a holder, except as to fraud, duress, mutual mistake of fact, or material misrepresentation by or involving such holder.

(e) THE SECRETARY OF THE TREASURY.—If at any time the moneys available to the Secretary are insufficient to enable him to discharge his responsibilities under subsection (c) of this section, he shall issue notes or other obligations to the Secretary of the Treasury in such forms and denominations, bearing such maturities, and subject to such terms and conditions as may be prescribed by the Secretary of the Treasury. Such obligations shall bear interest at a rate to be determined by the Secretary of the Treasury taking into consideration the current average market yield on outstanding marketable obligations of the United States of comparable maturities during the month preceding the issuance of such obligations. The Secretary of the Treasury is authorized and directed to purchase any such obligations and for such purpose is authorized to use as a public debt transaction the proceeds from the sale of any securities issued under the Second Liberty Bond Act, as amended. The purposes for which securities may be issued under such Act are extended to include any purchase of notes or other obligations issued under this subsection. At any time, the Secretary of the Treasury may sell any such obligations, and all sales, purchases, and redemptions of such obligations by the Secretary of the Treasury shall be treated as public debt transactions of the United States.

40 Stat. 288.
31 USC 774.

(f) AUTHORIZATION FOR APPROPRIATIONS.—There are hereby authorized to be appropriated to the Secretary such amounts as are necessary to discharge the obligations of the United States arising under this section.

(g) LAWFUL INVESTMENTS.—All obligations issued by the Association shall be lawful investments and may be accepted as security for all fiduciary, trust, and public funds, the investment or deposit of which shall be under the authority and control of the United States or any officer or officers thereof. All such obligations issued pursuant to this section shall be exempt securities within the meaning of laws administered by the Securities and Exchange Commission.

LOANS

SEC. 211. (a) GENERAL.—The Association is authorized, in accordance with the provisions of this section and such rules and regulations as it shall prescribe, to make loans to the Corporation, the National Railroad Passenger Corporation, and other railroads (including a

87 STAT. 1002

49 Stat. 911;
76 Stat. 572.
11 USC 205.

railroad in reorganization which has been found to be reorganizable under section 77 of the Bankruptcy Act pursuant to section 207(b) of this title) in the region, for purposes of assisting in the implementation of the final system plan; to a State or local or regional transportation authority pursuant to section 403 of this Act; and to provide assistance in the form of loans to any railroad which (A) connects with a railroad in reorganization, and (B) is in need of financial assistance to avoid reorganization proceedings under section 77 of the Bankruptcy Act (11 U.S.C. 205). No such loan shall be made by the Association to a railroad unless such loans shall, where applicable, be treated as an expense of administration. The rights referred to in the last sentence of section 77(j) of the Bankruptcy Act (11 U.S.C. 205(j)) shall in no way be affected by this Act.

(b) APPLICATIONS.—Each application for such a loan shall be made in writing to the Association in such form and with such content and other submissions as the Association shall prescribe to protect reason-

Publication in
Federal Regis-
ter.

ably the interests of the United States. The Association shall publish a notice of the receipt of each such application in the Federal Register and shall afford interested persons an opportunity to comment thereon.

(c) TERMS AND CONDITIONS.—Each loan shall be extended in such form, under such terms and conditions, and pursuant to such regulations as the Association deems appropriate. Such loan shall bear interest at a rate not less than the greater of a rate determined by the Secretary of the Treasury taking into consideration (1) the rate prevailing in the private market for similar loans as determined by the Secretary of the Treasury, or (2) the current average yield on outstanding marketable obligations of the Association with remaining periods of maturity comparable to the average maturities of such loans, plus such additional charge, if any, toward covering costs of the Association as the Association may determine to be consistent with the purposes of this Act.

(d) MODIFICATIONS.—The Association is authorized to approve any modification of any provision of a loan under this section, including the rate of interest, time of payment of interest or principal, security, or any other term or condition, upon agreement of the recipient of the loan and upon a finding by the Association that such modification is equitable and necessary or appropriate to achieve the policy declared in subsection (f) of this section.

(e) PREREQUISITES.—The Association shall make a finding in writing, before making a loan to any applicant under this section, that—

(1) the loan is necessary to carry out the final system plan or to prevent insolvency;

(2) it is satisfied that the business affairs of the applicant will be conducted in a reasonable and prudent manner; and

(3) the applicant has offered such security as the Association deems necessary to protect reasonably the interests of the United States.

(f) POLICY.—It is the intent of Congress that loans made under this section shall be made on terms and conditions which furnish reasonable assurance that the Corporation or the railroads to which such loans are granted will be able to repay them within the time fixed and that the goals of the final system plan are reasonably likely to be achieved.

RECORDS, AUDIT, AND EXAMINATION

SEC. 212. (a) RECORDS.—Each recipient of financial assistance under this title, whether in the form of loans, obligations, or other arrangements, shall keep such records as the Association or the Secretary shall prescribe, including records which fully disclose the amount and dis-

87 STAT. 1003

position by such recipient of the proceeds of such assistance and such other records as will facilitate an effective audit.

(b) AUDIT AND EXAMINATION.—The Association, the Secretary, and the Comptroller General of the United States, or any of their duly authorized representatives shall, until the expiration of 3 years after the implementation of the final system plan, have access for the purpose of audit and examination to any books, documents, papers, and records of such recipients which in the opinion of the Association, the Secretary, or the Comptroller General may be related or pertinent to the loans, obligations or other arrangements referred to in subsection (a) of this section. The Association or any of its duly authorized representatives shall, until any financial assistance received under this title has been repaid to the Association, have access to any such materials which concern any matter that may bear upon—

(1) the ability of the recipient of such financial assistance to make repayment within the time fixed therefor;

(2) the effectiveness with which the proceeds of such assistance is used; and

(3) the implementation of the final system plan and the realization of the declaration of policy of this Act.

EMERGENCY ASSISTANCE PENDING IMPLEMENTATION

SEC. 213. (a) EMERGENCY ASSISTANCE.—The Secretary is authorized, pending the implementation of the final system plan, to pay to the trustees of railroads in reorganization such sums as are necessary for the continued provision of essential transportation services by such railroads. Such payments shall be made by the Secretary upon such reasonable terms and conditions as the Secretary establishes, except that recipients must agree to maintain and provide service at a level no less than that in effect on the date of enactment of this Act.

(b) AUTHORIZATION FOR APPROPRIATIONS.—There are authorized to be appropriated to the Secretary for carrying out this section such sums as are necessary, not to exceed $85,000,000, to remain available until expended.

AUTHORIZATION FOR APPROPRIATIONS

SEC. 214. (a) SECRETARY.—There are authorized to be appropriated to the Secretary for purposes of preparing the reports and exercising other functions to be performed by him under this Act such sums as are necessary, not to exceed $12,500,000, to remain available until expended.

(b) OFFICE.—There are authorized to be appropriated to the Commission for the use of the Office in carrying out its functions under this Act such sums as are necessary, not to exceed $5,000,000, to remain available until expended. The budget for the Office shall be submitted by the Commission directly to the Congress and shall not be subject to review of any kind by any other agency or official of the United States. Moneys appropriated for the Office shall not be withheld by any agency or official of the United States or used by the Commission for any purpose other than the use of the Office. No part of any other moneys appropriated to the Commission shall be withheld by any other agency or official of the United States to offset any moneys appropriated pursuant to this subsection.

(c) ASSOCIATION.—There are authorized to be appropriated to the Association for purposes of carrying out its administrative expenses under this Act such sums as are necessary, not to exceed $26,000,000, to remain available until expended.

87 STAT. 1004

MAINTENANCE AND IMPROVEMENT OF PLANT

Sec. 215. Prior to the date upon which rail properties are conveyed to the Corporation under this Act, the Secretary, with the approval of the Association, is authorized to enter into agreements with railroads in reorganization in the region (or railroads leased, operated, or controlled by railroads in reorganization) for the acquisition, maintenance, or improvement of railroad facilities and equipment necessary to improve property that will be in the final system plan. Agreements entered into pursuant to this section shall specifically identify the type and quality of improvements to be made pursuant Ante, p. 1000. to such agreements. Notwithstanding section 210(b) of this title, the Association shall issue obligations under section 210(a) of this title in an amount sufficient to finance such agreements and shall require the Corporation to assume any such obligations. However, the Association may not issue obligations under this section in an aggregate amount in excess of $150,000,000. The Secretary may not enter into any agreements under this section until he issues regulations setting forth procedures and guidelines for the administration of this section. The Corporation shall not be required under title III of this Act to compensate any railroad in reorganization for that portion of the value of rail properties transferred to it under this Act which is attributable to the acquisition, maintenance, or improvement of such properties under this section.

TITLE III—CONSOLIDATED RAIL CORPORATION

FORMATION AND STRUCTURE

Sec. 301. (a) Establishment.—There shall be established within 300 days after the date of enactment of this Act, in accordance with the provisions of this section, a corporation to be known as the Consolidated Rail Corporation.

(b) Status.—The Corporation shall be a for-profit corporation established under the laws of a State and shall not be an agency or instrumentality of the Federal Government. The Corporation shall be deemed a common carrier by railroad under section 1(3) of the 41 Stat. 424. Interstate Commerce Act (49 U.S.C. 1(3)), shall be subject to the provisions of this Act and, to the extent not inconsistent with such Acts, shall be subject to applicable State law. The principal office of the Corporation shall be located in Philadelphia in the Commonwealth of Pennsylvania.

(c) Incorporators.—The members of the executive committee of the Association shall be the incorporators of the Corporation and shall take whatever steps are necessary to establish the Corporation, including the filing of articles of incorporation. The incorporators shall also serve as the Board of Directors of the Corporation until the stock and other securities of the Corporation are distributed to the estates of the railroads in accordance with section 303(c) of this title and shall adopt the intial bylaws of the Corporation.

(d) Board of Directors.—The Board of Directors of the Corporation shall consist of 15 individuals selected in accordance with the articles and bylaws of the Corporation: *Provided*, That so long as 50 per centum or more, as determined by the Secretary of the Treasury, of the outstanding indebtedness of the Corporation consists of obligations of the Association or other debts owing to or guaranteed by the United States, three of the members of such board shall be the Secretary, the Chairman and the President of the Association and five of the members of such board shall be individuals appointed as such by the President, by and with the advice and consent of the Senate.

87 STAT. 1005

(e) INITIAL CAPITALIZATION.—In order to carry out the final system plan the Corporation is authorized to issue stock and other securities. Common stock shall be issued initially to the estates of railroads in reorganization in the region in exchange for rail properties conveyed to the Corporation pursuant to the final system plan. Nothing in this subsection shall preclude the Corporation from repurchasing the common stock initially issued through payments out of profits in order to establish an employee stock ownership plan; and nothing in this subsection shall preclude the recipients of common stock initially issued from establishing an employee stock ownership plan.

(f) AUDIT AND EXPENDITURES.—So long as 50 per centum or more, as determined by the Secretary of the Treasury, of the outstanding indebtedness of the Corporation consists of obligations of the Association or other debts owing to or guaranteed by the United States, the Corporation shall be subject to the provisions of the Government Corporation Control Act for the purposes of a Federal Government audit. Section 201 of the Government Corporation Control Act (31 U.S.C. 856) is amended by inserting at the end thereof the following: ", and (9) the Consolidated Rail Corporation to the extent provided in the Regional Rail Reorganization Act of 1973.". *Ante,* p. 992.

(g) ANNUAL REPORT.—The Corporation shall transmit to the Congress and the President, not later than 90 days after the end of each fiscal year, a comprehensive and detailed report on all activities and accomplishments of the Corporation during the preceding fiscal year. Report to Congress and President.

POWERS AND DUTIES OF THE CORPORATION

SEC. 302. The Corporation shall have all of the powers and is subject to all of the duties vested in it under this Act, in addition to the powers conferred upon it under the laws of the State or States in which it is incorporated and the powers of a railroad in any State in which it operates. The Corporation is authorized and directed to—

(a) acquire rail properties designated in the final system plan to be transferred or conveyed to it;

(b) operate rail service over such rail properties except as provided under sections 304(e) and 601(d)(3) of this Act;

(c) rehabilitate, improve, and modernize such rail properties; and

(d) maintain adequate and efficient rail services.

So long as 50 per centum or more, as determined by the Secretary of the Treasury, of the outstanding indebtedness of the Corporation consists of obligations of the Association or other debts owing to or guaranteed by the United States, the Corporation shall not engage in activities which are not related to transportation.

VALUATION AND CONVEYANCE OF RAIL PROPERTIES

SEC. 303. (a) DEPOSIT WITH COURT.—Within 10 days after delivery of a certified copy of a final system plan pursuant to section 209(c) of this Act—

(1) the Corporation, in exchange for the rail properties of the railroads in reorganization in the region and of railroads leased, operated, or controlled by railroads in reorganization in the region to be transferred to the Corporation, shall deposit with the special court all of the stock and other securities of the Corporation and obligations of the Association designated in the final system plan to be exchanged for such rail properties;

(2) each profitable railroad operating in the region purchasing rail properties from a railroad in reorganization in the region, or from a railroad leased, operated, or controlled by a railroad in

87 STAT. 1006

reorganization in the region, as provided in the final system plan shall deposit with the special court the compensation to be paid for such rail properties.

(b) CONVEYANCE OF RAIL PROPERTIES.—(1) The special court shall, within 10 days after deposit under subsection (a) of this section of the securities of the Corporation, obligations of the Association, and compensation from the profitable railroads operating in the region, order the trustee or trustees of each railroad in reorganization in the region to convey forthwith to the Corporation and the respective profitable railroads operating in the region, all right, title, and interest in the rail properties of such railroad in reorganization and shall itself order the conveyance of all right, title, and interest in the rail properties of any railroad leased, operated, or controlled by such railroad in reorganization that are to be conveyed to them under the final system plan as certified to such court under section 209(d) of this Act.

(2) All rail properties conveyed to the Corporation and the respective profitable railroads operating in the region under this section shall be conveyed free and clear of any liens or encumbrances, but subject to such leases and agreements as shall have previously burdened such properties or bound the owner or operator thereof in pursuance of an arrangement with any State, or local or regional transportation authority under which financial support from such State, or local or regional transportation authority was being provided at the time of enactment of this Act for the continuance of rail passenger service or any lien or encumbrance of no greater than 5 years' duration which is necessary for the contractual performance by any person of duties related to public health or sanitation. Such conveyances shall not be restrained or enjoined by any court.

(3) Notwithstanding anything to the contrary contained in this Act, if railroad rolling stock is included in the rail properties to be conveyed, such conveyance may only be effected if the profitable railroad operating in the region or the Corporation to whom the conveyance is made assumes all of the obligations under any conditional sale agreement, equipment trust agreement, or lease in respect to such rolling stock and such conveyance is made subject thereto; and the provisions of this Act shall not affect the title and interests of any lessor, equipment trust trustee, or conditional sale vendee or assignee under such conditional sale agreement, equipment trust agreement or lease under 49 Stat. 911. section 77(j) of the Bankruptcy Act (11 U.S.C. 205(j)).

(4) Notwithstanding anything to the contrary contained in this Act, if a railroad in reorganization has leased rail properties from a lessor that is neither a railroad nor controlled by or affiliated with a railroad, and such lease has been approved by the lessee railroad's reorganization court prior to the date of enactment of this Act, conveyance of such lease may only be effected if the Corporation or the profitable railroad to whom the conveyance is made assumes all of the terms and conditions specified in the lease, including the obligation to pay the specified rent to the non-railroad lessor.

(c) FINDINGS AND DISTRIBUTION.—(1) After the rail properties have been conveyed to the Corporation and profitable railroads operating in the region under subsection (b) of this section, the special court, giving due consideration to the findings contained in the final system plan, shall decide—

(A) whether the transfers or conveyances—

(i) of rail properties of each railroad in reorganization, or of each railroad leased, operated, or controlled by a railroad in reorganization, to the Corporation in exchange for the securities and the other benefits accruing to such rail-

87 STAT. 1007

road as a result of such exchange, as provided in the final
system plan and this Act, and

(ii) of rail properties of each railroad in reorganization,
or of each railroad leased, operated, or controlled by a railroad in reorganization, to a profitable railroad operating in
the region, in accordance with the final system plan,
are in the public interest and are fair and equitable to the estate
of each railroad in reorganization in accordance with the standard
of fairness and equity applicable to the approval of a plan of
reorganization or a step in such a plan under section 77 of the
Bankruptcy Act (11 U.S.C. 205), or fair and equitable to a rail- 49 Stat. 911;
road that is not itself in reorganization but which is leased, oper- 76 Stat. 572.
ated, or controlled by a railroad in reorganization; and

(B) whether the transfers or conveyances are more fair and
equitable than is required as a constitutional minimum.

(2) If the special court finds that the terms of one or more exchanges
for securities and other benefits are not fair and equitable to an estate
of a railroad in reorganization, or to a railroad leased, operated, or
controlled by a railroad in reorganization, which has transferred rail
properties pursuant to the final system plan, it shall—

(A) enter a judgment reallocating the securities of the Corporation in a fair and equitable manner if it has not been fairly
allocated among the railroads transferring rail properties to the
Corporation; and

(B) if the lack of fairness and equity cannot be completely
cured by a reallocation of the Corporation's securities, order the
Corporation to provide for the transfer to the railroad of other
securities of the Corporation or obligations of the Association as
designated in the final system plan in such nature and amount as
would make the exchange or exchanges fair and equitable; and

(C) if the lack of fairness and equity cannot be completely
cured by reallocation of the Corporation's securities or by providing for the transfer of other securities of the Corporation or
obligations of the Association as designated in the final system
plan, enter a judgment against the Corporation.

(3) If the special court finds that the terms of one or more conveyances of rail properties to a profitable railroad operating in the
region in accordance with the final system plan are not fair and equitable, it shall enter a judgment against such profitable railroad. If the
special court finds that the terms of one or more conveyances or
exchanges for securities or other benefits are fairer and more equitable
than is required as a constitutional minimum, then it shall order the
return of any excess securities, obligations, or compensation to the
Corporation or a profitable railroad so as not to exceed the constitutional minimum standard of fairness and equity.

(4) Upon making the findings referred to in this subsection, the
special court shall order distribution of the securities, obligations, and
compensation deposited with it under subsection (b) of this section to
the trustee or trustees of each railroad in reorganization in the region
who conveyed right, title, and interest in rail properties to the Corporation and the respective profitable railroads under such subsection.

(d) APPEAL.—A finding or determination entered pursuant to subsection (c) of this section may be appealed directly to the Supreme
Court of the United States in the same manner that an injunction
order may be appealed under section 1253 of title 28, United States
Code: *Provided*, That such appeal is exclusive and shall be filed in the 62 Stat. 928.
Supreme Court not more than 5 days after such finding or determination is entered by the special court. The Supreme Court shall dismiss

87 STAT. 1008

any such appeal within 7 days after the entry of such an appeal if it determines that such an appeal would not be in the interest of an expeditious conclusion of the proceedings and shall grant the highest priority to the determination of any such appeals which it determines not to dismiss.

TERMINATION OF RAIL SERVICE

Sec. 304. (a) Discontinuance.—Except as provided in subsections (c) and (f) of this section, (1) rail service on rail properties of a railroad in the region which transfers to the Corporation or to profitable railroads operating in the region all or substantially all of its rail properties designated for such conveyance in the final system plan, and (2) rail service on rail properties of a profitable railroad operating in the region which transfers substantially all of its rail properties to the Corporation or to other railroads pursuant to the final system plan may be discontinued to the extent such discontinuance is not precluded by the terms of the leases and agreements referred to in section 303(b)(2) of this title if—

(A) the final system plan does not designate rail service to be operated over such rail properties; and

(B) not sooner than 30 days following the effective date of the final system plan the trustee or trustees of the applicable railroad in reorganization or a profitable railroad give notice in writing of intent to discontinue such rail service on a date certain which is not less than 60 days after the date of such notice; and

(C) the notice required by paragraph (B) of this subsection is sent by certified mail to the Governor and State transportation agencies of each State and to the government of each political subdivision of each State in which such rail properties are located and to each shipper who has used such rail service during the previous 12 months.

(b) Abandonment.—(1) Rail properties over which rail service has been discontinued under subsection (a) of this section may not be abandoned sooner than 120 days after the effective date of such discontinuance except as provided in subsections (c) and (f) of this section. Thereafter, except as provided in subsection (c) of this section, such rail properties may be abandoned upon 30 days' notice in writing to all those required to receive notice under paragraph (2)(C) of subsection (a) of this section.

(2) In any case in which rail properties proposed to be abandoned under this section are designated by the final system plan as rail properties which are suitable for use for other public purposes (including roads or highways, other forms of mass transportation, conservation, and recreation), such rail properties shall not be sold, leased, exchanged, or otherwise disposed of during the 180-day period beginning on the date of notice of proposed abandonment under this section unless such rail properties have first been offered, upon reasonable terms, for acquisition for public purposes.

(c) Limitations.—Rail service may be discontinued and rail properties may be abandoned under subsections (a) and (b) of this section notwithstanding any provision of the Interstate Commerce Act (49 U.S.C. 1 et seq.) or the constitution or law of any State or the decision of any court or administrative agency of the United States or of any State. No rail service may be discontinued and no rail properties may be abandoned pursuant to this section—

(1) after 2 years from the effective date of the final system plan or more than 2 years after the final payment of any rail service continuation subsidy is received, whichever is later; or

24 Stat. 379.

87 STAT. 1009

(2) if a shipper, a State, the United States, a local or regional transportation authority, or any responsible person offers—

(A) a rail service continuation subsidy which covers the difference between the revenue attributable to such rail properties and the avoidable costs of providing service on such rail properties plus a reasonable return on the value of such rail properties;

(B) a rail service continuation subsidy which is payable pursuant to a lease or agreement with a State, or a local or regional transportation authority, under which financial support was being provided at the time of the enactment of this Act for the continuance of rail passenger service; or

(C) to purchase, pursuant to subsection (d) of this section, such rail properties in order to operate rail service over such properties.

If a rail service continuation subsidy is offered, the government or person offering the subsidy shall enter into an operating agreement with the Corporation or any responsible person (including a government entity) under which the Corporation or such person (including a government entity) will operate rail service over such rail properties and receive the difference between the revenue attributable to such properties and the avoidable costs of providing service on such rail properties and the trustee of any railroad in reorganization shall receive a reasonable rate of return on the value of any rail properties for which a rail service is operated under such subsidy.

(d) PURCHASE.—If an offer to purchase is made under subsection (c)(2)(C) of this section, such offer shall be accompanied by an offer of a rail service continuation subsidy. Such subsidy shall continue until the purchase transaction is completed, unless a railroad assumes operations over such rail properties on its own account pursuant to an order or authorization of the Commission. Whenever a railroad in reorganization in the region or a profitable railroad gives notice of intent to discontinue service pursuant to subsection (a) of this section, such railroad shall, upon the request of anyone apparently qualified to make a purchase offer promptly make available its most recent reports on the physical condition of such property together with such traffic and revenue data as would be required under subpart B of part 1121 of chapter X of title 49 of the Code of Federal Regulations and such other data necessary to ascertain the avoidable costs of providing service over such rail properties.

(e) ABANDONMENT BY CORPORATION.—After the rail system to be operated by the Corporation under the final system plan has been in operation for 2 years, the Commission may authorize the Corporation to abandon any rail properties as to which it determines that rail service over such properties is not required by the public convenience and necessity. The Commission may, at any time after the effective date of the final system plan, authorize additional rail service in the region or authorize the abandonment of rail properties which are not being operated by the Corporation or by any other person. Determinations by the Commission under this subsection shall be made pursuant to applicable provisions of the Interstate Commerce Act (49 U.S.C. 1). 24 Stat. 379.

(f) INTERIM ABANDONMENT.—After the date of enactment of this Act, no railroad in reorganization may discontinue service or abandon any line of railroad other than in accordance with the provisions of this Act, unless it is authorized to do so by the Association and unless no affected State or local or regional transportation authority reasonably opposes such action, notwithstanding any provision of any other Federal law, the constitution or law of any State, or decision or order of, or the pendency of any proceeding before any Federal or State court, agency, or authority.

87 STAT. 1010
TITLE IV—LOCAL RAIL SERVICES

FINDINGS AND PURPOSE

SEC. 401. (a) FINDINGS.—The Congress finds and declares that—
(1) The Nation is facing an energy shortage of acute proportions in the next decade.

(2) Railroads are one of the most energy-efficient modes of transportation for the movement of passengers and freight and cause the least amount of pollution.

(3) Abandonment, termination, or substantial reduction of rail service in any locality will adversely affect the Nation's long-term and immediate goals with respect to energy conservation and environmental protection.

(4) Under certain circumstances the cost to the taxpayers of rail service continuation subsidies would be less than the cost of abandonment of rail service in terms of lost jobs, energy shortages, and degradation of the environment.

(b) PURPOSE.—Therefore, it is declared to be the purpose of the Congress to authorize the Secretary to maintain a program of rail service continuation subsidies.

RAIL SERVICE CONTINUATION SUBSIDIES

SEC. 402. (a) GENERAL.—The Secretary shall provide financial assistance in accordance with this section for the purpose of rail service continuation subsidies. For purposes of subsection (b)(1) of this section the Federal share of a rail service continuation subsidy shall be 70 per centum and the State share shall be 30 per centum. For purposes of subsection (b)(2) of this section a State receiving discretionary assistance shall be required to contribute at least 30 per centum of the cost of the program for which the Federal assistance is provided.

(b) ENTITLEMENT.—(1) Each State in the region is entitled to an amount for rail service continuation subsidies from 50 per centum of the sums appropriated each fiscal year for such purpose in the ratio which the total rail mileage in such State, as determined by the Secretary and measured in point-to-point length (excluding yard tracks and sidings), bears to the total rail mileage in all the States in the region, measured in the same manner, except that the entitlement of each State shall be no less than 3 per centum, and the entitlement of no State shall be more than 10 per centum, of 50 per centum of the funds appropriated. In the event that the total amount allocated under this formula, due to the application of the maximum and minimum limitations which it establishes, is greater or less than 50 per centum of the funds appropriated, the excess or deficiency, as the case may be, shall be added to or deducted from the Secretary's discretionary fund provided for in paragraph (2) of this subsection. The entitlement of any State which is withheld in accordance with this section and any sums not used or committed by a State during the preceding fiscal year shall be paid into the discretionary fund provided for in paragraph (2) of this subsection.

(2) The Secretary is authorized to provide discretionary financial assistance to a State or a local or regional transportation authority in the region for the purpose of continuing local rail services, including assistance for the purposes enumerated in section 403 of this title.

(c) ELIGIBILITY.—A State in the region is eligible to receive rail service continuation subsidies pursuant to subsection (b) of this section in any fiscal year if—

87 STAT. 1011

(1) the State has established a State plan for rail transportation and local rail services which is administered or coordinated by a designated State agency and such plan provides for the equitable distribution of such subsidies among State, local, and regional transportation authorities;

(2) the State agency has authority and administrative jurisdiction to develop, promote, supervise, and support safe, adequate, and efficient rail services; employs or will employ, directly or indirectly, sufficient trained and qualified personnel; and maintains or will maintain adequate programs of investigation, research, promotion, and development with provision for public participation;

(3) the State provides satisfactory assurance that such fiscal control and fund accounting procedures will be adopted as may be necessary to assure proper disbursement of, and accounting for, Federal funds paid under this title to the State; and

(4) the State complies with the regulations of the Secretary issued under this section.

(d) REGULATIONS.—Within 90 days after the date of enactment of this Act. the Secretary shall issue, and may from time to time amend, regulations with respect to basic and discretionary rail service continuation subsidies.

(e) PAYMENT.—The Secretary shall pay to each State in the region an amount equal to its entitlement under subsection (b)(1) of this section. Any amounts which are not expended or committed by a State pursuant to subsection (b) during the ensuing fiscal year shall be returned by such State to the Secretary, who may use such amounts in accordance with subsection (b)(2) of this section.

(f) TERM.—A rail service continuation subsidy between a State, or a local or regional authority, and the Corporation or other responsible person (including a government entity) may not exceed a term of 2 years.

(g) RECORD. AUDIT. AND EXAMINATION.—(1) Each recipient of financial assistance under this section. whether in the form of grants, subgrants. contracts. subcontracts. or other arrangements. shall keep such records as the Secretary shall prescribe. including records which fully disclose the amount and disposition by such recipient of the proceeds of such assistance. the total cost of the project or undertaking in connection with which such assistance was given or used. the amount of that portion of the cost of the project supplied by other sources, and such other records as will facilitate an effective audit.

(2) The Secretary and the Comptroller General of the United States,   GAO audit. or any of their duly authorized representatives shall, until the expiration of 3 years after completion of the project or undertaking referred to in paragraph (1) of this subsection. have access for the purpose of audit and examination to any books. documents, papers, and records of such receipts which in the opinion of the Secretary or the Comptroller General may be related or pertinent to the grants, contracts, or other arrangements referred to in such paragraph.

(h) WITHHOLDING.—If the Secretary, after reasonable notice and opportunity for a hearing to any State agency, finds that a State is not eligible for rail service continuation subsidies under subsections (c) and (d) of this section. payment to such State shall not be made until there is no longer any failure to comply.

(i) AUTHORIZATION FOR APPROPRIATIONS.—(1) There is authorized to be appropriated to carry out the purposes of this section such sums as are necessary, not to exceed $90,000.000 for each of the 2 fiscal years including and following the effective date of the final system plan. Such sums as are appropriated shall remain available until expended.

87 STAT. 1012

(2) One-half of the sums appropriated pursuant to the authorization of this subsection shall be reserved for allocation to States in the region under subsection (b)(1) of this section. One-half of the sums appropriated pursuant to the authorization of this subsection shall be reserved for distribution by the Secretary under subsection (b)(2) of this section.

(j) DEFINITION.—As used in this section, "rail service continuation subsidies" means subsidies calculated in accordance with the provisions of section 205(d)(3) of this Act to cover costs of operating adequate and efficient rail service, including where necessary improvement and maintenance of tracks and related facilities.

ACQUISITION AND MODERNIZATION LOANS

SEC. 403. (a) ACQUISITION.—If a State which is eligible for assistance under section 402(c) of this title or a local or regional transportation authority has made an offer to purchase any rail properties of a railroad pursuant to section 304(c)(2)(C) of this Act or other lawful authority, the Secretary is authorized to direct the Association to provide loans to such State or local or regional transportation authority not to exceed 70 per centum of the purchase price: *Provided, however,* That any recipient of such loan is no longer eligible for a rail service continuation subsidy pursuant to section 402 of this title.

(b) MODERNIZATION.—In addition to such acquisition loans, the Secretary is authorized to direct the Association to provide additional assistance not to exceed 70 per centum of the cost of restoring or repairing such rail properties to such condition as will enable safe and efficient rail transportation operations over such rail properties. Such financial assistance may be in the form of a loan or the guarantee of a loan. The Association shall provide such financial assistance as the Secretary may direct under this section and shall adopt regulations describing its procedures for such assistance. With the approval of the Secretary, a State may expend sums received by it under section 402 of this title for acquisition and modernization pursuant to this section.

TITLE V—EMPLOYEE PROTECTION

DEFINITIONS

49 USC 1,
301.

SEC. 501. As used in this title unless the context otherwise requires—

(1) "acquiring railroad" means a railroad, except the Corporation, which seeks to acquire or has acquired, pursuant to the provisions of this Act, all or a part of the rail properties of one or more of the railroads in reorganization, the Corporation, or a profitable railroad;

(2) "employee of a railroad in reorganization" means a person who, on the effective date of a conveyance of rail properties of a railroad in reorganization to the Corporation or to an acquiring railroad, has an employment relationship with either said railroad in reorganization or any carrier (as defined in parts I and II of the Interstate Commerce Act) which is leased, controlled, or operated by the railroad in reorganization except a president, vice president, treasurer, secretary, comptroller, and any other person who performs functions corresponding to those performed by the foregoing officers;

(3) "protected employee" means any employee of an acquiring railroad adversely affected by a transaction and any employee of a railroad in reorganization who on the effective date of this Act have not reached age 65;

(4) "class or craft of employees" means a group of employees, recognized and treated as a unit for purposes of collective bargaining,

87 STAT. 1013

which is represented by a labor organization that has been duly authorized or recognized pursuant to the Railway Labor Act as its representative for purposes of collective bargaining; 44 Stat. 577.
45 USC 151.

(5) "representative of a class or craft of employees" means a labor organization which has been duly authorized or recognized as the collective bargaining representative of a class or craft of employees pursuant to the Railway Labor Act;

(6) "deprived of employment" means the inability of a protected employee to obtain a position by the normal exercise of his seniority rights with the Corporation after properly electing to accept employment therewith or, the subsequent loss of a position and inability, by the normal exercise of his seniority rights under the applicable collective bargaining agreements, to obtain another position with the Corporation: *Provided, however,* That provisions in existing collective bargaining agreements of a railroad in reorganization, which do not require a protected employee, in the normal exercise of seniority rights, to make a change in residence, in order to maintain his protection, will be preserved and will also be extended and be applicable to all other protected employees of that same craft or class. It shall not, however, include any deprivation of employment by reason of death, retirement, resignation, dismissal or disciplinary suspension for cause, failure to work due to illness or disability, nor any severance of employment covered by subsections (d) and (e) of section 505 of this title;

(7) "employee adversely affected with respect to his compensation" means a protected employee who suffers a reduction in compensation;

(8) "transaction" means actions taken pursuant to the provisions of this Act or the results thereof; and

(9) "change in residence" means transfer to a work location which is located either (A) outside a radius of 30 miles of the employee's former work location and farther from his residence than was his former work location or (B) is located more than 30 normal highway route miles from his residence and also farther from his residence than was his former work location.

EMPLOYMENT OFFERS

SEC. 502. (a) APPLICABLE LAW.—The Corporation and, where applicable, the Association shall be subject to the provisions of the Railway Labor Act and shall be considered employers for purposes of the Railroad Retirement Act, Railroad Retirement Tax Act, and the Railroad Unemployment Insurance Act. The Corporation, in addition, shall, except as otherwise specifically provided by this Act, be subject to all Federal and State laws and regulations applicable to carriers by railroad. 48 Stat. 1283.
26 USC 3201.
45 USC 367.

(b) MANDATORY OFFER.—The Corporation shall offer employment, to be effective as of the date of a conveyance or discontinuance of service under the provisions of this Act, to each employee of a railroad in reorganization who has not already accepted an offer of employment by the Association, where applicable, or an acquiring railroad. Such offers of employment to employees represented by labor organizations will be confined to their same craft or class. The Corporation shall apply to said employees the protective provisions of this title.

(c) ASSOCIATION.—After the transfer of rail properties pursuant to section 303, the Association, in employing any additional employees, shall give priority consideration to employees of a railroad in reorganization and the provisions of this title shall apply to any such employees employed by the Association as if they were employees of the Corporation.

ASSIGNMENT OF WORK

Sec. 503. The Corporation shall have the right to assign, allocate, reassign, reallocate, and consolidate work formerly performed on the rail properties acquired pursuant to the provisions of this Act from a railroad in reorganization to any location, facility, or position on its system provided it does not remove said work from coverage of a collective-bargaining agreement and does not infringe upon the existing classification of work rights of any craft or class of employees at the location or facility to which said work is assigned, allocated, reassigned, reallocated, or consolidated and shall have the right to transfer to an acquiring railroad the work incident to the rail properties or facilities acquired by said acquiring railroad pursuant to this Act, subject, however, to the provisions of section 508 of this title.

COLLECTIVE-BARGAINING AGREEMENTS

Sec. 504. (a) INTERIM APPLICATION.—Until completion of the agreements provided for under subsection (d) of this section, the Corporation shall, as though an original party thereto, assume and apply on the particular lines, properties, or facilities acquired all obligations under existing collective-bargaining agreements covering all crafts and classes employed thereon, except that the Agreement of May 1936, Washington, D.C. and provisions in other existing job stabilization agreements shall not be applicable to transactions effected pursuant to this Act with respect to which the provisions of section 505 of this title shall be superseding and controlling. During this period, employees of a railroad in reorganization who have seniority on the lines, properties, or facilities acquired by the Corporation pursuant to this Act shall have prior seniority roster rights on such acquired lines, properties, or facilities.

(b) SINGLE IMPLEMENTING AGREEMENT.—On or before the date of the adoption of the final system plan by the Board of Directors of the Association as provided in section 207(c) of this Act, the representatives of the various classes or crafts of the employees of a railroad in reorganization involved in a conveyance pursuant to this Act and representatives of the Corporation shall commence negotiation of a single implementing agreement for each class and craft of employees affected providing (1) the identification of the specific employees of the railroad in reorganization to whom the Corporation offers employment; (2) the procedure by which those employees of the railroad in reorganization may elect to accept employment with the Corporation; (3) the procedure for acceptance of such employees into the Corporation's employment and their assignment to positions on the Corporation's system; (4) the procedure for determining the seniority of such employees in their respective crafts or classes on the Corporation's system which shall, to the extent possible, preserve their prior seniority rights; and (5) the procedure for determining equitable adjustment in rates of comparable positions. If no agreement with respect to the matters referred to in this subsection is reached by the end of 30 days after the commencement of negotiations, the parties shall within an additional 10 days select a neutral referee and, in the event they are unable to agree upon the selection of such referee, then the National Mediation Board shall immediately appoint a referee. After a referee has been designated, a hearing on the dispute shall commence as soon as practicable. Not less than 10 days prior to the effective date of any conveyance pursuant to the provisions of

87 STAT. 1015

this Act, the referee shall resolve and decide all matters in dispute with respect to the negotiation of said implementing agreement or agreements and shall render a decision which shall be final and binding and shall constitute the implementing agreement or agreements between the parties with respect to the transaction involved. The salary and expenses of the referee shall be paid pursuant to the provisions of the Railway Labor Act.

(c) RELATIONSHIP TO OTHER PROVISIONS.—Notwithstanding failure for any reason to complete implementing agreements provided for in subsection (b) of this section, the Corporation may proceed with a conveyance of properties, facilities, and equipment pursuant to the provisions of this Act and effectuate said transaction: *Provided*, That all protected employees shall be entitled to all of the provisions of such agreements, as finally determined, from the time they are adversely affected as a result of any such conveyance.

44 Stat. 577, 45 USC 151.

(d) NEW COLLECTIVE-BARGAINING AGREEMENTS.—Not later than 60 days after the effective date of any conveyance pursuant to the provisions of this Act, the representatives of the various classes or crafts of the employees of a railroad in reorganization involved in a conveyance and representatives of the Corporation shall commence negotiations of new collective-bargaining agreements for each class and craft of employees covering the rates of pay, rules, and working conditions of employees who are employees of the Corporation, which collective-bargaining agreements shall include appropriate provisions concerning rates of pay, rules, and working conditions but shall not include any provisions for job stabilization resulting from any transaction effected pursuant to this Act which may exceed or conflict with those established or prescribed herein.

EMPLOYEE PROTECTION

SEC. 505. (a) EQUIVALENT POSITION.—A protected employee whose employment is governed by a collective-bargaining agreement will not, except as explicitly provided in this title, during the period in which he is entitled to protection, be placed in a worse position with respect to compensation, fringe benefits, rules, working conditions, and rights and privileges pertaining thereto.

(b) MONTHLY DISPLACEMENT ALLOWANCE.—A protected employee, who has been deprived of employment or adversely affected with respect to his compensation shall be entitled to a monthly displacement allowance computed as follows:

(1) Said allowance shall be determined by computing the total compensation received by the employee, including vacation allowances and monthly compensation guarantees, and his total time paid for during the last 12 months immediately prior to his being adversely affected in which he performed compensated service more than 50 per centum of such months, based upon his normal work schedule, and by dividing separately the total compensation and the total time paid for by 12, thereby producing the average monthly compensation and average monthly time paid for; and, if an employee's compensation in his current position is less in any month in which he performs work than the aforesaid average compensation, he shall be paid the difference, less any time lost on account of voluntary absences other than vacations, but said protected employee shall be compensated in addition thereto at the rate of the position filled for any time worked in excess of his average monthly time, *Provided, however*, That—

87 STAT. 1016

(A) in determining compensation in his current employment the protected employee shall be treated as occupying the position, producing the highest rate of pay to which his qualifications and seniority entitle him under the applicable collective bargaining agreement and which does not require a change in residence;

(B) the said monthly displacement allowance shall be reduced by the full amount of any unemployment compensation benefits received by the protected employee and shall be reduced by an amount equivalent to any earnings of said protected employee in any employment subject to the Railroad Retirement Act and 50 per centum of any earnings in any employment not subject to the Railroad Retirement Act;

48 Stat. 1283.

(C) a protected employee's average monthly compensation shall be adjusted from time to time thereafter to reflect subsequent general wage increases;

(D) should a protected employee's service total less than 12 months in which he performs more than 50 per centum compensated service based upon his normal work schedule in each of said months, his average monthly compensation shall be determined by dividing separately the total compensation received by the employee and the total time for which he was paid by the number of months in which he performed more than 50 per centum compensated service based upon his normal work schedule; and

(E) the monthly displacement allowance provided by this section shall in no event exceed the sum of $2,500 in any month except that such amount shall be adjusted to reflect subsequent general wage increases.

(2) A protected employee's average monthly compensation under this section shall be based upon the rate of pay applicable to his employment and shall include increases in rates of pay not in fact paid but which were provided for in national railroad labor agreements generally applicable during the period involved.

(3) If a protected employee who is entitled to a monthly displacement allowance served as an agent or a representative of a class or craft of employees on either a full- or part-time basis in the 12 months immediately preceding his being adversely affected, his monthly displacement allowance shall be computed by taking the average of the average monthly compensation and average monthly time paid for of the protected employees immediately above and below him on the same seniority roster or his own monthly displacement allowance, whichever is greater.

(4) An employee and his representative shall be furnished with a protected employee's average monthly compensation and average monthly time paid for, computed in accordance with the terms of this subsection, together with the data upon which such computations are based, within 30 days after the protected employee notifies the Corporation in writing that he has been deprived of employment or adversely affected with respect to his compensation.

(c) DURATION OF DISPLACEMENT ALLOWANCE.—The monthly displacement allowance provided for in subsection (b) of this section shall continue until the attainment of age 65 by a protected employee with 5 or more years of service on the effective date of this Act and, in the case of a protected employee who has less than 5 years service on such date, shall continue for a period equal to his total prior years of service: *Provided*, That such monthly displacement allowance shall termi-

87 STAT. 1017

nate upon the protected employee's death, retirement, resignation, or dismissal for cause; and shall be suspended for the period of disciplinary suspension for cause, failure to work due to illness or disability, voluntary furlough, or failure to retain or obtain a position available to him by the exercise of his seniority rights in accordance with the provisions of this section.

(d) TRANSFER.—(1) A protected employee who has been deprived of employment may be required by the Corporation, in inverse seniority order and upon reasonable notice, to transfer to any bona fide vacancy for which he is qualified in his same class or craft of employee on any part of the Corporation's system and shall then be governed by the collective-bargaining agreement applicable on the seniority district to which transferred. If such transfer requires a change in residence, any such protected employee may choose (A) to voluntarily furlough himself at his home location and have his monthly displacement allowance suspended during the period of voluntary furlough, or (B) to be severed from employment upon payment to him of a separation allowance computed as provided in subsections (e) and (f) of this section, which separation allowance shall be in lieu of all other benefits provided by this title.

(2) Such protected employee shall not be required to transfer to a location requiring a change in residence unless there is a bona fide need for his services at such location. Such bona fide need for services contemplates that the transfer be to a position which has not and cannot be filled by employees who are not required to make a change in residence in the seniority district involved and which, in the absence of this section, would have required the employment of a new employee.

(3) Such protected employee who, at the request of the Corporation, has once accepted and made a transfer to a location requiring a change in residence shall not be required again to so transfer for a period of 3 years.

(4) Transfers to vacancies requiring a change in residence shall be subject to the following:

(A) The vacancy shall be first offered to the junior qualified protected employee deprived of employment in the seniority district where the vacancy exists, and each such employee shall have 20 days to elect one of the options set forth in paragraph (1) of this subsection. If that employee elects not to accept the transfer, it will then be offered in inverse seniority order to the remaining qualified, protected employees deprived of employment on the seniority district, who will each have 20 days to elect one of the options set forth in paragraph (1) of this subsection.

(B) If the vacancy is not filled by the procedure in paragraph (4)(A) of this subsection, the vacancy will then be offered in the inverse order of seniority to the qualified protected employees deprived of employment on the system and each of such employees will be afforded 30 days to elect one of the options set forth in paragraph (1) of this subsection.

(C) The provisions of this paragraph shall not prevent the adoption of other procedures pursuant to an agreement made by the Corporation and representative of the class or craft of employees involved.

(e) SEPARATION ALLOWANCE.—A protected employee who is tendered and accepts an offer by the Corporation to resign and sever his employment relationship in consideration of payment to him of a separation allowance, and any protected employee whose employment

87 STAT. 1018

relationship is severed in accordance with subsection (d) of this section, shall be entitled to receive a lump-sum separation allowance not to exceed $20,000 in lieu of all other benefits provided by this title. Said lump-sum separation allowance, in the case of a protected employee who had not less than 3 nor more than 5 years of service as of the date of this Act, shall amount to 270 days' pay at the rate of the position last held and, in the case of a protected employee having had 5 or more years' service, shall amount to the number of days' pay indicated below at the rate of the position last held dependent upon the age of the protected employee at the time of such termination of employment:

60 or under	360 days' pay
61	300 days' pay
62	240 days' pay
63	180 days' pay
64	120 days' pay.

(f) TERMINATION ALLOWANCE.—The Corporation may terminate the employment of an employee of a railroad in reorganization, who has less than 3 years' service as of the effective date of this Act: *Provided, however,* That in such event the terminated employee shall be entitled to receive a lump sum separation allowance in an amount determined as follows:

2 to 3 years' service	180 days' pay at the rate of the position last held.
1 to 2 years' service	90 days' pay at the rate of the position last held.
Less than 1 year's service	5 days' pay at the rate of the position last held for each month of service.

(g) MOVING EXPENSE BENEFITS.—Any protected employee who is required to make a change of residence as the result of a transaction shall be entitled to the following benefits—

(1) Reimbursement for all expenses of moving his household and other personal effects, for the traveling expense of himself and members of his family, including living expenses for himself and his family, and for his own actual wage loss, not to exceed 10 working days. *Provided,* That the Corporation or acquiring railroad shall, to the same extent provided above, assume said expenses for any employee furloughed within 3 years after changing his point of employment as a result of a transaction, who elects to move his place of residence back to his original point of employment. No claim for reimbursement shall be paid under the provisions of this section unless such claim is presented to the Corporation or acquiring railroad within 90 days after the date on which the expenses were incurred.

(2)(A)(i) If the protected employee owns, or is under a contract to purchase, his own home in the locality from which he is required to move and elects to sell said home, he shall be reimbursed for any loss suffered in the sale of his home for less than its fair market value. In each case the fair market value of the home in question shall be determined as of a date sufficiently prior to the date of the transaction so as to be unaffected thereby. The Corporation or an acquiring railroad shall in each instance be afforded an opportunity to purchase the home at such fair market value before it is sold by the employee to any other person.

(ii) A protected employee may elect to waive the provisions of paragraph (2)(A)(i) of this subsection and to receive, in lieu thereof, an amount equal to his closing costs which are ordinarily paid for and assumed by a seller of real estate in the jurisdiction

87 STAT. 1019

in which the residence is located. Such costs shall include a real estate commission paid to a licensed realtor (not to exceed $3,000 or 6 per centum of sale price, whichever is less), and any prepayment penalty required by the institution holding the mortgage; such costs shall not include the payment of any "points" by the seller.

(B) If the protected employee holds an unexpired lease on a dwelling occupied by him as his home, he shall be protected from all loss and cost in securing the cancellation of said lease.

(C) No claim for costs or loss shall be paid under the provisions of this paragraph unless the claim is presented to the Corporation or an acquiring railroad within 90 days after such costs or loss are incurred.

(D) Should a controversy arise with respect to the value of the home, the costs or loss sustained in its sale, the costs or loss under a contract for purchase, loss or cost in securing termination of a lease, or any other question in connection with these matters, it shall be decided through joint conference between the employee, or his representative, and the Corporation or an acquiring railroad. In the event they are unable to agree, the dispute or controversy may be referred by either party to a board of competent real estate appraisers, selected in the following manner: One to be selected by the employee or his representative and one by the Corporation or acquiring railroad and these two, if unable to agree upon a valuation within 30 days, shall endeavor by agreement within 10 days thereafter to select a third appraiser, or to agree to a method by which a third appraiser shall be selected, and, failing such agreement, either party may request the National Mediation Board to designate within 10 days a third qualified real estate appraiser whose designation will be binding upon the parties. A decision of a majority of the appraisers shall be required and said decision shall be final and conclusive. The salary and expenses of the third or neutral appraiser, including the expenses of the appraisal board, shall be borne equally by the parties to the proceedings. All other expenses shall be paid by the party incurring them, including the compensation of the appraiser selected by such party.

(h) APPLICATION OF TITLE.—Should a railroad rearrange or adjust its forces in anticipation of a transaction with the purpose or effect of depriving a protected employee of benefits to which he otherwise would have become entitled under this title, the provisions of this title will apply to such employee.

CONTRACTING OUT

SEC. 506. All work in connection with the operation or services provided by the Corporation on the rail lines, properties, equipment, or facilities acquired pursuant to the provisions of this Act and the maintenance, repair, rehabilitation, or modernization of such lines, properties, equipment, or facilities which has been performed by practice or agreement in accordance with provisions of the existing contracts in effect with the representatives of the employees of the classes or crafts involved shall continue to be performed by said Corporation's employees, including employees on furlough. Should the Corporation lack a sufficient number of employees, including employees on furlough, and be unable to hire additional employees, to perform the work required, it shall be permitted to subcontract that part of such work which cannot be performed by its employees, including those on furlough, except where agreement by the representatives of the employees of the classes or crafts involved is required by applicable collective-bargaining agreements. The term "unable to hire additional employees" as used in this section contemplates establishment and maintenance by the Corporation of an apprenticeship, training, or recruitment program to provide an adequate number of skilled employees to perform the work.

ARBITRATION

SEC. 507. Any dispute or controversy with respect to the interpretation, application, or enforcement of the provisions of this title, except section 504(d) and those disputes or controversies provided for in subsection (g)(2)(D) of section 505 and subsection (b) of section 504 which have not been resolved within 90 days, may be submitted by either party to an Adjustment Board for a final and binding decision thereon as provided in section 3 Second, of the Railway Labor Act, in which event the burden of proof on all issues so presented shall be upon the Corporation or, where applicable, the Association.

44 Stat. 578;
80 Stat. 208.
45 USC 153.

ACQUIRING RAILROADS

SEC. 508. An acquiring railroad shall offer such employment and afford such employment protection to employees of a railroad from which it acquires properties or facilities pursuant to this Act, and shall further protect its own employees who are adversely affected by such acquisition, as shall be agreed upon between the said acquiring railroad and the representatives of such employees prior to said acquisition: *Provided, however,* That the protection and benefits provided for protected employees in such agreements shall be the same as those specified in section 505 of this title: *And provided further, however,* That unless and until such agreements are reached, the acquiring railroad shall not enter into purchase agreements pursuant to section 303 of this Act.

PAYMENTS OF BENEFITS

SEC. 509. The Corporation, the Association (where applicable), and acquiring railroads, as the case may be, shall be responsible for the actual payment of all allowances, expenses, and costs provided protected employees pursuant to the provisions of this title. The Corporation, the Association (where applicable), and acquiring railroads shall then be reimbursed for such actual amounts paid protected employees, not to exceed the aggregate sum of $250,000,000, pursuant to the provisions of this title by the Railroad Retirement Board upon certification to said Board by the Corporation, the Association (where applicable), and acquiring railroads of the amounts paid such employees. Such reimbursement shall be made from a separate account maintained in the Treasury of the United States to be know as the Regional Rail Transportation Protective Account. There is hereby authorized to be appropriated to such protective account annually such sums as may be required to meet the obligations payable hereunder, not to exceed in the aggregate, however, the sum of $250,000,000. There is further authorized to be appropriated to the Railroad Retirement Board annually such sums as may be necessary to provide for additional administrative expenses to be incurred by the Board in the performance of its functions under this section.

Appropriation.

87 STAT. 1021

TITLE VI—MISCELLANEOUS PROVISIONS

RELATIONSHIP TO OTHER LAWS

SEC. 601. (a) ANTITRUST.—(1) Except as specifically provided in paragraph (2) of this subsection, no provision of this Act shall be deemed to convey to any railroad or employee or director thereof any immunity from civil or criminal liability, or to create defenses to actions, under the antitrust laws.

(2) The antitrust laws are inapplicable with respect to any action taken to formulate or implement the final system plan where such action was in compliance with the requirements of such plan.

(3) As used in this subsection, "antitrust laws" includes the Act of July 2, 1890 (ch. 647, 26 Stat. 209), as amended; the Act of October 15, 1914 (ch. 323, 38 Stat. 730), as amended; the Federal Trade Commission Act (38 Stat. 717), as amended; sections 73 and 74 of the Act of August 27, 1894 (28 Stat. 570), as amended; the Act of June 19, 1936 (ch. 592, 49 Stat. 1526), as amended; and the antitrust laws of any State or subdivision thereof.

15 USC 2.
15 USC 12.
15 USC 58.
15 USC 8, 9.
15 USC 13.

(b) COMMERCE AND BANKRUPTCY.—The provisions of the Interstate Commerce Act (49 U.S.C. 1 et seq.) and the Bankruptcy Act (11 U.S.C. et seq.) are inapplicable to transactions under this Act to the extent necessary to formulate and implement the final system plan whenever a provision of any such Act is inconsistent with this Act.

24 Stat. 379.
30 Stat. 544.

(c) ENVIRONMENT.—(1) The provisions of section 102(2)(C) of the National Environmental Policy Act of 1969 (42 U.S.C. 4332 (2)(C)) shall not apply with respect to any action taken under authority of this Act before the effective date of the final system plan.

83 Stat. 853.

(d) NORTHEAST CORRIDOR.—(1) Rail properties designated in accordance with section 206(c)(1)(C) of this Act shall be leased or may (at its option) be purchased or otherwise acquired by the National Railroad Passenger Corporation. The Corporation shall negotiate an appropriate sale or lease agreement with the National Railroad Passenger Corporation as provided in the final system plan.

(2) Properties acquired by purchase, lease, or otherwise pursuant to this subsection shall be improved in order to meet the goal set forth in section 206(a)(3) of this Act, relating to improved high-speed passenger service, by the earliest practicable date after the date of enactment of this Act.

(3) The Secretary shall begin the necessary engineering studies and improvements upon enactment.

(4) The final system plan shall provide for any necessary coordination with freight or commuter services of use of the facilities designated in section 206(c)(1)(C) of this Act. Such coordination may be effectuated through a single operating entity, designated in the final system plan, or as mutually agreed upon by the interested parties.

(5) Construction or improvements made pursuant to this subsection may be made in consultation with the Corps of Engineers.

(e) EMERGENCY SERVICE.—Section 1(16) of the Interstate Commerce Act (49 U.S.C. 1(16)) is amended by inserting "(a)" before the word "Whenever" in the first sentence and adding the following new paragraph:

41 Stat. 477.

"(b) Whenever any carrier by railroad is unable to transport the traffic offered it because—

"(1) its cash position makes its continuing operation impossible;

"(2) it has been ordered to discontinue any service by a court: or

87 STAT. 1022

"(3) it has abandoned service without obtaining a certificate from the Commission pursuant to this section;

the Commission may, upon the same procedure as provided in paragraph (15) of this section, make such just and reasonable directions with respect to the handling, routing, and movement of the traffic available to such carrier and its distribution over such carrier's lines, as in the opinion of the Commission will best promote the service in the interest of the public and the commerce of the people subject to the following conditions:

"(A) Such direction shall be effective for no longer than 60 days unless extended by the Commission for cause shown for an additional designated period not to exceed 180 days.

"(B) No such directions shall be issued that would cause a carrier to operate in violation of the Federal Railroad Safety Act of 1970 (45
84 Stat. 971. U.S.C. 421) or that would substantially impair the ability of the carrier so directed to serve adequately its own patrons or to meet its outstanding common carrier obligations.

"(C) The directed carrier shall not, by reason of such Commission direction, be deemed to have assumed or to become responsible for the debts of the other carrier.

"(D) The directed carrier shall hire employees of the other carrier to the extent such employees had previously performed the directed service for the other carrier, and, as to such employees as shall be so hired, the directed carrier shall be deemed to have assumed all existing employment obligations and practices of the other carrier relating thereto, including, but not limited to, agreements governing rate of pay, rules and working conditions, and all employee protective conditions commencing with and for the duration of the direction.

"(E) Any order of the Commission entered pursuant to this paragraph shall provide that if, for the period of its effectiveness, the cost, as hereinafter defined, of handling, routing, and moving the traffic of another carrier over the other carrier's lines of road shall exceed the direct revenues therefor, then upon request, payment shall be made to the directed carrier, in the manner hereinafter provided and within 90 days after expiration of such order, of a sum equal to the amount
"Cost." by which such cost has exceeded said revenues. The term 'cost' shall mean those expenditures made or incurred in or attributable to the operations as directed, including the rental or lease of necessary equipment, plus an appropriate allocation of common expenses, overheads, and a reasonable profit. Such cost shall be then currently recorded by the carrier or carriers in such manner and on such forms as by general order may be prescribed by the Commission and shall be submitted to and subject to audit by the Commission. The Commission shall certify promptly to the Secretary of the Treasury the amount of payment to be made to said carrier or carriers under the provisions of this paragraph. Payments required to be made to a carrier under the provisions of this paragraph shall be made by the Secretary of the Treasury from funds hereby authorized to be appropriated in such amounts as may be necessary for the purpose of carrying out the provisions hereof.".

ANNUAL EVALUATION BY THE SECRETARY

Report to Congress.   Sec. 602. As part of his annual report each year, the Secretary shall transmit to Congress each year a comprehensive report on the effectiveness of the Association and the Corporation in implementing the purposes of this Act, together with any recommendations for additional legislative or other action.

87 STAT. 1023

FREIGHT RATES FOR RECYCLABLES

Sec. 603. The Commission shall, by expedited proceedings, adopt appropriate rules under the Interstate Commerce Act (49 U.S.C. 1 et seq.) which will eliminate discrimination against the shipment of recyclable materials in rate structures and in other Commission practices where such discrimination exists.

24 Stat. 379.

SEPARABILITY

Sec. 604. If any provision of this Act or the application thereof to any person or circumstances is held invalid, the remainder of this Act and the application of such provision to other persons or circumstances shall not be affected thereby.

Approved January 2, 1974.

LEGISLATIVE HISTORY:

HOUSE REPORTS: No. 93-620 (Comm. on Interstate and Foreign
            Commerce) and No. 93-744 (Comm. of Conference).
CONGRESSIONAL RECORD, Vol. 119 (1973):
    Nov. 8, considered and passed House.
    Dec. 11, considered and passed Senate, amended.
    Dec. 13, Proceedings vacated; reconsidered and passed
        Senate, amended.
    Dec. 20, House agreed to conference report.
    Dec. 21, Senate agreed to conference report.
WEEKLY COMPILATION OF PRESIDENTIAL DOCUMENTS, Vol. 10, No. 1 (1974):
    Jan. 2, Presidential statement.

O

APPENDIX E

Title IV of the 3R Act as Amended in 1975 and 1976

TITLE IV -- LOCAL RAIL SERVICES

FINDINGS AND PURPOSE

SEC. 401. (a) FINDINGS. -- The Congress finds and declares that --

(1) The Nation is facing an energy shortage of acute proportions in the next decade.

(2) Railroads are one of the most energy-efficient modes of transportation for the movement of passengers and freight and cause the least amount of pollution.

(3) Abandonment, termination, or substantial reduction of rail service in any locality will adversely affect the Nation's long-term and immediate goals with respect to energy conservation and environmental protection.

(4) Under certain circumstances the cost to the taxpayers of rail service continuation subsidies would be less than the cost of abandonment of rail service in terms of lost jobs, energy shortages, and degradation of the environment.

(b) PURPOSE. -- Therefore, it is declared to be the purpose of the Congress to authorize the Secretary to maintain a program of rail service continuation subsidies.

RAIL SERVICE CONTINUATION ASSISTANCE

SEC. 402(a) GENERAL. --

(1) The Secretary shall provide financial assistance in accordance with this section to assist in the provision of rail service continuation payments, the acquisition or modernization of rail properties, including the preservation of rights-of-way for future rail service, the construction or improvement of facilities necessary to accommodate the transportation of freight previously moved by rail service, and the cost of operating and

maintaining rail service facilities such as
yards, shops, docks, or other facilities useful
in facilitating and maintaining main line or local
rail service. The Federal share of the costs of
any such assistance shall be as follows: (A) 100
percent for the 12-month period following the
date that rail properties are conveyed pursuant
to section 303(b)(1) of this Act; and (B) 90
percent for the succeeding 12-month period.

(2) The Secretary shall, within one year
after the date of enactment of the Railroad
Revitalization and Regulatory Reform Act of 1976,
promulgate standards and procedures under which
the State share of such cost may be provided
through in-kind benefits such as forgiveness of
taxes, trackage rights, and facilities which
would not otherwise be provided.

(3) The Secretary, in cooperation with the
Secretary of Labor, the Association, and the
Commission,, shall assist States and local or
regional transportation authorities in
negotiating initial operating or lease agreements
and shall report to the Congress not later than
30 days after the date of enactment of the
Railroad Revitalization and Regulatory Reform Act
of 1976 on the progress of such negotiations.
The Secretary may, with the concurrence of a
State, enter directly into operating or lease
agreements with railroads designated to provide
service under section 304(d) of this Act, and
with the trustees of railroads in reorganization
in the region over whose rail properties such
service will be provided, to assure the
uninterrupted continuation of rail service after
such date of conveyance. Such agreements may be
entered into only during the period when the
Federal share is 100 percent. Payments shall be
made from the funds to which a State would
otherwise be entitled under this section.

(b) ENTITLEMENT. --

(1) Each State in the region which is,
pursuant to subsection (c) of this section,
eligible to receive rail service continuation
assistance is entitled to an amount equal to the
total amount authorized and appropriated for such
purpose multiplied by a fraction whose numerator
is the rail mileage in such State which is
eligible for rail service continuation assistance
under this section and whose denominator is the
rail mileage in all of the States in the region
which are eligible for rail service continuation
assistance under this section. Notwithstanding
the preceding sentence, the entitlement of each
State shall not be less than 3 percent of the
funds appropriated. Not more than 5 percent of
a State's entitlement may be used for rail
planning activities. For purposes of this
subsection, rail mileage shall be measured by the

Secretary in consultation with the Interstate
Commerce Commission. Any portion of the
entitlement of any State which is withheld, in
accordance with this section, and any such sums
which are not used or committed by a State shall
be reallocated immediately, to the extent
practicable among the other States in accordance
with the formula set forth in this subsection.
In addition to amounts provided pursuant to such
rail mileage formula, funds shall also be made
available to each State for the cost of operating
and maintaining rail service facilities such as
yards, shops, and docks which are useful in
facilitating and maintaining main line or local
rail services and which are contained in each
State's rail plan, except that (A) any such
assistance shall extend for a period of only 12
months following the date rail properties are
conveyed under section 303(b)(1) of this Act, and
(B) no railroad shall be required to operate such
facilities. With respect to the limitation on
assistance for rail service facilities under the
preceding sentence, the Secretary shall not later
than 90 days prior to the end of such 12-month
period, submit a report to the Congress in
conjunction with a designated State agency,
recommending future action with respect to such
facilities.

(2) For a period of not more than 1 year
following the date rail properties are conveyed
pursuant to section 303(b)(1) of this Act, the
Secretary is authorized to provide financial
assistance, from the funds to which a State would
otherwise be entitled under this section for the
continuation of local rail services, to any
person determined by the Secretary to be
financially responsible who will enter into any
operating and lease agreements with railroads
designated to provide service under section
304(d) of this Act, regardless of the
eligibility of the State, where the applicable
rail properties are located, to receive
assistance under subsection (c) of this section.
In any case in which a State is eligible to
receive rail service continuation assistance
under subsection (c) of this section, States
shall have priority to receive such payments over
any other person eligible under this paragraph
and no other person eligible under this paragraph
shall receive such payments unless his
application therefor has been approved by the
State agency designated under subsection (c) to
administer the State plan.

(c) ELIGIBILITY. --

(1) A State in the region is eligible to
receive financial assistance pursuant to
subsection (b) of this section if, in any fiscal
year --

(A) the State has established a State plan for rail transportation and local rail services (herein referred to as the "State rail plan") which is administered or coordinated by a designated State agency and such plan includes a suitable process for updating, revising, and amending such plan and provides for the equitable distribution of such financial assistance among State, local, and regional transportation authorities;

(B) the State agency (i) has authority and administrative jurisdiction to develop, promote, supervise, and support safe, adequate, and efficient rail services, (ii) employes or will employ, directly or indirectly, sufficient trained and qualified personnel, and (iii) maintains or will maintain adequate programs of investigation, research promotion, and development with provision for public participation;

(C) the State provides satisfactory assurance that such fiscal control and fund accounting procedures will be adopted as may be necessary to assure proper disbursement of, and accounting for, Federal funds paid under this title to the State; and (D) the State complies with the regulations of the Secretary issued under this section.

(2) The rail freight services which are eligible for rail service continuation assistance pursuant to this section are --

(A) those rail services of railroads in reorganization in the region, or persons leased, operated, or controlled by any such railroad, which the final system plan does not designate to be continued;

(B) those rail services, or rail properties referred to in section 304(a)(2) of this Act;

(C) those rail services in the region which have been, at any time during the 5-year period prior to the date of enactment of this Act, or which, are subsequent to the date of enactment of this Act owned, leased, or operated by a State agency or by a local or regional transportation authority, or with respect to which a State, a political subdivision thereof, or a local or regional transportation authority has invested (at any time during the 5-year period prior to the date of enactment of this Act), or invests (subsequent to the date of enactment of this Act), substantial sums for improvement or maintenance of rail service; or

(D) those rail services in the region with respect to which the Commission authorizes the discontinuance of rail services or the abandonment of rail properties, effective on or after the date of enactment of this Act.

(3) The rail freight properties which are eligible to be acquired or modernized with financial assistance pursuant to subsection (b) of this section are those rail properties which are used for services eligible for rail service continuation assistance, pursuant to paragraph (2) of this subsection, including those properties which are identified, in the applicable State rail plan as having potential for future use for rail freight service.

(4) The facilities which are eligible to be constructed or improved with financial assistance pursuant to subsection (b) of this section are those facilities in the region (including intermodal terminals and highways or bridges) which are needed in order to provide rail freight service which will no longer be available because of the discontinuance of rail freight service under section 304 of this Act or other lawful authority. No funds provided under this paragraph may be used to pay the State share of any highway projects under title 23, United States Code.

(5) Rail properties are eligible to be acquired with financial assistance pursuant to subsection (b) of this section if (A) they are to be used for intercity or commuter rail passenger service, and (B) they pertain to a line in the region (other than rail properties designated in accordance with section 206(c (1)(C) of this Act) which, if so acquired (i) would enable the National Railroad Passenger Corporation to serve, more efficiently, a route which it operated on November 1, 1975, (ii) would provide intercity rail passenger service designated by the Secretary under title IV of the Rail Passenger Service Act, or (iii) would provide such service over a route designated for service pursuant to section 403(c) of the Rail Passenger Service Act (45 U.S.C. 563(c)).

(d) REGULATIONS. -- Within 90 days after the date of enactment of this Act, the Secretary shall issue, and may from time to time amend, regulations with respect to the provision of financial assistance under this title.

(e) PAYMENT. -- The Secretary shall pay to each eligible State in the region an amount equal to its entitlement under subsection (b) of this section.

(f) RECORDS, AUDIT, AND EXAMINATION. --

(1) Each recipient of financial assistance under this section, whether in the form of grants, subgrants, contracts, subcontracts, or other arrangements, shall keep such records as the Secretary shall prescribe, including records which fully disclose the amount and disposition by such recipient of the proceeds of such assistance, the total cost of the project or undertaking in connection with which such assistance was given or used, the amount of that portion of the cost of the project supplied by other sources, and such other records as will facilitate an effective audit. Such records shall be maintained for 3 years after completion of such a project or undertaking.

(2) The Secretary and the Comptroller General of the United States, or any of their duly authorized representatives, shall have access for the purpose of audit and examination to any books, documents, papers, and records of such receipts which in the opinion of the Secretary or the Comptroller General may be related or pertinent to the grants, contracts, or other arrangements referred to in such paragraph.

(g) WITHHOLDING. -- If the Secretary, after reasonable notice and an opportunity for a hearing to any State agency, finds that a State is not eligible for financial assistance under subsections (c) and (d) of this section, payment to such State shall not be made until there is no longer any failure to comply.

(h) AUTHORIZATION OF APPROPRIATIONS. -- There is authorized to be appropriated to the Secretary to carry out the purposes of this section an amount not to exceed $180,000,000 without fiscal year limitation. Such sums as are appropriated shall remain available until expended.

(i) DEFINITION. -- As used in this section, the term "rail service continuation assistance" includes expenditures made by a State (or a local or regional transportation authority), at any time during a 1-year period preceding the date of enactment of this Act, or subsequent to the date of enactment of this Act, for acquisition, rehabilitation, or modernization of rail facilities on which rail freight services would have been curtailed or abandoned but for such expenditures.

(b) Section 403(a) of the Regional Rail

Reorganization Act of 1973 (45 U.S.C. 763), is amended by striking the colon and the proviso and inserting in lieu thereof a period.

(c) Section 403(b) of the Regional Rail Reorganization Act of 1973 (45 U.S.C. 763(b)) is amended by striking the last sentence thereof and inserting in lieu thereof the following: "Notwithstanding any other provision of this title, a State may expend sums received by it under paragraphs (1) and (2) of section 402(b) of this title for acquisition and modernization pursuant to this section, or for any project designated pursuant to a State rail plan.

ACQUISITION AND MODERNIZATION LOANS

SEC. 403. (a) ACQUISITION. -- If a State which is eligible for assistance under section 402(c) of this title or a local or regional transportation authority has made an offer to purchase any rail properties of a railroad pursuant to section 304(c)(2)(C) of this Act or other lawful authority, the Secretary is authorized to direct the Association to provide loans to such State or local or regional transportation authority not to exceed 70 per centum of the purchase price; Provided, however, That any rail service for which a State agency or local or regional transportation authority receives such loan is no longer eligible for a rail service continuation subsidy pursuant to section 402 of this title.

(b) MODERNIZATION. -- In addition to such acquisition loans, the Secretary is authorized to direct the Association to provide additional assistance not to exceed 70 per centum of the cost of restoring or repairing such rail properties to such condition as will enable safe and efficient rail transportation operations over such rail properties. Such financial assistance may be in the form of a loan or the guarantee of a loan. The Association shall provide such financial assistance as the Secretary may direct under this section and shall adopt regulations describing its procedures for such assistance. With the approval of the Secretary, a State may expend sums received by it under section 402 of this title for acquisition and modernization pursuant to this section.

APPENDIX F
The Local Rail Service
Assistance Act of 1978

Public Law 95–607
95th Congress

An Act

To amend section 5 of the Department of Transportation Act, relating to rail service assistance, and for other purposes.

Nov. 8, 1978

[S. 2981]

Be it enacted by the Senate and House of Representatives of the United States of America in Congress assembled,

Department of Transportation Act, amendment. Local Rail Service Assistance Act of 1978.
49 USC 1651 note.

TITLE I—LOCAL RAIL SERVICE ASSISTANCE

SHORT TITLE

Sec. 101. This title may be cited as the "Local Rail Service Assistance Act of 1978".

EXPANSION OF ASSISTANCE

Sec. 102. Section 5(f) of the Department of Transportation Act (49 U.S.C. 1654(f)) is amended—

(1) in paragraph (2), by striking out "purchasing a line of railroad or other rail properties" and inserting in lieu thereof "acquiring, by purchase, lease, or in such other manner as the State considers appropriate, a line of railroad or other rail properties, or any interest therein,";

(2) in paragraph (3), by striking out "and" immediately after the semicolon;

(3) in paragraph (4), by striking out the period and inserting in lieu thereof "; and"; and

(4) by adding at the end thereof the following new paragraph:

"(5) the cost of constructing rail or rail related facilities (including new connections between two or more existing lines of railroad, intermodal freight terminals, sidings, and relocation of existing lines) for the purpose of improving the quality and efficiency of rail freight service.".

COST SHARING

Sec. 103. Section 5(g) of the Department of Transportation Act (49 U.S.C. 1654(g)) is amended to read as follows:

"(g) The Federal share of the costs of any rail service assistance program shall be 80 per centum, except that the Federal share of costs for financial assistance under paragraph (1) of subsection (f) of this section for any project described in subsection (k)(1) of this section shall be 80 per centum for the first and second years such project is conducted and 70 per centum for the third year such project is conducted. The State share of the costs may be provided in cash or through any of the following benefits, to the extent that such benefits would not otherwise be provided: (1) forgiveness of taxes imposed on a common carrier by railroad or on its properties; (2) the provision by the State or by any person or entity on behalf of such State, for use in its rail service assistance program, of real property or tangible personal property of the kind necessary for the safe and efficient operation of rail freight service; (3) trackage rights secured by the State for a common carrier by railroad; or (4) the cash equivalent of State

Federal share.

State share.

salaries for State public employees working in the State rail service assistance program, but not including overhead and general administrative costs. If a State, or any person or entity on behalf of a State, provides more than such State's percentage share of the cost of its rail service assistance program during any fiscal year, the amount in excess of such share shall be applied toward such State's share of the costs of its program for subsequent fiscal years.".

FORMULA ALLOCATION

SEC. 104. Section 5(h) of the Department of Transportation Act (49 U.S.C. 1654(h)) is amended to read as follows:

"(h)(1) For the period beginning October 1, 1978, and ending September 30, 1979, each State which is eligible to receive rail service assistance under this section is entitled to an amount equal to the total amount authorized and appropriated for such purposes, multiplied by a fraction the numerator of which is the rail mileage in such State which was eligible for rail service assistance under this section prior to October 1, 1978, and the denominator of which is the rail mileage in all of the States which was eligible for rail service assistance under this section prior to such date. Notwithstanding the provisions of the preceding sentence, the entitlement of each State shall not be less than 1 percent of the funds appropriated.

"(2) Effective October 1, 1979, each State which is eligible to receive rail service assistance under this section is entitled annually to a sum from available funds as determined pursuant to this subsection. Available funds are funds appropriated for rail service assistance for that fiscal year and any funds to be reallocated for that fiscal year in accordance with this subsection. Subject to the limitations set forth in paragraph (3) of this subsection, the Secretary shall calculate each State's entitlement as follows:

"(A) two-thirds of the available funds, multiplied by a fraction (i) the numerator of which is the sum of the rail mileage in the State which, in accordance with section 1a(5)(a) of the Interstate Commerce Act (49 U.S.C. 1a(5)(a)), is either 'potentially subject to abandonment' or with respect to which a carrier plans to submit, but has not yet submitted, an application for a certificate of abandonment or discontinuance, and (ii) the denominator of which is the total of such rail mileage in all the States; and

"(B) one-third of available funds, multiplied by a fraction (i) the numerator of which is the rail mileage in the State with respect to which the Interstate Commerce Commission, within 3 years prior to the first day of the fiscal year for which funds are allocated or reallocated under this section, has found that the public convenience and necessity permit the abandonment of, or the discontinuance of rail service on, such rail mileage (including, until September 30, 1981, the rail mileage which was eligible for assistance under section 402 of the Regional Rail Reorganization Act of 1973 (45 U.S.C. 762), and all rail mileage in the State which has, prior to October 1, 1978, been included for formula allocation purposes under this section); and (ii) the denominator of which is the total rail mileage in all the States eligible for rail service assistance under this section which the Interstate Commerce Commission has made such a finding (including, until September 30, 1981, the rail mileage in all the States which was eligible for financial assistance under section 402 of the Regional Rail Reorganization Act of 1973 (45 U.S.C. 762), and the rail mileage in all the States which has, prior to October 1, 1978, been included for formula allocation purposes under this section). Notwithstanding the preceding provisions of this paragraph, the entitlement of each State in a fiscal year shall not be less than 1 percent of the funds appropriated for such fiscal year.

"(3)(A) For purposes of paragraphs (1) and (2) of this subsection, rail mileage shall be measured by the Secretary as of the first day of each fiscal year. In making calculations under this subsection, no rail mileage shall be included more than once in either the numerator or the denominator of a fraction.

"(B) Entitlement funds are available to a State during the fiscal year for which the funds are appropriated. In accordance with the formula stated in this subsection, the Secretary shall reallocate, to each State which is eligible to receive rail service assistance under this section, a share of any entitlement funds which have not been the subject of an executed grant agreement between the Secretary and the State before the end of the fiscal year for which the funds were appropriated. Reallocated funds are available to the State for the same purpose and for the same time period as an original allocation and are subject to reallocation if not made the subject of an executed grant agreement between the Secretary and the State before the end of the fiscal year for which the funds were reallocated. Funds appropriated in fiscal year 1978 and prior years which are not the subject of an executed grant agreement as of October 1, 1978, shall remain available to the States during fiscal year 1979.

Reallocation of funds.

"(4) Two or more States which are eligible to receive rail service assistance under this section may, where not in violation of State law, enter into an agreement to combine any portion of their respective Federal entitlements under this subsection for purposes of conducting any project which is eligible for assistance under subsection (k) of this section and which will benefit each State which is a party to such agreement.".

State agreements.

PLANNING ASSISTANCE

SEC. 105. Section 5(i) of the Department of Transportation Act (49 U.S.C. 1654(i)) is amended to read as follows:

"(i) During each fiscal year, a State may expend not to exceed $100,000, or 5 percent, whichever is greater, of its annual entitlement under subsection (h) of this section to meet the cost of establishing, implementing, revising, and updating the State rail plan required by subsection (j) of this section.".

Ante, p. 3060.

Infra.

STATE ELIGIBILITY

SEC. 106. (a) Paragraph (2) of section 5(j) of the Department of Transportation Act (49 U.S.C. 1654(j)(1)) is amended—

(1) by inserting "(A)" immediately after "(2)"; and

(2) by adding immediately before the semicolon at the end thereof the following: ", and (B) such State plan includes, as

9.

soon as practicable after the date of enactment of the Local Rail Service Assistance Act of 1978, a methodology for determining the ratio of benefits to costs of projects which are proposed to be initiated after such date of enactment and which are eligible for assistance under paragraphs (2) through (4) of subsection (k) of this section".

4   (b) During the period prior to the inclusion in a State rail plan of the methodology referred to in the amendment made by subsection (a) of this section, the Secretary of Transportation shall continue to fund projects on a case-by-case basis where he has determined, based upon analysis performed and documented by the State, that the public benefits associated with the project outweigh the public costs of such project.

PROJECT ELIGIBILITY

SEC. 107. Section 5(k) of the Department of Transportation Act (49 U.S.C. 1654(k)) is amended to read as follows:

"(k)(1) A project is eligible for financial assistance under paragraph (1) of subsection (f) of this section only if—

"(A) (i) the Interstate Commerce Commission has found, since February 5, 1976, that the public convenience and necessity permit the abandonment of, or the discontinuance of rail service on, the line of railroad which is related to the project; or (ii) the line of railroad or related project was eligible for assistance under section 402 of the Regional Rail Reorganization Act of 1973 (45 U.S.C. 762); and

"(B) the line of railroad or related project has not previously received financial assistance under paragraph (1) of subsection (f) of this section for more than 36 months, except that a line of railroad or related project which was eligible for financial assistance under section 402 of the Regional Rail Reorganization Act of 1973 (45 U.S.C. 762) or under this section prior to October 1, 1978, shall be eligible only until September 30, 1981.

"(2) A project is eligible for financial assistance under paragraph (2) of subsection (f) of this section only if—

"(A) the Interstate Commerce Commission has found, since February 5, 1976, that the public convenience and necessity permit the abandonment of, or the discontinuance of rail service on, the line of railroad related to the project;

"(B) the line of railroad related to the project is listed for possible inclusion in a rail bank in part III, section C of the Final System Plan issued by the United States Railway Association under section 207 of the Regional Rail Reorganization Act of 1973 (45 U.S.C. 717); or

"(C) the line of railroad related to the project was eligible to be acquired under section 402(c)(3) of the Regional Rail Reorganization Act of 1973 (45 U.S.C. 762(c)(3)), except that a line of railroad or related project which was eligible for financial assistance under such section 402 or under this section prior to October 1, 1978, shall be eligible only until September 30, 1981.

"(3) A project is eligible for financial assistance under paragraphs (3) and (5) of subsection (f) of this section only if—

"(A) the line of railroad related to the project is certified by the railroad as having carried 3 million gross ton miles of freight or less per mile during the prior year;

"(B) the line of railroad related to the project is certified by the railroad as having carried less than 5 million gross ton miles of freight per mile during the prior year and the Secretary has determined that the project is essential to carry out proposals made under authority of subsections (a) through (e) of this section;

"(C) an application for a certificate of abandonment or discontinuance with respect to the line of railroad related to the project has been filed with the Interstate Commerce Commission prior to January 1, 1979 (whether or not such application has been granted);

"(D) the line of railroad related to the project is listed for possible inclusion in a rail bank in part III, section C of the Final System Plan issued by the United States Railway Association under section 207 of the Regional Rail Reorganization Act of 1973 (45 U.S.C. 717); or

"(E) the line of railroad related to the project was eligible to be acquired under section 402(c)(3) of the Regional Rail Reorganization Act of 1973 (45 U.S.C. 762(c)(3)).
Any project involving a line of railroad described in subparagraph (C), (D), or (E) of this paragraph shall only be eligible for financial assistance until September 30, 1981.

"(4) A project is eligible for financial assistance under paragraph (4) of subsection (f) of this section only if—

"(A) the Interstate Commerce Commission has found, since February 5, 1976, that the public convenience and necessity permit the abandonment of, or the discontinuance of rail service on, the line of railroad which is related to the project: or

"(B) the line of railroad or related project was eligible for financial assistance under section 402 of the Regional Rail Reorganization Act of 1973 (45 U.S.C. 762), except that a line of railroad or related project which was eligible for assistance under such section 402 or under this section prior to October 1, 1978, shall be eligible only until September 30, 1981.

"(5) On or before August 1 of each year, each common carrier by railroad subject to part I of the Interstate Commerce Act shall pre- **49 USC 1.** pare, update, and submit to the Secretary a listing of those rail lines of such carrier which, based on level of usage, carried 3 million gross ton miles of freight or less per mile during the prior year.".

REHABILITATION ASSISTANCE

SEC. 108. Section 5 of the Department of Transportation Act (49 U.S.C. 1654) is amended by redesignating subsection (o) as subsection (p), and by inserting immediately after subsection (n) the following new subsection:

"(o) A State shall use financial assistance provided under paragraph (3) of subsection (f) of this section in accordance with the following provisions:

"(1) The financial assistance shall be used to rehabilitate or improve rail properties in order to improve rail freight service within the State.

"(2) The State shall, in its discretion, grant or loan funds to the owner of rail properties or operator of rail service related to the project.

"(3) The State shall determine all financial terms and conditions of a grant or loan, except that the timing of all advances with respect to grants in and under this subsection shall be in accordance with Department of Treasury regulations.

"(4) The State shall place the Federal share of repaid funds in an interest-bearing account or, with the approval of the Secretary, permit any borrower to place such funds, for the benefit and use of the State, in a bank which has been designated by the Secretary of the Treasury in accordance with section 10 of the Act of June 11, 1942 (12 U.S.C. 265). The State shall use such funds and all accumulated interest to make further loans or grants under paragraph (3) of subsection (f) of this section in the same manner and under the same conditions as if they were originally granted to the State by the Secretary. The State may, at any time, pay to the Secretary the Federal share of any unused funds and accumulated interest. After the termination of a State's participation in the rail service assistance program established by this section, such State shall pay the Federal share of any unused funds and accumulated interest to the Secretary.".

TECHNICAL AMENDMENTS

Sec. 109. (a) Section 5 of the Department of Transportation Act (49 U.S.C. 1654) is amended—

063.

(1) in subsection (g), subsection (m) (1), and the first sentence of subsection (p) (as redesignated by section 108 of this title), by striking out "(o)" each place it appears and inserting in lieu thereof "(p)"; and

(2) by amending the third sentence of subsection (p) (as so redesignated) to read as follows: "In addition, any appropriated sums remaining after the repeal of section 402 of the Regional Rail

62.

Reorganization Act of 1973 and of section 810 of the Railroad

653a.

Revitalization and Regulatory Reform Act of 1976 are authorized to remain available to the Secretary for purposes of subsections (f) through (p) of this section.".

(b)(1) Section 810 of the Railroad Revitalization and Regulatory Reform Act of 1976 (49 U.S.C. 1653a) is repealed.

(2) The table of contents for title VIII of the Railroad Revitalization and Regulatory Reform Act of 1976 is amended by striking out "Sec. 810. Rail bank.".

EFFECTIVE DATE

654

Sec. 110. The provisions of this title shall take effect on October 1, 1978.

TITLE II—AMENDMENTS TO THE REGIONAL RAIL REORGANIZATION ACT OF 1973

AMENDMENTS TO THE REGIONAL RAIL REORGANIZATION ACT OF 1973

Sec. 201. Section 304(e) of the Regional Rail Reorganization Act of 1973 (45 U.S.C. 744(e)) is amended—

(1) by striking out the comma at the end of paragraph (4) (B) and inserting in lieu thereof "; or"; and

(2) by adding immediately after paragraph (4)(B) the following new subparagraph:

"(C) offers a rail service continuation payment, pursuant to subsection (c)(2)(A) of this section and regulations issued by the Office pursuant to section 205(d)(5) of this Act, for the operation of rail passenger service provided under an agreement or lease pursuant to section 303(b)(2) of this title or subsection (c)(2)(B) of this section where such offer is made for the continuation of the service beyond the period required by such agreement or lease, except that such services shall not be eligible for assistance under section 17(a)(2) of the Urban Mass Transportation Act of 1964 (49 U.S.C. 1613(a)(2))."; and

45 USC 715.
45 USC 743.

(3) by adding at the end thereof the following new paragraphs:

"(7)(A) If a State (or a local or regional transportation authority) in the region offers to provide payment for the provision of additional rail passenger service, the Corporation shall undertake to provide such service pursuant to this subsection (including the discontinuance provisions of paragraph (2) of this subsection). An offer to provide payment for the provision of additional rail passenger service shall be made in accordance with subsection (c)(2)(A) of this section and under regulations issued by the Office pursuant to section 205(d)(5) of this Act, and shall be designed to avoid any additional costs to the Corporation arising from the construction or modification of capital facilities or from any additional operating delays or costs arising from the absence of such construction or modification. The State (or local or regional transportation authority) shall demonstrate that it has acquired, leased, or otherwise obtained access to all rail properties, other than those designated for conveyance to the National Railroad Passenger Corporation pursuant to sections 206(c)(1)(C) and 206(c)(1)(D) of this Act and to the Corporation pursuant to section 303(b)(1) of this title, necessary to provide the additional rail passenger service and that it has completed, or will complete prior to the inception of the additional rail service, all capital improvements necessary to avoid significant costs which cannot be avoided by improved scheduling or other means on other existing rail services (including rail freight service) and to assure that the additional service will not detract from the level and quality of existing rail passenger and freight service.

42 USC 716.

"(B) As used in this paragraph, the term 'additional rail passenger service' means rail passenger service (other than rail passenger service provided pursuant to the provisions of paragraphs (2) and (4) of this subsection), including extended or expanded service and modified routings, which is to be provided over rail properties conveyed to the Corporation pursuant to section 303(b)(1) of this title, or over (i) rail properties contiguous thereto conveyed to the National Railroad Passenger Corporation pursuant to this Act, or (ii) any other rail properties contiguous thereto to which a State (or local or regional transportation authority) has obtained access.

"Additional rail
passenger
service."

"(C) Notwithstanding any other provision of this paragraph, the Corporation shall not be required to operate additional rail passenger service over rail properties leased or acquired from or owned or leased by a profitable railroad in the region.

"(8) The Secretary shall, in consultation with the Association, conduct a study to determine the best means of compensating the Corporation for liabilities which it may incur for damages to persons or property, resulting from the operation of rail passenger service required to be operated pursuant to this subsection or section 303 (b)(2) of this title, which are not underwritten by private insurance carriers or are not indemnified by a State (or local or regional transportation authority). Such study shall identify the nature of the risks to the Corporation, the probable degree of uninsurability of such risks, and the desirability and feasibility of various indemnification programs, including subsidy offers made pursuant to this section, self-insurance through a passenger tax or other mechanism, or government indemnification for such liabilities. Within one year after the date of enactment of this paragraph, the Secretary shall prepare a report with appropriate recommendations and shall submit such report to the Congress. Such report shall specify the most appropriate means of indemnifying the Corporation for such liabilities in a manner which shall prevent the cross-subsidization of passenger services with revenues from freight services operated by the Corporation.".

TITLE III—AMENDMENTS TO THE RAILROAD REVITALIZATION AND REGULATORY REFORM ACT OF 1976; RELATED PROVISIONS

INCREASE IN FUNDING LIMITATION ON PURCHASE OF TRUSTEE CERTIFICATES; EXTENSION OF AUTHORITY TO ISSUE AND SELL FUND ANTICIPATION NOTES

Sec. 301. (a) Section 505 of the Railroad Revitalization and Regulatory Reform Act of 1976 (45 U.S.C. 825) is amended—

(1) in subsection (d)(3), by striking out the last sentence; and

(2) in subsection (e), by striking out "purchase under this title after September 30, 1978." and inserting in lieu thereof ", after September 30, 1979, make commitments to purchase under this title,".

(b) Sections 507(a) and 507(d) of the Railroad Revitalization and Regulatory Reform Act of 1976 (7 U.S.C. 827 (a) and (d)) are amended by striking out "1978" and inserting in lieu thereof "1979".

(c) Section 509 of the Railroad Revitalization and Regulatory Reform Act of 1976 (45 U.S.C. 829) is amended by striking out "March 31" each place it appears and inserting in lieu thereof "September 30".

SECURITY FOR TRUSTEE CERTIFICATES

Sec. 302. Section 505(d)(2) of the Railroad Revitalization and Regulatory Reform Act of 1976 (45 U.S.C. 825(d)(2)) is amended—

(1) in the last sentence of subparagraph (B), by striking out "No certificate" and inserting in lieu thereof "Except as provided in subparagraph (C) of this paragraph, no certificate"; and

(2) by adding at the end thereof the following new subparagraph:

"(C) The Secretary may purchase certificates under this section without making the finding referred to in clause (iii) of subparagraph (B) only if such certificates are senior in rights to all outstanding capital stock, common and preferred, of the debtor corporation, and all unsecured debt incurred before the date of commencement of railroad reorganization proceedings pursuant to section 77 of the Bankruptcy Act, but subordinate to all senior debt of the debtor corporation whenever such senior debt is incurred. As used in this subparagraph, the term 'senior debt' means— 11 USC 205.
"Senior debt."

"(i) all costs of administration, incurred or to be incurred by a trustee, and secured debt assumed by a trustee, in connection with the reorganization proceedings and the operation of a debtor's business by a trustee during the pendency of such proceedings; and

"(ii) all secured debt incurred before the date of commencement of railroad reorganization proceedings pursuant to section 77 of the Bankruptcy Act and determined by the court to be a proper claim against the estate and an obligation of the debtor corporation.".

FRA REVIEW

Sec. 303. The Federal Railroad Administration shall promptly review the condition of the Chicago, Milwaukee, and Saint Paul Railroad and consider assisting such railroad with loans for roadbed and track improvement. 45 USC 825 note.

TITLE IV—AMENDMENTS TO THE INTERSTATE COMMERCE ACT

RENEWAL

Sec. 401. (a) Section 15(8)(c) of the Interstate Commerce Act (49 U.S.C. 15(8)(c)) is amended—

(1) in clause (i), by striking out "within 2 years after the date of the enactment of this subdivision" and inserting in lieu thereof "prior to July 1, 1980";

(2) in clause (ii), by inserting "and" after the semicolon; and

(3) by striking out clauses (iii) and (iv) and inserting in lieu thereof a new clause (iii) to read as follows:

"(iii) the aggregate of increases or decreases in any rate filed pursuant to clause (i) or (ii) of this subdivision during any calendar year is not greater than 7 per centum of the rate in effect on January 1 of that year.".

(b) The last sentence of section 15(8)(d) of the Interstate Commerce Act (49 U.S.C. 25(8)(d)) is amended by striking out "clauses (iii) or (iv)" and inserting in lieu thereof "clause (iii)". 49 USC 15.

CAR SERVICE

Sec. 402. Section 1(14) of the Interstate Commerce Act (49 U.S.C. 1(14)) is amended by redesignating subdivision (b) as subdivision (c), and by inserting immediately after subdivision (a) the following new subdivision:

Petition.
Notice
and hearing.

"(b) If the Commission finds, upon the petition of an interested party and after notice and a hearing on the record, that a common carrier by railroad subject to this part has materially failed to furnish safe and adequate car service as required by paragraph (11) of this section, the Commission may require such carrier to provide itself with such facilities and equipment as may be reasonably necessary to furnish such service, if the evidence of record establishes, and the Commission affirmatively finds, that—

"(i) the provision of such facilities or equipment will not materially and adversely affect the ability of such carrier to otherwise provide safe and adequate transportation services;

"(ii) the expenditure required for such facilities or equipment, including a return which equals such carrier's current cost of capital, will be recovered; and

"(iii) the provision of such facilities or equipment will not impair the ability of such carrier to attract adequate capital.".

Approved November 8, 1978.

LEGISLATIVE HISTORY:

HOUSE REPORT No. 95-1482 accompanying H.R. 11979 (Comm. on Interstate and Foreign Commerce).
SENATE REPORT No. 95-1159 (Comm. on Commerce, Science, and Transportation).
CONGRESSIONAL RECORD, Vol. 124 (1978):
    Sept. 23, considered and passed Senate.
    Oct. 11, 13, H.R. 11979 considered and passed House; passage vacated, and S. 2981, amended, passed in lieu.
    Oct. 15, Senate concurred in House amendments.

BIBLIOGRAPHY

Books and Reports

Banks (R.L.) and Associates. *Development and Evaluation of an Economic Abstraction of Light Density Line Operations.* Report FRA-OE-73–3, prepared for the Federal Railroad Administration, June 1973.

Battelle Columbus Laboratories. *An Environmental Assessment of the Potential Effects of the Railroad System Plan.* Columbus, Ohio: Battelle, 1974.

Black, William R. and Runke, James F. *The States and Rural Rail Preservation: Alternative Strategies.* Lexington, KY.: The Council of State Governments, October 1975.

Boyer, Kenneth D. and Sheperd, William G. (eds.) *Economic Regulation: Essays in Honor of James R. Nelson.* East Lansing, Mich.: The Institute of Public Utilities, Graduate School of Business Administration, Michigan State University, 1981.

Cherington, Charles R. *Regulation of Railroad Abandonments.* Cambridge: Harvard University Press, 1948.

Conant, Michael. *Railroad Mergers and Abandonments.* Berkeley: University of California Press, 1964.

CONSAD Research Corporation. *Analysis of Community Impacts Resulting From the Loss of Rail Service.* Pittsburgh: Consad Research Corporation, 1974, 4 vols.

Daughen, Joseph R. and Binzen, Peter. *The Wreck of the Penn Central.* Boston: Little, Brown and Co., 1971.

Davies, Gerald K., *et. al. Viability of Light Density Rail Lines: The United States Railway Association's Analytic Policies and Procedures.* Washington, D.C.: United States Railway Association, March 1976.

Due, John R. *A Case Study of the Effects of the Abandonment of a Railway Line—Sherman and Wasco Counties, Oregon,* Champaign, Ill.: College of Commerce and Business Administration, University of Illinois at Champaign-Urbana, Transportation Research Paper No. 5, 1974.

Due, John F. *Long Term Impact of Abandonment of Railway Lines.* Champaign, Ill.: College of Commerce and Business Administration, University of Illinois at Champaign-Urbana, Transportation Research Paper No. 7, 1975.

Faucett (Jack) Associates, Inc. *Potential Economic Impact of the Termination of Rail Service to Twelve Selected Communities.* Chevy Chase, Md.: Jack Faucett Associates, Inc., 1973.

Ferguson, Allen R.; Jones, Jr., Norman H.; Slavsky, Barry I.; Reece III, Lawrence H.; Rothenberg, Stanley; and, Topping, Frances. *Community Impacts of Abandonment of Railroad Service.* Washington, D.C.: Public Interest Economics Center, 1974.

Friedlaender, Ann F. *The Dilemma of Freight Transport Regulation.* Washington, D.C.: The Brookings Institution, 1969.

Friedlaender, Ann F. and Spady, Richard H. *Freight Transport Regulation.* Cambridge, Mass.: The MIT Press, 1981.

Harr, John E. *The Great Railway Crisis: An Administrative History of the United States Railway Association.* National Academy of Public Administration, March 1978.

Hilton, George W. *Amtrak: The National Railroad Passenger Corporation.* Washington, D.C.: American Enterprise Institute for Public Policy Research, 1980.

Humphrey, Thomas J. *Framework for Predicting the External Impacts of Railroad Abandonments.* Cambridge, Mass.: Transportation Systems Division, Department of Civil Engineering, Massachusetts Institute of Technology, 1975.

JWK International Corp. and Roger Creighton Assoc., Inc. *Rail Planning Manual, Vol. I, Guide for Decision-Makers, and Vol. II, Guide for Planners.* Reports FRA-RFA-76-06, FRA-RFA-78-01, prepared for the Federal Railroad Administration, December 1976 and July 1978.

Keeler, Theodore E. *Railroads, Freight and Public Policy.* Washington, D.C.: The Brookings Institution, 1983.

Levine, Harvey A.; Eby, Clifford C.; Rockey, Craig F.; and Dale, John L. *Small Railroads.* Chelsea, Mich.: Book Crafters, Inc., 1982.

MacAvoy, Paul W. and Snow, John W. *Railroad Revitalization and Regulatory Reform.* Washington, D.C.: American Enterprise Institute, 1977.

Pigozzi, B.W.; Martin, R.N.; and, Schuler, H.J. *Indiana Rail Plan: Methodology Review.* Bloomington, Indiana: Center for Urban and Regional Analysis, Indiana University, Rail Planning and Policy Series, No. 2, October 1976.

Purnell, Lynn O. *A Methodology for Evaluating the Impact of Rail Abandonment on Rural Highways.* West Lafayette, Indiana: School of Civil Engineering, 1976, Report JHRP-76-4.

Runke, James F. and Zucker, Norbert Y. (eds.). *Proceedings of the Regional Rail Planning Seminars, Fall 1976.* Lexington, Ky.: The Council of State Governments and the Federal Railroad Administration, April 1977.

Simat, Helliesen and Eichner, Inc. *Additional Retrospective Rail Line Abandonment Studies.* Boston: Simat, Helliesen and Eichner, Inc., 1975.

Simat, Helliesen and Eichner, Inc. *Retrospective Rail Line Abandonment Study (revised).* Boston: Simat, Helliesen and Eichner, Inc., 1973.

Smith (Wilbur) and Associates. *Economic Study of Alternative Modes for Rail Traffic and Their Costs.* Washington, D.C.: Wilbur Smith and Associates, 1974.

Sobel, Robert. *The Fallen Colossus.* New York: Weybright and Talley, 1977.

Thornton, W.L. *How to Deal with the Railroad Crisis: An Open Letter to Congress.* St. Augustine, Fla.: Florida East Coast Railway Company, June 1975.

Watt, William J. *Bowen: The Years as Governor.* Indianapolis: Bierce Associates, 1981.

Weinblatt, H.B. and Matzzie, D.E. *Effects of Railroad Abandonment on the Modal Distribution of Traffic and Related Costs.* Pittsburgh, Pa.: CONSAD Research Corporation, 1977.

Journals and Newspapers

Albright, Joseph. "A Hell of a Way to Run a Government," *New York Times*, November 3, 1974.

Bethell, Tom. "The Gravy Train," *The Washington Monthly*, Vol. 8, No. 3, 1976, pp. 6–11.

Black, William R. "Local Rail Service Assistance: Objectives and Initial Trends," *Transportation Research A*, Vol. 13A, 1979, pp. 351–360.

Bloch, Theodore S. and Stein, Robert Jay. "The Public Counsel Concept in Practice: The Regional Rail Reorganization Act of 1973," *William and Mary Law Review*, Vol. 16, No. 2, 1974, pp. 215–236.

Bunker, A.R. and Hill, L.D. "Impact of Rail Abandonment on Agricultural Production and Associated Grain Marketing and Fertilizer Supply Firms," *Illinois Agricultural Economics*, Vol. 15, No. 1, 1975, pp. 12–20.

"Commission Drops '34-Carload Rule' From Evaluation in Rail Abandonments," *Traffic World*, Vol. 168, No. 7, Whole Number 3630, November 15, 1976, pp. 34–35.

Conant, Michael. "Structural Reorganization of the Northeast Railroads," *ICC Practitioner's Journal*, Vol. 43, No. 2, 1976, pp. 207–223.

Ellison, Bruce. "Conrail is a Threat, N&W Official Says," *Cleveland Plain Dealer*, March 19, 1976.

Ericson, Helen. "Talks on Northeast Rail Track Purchase Slated," *Journal of Commerce* (New York), February 25, 1976.

"Expanded Aid to Local Freight Rail Lines Enacted," *Congressional Quarterly*, Nov. 18, 1978, pp. 3317–3318.

"Factories in Ohio Face Loss of Railroad Lines," *Youngstown Vindicator*, January 20, 1976.

"FRA Authorizes Rail Subsidy Payments to Continue Post April 1 Operations," *Traffic World*, Vol. 166, No. 1, Whole Number 3598, April 5, 1976, p. 8.

Harris, Robert G. "Economics of Traffic Density in the Rail Freight Industry," *The Bell Journal of Economics*, Vol. 8, No. 2, 1977, pp. 556–564.

"Help for Ohio Railroads," *Youngstown Vindicator*, November 10, 1975.

Hirschey, M.J. "Rail Service Subsidies—A Critical Analysis of the Program," *Quarterly Review of Economics and Business*, Vol. 18, No. 2, 1978, pp. 41–53.

"ICC Institutes Rulemaking to Provide New Rail Subsidy Payment Standards," *Traffic World*, Vol. 178, No. 3, Whole Number 3756, April 16, 1979, pp. 35–38.

Jones, William H. "Public-Be-Damned Attitude," *Washington Post*, March 24, 1976.

Jordan, Robert A. "147 Miles of Mass. Track Cut in Penn Central Freight Plan," *Boston Sunday Globe*, December 10, 1975.

Keisling, Phil. "How to Make a Billion from a Bankrupt Railroad," *The Washington Monthly*, July-August 1982, pp. 24–35.

Kelly, Paul A. "State Agrees to Acquire Pennsy Right of Way," *Providence Journal-Bulletin*, November 29, 1975.

Kiffney, John. "Rail Service Plan Wins Praise," *Providence Journal*, February 4, 1976.

Kizzia, Tom. "The Delmarva Short Lines: A New Breed," *Railway Age*, Vol. 181, No. 17, September 8, 1980, pp. 82–87.

Knudsen, Daniel C. "The Virginia Rail Subsidy Program: A Review," *Virginia Social Science Journal*, Vol. 16, No. 1, 1981, pp. 60–69.

"Labor Impasses Blocks Sale of Track in Northeast to Chessie and Southern," *Traffic World*, Vol. 165, No. 7, Whole Number 3591, pp. 11–12, February 16, 1976.

"Local Rail Services Program: Perspective of States and Railroads," *Transportation Research Circular*, No. 209, August 1979.

Loving, Jr., Rush. "Michigan's Wacky Ride on the Little Railroad That Couldn't," *Fortune*, October 23, 1978.

McDiarmid, Hugh. "Milliken's Plan to Buy Railroad Picks Up Steam," *Detroit Free Press*, February 21, 1976.

Mitchell, Susan. "Public Participation: The Regional Rail Reorganization Approach (I Think I Can . . . I Know I Can)," *ICC Practitioner's Journal*. Vol. 44, No. 1, 1976, pp. 10–50.

Neuschel, Robert P. "Politically Expedient Legislation-Transportation's Waterloos," *Progressive Railroading*, March 1974, pp. 34–36.

"New Rail Agency Sidetracked, Executive Director Asserts," *Cleveland Plain Dealer*, April 7, 1976.

"Penn Central's Estate Agrees to $2.1 Billion Payment for Property," *Traffic World*, Vol. 184, No. 8, Whole Number 3840, 1980. p. 114.

Price, Jeffrey P. and Berardino, Frank J. "Defining Economic Terms Used in the Railroad Revitalization and Regulatory Reform Act," *Transportation Law Journal*, Vol. 9, 1977, pp. 133–166.

Putsay, Michael W. "Regional Rail Reorganization and the Northeast Rail Problem," *The Logistics and Transportation Review*, Vol. 11, No. 3, 1975, pp. 213–228.

"Railroad Flagman Bill," editorial, *Evening Bulletin* (Philadelphia), December 10, 1975.

"Railroad Task Force Revived," *Hartford* (Connecticut) *Times*, January 21, 1976.

Rossi, Louis. "New York State's Rail Programs," *AASHTO Quarterly*, Vol. 59, No. 2, 1980, pp. 6–8.

"Sale, Assets Transfer By 7 Railroads Barred," *Philadelphia Inquirer*, December 24, 1975.

Sammon, John P. "Life Without the Railroad: Economic Effect of Rail Abandonment on the Community," *Transportation Research News*, No. 85, 1979, pp. 5–6.

Sandler, J. "A Test of Significance of the Difference Between Means of Correlated Measures, Based on Simplification of Students t," *British Journal of Psychology*, Vol. 46, 1955, pp. 225–226.

Seymer, Nigel. "Intermodal Comparisons of Energy Intensiveness in Long-Distance Transport," *Transportation Research*, Vol. 10, No. 4, 1976, pp. 275–279.

"Shapp to Sign Flagman Alert Liability Bill," *Pittsburgh Press*, November 16, 1975.

Smith, Michael; Butler, Steward E.; and, Harvey, Thomas N. "Benefit-Cost Analysis in Rail Branch-Line Evaluation," *Transportation Research Record*, 758, 1980, pp. 29–34.

"Southern, Chessie Having Problems Getting Labor Pacts for Bankrupts," *Journal of Commerce* (New York), January 30, 1976.

Southwick, Thomas P. "Subsidies Will Save Lines Excluded from Conrail," *Patriot Ledger* (Quincy, Mass.), February 10, 1976.

"Special Court Suggests Flexible Guidelines in Conrail Valuation Case," *Traffic World*, Vol. 172, No. 4, Whole Number 3679, 1977, pp. 86–87.

"State Asks $26 Million Rail Aid," *Detroit Free Press*, December 11, 1975.

Trimble, Walter. "Rail Plan Watched Closely," *Columbus Dispatch*, January 30, 1976.

"U.S. Cash will Save Rail Ferry," *Detroit Free Press*, February 5, 1976.

"USRA Accepts Ann Arbor Takeover but Rejects N&W Proposal in New England," *Traffic World*, Vol. 165, No. 9, Whole Number 3593, p. 20, March 1, 1976.

Whisman, Anne. "The Little Rail Line That Did," *Appalachia*, Vol. 13, No. 3, 1980. pp. 15–25.

"Why the Penn Central is Falling Apart," *Business Week*, No. 2350, September 28, 1974, pp. 62–66.

Federal Government Documents

Congressional Budget Office. *Railroad Reorganization: Congressional Action and Federal Expenditures Related to the Final System Plan of the U.S. Railway Association.* Washington, D.c.: U.S. Government Printing Office, Background Paper No. 2, January 15, 1976.

Federal Railroad Administration, U.S. Department of Transportation. "Acquisition and Modernization Loan Assistance: Procedures and Requirements for Filing of Applications and Disbursements," *Federal Register*, Vol. 40, No. 169, pp. 39898–39901, August 29, 1975.

Federal Railroad Administration, U.S. Department of Transportation. "Assistance to States and Persons in the Northeast and Midwest Region for Local Rail Services Under Section 402 of the Regional Rail Reorganization Act of 1973," *Federal Register*, Vol. 41, No. 45, pp. 9692–9699, March 5, 1976.

Federal Railroad Administration, U.S. Department of Transportation. "Assistance to States for Local Rail Service," *Federal Register*, Vol. 44, No. 170, (pp. 51126–51127,) August 30, 1979.

Federal Railroad Administration, U.S. Department of Transportation. "Continuation of Local Rail Services: Procedures and Requirement Regarding Filing of Applications," *Federal Register*, Vol. 39, No. 67, pp. 12528–12532, April 5, 1974.

Federal Railroad Administration, U.S. Department of Transportation. "Continuation of Local Rail Service: Procedures and Requirements Regarding Applications and Disbursements," *Federal Register*, Vol. 40, No. 19, pp. 4232–4237, January 28, 1975.

Federal Railroad Administration, U.S. Department of Transportation, Penn Central Transportation Company, Supplemental Report and Order, Docket No. RST-1, Waiver Petition No. 17, December 31, 1975.

Federal Railroad Administration, U.S. Department of Transportation. *State Rail Assistance Program Manual.* Washington, D.C.: U.S. Department of Transportation, October 1978.

Federal Railroad Administration, U.S. Department of Transportation. "Substitute

Service Assistance," *Federal Register*, Vol. 43, No. 4, (pp. 1108–1109,) January 6, 1978.

Fischer, John W., *Local Rail Service: The State Experience*. Congressional Research Service, Report No. 80–22 E, February 1, 1980.

In re Penn Central Transportation Company, Bky. No. 70–347, Order of Judge John P. Fullman, No. 2927, April 25, 1977.

Interstate Commerce Commission. "Acquisition of Rail Properties by Profitable Railroads in the Region as Proposed by the United States Railway Association". *Ex Parte No. 293 (Sub. No. 4)*, decided May 16, June 17, and July 16, 1975.

Interstate Commerce Commission. "Common Carrier Status of States, State Agencies and Instrumentalities, and Political Subdivisions," *Finance Docket 28990F*, Served August 7, 1980.

Interstate Commerce Commission. *Designated Operator Docket File*, unpublished.

Interstate Commerce Commission. *Evaluation of the U.S. Railway Association's Final System Plan*. Washington, D.C.: U.S. Government Printing Office, 1975.

Interstate Commerce Commission. "Notice: Continuation of Rail Service Under Subsidy by Designated Operator." Service Date: March 8, 1976.

Interstate Commerce Commission. *Rail Transportation Services on the Delmarva Peninsula*. Washington, D.C.: Interstate Commerce Commission, April 1977.

Interstate Commerce Commission. "Standards for Determining Rail Services Continuation Subsidies: Report and Order," *Federal Register*, Vol. 41, No. 246, (pp. 55686–55694,) December 31, 1976.

Interstate Commerce Commission. "Trustees Directed to Make Rail Properties Available for Continued Rail Service," *Ex Parte No. 293 (Sub. No. 10)*, Service Date: March 17, 1976.

Interstate Commerce Commission. *Uniform System of Accounts for Railroad Companies*. Washington, D.C.: U.S. Government Printing Office. Issue of 1968 as revised November 1, 1974.

McLaughlin, Charles. *Survey of FRA Grant Programs*. Washington, D.C.: U.S. Department of Transportation, March 8, 1978.

McGowan, JoAnne and Richards, Hoy A. *Proceedings of the 1975 National Rail Planning Conference*. Washington, D.C.: U.S. Government Printing Office, 1975.

Office of Management and Budget. *Additional Details on Budget Savings, Fiscal Year 1982, Budget Revisions*, Washington, D.C.: Executive Office of the President, Office of Management and Budget, April 1981.

Office of Public Counsel, Rail Services Planning Office, Interstate Commerce Commission. *Guide for Evaluating the Community Impact of Rail Service Discontinuance*. Washington, D.C.: U.S. Government Printing Office, January 10, 1975.

Office of State Assistance Programs, Federal Railroad Administration. *Benefit-Cost Guidelines, Rail Branch Line Continuation Assistance Programs*. Washington, D.C.: U.S. Department of Transportation, April 1979.

Office of the Inspector General. *Report on Audit of Rail Services Assistance Program Accomplishments, Problems and Future Directions*. Washington, D.C.: U.S. Department of Transportation, Report No. AM-FR-1–105, September 9, 1981.

Rail Services Planning Office, Interstate Commerce Commission. *Evaluation of* the Secretary of Transportation's Rail Services Report, Washington, D.C.: U.S. Government Printing Office, 1974.

Rail Services Planning Office, Interstate Commerce Commission. *Evaluation of the U.S. Railway Association's "Preliminary System Plan" and Supplement.* Washington, D.C.: U.S. Government Printing Office, 1975.

Rail Services Planning Office, Interstate Commerce Commission. *The Public Response to the Secretary of Transportation's Rail Services Report, Vol. I, New England States; Vol. II, Mid-Atlantic States; Vol. III, Midwestern States,* Washington, D.C.: U.S. Government Printing Office, 1974.

Rail Services Planning Office, Interstate Commerce Commission. *Rail Merger Study.* Issue papers and a final report, 10 vols., Washington, D.C.: U.S. Government Printing Office, 1977.

Rail Services Planning Office, Interstate Commerce Commission. *Report of the Office of Public Counsel.* Washington, D.C.: The Interstate Commerce Commission, July 12, 1974; November 1974; January 1975; June 1975; March 1976.

Rail Services Planning Office, Interstate Commerce Commission. *Report to the President and Congress on the Effectiveness of the Rail Passenger Service Act of 1970.* Washington, D.C.: U.S. Government Printing Office, March 15, 1978.

Rail Services Planning Office, Interstate Commerce Commission. "Standards for Determining Rail Service Continuation Subsidies, *Federal Register,* Vol. 40, No. 5, pp. 1624–1636, January 8, 1975; Vol. 40, p. 14186, March 28, 1975; Vol. 41, p. 3402, January 22, 1976; Vol. 41, p. 12836, March 26, 1976.

Rail Services Planning Office, Interstate Commerce Commission. *Statement of the Office of Public Counsel.* Washington, D.C.: The Interstate Commerce Commission, July 25, 1974.

Secretary, U.S. Department of Transportation. *Final Standards, Classification and Designation of Lines of Class I Railroads in the United States, Vol. I and II.* Washington, D.C.: U.S. Government Printing Office, 1977.

Secretary, U.S. Department of Transportation. *Preliminary Standards, Classification, and Designation of Lines of Class I Railroads in the United States.* Washington, D.C.: U.S. Government Printing Office, 1976.

Sullivan, James R. "The Prepaid Revenue Supplement Program," in Federal Railroad Administration. *Symposium on Economic and Public Policy Factors Influencing Light Density Rail Line Operations.* Washington, D.C.: U.S. Government Printing Office, 1973, pp. 28–33.

United States Railway Association. *Annual Report June 30, 1974, with a Supplemental Report Through October 1974.* Washington, D.C.: U.S. Government Printing Office, November 1974.

United States Railway Association. *Final System Plan, Official Errata Supplement to Vol. I and II.* Washington, D.C.: U.S. Government Printing Office, December 1, 1975.

United States Railway Association. *Final System Plan: Material Approved for Submission to the Board of Directors, USRA and Interstate Commerce Commission by the Executive Committee United States Railway Association.* Washington, D.C.: United States Railway Association, June 26, 1975.

United States Railway Association. *Final System Plan, Supplemental Report.* Washington, D.C.: U.S. Government Printing Office, July 26, 1975.

United States Railway Association. *1981 Conrail Performance Review.* Washington, D.C.: United States Railway Association, 1982.

United States Railway Association. *Preliminary System Plan, Vol. I, II, and Supplement.* Washington, D.C.: U.S. Government Printing Office, February 26, 1975.

United States Railway Association. *Report to Congress on Conrail Performance.* Washington, D.C.: United States Railway Association, 1980.

United States Railway Association. *Second Annual Report, June 30, 1975.* Washington, D.C.: U.S. Government Printing Office, October 1975.

United States Railway Association. *Seventh Annual Report 1980.* Washington, D.C.: United States Railway Association, 1980.

United States Railway Association. *Sixth Annual Report 1979.* Washington, D.C.: United States Railway Association, 1978.

United States Railway Association. *Third Annual Report, June 30, 1976.* Washington, D.C.: U.S. Government Printing Office, September 1976.

U.S. Congress. House. Committee on Appropriations. *Department of Transportation and Related Agencies Appropriations for 1977.* 94th Cong., 2nd sess., 1976, Part 3.

U.S. Congress. House. Committee on Appropriations. *Department of Transportation and Related Agencies Appropriations for 1978.* 95th Cong., 1st sess., 1977, Part 3.

U.S. Congress. House. Committee on Appropriations. *Department of Transportation and Related Agencies Appropriations for 1982.* 97th Cong., 1st sess., 1981, Part 5.

U.S. Congress. House. Committee on Appropriations. *Department of Transportation and Related Agencies Appropriations for 1982.* 97th Cong., 1st sess., 1981, Part 8, Budget Revisions.

U.S. Congress. House. Committee on Appropriations. *Department of Transportation and Related Agencies Appropriations for 1983.* 97th Cong., 2nd sess., 1982, Part 5.

U.S. Congress. House. Committee on Energy and Commerce. *Local Rail Service Assistance Act Authorization.* 97th Cong., 1st sess., 1981, Serial 97–23.

U.S. Congress. House. Committee on Interstate and Foreign Commerce. *Local Rail Service Assistance Act of 1978.* 95th Cong., 2nd sess., 1978, Report No. 95–1482.

U.S. Congress. House. Committee on Interstate and Foreign Commerce. *Local Rail Service Continuation Assistance.* 95th Cong., 1st sess., 1978, Serial No. 95–74.

U.S. Congress. House. Committee on Interstate and Foreign Commerce. *Local Rail Service Assistance.* 95th Cong., 2nd sess., 1978, Serial No. 95–156.

U.S. Congress. House. Committee on Interstate and Foreign Commerce. *Northeast Rail Problems, Legislative Proposals.* 93rd Cong., 1st sess., 1973, Committee Print No. 8.

U.S. Congress. House. Committee on Interstate and Foreign Commerce. *Rail Revitalization and Regulatory Reform Act of 1975.* 94th Cong., 1st sess., 1975, Report No. 94–725.

U.S. Congress. House. Committee on Interstate and Foreign Commerce. *Regional Rail Reorganization Act Amendments of 1975,* 94th Cong., 1st sess., 1975, Report No. 94–7.

U.S. Congress. House. Committee on Interstate and Foreign Commerce. *USRA Final System Plan.* 94th Cong., 1st sess., 1975, Serial 94–44.

U.S. Congress. Joint Resolution. "To Extend the Regional Rail Reorganization Act's Reporting Date and for Other Purposes." *Public Law 93–488*, enacted October 26, 1974.

U.S. Congress. "Railroad Revitalization and Regulatory Reform Act." *Public Law 94–210*, enacted February 5, 1976.

U.S. Congress. "Regional Rail Reorganization Act Amendments of 1975." *Public Law 94–5*, enacted February 28, 1975.

U.S. Congress. "Regional Rail Reorganization Act." *Public Law 93–236*, enacted January 2, 1974.

U.S. Congress. Senate. Committee on Appropriations. *Department of Transportation and Related Agencies Appropriations for Fiscal Year 1978.* 95th Cong., 1st sess., 1977, Part 1.

U.S. Congress. Senate. Committee on Appropriations. *Department of Transportation and Related Agencies Appropriations for Fiscal Year 1978.* 95th Cong., 1st sess., Part 4, 1977.

U.S. Congress. Senate. Committee on Appropriations. *Department of Transportation and Related Agencies Appropriations for Fiscal Year 1979.* 95th Cong., 2nd sess., 1978, Part 1.

U.S. Congress. Senate. Committee on Appropriations. *Department of Transportation and Related Agencies Appropriations for Fiscal Year 1982.* 97th Cong., 1st sess., 1982, Part 1.

U.S. Congress. Senate. Committee on Commerce. *Local Rail Services Act of 1978.* 95th Cong., 2nd sess., Report No. 95–1159, 1978.

U.S. Congress. Senate. Committee on Commerce. *Northeastern and Midwestern Railroad Transportation Crisis.* 93rd Cong., 1st sess., 1974, Serial 93–8, Part 3.

U.S. Congress. Senate. Committee on Commerce. *Northeastern Railroad Transportation Crisis.* 93rd Cong., 1st sess., 1973, Serial 93–8, Part 1 and Part 2.

U.S. Congress. Senate. Committee on Commerce. *The Penn Central and Other Railroads.* 92nd Cong., 2nd sess., 1973, Committee Print.

U.S. Congress. Senate. Committee on Commerce. *Railroads 1975.* 94th Cong., 1st sess., 1975, Report No. 94–31, Part 1, 2, 3, and 4.

U.S. Congress. Senate. Committee on Commerce. *Regional Rail Reorganization Act Amendments of 1975.* 94th Cong., 1st sess., 1975, Report 94–5.

U.S. Congress. Senate. Committee on Commerce, Science, and Transportation. *Local Rail Services Act of 1978.* 95th Cong., 2nd sess., 1978, Report No. 95–1159.

U.S. Congress. Senate. Committee on Commerce, Science, and Transportation. *Railroad Amendments Act of 1978.* 95th Cong., 2nd sess., 1978, Serial No. 95–114.

U.S. Congress. Senate. Committee of Conference, *Railroad Revitalization and Regulatory Reform Act of 1975.* Report of the Committee of Conference on S. 2718. 94th Cong., 1st sess., 1975, Report No. 94–585.

U.S. Congress. Senate. Committee of Conference, *Railroad Revitalization and Regulatory Reform Act of 1976.* Report of the Committee of Conference on S. 2718. 94th Cong., 2nd sess., 1976, Report 94–595.

U.S. Department of Transportation. *A Prospectus for Change in the Freight Railroad Industry.* Washington, D.C.: U.S. Department of Transportation, October 1978.

U.S. Department of Transportation. *Railroad Abandonments and Alternatives: A*

Report on Effects Outside the Northeastern Region. Washington, D.C.: U.S. Department of Transportation, 1976.

U.S. Department of Transportation. *Rail Service in the Midwest and Northeast Region.* 3 Vols. Washington, D.C.: U.S. Government Printing Office, February 1974.

U.S. General Açcounting Office. *Improved Controls Needed Over Federal Financial Assistance to Railroads.* Washington, D.C.: U.S. General Accounting Office, 1976, Report CED-76–161.

State Government Documents

Black, W.R.: Eisenach, S.D.; and, Knudsen, D.C. *Illinois Central Gulf Indianapolis District Rehabilitation Program and Cost Estimate - The State's Benefit-Cost Analysis.* Indianapolis, Ind.: Public Service Commission of Indiana, July 1979.

Black, W.R.; Eisenach, S.D.; and, Knudsen, D.C. *Indiana's Local Rail Service Assistance Program - The State's Benefit-Cost Analysis.* Indianapolis, Ind.: Public Service Commission of Indiana, August 1979.

Black, W.R.; Eisenach, S.D.; Knudsen, D.C.; Robbins, J.C. *Manual for State Benefit-Cost Analysis of Railroad Projects.* Indianapolis, Ind.: Public Service Commission of Indiana, September 1979.

Boston University Bureau of Business. "The Economic Impact of Discontinuance of the Rutland Railway," *Studies on the Economic Impact of Railway Abandonment and Service Discontinuance.* Washington, D.C.: U.S. Department of Commerce, 1965.

Department of Transportation, State of Wisconsin. *Rail Planning Procedures Report.* Report FRA-RFA-40025–75, prepared for the Federal Railroad Administration, September 1975.

Division of Regional Transport Research. *Indiana State Rail Plan 1983 Update.* Indianapolis, Ind.: Indiana Department of Transportation, 1982.

Ernst and Whinney. *Evaluation of the State Rail Assistance Program - Findings and Guidelines for Program Evaluation and Financial Management.* Prepared for the Office of State Assistance Programs, Federal Railroad Administration, January 1980.

Governor's Rail Task Force. *USRA Segments in Indiana: State Analysis and Recommendations.* Bloomington, Indiana: Center for Urban and Regional Analysis, Indiana University, August 1974.

Illinois Department of Transportation. *Illinois Rail System Plan.* Springfield, Ill.: Illinois Department of Transportation, December 1975.

Maryland Department of Transportation. *Maryland State Rail Plan.* Baltimore-Washington International Airport, Md.: Maryland Department of Transportation, August 1977.

Michigan Department of State Highways and Transportation. *Michigan Railroad Needs: A Planning Report.* Lansing, Mich.: Michigan Department of State Highways and Transportation, January 2, 1975.

Michigan Department of State Highways and Transportation. *Michigan Railroad Plan: Phase II,* Lansing, Mich.: Michigan Department of State Highways and Transportation, December 9, 1975.

New York State Railroad Task Force. *Railroad Mainline System Planning and the*

Role of the Erie Lackawanna Main Line via Port Jervis. Albany: New York State Department of Transportation, 1974.

Northeast Rail Task Force. *Report on the Profitability of New York State Branch Line Operations.* Albany: New York State Department of Transportation, 1974.

Ohio Department of Transportation. *Phass II Ohio Branch Line Plan,* Columbus, Ohio: Ohio Department of Transportation, December 1975.

Rail Division, New York State Department of Transportation. *New York State Rail Plan Update.* Albany: New York State Department of Transportation, 1978.

Rossi, Louis. *Report on Profitability of New York State Branch Lines.* Albandy, N.Y.: State Department of Transportation, February 13, 1974.

Shapp, Milton J., *et al. A United States Rail Trust Fund,* Harriburg: Bureau of Planning Statistics, Pennsylvania Department of Transportation, 1975.

Shapp, Milton J., *et al. Pennsylvania's Plan for a Balanced Eastern Rail System,* Harrisburg: Bureau of Planning Statistics, Pennsylvania Department of Transportation, 1975.

Transportation Planning Office, State of Indiana. *Indiana Transportation Fact Book.* Indianapolis: Transportation Planning Office, 1982.

Wisconsin Department of Transportation. *Short Line Railroads as an Alternative to Loss of Rail Service - Pros and Cons.* Madison, Wis.: Wisconsin Department of Transportation, November 1975.

Miscellaneous and Unpublished

Association of American Railroads. *Information Letter,* various issues, 1972–1980.

Association of American Railroads. *Rail News Update.* Washington, D.C., various issues from Feb. 6, 1980.

Black, William R., internal memorandum to Leo F. Mullin, Activation Task Force, Consolidated Rail Corporation, March 15, 1976.

Blaze, James R. "Conrail," presented at the Rail Abandonment Conference, Madison, Wisconsin, March 18, 1977.

Bunker, Arvin R. *Impact of Rail Line Abandonment on Agricultural Production and Associated Grain Marketing and Fertilizer Supply Firms,* (unpublished Ph.D. thesis, Department of Agricultural Economics, University of Illinois at Champaign-Urbana, 1975).

"Bylaws of the Conference of States on Regional Rail Reorganization," (xerox), September 1974.

"Comments on the Conrail Operating Agreement." A letter from the Federal Railroad Administration to the Consolidated Rail Corporation; undated; received during week of January 12, 1976.

Hopkins, John B.; Newfell, A.T.; and, Hazel, Morrin. "Fuel Consumption in Rail Freight Service," presented at the 56th annual meeting of the Transportation Research Board, 1977.

Matzzie, Donald E.; Weinblatt, Herbert B.; Harman John; Jones, J. Richard. "Light Density Railroad Line Abandonment: Scaling the Problem," presented at the 56th annual meeting of the Transportation Research Board, 1977.

Morlok, Edward K. "An Engineering Analysis and Comparison of Railroad and Truck Line-Haul Work (Energy) Requirements," presented at the 56th annual meeting of the Transportation Research Board, 1977.

"Shapp Attacks U.S. Railways Association's Plan," Press Release, Office of the Governor, Commonwealth of Pennsylvania, March 25, 1975.

Williams, Jr., G.M. "A Perspective on the Relationship Between the States and Conrail in Developing and Implementing Rail Programs Stemming from Recent Federal Legislation," a paper presented at a meeting of the Committee on the State Role in Rail Transport of the Transportation Research Board, Lake Tahoe, California, September 6, 1978.

Zell, Martin, Assistant Commissioner, New York State Department of Transportation. Letter to members of the state rail agencies in the reorganization region. Albany, June 24, 1974.

Zodikoff, Benjamin. "New York State's Rail Assistance Programs," presented at the AASHTO Annual Meeting Birmingham, Alabama, November 16, 1976.

INDEX